HOW TO WIN CAMPAIGNS

2

3 - Fl

If n
2

'Finding creative and practical ways to engage the public to challenge vested interests that threaten a fairer and safer world is increasingly urgent – and daunting. With disarming clarity, Chris Rose sets out how it can be done. This is a must-read for anyone campaigning for solutions that serve the public interest.'

Michael Keating, Director, Africa Progress Panel

'Chris Rose has devised an enormously insightful and helpful guide from his many years of experience running great campaigns. The tools in this book are powerful allies for any campaigner, and will prevent expensive mistakes by beginners and veterans alike.'

Caroline Fiennes, Executive Director, Global Cool

'Environmentalists have a bad habit of understanding more about the issues than they do about people. Then they wonder why their campaigns fail. Chris Rose not only knows about both, he knows how to connect them'.

Tom Burke, ex-Director of FoE and the Green Alliance,
co-founder of E3G Third Generation Environmentalism

'Rose is one of the top pros, and this book is full of expert guidance and examples. Any selection of these "100 steps to success" should make you more of a pro and less of an amateur.'

Rick Minter, editor of ECOS, British Association of Nature Conservationists

'They've got Karl Rove. We've got Chris Rose. Bet on us!'

John Passacantando, former Executive Director, Greenpeace USA

'Be it an advertising, electoral or sway campaign, this book is an excellent guide for anyone wanting to rally together public support for an important cause … Useful for the experienced campaigner and novice alike, this systematic and practical guide shows that campaigning has a key role to play in contemporary politics.'

The Waste Paper

'Rose delivers more in this book than most of us will ever know about campaigning. He successfully presents what is often seen as a black art as both tangible and doable.'

John Wyatt, Partner, Wyatt & Wyatt Corporate Communications

'Tells of the nuts and bolts of getting heard and achieving results in a marvellously readable way. An inspiring read for all budding campaigners.'

Tim O'Riordan, Professor of Environmental Sciences at the University of East Anglia

'A "must read" for those who want to use communications techniques to change the world we live in.'

Ed Gyde, Director, Munro & Forster Communications

'Applicable to any issue and from any point of view, the book's 100 key steps and tools provide promising models of motivation, analysis and communication for any campaign, large or small.'

Countryside Voice

'A thoroughly engaging piece of work, infused with the enthusiasm of the author for a subject he clearly knows very well.'

Resource

HOW TO WIN CAMPAIGNS
Communications for Change

CHRIS ROSE
SECOND EDITION

publishing for a sustainable future

London • Washington DC

First published by Earthscan in the UK and USA in 2010

For a full list of publications please contact:
Earthscan
2 Park Square, Milton Park, Abingdon, Oxon OX14 4RN
711 Third Avenue, New York, NY 10017

Earthscan is an imprint of the Taylor & Francis Group, an informa business

A catalogue record for this book is available from the British Library

Library of Congress Cataloging-in-Publication Data
Rose, Chris, 1956-
    How to win campaigns: communications for change / Chris Rose. – 2nd ed.
      p. cm.
    Includes bibliographical references and index.
    ISBN 978-1-84971-193-7 (hardback) – ISBN 978-1-84971-114-2 (pbk.) 1.   Social action.
2.   Communication in social action. 3.   Social marketing. 4.   Persuasion
(Psychology) 5.   Publicity. I.   Title.
    HN18.R628 2010
    659–dc22

                                        2010036550

ISBN 13: 978-1-84971-193-7 (hbk)
ISBN 13: 978-1-84971-114-2 (pbk)

Printed and bound in the UK by TJ International, Padstow, Cornwall

Typeset by Domex e-Data, India
Cover design by Rogue Four Design

For Amazon, Willow and Sarah, and for all the campaigners
who have given their safety, lives, freedom or comforts
to try and make the world a better place

Contents

Acknowledgements

I am particularly grateful to Rick le Coyte for his help in reviewing the content of this book for its second edition, and for contributing to many of the sections, especially those concerned with 'new media'. I would also like to thank my friends Pat Dade and Les Higgins at Cultural Dynamics Strategy and Marketing for their very generous help in contributing material from their researches into values, and the numerous readers of the campaign strategy newsletters (see www.campaignstrategy.org) whose ideas I have plundered. Also my family, who have put up with me spending far too much time alone with my computer. Lastly, I am very grateful for all the support and assistance of Jonathan Sinclair Wilson, Alison Kuznets and their colleagues at Earthscan.

Preface to the Second Edition

When I first told my colleagues in conservation and academia that I was taking a job as a 'campaigner' in the early 1980s, they shook their heads sadly as if saying goodbye to a condemned man. The scientists foresaw a complete loss of credibility, the others professional oblivion. Perhaps they were right, but it has been fun. And strangely, since this book was first published in 2005, 'campaigning' has moved so far into the mainstream that almost anyone concerned with 'public life' – from government ministers to blue chip companies – can be found using the same techniques, even happily calling them 'campaigns', that were once the preserve of the disempowered and the marginalized. So a lot more people are 'campaigning'.

The most obvious development since 2005 has been the maturing of 'new media' into 'online', but although this has changed the order in which things can be done, and how they can be done, it has not really altered the fundamentals of campaign strategy. In line with both the preceding points, there has been an explosion of resources available to anyone wanting to discover the how-to of campaigning, with a huge increase in training and online resources. As campaigning has become more established, there are even the first college courses actually trying to teach it.

The application of communications psychology to campaigning, particularly spurred by the need to 'change behaviours', such as motivational values, heuristics and framing, has also begun to penetrate campaign practice, although established non-governmental organizations (NGOs) in particular are remarkably conservative, and often lag far behind what the private sector or even public bodies are willing to try.

What was once seen by the establishment as illegitimate has become respectable, and is always in danger of becoming dull. This book is a collection of guidelines arrived at by trial and error rather than rules, and there is no rule that I know of as to what makes a good campaigner except, as a friend of mine once said during an exasperating session trying to advise a very respectable NGO on how to hire for a 'campaigner' post, 'if someone's going to campaign, they've got to want to "act up"'.

Introduction

There are but two powers in the world, the sword and the mind. In the long run the sword is always beaten by the mind. (Napoleon Bonaparte)

There are two forces in the world today – US military power, and world public opinion. (*Time Magazine*, 2003)

Every day, millions of people are touched by campaigns. It is important that campaigns succeed. Lives may depend upon the outcome of campaigns over access to health, medicines, clean water or justice. The survival of nature depends on the success of campaigns to change policies and industries that are destroying our atmosphere, oceans, forests and other 'public goods'. If campaigners for education, child rights and fairer trade are to fail, then the poorest of the poor will be condemned to a more miserable future.

Yet most campaigning does fail, and there is remarkably little effort to learn why, or to analyse and replicate the campaigns that are successful. This book cannot provide a comprehensive answer but it collects together some campaign 'tools' that have a track record of helping campaigns work. It is good that thousands, perhaps millions, of people devote their lives to campaigns; it is tragic if their efforts are mostly wasted, and a scandal if that could be avoided.

Campaigns mostly involve communication: a conversation with society. This differs from the communication we carry out one to one with our friends or colleagues. This communication is used to persuade large numbers of people to act as a matter of urgency, so many campaign techniques are those of influencing people without having to stop and make friends first, and in this respect campaigning is like public relations (PR). But unlike PR, campaigning is an expression of popular democracy; it creates new channels of influence for the public, in the public interest. Campaigns work in the public interest by borrowing power from the people for good causes. In a world where politics are increasingly professionalized[1] and lean increasingly towards promotion of private economic interests, campaigning has often become the common politics of the people.

Advertising campaigns sell things, electoral campaigns get politicians elected, but the sorts of campaigns this book is about bring neither money nor formal power. Instead, they harness a collective will and effort as an engine of change for public benefit.

What sway campaigns have depends upon the scale and intensity of their public support. This is their source of energy and an inbuilt test of legitimacy. Generally the rich and powerful do not campaign – they do not have to. Many campaigns are a reaction against an abuse of power.

For most voluntary non-governmental organizations (NGOs), their only resource to secure real change is public persuasion. Business has money, government has law but campaigns have only public support. Communication is the campaigners' instrument for change, not simply a way to publicize an opinion.

The best campaigns seem to communicate themselves. Others go down in a blaze of publicity but achieve no real change; many more struggle on in obscurity. A high failure rate is to be expected. Campaigning is a high-risk venture. In business, most new enterprises will fail. In nature, few species of wildlife reaching a new land will ever become established – most, as with campaigns, will die out.

In business or ecology, though, we expect to know the reasons for success and failure. We have studies and colleges devoted to the subject. Much the same is true of politics – getting elected is not generally regarded as an accident. Yet with campaigns the reasons for success and failure are often treated as an impenetrable mystery.

Such explanations as are given often descend into glib circularities such as 'to be effective, campaigns must communicate effectively' or effective campaigns need to be 'well planned, adequately resourced and engaging for the public'. This is about as useful for planning real activity and expenditure as saying that in order to be healthy, people must not get diseases and should avoid getting ill.

The UK National Council for Voluntary Organisations summarized its findings from a review of campaign literature on campaign effectiveness thus:[2]

> *If there is an obvious problem and a good case that resolving it will bring benefit, progress will be easier. It helps to have a viable solution and an outline of a course of action. A constructive alternative is the price of success. You should pick the target and fix responsibility. The ideal target will be receptive, vulnerable to pressure in some way, and have the power actually to get things done. It helps if there support at some level within the target institution, even if not actually from the decision-maker him- or herself. The target may have delay, rather than resolution, in mind. The issue must stand out and this is more likely if there is a short and easily understood chain of argument linking the problem to the solution you are advocating and when there is an external rationale and sense of urgency. External milestones can create urgency without which people won't act.*

Campaigns are wars of persuasion. Use of communication is often the key to success or failure. By itself, public concern is rarely effectively focused: hence this book is mostly about how to use communication to enlist and focus the support of others. While there are lots of books about issues, this one is about the tactics and strategies of campaigning and communication, looking as much as possible at underlying principles.

Even though it is evident that most campaigning relies on communication, and some organizations excel at it, many NGOs ignore it in favour of issue knowledge. So a route map or strategic advice on how to organize it is hard to come by. Some 'campaign manuals'[3] contain valuable advice, but most tend towards details of individual communication practices or specialisms such as lobbying at international negotiations[4] or domestic issue-by-issue advice.[5] 'Grass-roots' and direct action-based campaign groups have produced a lot of useful websites, but these too tend to be either practical (how to encase your arm in concrete) or polemical (why capitalism must be defeated). Useful new web resources appear all the time: one of the best is www.thechangeagency.org. I try to list them at my website www.campaignstrategy.org. Please send me your ideas at chris@campaignstrategy.co.uk.

The commercial marketing and public relations literature is large, but campaigns for corporates are very different because they don't have to appeal to anyone's better nature. They rely on self-interest and normally start from the position of an insider. 'Social marketing' uses a number of similar techniques for non-profit purposes but generally does not challenge power or vested interests, or even seek specific outcomes.

Even some voluntary campaigning organizations, which rely so much on communication, don't treat it with the seriousness it deserves. Many managers and directors believe that communication is a low-value extra, something 'handled' by the press office, while other staff are given little or no training in it. All politicians are said to be susceptible to the conceit that they are economists. The NGO equivalent is to assume that everyone can communicate. One commentator[6] has put it like this:

> Communications is seen as 'soft'. While programme development and practice are seen as requiring expertise and the thoughtful consideration of best practices, communications is an 'anyone can do it if you have to' task. It is time to retire this thinking. Doing communications strategically requires the same investment of intellect and study that these other areas of non-profit practice have been accorded.

Today most managers are at least dimly aware that they *ought* to have a 'communications strategy'. It's seen as good practice. Unfortunately even many campaigners also think that a communications strategy equals a media strategy. In reality using the 'media', that is press, radio, television and so on, may not be the most effective way to communicate.[7] As a consultant and campaigner for over 20 years, I've lost count of the number of directors who assess the success of campaigns by weight of press clippings, or the number of website 'hits', and campaigners who are better able to tell you about how the media is covering their campaign than what effect that campaign is having in terms of change.

The mistaken assumption that communications simply means media is more likely where an organization has a specialist media department, while other departments may not be called 'communications' although that is mostly what they do – for example 'campaigns', 'marketing' or 'public information'.

Campaigning is a mongrel craft drawing from many other disciplines, so it's no surprise that lawyers tend to think campaigning hinges on making arguments, scientists want to progress campaigns by research, writers and academics by publishing, and teachers may believe education is how to change the world. Each can play a part in campaigns, it is true. Yet effective campaigns are usually better executed by showing rather than arguing, by motivation rather than education, and by mobilization rather than accumulation of knowledge. Doing this to order means planning communication like a composer or film director.

There is no absolute right answer to effective communication. Communication strategy for campaigns is like chess but with your opponents changing all the time, and with rules that are a matter of opinion. My general advice is:

- Keep it short and simple;
- Be visual;
- Create events;
- Tell stories about real people;
- Be *pro*active – don't just respond;
- Get your communication in the right order; and
- Communicate in the agenda of the outside world – don't export the internal agenda, plan, jargon or 'message'.

Easy to say; harder to do.

A common pitfall is to get stuck arguing over 'messages'. It's best to avoid discussing 'your message' altogether and instead focus on the elements that are often critical to the success or failure of communication. The Context, Action, Trigger, Channel, Audience, Messenger and Programme all need to be got right (see Chapter 1) – discuss these and the 'message' will often emerge.

Effective campaigns, and effective campaigning organizations, need a structure. Composers use concertos or symphonies. Campaigners can use communication strategies. Done badly, these can be dull plans, tick-box exercises and lists of impossible aspirations. Done well they can be fun, inspiring, lyrical and useful. Campaigns should also be exciting – an adventure. Aim to conduct your campaign like an opera – a political opera, painted in dramatic polarities.[8]

A communications strategy is about planning and knowing what you communicate, who to, why, and what can make it effective. It is using communication instrumentally – as an instrument to make change happen. It needs mechanical inputs such as identifying particular audiences or channels, but should also flow from your values, from the essence of your organization and cause, from the heart as well as the head.

Communications strategies can exist at many levels. For campaign groups the three most important are:

1   Organizational – the whole communication of the organization;
2   Campaign – for example, a campaign on child labour; and
3   Project – for example, around a specific European Union Council decision.

At a micro-level, campaign communication can literally be a conversation. At organizational level, it is an indirect 'conversation', a relationship built up over years. Your campaign communication may be carefully conceived all on its own, but it will arrive as part of a compound mosaic of impressions and information received from many sources. Everything your organization says or does – be it intended as communication or unintended – and anything said about it, will be added into the mental mix.

Maybe it includes direct engagements such as an encounter with a street money collector, or a campaign team, or even helping in a campaign activity. What were the people like? How were you treated? Who else was there? It all forms an impression, the result of a lot of fragments.

Impressions that count are mostly the result of events, things that happen: the equivalent of a few 'snapshots'. We 'make sense' of them by filling in the 'missing gaps' and explaining fragments by using other information, maybe about the issue in general, or our own life experiences. That way we make an overall picture that adds up. Campaigners can make deliberate use of this habit of 'first we see, then we understand' (see 'Framing', Chapter 1).

The steps to change determine the campaign strategy, and that in turn needs to determine communications. Here's a shorthand way[9] to link communications to a campaign strategy:

•   Locate decision – locate the action (often a decision) you want to achieve. What decision do you want made, and by whom?
•   Identify mechanism – what mechanisms will get you the decision? What is the best way to get to the people you wish to influence?
•   Determine audience – who do you need to convince/affect to get your mechanism into operation? If you do not reach the target audience, the mechanism will not operate, no matter how good the campaign materials are. Getting the mechanism to operate may require you to influence a different audience from the ultimate target.
•   Work back to proposition – what is the best way to motivate your audience? Tailor the original arguments/communications that you want to use for your target audience. What angle will your target audience respond best to?

- Define activities and materials – knowing the decision you want, the mechanics of that decision and what will motivate your target audience means you can now decide the appropriate materials for the campaign.

This book has no academic pedigree but shares practical lessons learned from successful campaigns and repeated failures, in the hope that it may help campaigns be less frustrating, more rewarding and, above all, more effective. A lot of the examples are from Greenpeace, simply because they were ones I had easiest access to. They all illustrate principles that can apply to any campaign. A well-resourced book of campaign case studies could cast the net far wider.

The essentials of campaigning have a history as long as human communications itself – perhaps from the first time that someone questioned the direction of a group or tribe and said to others: 'Come with me – let's go this way instead.' An alternative objective, a call to action, the need to get attention, to reach the right audience with the right message at the right moment – these are some of the fundamentals.

The pages of this book mostly contain 'thinking tools'. Using them doesn't require any equipment, any qualifications or even any money. They apply to any topic and from the scale of a one-person one-street project up to the major campaigns of pressure groups, advocacy organizations involving hundreds of people.

Campaigns did not begin with pressure groups, marketing or 'modern' advertising. History is littered with the antecedents of campaigning. Plenty are military, for at their root, campaigns are about power and contested 'outcomes'. Many campaigners like to name *The Art of War*[10] by fifth century Chinese general Sun Tzu, as their favourite text, though fewer seem to put his principles into practice. As a copy-writer Shakespeare penned many effective calls to action, 'once more unto the breach, dear friends, once more' being one of the better ones.

To campaign effectively it is not enough to be concerned, or even to spread that concern to others: instead one needs to motivate people to take action, and that requires a solution which looks feasible, as well as a problem that is compelling. Good campaigning involves figuring out when to work on the problem, and when to work on the solution (Chapter 6). Nor is campaigning necessarily punitive – any campaigner whose objective is to punish the opponent is unlikely to achieve an early surrender or to win many friends. Campaigning is a business for those who want to get even, not mad. It's the marketing of motivation, which means understanding motivation (Chapter 3). As Saul Alinsky wrote in the now old but still readable tract *Rules for Radicals*,[11] 'With very rare exceptions, the right things are done for the wrong reasons.'

Campaigning is not always a particularly polite or noble business, and some may baulk at the thought of using techniques that in some cases were developed for the darker arts of politics, war or commerce. In fact, these days campaigns are pilfered by government and business far more than the other way around. All I can say is that my sympathy lies with those who ask: 'Why should the devil have all the best tunes?'[12]

WHAT CAMPAIGNING GETS YOU

The essential difference between campaigning and 'advocacy' is public engagement. A campaign needs public support to succeed, and it is a form of politics for the public. There are many reasons people campaign, most of which boil down to righting an injustice. Organizations campaign because it works: it can get you change that goes beyond business as usual, the fruits of persuasion that cannot be bought or obtained by mere argument, protest or admonishment. Here are some reasons why campaigning can work:

- It creates gearing – multiplies the impact of efforts at change by enlisting the help of many people, thereby making it possible to achieve particular changes more quickly, or bigger changes altogether;
- It sets agendas – it aligns the public about what needs to be done;
- If action-based, it is a more powerful form of communication than just dialogue based on opinions;
- It can remedy a democratic deficit, compensating for the corporatization and professionalization of politics and the consequent spiralling lack of trust in the formal political system;
- Politics respond more and more via the media and less directly to the public, so having a dialogue in society is more and more important in creating political backing for a proposal;
- Trust in the media, especially paid-for messages is declining, so communication with a clear personal endorsement, such as through participative networks, is more persuasive;
- For the time being, NGOs – and this includes many campaign groups – are generally more trusted than most other elements of society, such as businesses, politicians and paid-for scientists;
- It is established as a way of raising and testing injustices and action-deficits, and is now almost indispensable in trying to protect 'public goods',[13] because politics have broadly become the promoter of private interests;
- Atomization of society has raised the importance of mass and networked media as a way of being heard;
- Globalization of communications technology and narrowcasting has increased the opportunity to be heard if you are organized but reduced it otherwise, and made achieving 'cross-over' between 'unlike' segments of society more difficult, eroding 'common values';

- It creates a community and ecology of action – it means people are 'not alone'; and
- It gives agency – greater influence over the world.

Politics and business are converging with the form and techniques, although not the purpose of campaigns. As societies become driven less by survival needs and more by need to fulfil potential, they increasingly deal with things for which there is no direct market price, and this is the territory of campaigns. In 2009 the income of the 'third sector' of voluntary and community groups was put[14] at £100 billion a year in the UK alone, with assets twice that size and a workforce larger than the banking and finance sectors. These groups very much rely on effective communication for their influence. Equally the public communication techniques of campaigning become more salient in a 24/7 global 'public conversation world' in which, as public affairs executive Simon Bryceson says, 'politicians cast themselves in a "perpetual campaign", competing to stay in line with "public opinion"'.[15]

WHAT CAMPAIGNERS NEED TO KNOW

For strategy, campaigners need to understand power. You may have a good argument or a cause you care about, but why should anyone listen or take notice? An interests analysis (see Chapter 5) should identify who is in control of what and who is benefiting from the status quo. It should help you answer the question 'Why hasn't the change I want already taken place?' Posing a threat to established power or interests will make people take notice. Remember what Stalin responded when told that the Vatican opposed his actions in World War II: 'How many divisions does the Pope have?'

For engagement, campaigners need to understand motivation – their own, and that of others. If this is not well understood, it's unlikely that sufficient people can be motivated to lend the necessary support. Frequently it is not a question of which 'facts' are presented or what 'argument' is made but the terms in which a case is made – what 'the issue' is framed as, whether it meets the psychological needs of an audience, and whether factors such as the channel, messenger or context are right. Effective campaigning is rarely the result of a blind experiment that people come flocking to support. More often it results from identifying key audiences for change and then finding out what will motivate them. Neither 'education' nor 'changing minds' often come into it (see Chapter 11).

To engage in the business of public politics – and play out issues of who is right and wrong, and where society should be heading – campaigners need to understand 'the media' and the ritualized hidden formats of news reporting. To lure and feed the media machine, campaigns require events, the stuff of news and politics. The capacity to create events that lead observers to conclude they support the campaign, and then to act, marks out truly effective campaign groups from those that simply protest.

To make use of public sympathy and support, campaign groups need to organize themselves, with engagement mechanisms and supporter communication. They need to be able to analyse and achieve simplicity without simplification, to create compelling propositions (Chapter 7) that capture the problem, solution, responsible parties, consequent benefit and action needed, in a succinct phrase or image. To reach large numbers of people, they need to think visually and use visual language (Chapter 6).

To compete for scarce human attention, campaigns need to offer agency – more sway over the world – and to offer solutions not available via formal politics or the market. To persist and endure, campaigns need both organization and a vision, as well as a brand (see Chapter 12).

Campaigners need to identify what needs to be done or how the world should be different, what would have an effect in making that happen, and how to do it. This is 'Level 1'. They then need to assemble the forces and mechanisms to make the necessary changes happen (Level 2). It is pretty easy to reach the first level: to specify what a better world would look like. It's harder to uncover the truth about the politics and dynamics of potential change. And it's very much harder to put together a campaign machine capable of making that change a reality (Level 3). Yet it is only at this third level that campaigns transform from being protests, well-publicized arguments or demonstrations of wishful thinking into agents of change. It is also only then that they are taken seriously by opponents.

There are suggestions and techniques for all of the above in this book, though many are necessarily mere sketches of what is required. All this requires strategy, method and calculation, but the most powerful campaigns also reach the heart by clearly coming from the heart as well as the head (see 'The glass onion', Chapter 12).

To do this, campaign groups need to be able to operate on principle as well as by strategy, and to achieve that, they need to understand, express and use their own values. Campaigns can change politics and power structures by strategy calculated from an understanding of interests, and in this they are like PR operations by major companies, or like politics. But they can also change the same targets through the shaping pressure of values, formulating new concerns and norms, and from this territory professional politics and commerce are largely excluded.

The two processes – influence by changing interests and by changing values – are linked because it is events and conversations in society that gradually surface and coalesce values as new norms, often over decades or generations.

Campaigners also need to understand the issue of their campaign – which this book is not about – but it is a great mistake to assume that this is the most important thing. Too much focus on the issue, instead of on changing the issue, is almost invariably a recipe for failure.

JOHN MUIR AND SEVEN PRINCIPLES OF CAMPAIGNING

To my mind, the first 'modern' campaigner was John Muir. In the 19th century he used the media, and personal action, to mobilize support in a cause that changed great events in the US, with reverberations that have spread around the world.

Muir was an irascible Scot from Dunbar who emigrated to the US as a child. He lived drama and adventure, activism, science and politics. He was a one-man 19th century David Attenborough, Petra Kelly and tree-hugger rolled into one.

John Muir was for Nature with a big N, science, beauty and learning. Muir confounded his Calvinistic parents, who believed maths to be the devil's work, by learning in secret. After failing at farming, his family trekked west to an unsuccessful get-rich-quick opportunity – the California gold rush. Later, Muir had the first recorded 'wilderness experience' when he spent the American Civil War in the Canadian forests after losing an eye in a spinning accident. 'Going out,' he wrote just before he died, 'I was really going in.'

As a communicator, Muir connected personal action with 'global' responsiblities. He walked across the US and began his journal with his address: 'John Muir, Earth, Planet, Universe' – perhaps the best known self-declaration of citizenship of nature by a Westerner since the Celts.

As an activist, Muir climbed into the Yosemite region in the forests of the Sierra Nevada with a Chinese and a Spanish-American. Together they helped fight off loggers of giant redwoods at Mariposa Grove above Yosemite, including use of muskets. The massive redwoods – some fallen as the loggers left them, others still towering like giant, tufted icebergs of wood – are still there today.

Scaling many famous peaks for the first time, Muir proved glaciers actually moved and convinced President Theodore Roosevelt to back conservation, create national forests and expand national parks.

Muir used his adventure writing in east coast magazines and newspapers such as *The New York Tribune* to reach a wider mass public, arguing for Nature in the face of wholesale railway-driven development. That way he met a lawyer, who helped take the cause 'to the Hill' to seek legislation in Washington. So Muir combined the components of subsequent environmental 'campaigns': communication, inspiration, definition of an issue at individual and global scales, use of ethics and law, politics, journalism and the media to play out a struggle between the public conscience and private interests.

Muir founded the Sierra Club, and then split from it over its support for a dam at Hetch Hetchy in Yosemite Valley. The San Francisco authorities blamed a lack of water – rather than their lack of a fire brigade and proper planning – for the fires that followed the great San Francisco earthquake. Hence, they needed a dam. It was the environmental cause célèbre of its day.

Others later split from the Sierra Club to form Greenpeace and Friends of the Earth.

Muir's work largely inspired the global national parks and conservation movement. So no emigrant child from Dunbar: no Rainbow Warrior, no World Heritage Sites – perhaps even no defence of the ozone layer. Despite his achievements, Muir is largely unsung as a hero or significant social figure.[16]

Why seven principles? It seems a good number.[17] Ideally, a campaign needs to:

1   Be multidimensional: communicating in all the dimensions of human understanding and decision-making. Political, emotional, economic, spiritual, psychological, technical, scientific, maybe more. Even if it begins in one, it must be able to translate into the others. It must understand the intuitive and personal (for example flowing from psychology and culture), and the counter-intuitive (for example from science) and be able to deal in both.

2   Engage by providing agency – it needs to give its supporters greater power over their own lives. It must offer a credible, feasible and attractive way to make a new and additional difference (see Chapter 2).

3   Have moral legitimacy, which it gets not by whom it represents but by meeting a need. Campaigners and their supporters have to be convinced the campaign is needed to make something happen in society that ought to be happening but that is not. The more widely shared this feeling becomes, the greater the moral authority of the campaign and the more that can be done. Most campaigns are planned in the mind, won in people's hearts and rationalized again in the mind.

4   Provoke a conversation in society (see Chapter 4). I say they provoke a conversation rather than conduct it because, to be really effective, campaigns often need society to rethink its views and actions on a particular issue. When campaigns achieve 'cross-over' or a self-sustaining chain reaction of participation, then of course the campaigning organization has lost 'control' and the 'issue' is no longer its property, but it has probably succeeded in changing that society forever. Start talking with society, end by society talking to itself.

5   Have verve, élan, infectious energy. It may feed aspirations, or provide security but, above all, it needs an inspired vanguard. If your campaign doesn't excite you, then it probably won't engage others.

6   Be strategic. It must plan a way to assemble enough forces to change what it wants to change. It must involve a battle-winning strategy at one level, and a war-winning strategy composed of a series of battles (see critical paths, Chapter 5).

7   Be communicable, first verbally, as a story – which enables it to be passed on, remembered, perhaps mythologized, not forgotten, mused over, rekindled, reinvented; second, visually: both as emotionally powerful framing images and as 'evidences'. These visual signs are short cuts to understanding. Campaigns that can be communicated like this can be literally understood without words so have no trouble crossing over

languages or, for the most part, across cultures. They also become 'semiostic' – people read their own meaning into the images, enabling a campaign to unite rather than to divide.

With qualities such as these, a campaign can resonate, spread and survive setbacks, able to reinvent itself and grow 'reflexively'. Even if crushed, oppressed or deserted by supporters, such a campaign may live on as an inspiration and rise again. When campaigns are successful in these terms, they can offer some people a lifestyle or belief system, and in some cases organizations, individuals and the campaigns become indistinguishable.

1

HOW TO BEGIN

WHERE TO START

A book can have only one beginning, but campaigns can have many different beginnings. First you need to find your own beginning, and that depends on where you are at:

- If you know your issue but you don't know exactly what you want to achieve, begin by defining your objective (see Chapter 5, 'The ambition box');
- If you need to campaign because you are faced with a known specific problem, and that tells you your objective but you don't know how to get that changed, then begin with the campaign motivation sequence (this chapter);
- If you have a concern but don't know how the issue works – the forces and processes behind the problem – then start with issue mapping and gathering intelligence (Chapter 4);
- If you already run a campaign and feel a need to change strategy or tactics, try looking at factors such as resources and assets (Chapter 9);
- If you have an organization that thinks it might like to campaign but is not sure, then step back and examine the bigger picture (Chapter 12), and try locating your approach in the ambition box.

See also the campaign planning star in Chapter 5, which illustrates factors needed in generating a campaign plan and proposition.

WHAT COMMUNICATION IS

The two words 'information' and 'communication' are often used interchangeably, but they signify quite different things. Information is giving out; communication is getting through. (Sidney J. Harris, American journalist and author)

Good communication isn't noticed. It's like good design: we only notice bad design. The London Underground map is often cited as a classic. We don't notice it because it fits its purpose so well (use it to *walk* around London, and you find it bears little resemblance to 'reality').

Forget old saws such as 'getting your message across'. Campaigners who focus on 'sending messages' will never succeed: they will persuade no one but themselves. Successful communication needs to be two-way: more telephone than megaphone, with the active involvement of both parties.

Real communication, it has been said,[1] is rare and involves 'the transferring of an idea from the mind of the sender to the mind of the receiver'.

If someone does not want to receive your message, they won't. Would-be communicators therefore need to understand the motivations of their audience.

All too often, communication is treated as a technical, one-way process beautifully designed to reflect the views of the sender, unsullied by the need to be effective with the receiver.

'Delivering messages', 'sending information', 'targeting advertising': it becomes like targeting missiles – fire and forget – except that forgetting is the last thing that should be happening. Campaigners should spend at least as much time listening to the public and the target, allies and opponents they seek to influence as they spend in working on communications back in the office.

The word 'audience' wrongly implies that receivers are passive. A dialogue is usually best, and if that's impossible, repetition may succeed in 'reaching' the audience.

A popular basic model of communications is illustrated in Figure 1.1.

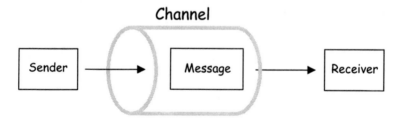

Figure 1.1 *Basic model of communications*

We all know that serious misunderstandings can occur even in one-to-one communication. Introduce a third party – such as a newspaper or radio station and its journalists – and volume may increase but noise gets into the channel because of journalists' interpretations, or pollution by the thousands of other messages to which we are exposed each day.[2]

To improve communication, obtain feedback, whether volunteered or obtained through qualitative research.

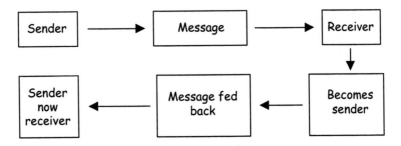

Figure 1.2 *Communication model incorporating feedback*

Des Wilson, founder of Shelter, said: 'Remember, the bigger the audience, the simpler the message.'[3] So with public media, messages need to become simpler, compared to the complexities you can deal with in conversations at home or in the office.

IF YOU FIND A FIRE

The short words are best, and the old words are the best of all.
(Sir Winston Churchill)

Motivational communication follows some well-established sequences, developed and refined by generations of salespeople. A useful version for campaigns is:

awareness → alignment → engagement → action

Take the example of a fire safety notice that you might find in a hotel.

These notices keep it simple. They look something like the example shown in Figure 1.3 (overleaf). At first sight, constructing this message seems easy but, in fact, it is carefully designed. It instructs to raise the alarm first – this is in the best interests of the hotel residents. It doesn't say 'call the fire brigade' – which might be in the best financial interests of the hotel owner, but which could mean searching for a phone in smoke-filled corridors. It puts lives over property. Then it says to go to the place of safety – and only then call the fire brigade.

So it's communication with a *purpose* (here = save lives). You need to know *why* you are trying to communicate, what the objective is in terms of an *action*, what you want someone to *do*, before you can communicate effectively.

Also, the sign is very simple and it instructs rather than offering a discussion, which would not be appropriate in an emergency. It is unambiguous. Lastly, it follows the sequence shown in Table 1.1.

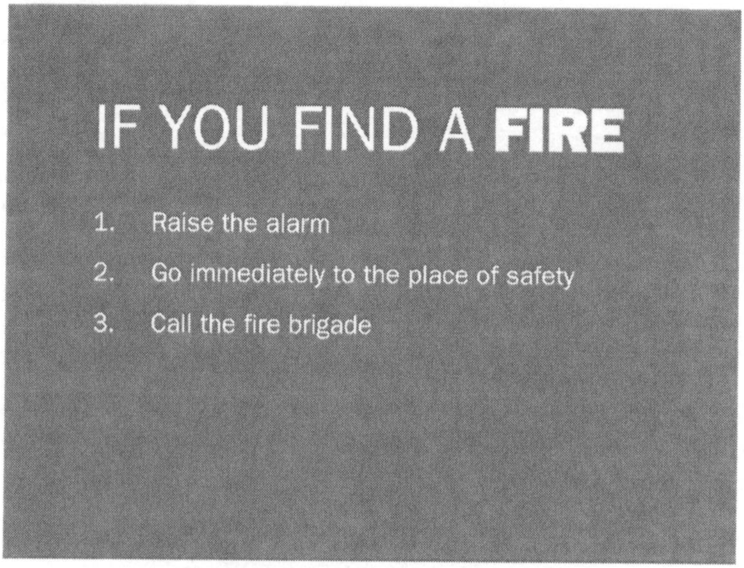

IF YOU FIND A **FIRE**

1.   Raise the alarm

2.   Go immediately to the place of safety

3.   Call the fire brigade

Figure 1.3 *Example of a fire safety notice*

Table 1.1 *Sequence followed by fire safety notice*

If you find a fire	Awareness
We are all in danger	Alignment
Let's go this way	Engagement
We are leaving	Action

Awareness establishes the subject. Alignment establishes that it is relevant to everyone. Engagement is an appeal to join in – and requires a commonly available mechanism (see Chapter 2). The action is what is needed. Omit or reorder any of these steps and problems result.

If all our communication was so simple, we'd all be more effective. Yet all too often our communication is not like this but more like the alternative fire sign shown in Figure 1.4.

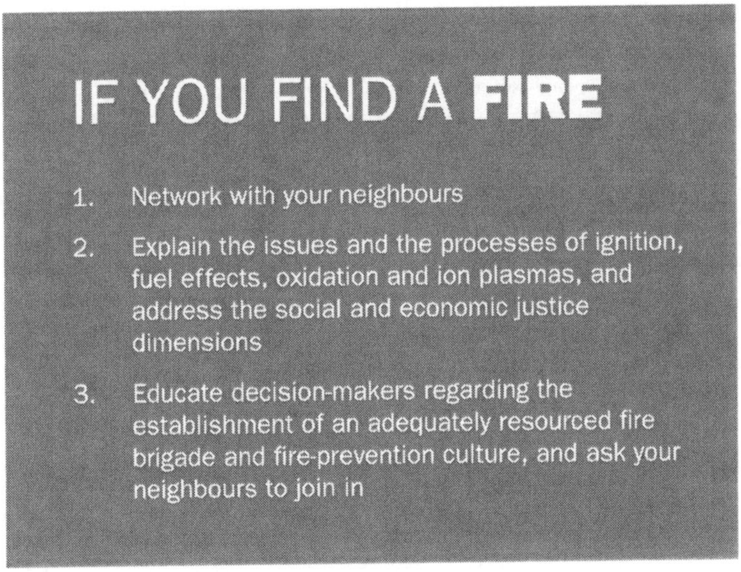

IF YOU FIND A **FIRE**

1. Network with your neighbours

2. Explain the issues and the processes of ignition, fuel effects, oxidation and ion plasmas, and address the social and economic justice dimensions

3. Educate decision-makers regarding the establishment of an adequately resourced fire brigade and fire-prevention culture, and ask your neighbours to join in

Figure 1.4 *Alternative fire safety notice*

This addresses the same subject: it, too, is about fire. It's 'on message'. But it is not very clear and would probably lead to people frying in their rooms. It is a message about an issue, not communication designed to get a result in terms of a specific action. It invites 'education' and 'networking': things that involve reflection and discussion, and are open to interpretation. This can occur when:

*   An internal agenda is transmitted to the outside world – easily done if exhausted by getting it through the system;
*   A policy or plan is transmitted as a 'message';
*   Everyone has a say and the message mentions every important issue; or
*   There is an attempt to educate rather than to motivate.

Motivational campaign sequence

Many of the best campaigns are planned as a simple chronology of events. Often there are only one or two fixed dates and the rest is a chain of objectives that need to be reached, like climbing from one level to another or stepping from one stone to the next, with no firm way of predicting just when that will occur.

Plan *backwards* from the call to action. That should be either a fixed date (such as an event) or a date that can be estimated sufficiently well to have all the necessary communications, assets and capabilities in place when it arrives. The possible start date is then generated by adding together the critical time periods needed for each stage before the call to action opportunity.

Campaigns usually need to start with awareness. Awareness of the problem, preferably made more compelling by showing the victim.[4]

The campaign sequence[5] illustrated in Figure 1.5 shows how to plan using the basic formula of the fire notice: awareness → alignment → engagement → action. Each part needs to fit to the next like a jigsaw – the 'enemy' needs to be the particular one that fits with that victim, the solution really does have to solve the specific problem, and so on.

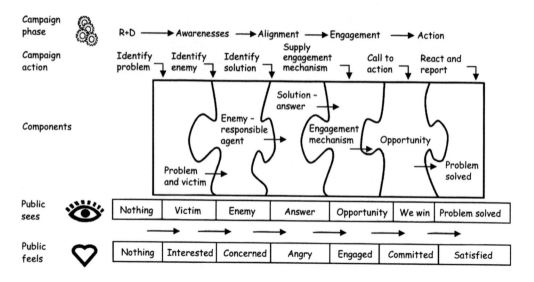

Figure 1.5 *Motivation sequence campaign model*

So in this classic communication path, the story begins when we see the problem – we see 'victims'. These might be human or physical, or animal or even plants. Fish dying from pollution, or a building damaged by acid rain, for example, or someone suffering torture. This is the awareness-building phase.

Next we see what or who is responsible, the 'enemy' or causal agent that is to blame – with no cause, a problem is not an issue. This is followed by a period of reinforcement by repetition or 'demonization': former UK Prime Minister Margaret Thatcher was an expert at this; she demonized striking miners, for example. This phase ought to last until the problem is established in the mind of our audience. By this time the public state of mind is one of concern.

If the 'bad news' just continues, the audience gets fed up and withdraws or switches off – the problem is just another tragedy. Concern with no solution will lead to withdrawal; with no constructive outlet it will create frustration, most probably towards the messenger. You can't hold people's emotional attention in that way for long.

If an 'answer' is supplied by revealing a solution, the campaign can progress because we get angry. It's no longer a tragedy but an *avoidable* problem: 'it doesn't have to be like this'. In journalistic terms you have the elements of a scandal (Chapter 8).

Alignment gets everyone looking in the same direction, agreeing what the problem is, who suffers, who's to blame and what the solution is. Skip any of this part and the audience won't see what you are doing as relevant to them.

An unaligned audience can be misread as not 'caring' about the problem if they don't engage after a call to action. In contrast, very strong alignment will result in spontaneous attempts to take action. For example, in 1995 during French nuclear tests at Moruroa, protests were organized outside French embassies all over the world, but soon thousands of people were taking action against any sort of French target they could reach. Art students in genteel English Bournemouth painted a mushroom cloud into the background of a Renault poster advertisement, while from Holland a group of Dutchmen cycled off to conquer Mont Blanc.

For the campaign to call for action it must have a suitable engagement mechanism ready; and when the timing is just right, give a clear call. In a public advocacy campaign, this might be a call to lobby a politician to pressure the government, visit a shop to lobby the manager about a brand or contact a company about corporate behaviour.

10:10 (www.1010uk.org) was launched in the run up to the 2009 'Conference of the Parties' of the UNFCCC. This was another 'moment of alignment': many people in the

---

BOX 1.1 – IT DOESN'T HAVE TO BE LIKE THIS

In the 1990 European Election, the UK Green Party won a record-breaking percentage of the vote in the UK. Its election broadcast of that year was perhaps the Greens' only really great piece of communication. A series of children appeared and did 'pieces to camera'. Each illustrated the simple point that the environment was polluted, and, by implication, didn't need to be and wouldn't be under the Greens. 'This is a glass of water,' said one child. An adult hand poured in a white powder from above. 'Add some nitrates, and some fertilizer,' said the boy. 'Now it's tap water – and I have to drink it.' Each sequence ended with the caption: 'It doesn't have to be like this.' Victim = child, enemy = anonymous industry figure, solution = vote Green, opportunity = election.

Similarly, seen by hundreds of millions on TV, a woman who had given birth in a flood-bound tree was rescued, along with her baby, by a helicopter winchman in Mozambique in 2000. A tragedy was clearly averted – it didn't need to happen. The incident was compelling, motivating because change was possible.

UK were strongly aligned to the need to 'do something' and 10:10 (making a 10 per cent carbon reduction in 2010) gave them a high profile platform (being promoted by a national newspaper and coming off the back of a film, *The Age of Stupid*) to do so. As a result, thousands of organizations, ranging from professional football clubs to government departments and supermarkets, did so, as well as many individuals. 10:10s then started springing up in other countries. In this case there was no need to go out and create alignment. The 'Red' campaign, raising funds for HIV-AIDS drugs for Africa, is a similar example (www.joinred.com): essentially an engagement device.

For a fund-raising group, if the campaign is at all successful, this may be when it goes back to its supporters or stakeholders to explain the success and ask for further help. If campaigners become too obsessed with the media, they may neglect engagement mechanisms, and the campaign generates publicity but no effective pressure. In this way, the campaign rolls out like a story, told from the beginning, with each step revealing something new. It does *not* start by communicating the whole route – if it did, there wouldn't be any change because there wouldn't be engagement, there would be no build-up or focus of pressure.

Unlike a play or a film, which progresses irrespective of audience interest, a campaign must not press on until the present stage is successfully completed. It has to gather support for each step – 'take people with you'. Sometimes this is a long, slow process. An over-ambitious project may try to take too many people along too far, too fast. An overcautious one may do the opposite.

COMMUNICATE BY DOING: MAKE EVENTS HAPPEN

Events work as communication: they are the stuff of politics, the essential nutrients of news. Asked what was the most difficult thing about running the country, British Prime Minister Harold Macmillan famously replied, 'Events, my dear boy, events.'

Creating events is the best way to be proactive and, as a rule, the winner in any persuasion struggle will be she or he who takes the initiative and sets the agenda. If your time is spent reacting to the events of others, you are unlikely to win. Pundits comment on change, campaigners make it happen.

Hope, injustice or anxiety may be the fuel but events should be the engine of campaigns. With luck, your campaign may register a big enough wave to blow your opponents off course. You stand most chance of doing that with a significant event, not a continuous effort.

The best campaigns communicate themselves because they involve doing, not advocacy. Deeds speak louder than words. We remember events and outcomes, not opinions. As one ex-director of Friends of the Earth, Tom Burke, is fond of saying: 'Nobody remembers what David and Goliath were fighting about – everyone knows who won.' News is about doing: we don't come across a crowd and ask 'What are people thinking?' We ask, 'What's happening?' Yet so many campaigners try to convey information, facts and even data, not actions and events.

Events help make media work far easier. I have often found myself trying to sell a story to a journalist and getting them interested, only to find that I can't answer the obvious question: 'So, what are you doing?' or 'What will happen?', because the campaign hadn't yet been planned as a series of events. Events can be news, your opinion isn't, and nor is an issue.

To make an event occur, we need to think in terms of doing things, activities that take us from point to point along a critical path. For people schooled in issues and facts, this can be a difficult transition, as they tend to produce arguments instead. Bear in mind the remark of political philosopher Macaulay: 'Argument is constructed in one way and government in entirely another' (and, he might now say, so is business). Your campaign planning should be based on events, not production of arguments.

CAMPAIGNING IS NOT EDUCATION

Campaigning involves stimulating action, best achieved by narrowing the focus and eliminating distractions and reducing options, as in advertising (Figure 1.6). Typically, it starts (left column) with a problem and moves a target audience through the stages of awareness (and alignment, not shown here), concern and so on, to action.

In contrast, education expands awareness of options and complexity (right-hand column). It typically takes a problem and shows that it is not so simple as you may have first thought.

BOX 1.2 – NATURAL INJUSTICE

Sometimes a campaign can be made noteworthy and arresting by personalizing it. This may be because we identify emotionally with individuals whereas we tend to ignore mass suffering, or because it resonates with long-established 'frames' that have emotional profile. On 19 March 2007, for example, the UK newspaper The Independent[6] carried a short article with the headline 'Czech village votes to ban US missile defence site'. Here we have David and Goliath and the cat calling on the king.

By taking a vote among its 100 or so residents (71 against, one in favour), the village of Trokavec converted an issue of politics into something far more personal. We can imagine living in the village, and picture the impact of a huge military installation dropped in by a superpower. The stark polarity of a superpower and a village instantly says 'this is unjust'. The same piece mentioned that two-thirds of Czechs oppose the plan, but that national statistic has nothing like the emotional impact of the tiny village trying to speak out. The campaign lesson? Personalize and create events that cause the reader, viewer or listener to do an instant calculus of right and wrong. Similarly, research[7] has shown that we will more readily help one person than help two, or a thousand.

The educational model is great for education but not for campaigning. It reaches understanding but not action. Using it to try and decide or stimulate action is likely to lead to confusion and frustration.

Attend meetings of university professors discussing a practicality to see this in practice. In one university I know, a discussion over what to do with a gap left by a 1940s World War II bomb, subsequently occupied by a car park, remained unresolved until the 1980s.

Contesting professors tend to make things complex, and dazzle each other with clever reframing, find angles nobody had thought of, or make reference to additional bodies of information that must be taken into account. Perpetual questioning is how knowledge advances. The same discussion in a bank or a double-glazing company would probably be over in minutes. Questioning fundamentals and reflecting on things is not how business, politics or war advances.

On the other hand, listen to the professors discussing the meaning of life or public motivations, or what music is, and you will probably leave impressed, turning over new insights in your mind, maybe seeing your whole existence in a new way. Ask the bankers

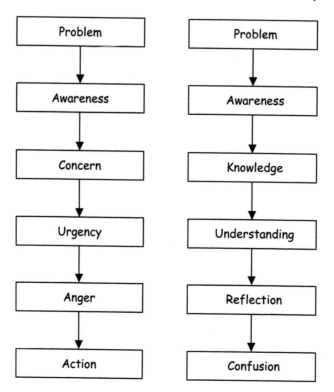

Figure 1.6 *Comparing a campaign model (left) with an education model (right)*

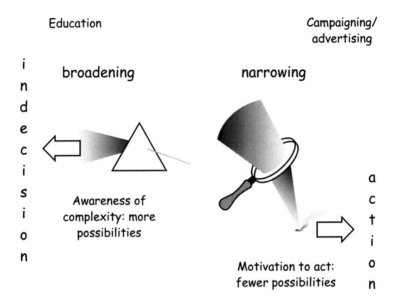

Figure 1.7 *Education and campaigning work in opposite directions*

and the sales directors to hold the same discussion (or even 'what business is') and you will quickly find it bottoms out in cliché, leaden tautologies and the sort of wisdom you can find in a fortune cookie (Figure 1.7).

Beware campaigners who want to educate others to see the issue in the right way before accepting their support. To be driven by principle is an admirable thing. but to campaign by trying to make others adopt your principles is not likely to be effective. As Gerd Leipold has written: 'Campaign organizations have to be opportunistic, not in terms of their beliefs and values but in terms of reaching audiences.'[8]

CAMPCAT ESSENTIAL COMMUNICATION COMPONENTS

Discussion of what will be an 'effective' communication can easily become circular. Try to avoid the pivotal word 'message'. If a discussion starts by asking 'What messages do we want to use?', it is quite likely to lead to a one-way process rather than two-way communication.

For communication to have the right effect, at least seven key components need to work together: CAMPCAT.

- Channel – **how** the message gets there;
- Action – **what** we want to happen (and what the audience is asked to do);

- Messenger – who **delivers** the message;
- Programme – **why** we're doing it (essential to know this to assess effectiveness);
- Context – **where** and when the message arrives (including what else is going on);
- Audience – **who** we are communicating with;
- Trigger – what will **motivate** the audience to act.

The actual message is, like a binary warhead, the call-to-action (effectively 'do this'), plus the trigger or motivator (effectively 'why you should'). They may be communicated by an example or argument, or visually, but not often as an instruction or admonishment.

The programme is internal. The audience and the action should be determined by the critical path of the campaign (Chapter 5). Qualitative research (Chapter 4) should determine the trigger, context, messenger and channel. Campaigners have to accept that they will not always be the best messenger: in the words of Ayerman and Jamison's classic study of Greenpeace, they need to be users of research: 'intelligencers'. There's no point going on the radio or TV to make your point for the sake of publicity: it's having an effect that counts.[9]

Some campaigners enjoy sending messages so much that they scarcely ever stop to try and find out what message was received by the assumed target audience. The messengers themselves can then become 'noise in the channel'. You see the campaigner on TV. You get the message – that she or he is campaigning – but what about? Quite probably, we don't remember.[10]

Timing (part of context) can alter the effect. Anti-smoking radio commercials were found to be more effective on Sunday mornings, when many listeners regretted the amount they had smoked the night before, than on Saturday evening; an equally relevant time when people were just about to go for a night out.[11]

Each of these CAMPCAT elements should be researched rather than guessed at (although P the Programme is internally decided). In 2005 for example, CDSM and Campaign Strategy ran a survey of attitudes to air travel for Greenpeace UK.[12] As part of this we asked people this: 'Greenpeace believes that pollution from aircraft is a serious contributor to climate change. Given that, which of the following do you agree with?' and got the responses as shown in Table 1.2.

We also asked the same question but changed the messenger to 'independent scientists' and obtained more or less identical results, indicating that in this case Greenpeace did not need to change the messenger or to seek third-party endorsement: it was credible. In other cases – about finance for example – you might expect that the 'brand Greenpeace' would have a less good fit and that using a different messenger could help effectiveness.

In a similar way, choice of 'Channel' has many embedded effects. For instance, UK research into trust of channels by the Henley Centre showed 90 per cent trust for husband, wife or partner, 82 per cent for friends, 69 per cent for work colleagues, 50% for TV news, 27 per cent for retailers or manufacturers, and only 14 per cent for government or advertising. So 'information' or 'content' delivered through one channel may have a very different effect compared to delivering it through a different channel.

Table 1.2 *Attitudes to air travel*

Air travel is now too cheap	33%
There should be a tax on fuel for air travel	52%
Air travel should be rationed by government	20%
No more airports should be built	44%
We should limit our air travel voluntarily	61%
There should be a pollution warning on air tickets	61%
Don't know	2%
None of these	10%

REMEMBER THE CHICKENS

In most campaigning, it's best to abide by the marketing dictum 'start from where your audience is' and find a way to lead to the action you want people to take, or the conclusion you need them to reach, by starting from something they are already interested in, or concerned about. Campaigners who project their concerns and perspectives onto others – trying to 'sell', adding arguments and pointing to benefits, rather than researching audience perceptions – tend to fail.

Research is essential to find out how others perceive your proposition and how they talk about it. For example, there was once a successful aid agency development project in part of East Africa.[13] Following its success, the agency wanted to explain this idea to villagers elsewhere. So it sent a crew to make a short film explaining the project, and equipped a vehicle as a mobile cinema to show it.

The film was made and toured to the target villages. Afterwards, a survey found that what villagers most remembered about the film was 'the chickens'. The agency was puzzled: chickens had nothing to do with the project at all.

Eventually the agency looked at the film. A cut-away shot showed an agency Land Rover speeding past a hut, and as it did so, a large group of chickens flew across the screen. Unfortunately, in the target village area, chickens were a sign of wealth, and this therefore was by far the most interesting feature of the film. The villagers had been shown wealth on the scale of *Dynasty* or *Dallas*, only measured in chickens. Because it did not understand the language of the area (or the priorities of the villagers), the agency had no idea of what its film really showed.

I once helped win a debate before a live audience because our opponent – a wealthy English farmer – illustrated his case against planning controls by attacking suburbs, apparently unaware that the audience came mostly from the London suburbs.[14] The

BOX 1.3 – DO WHAT WORKS FOR THE TARGET AUDIENCE, NOT WHAT WORKS FOR YOU

It's very easy to play to your own constituency and resonate with them but not to change the support your opponent enjoys. In the UK numerous climate and transport campaigners have criticised Jeremy Clarkson, a TV motoring journalist who has positively celebrated conspicuous consumption of fossil fuels. In 2005 students and environmentalists petitioned Oxford Brookes University to stop him being awarded an Honorary Degree[15] and in 2009 activists from the group Climate Rush, who model themselves on the political Suffragettes, dumped horse manure on the drive of his large Oxfordshire house. Clarkson himself revels in being opposed by environmentalists and is something of an icon to Prospectors (see page 72) who are angered by concerned ethical campaigners telling them they should not want a big flashy car and so on. If the aim was to make someone like Clarkson less attractive to people with such motivations – gaining the esteem of others, or gaining self-esteem – then a better approach would be to associate him with someone who plausibly shared his predelictions, but who is laughed at. An example might be the 1960s spoof Bond figure 'Austin Powers'[16]: he would love big cars but is patently a fool.

exception to this rule is if you want to change minds. In this case it's important not to trigger familiar frames (Chapter 11). Contrary to popular assumption, good campaigning rarely involves changing minds. More often, it works through new applications of existing beliefs, perceptions and motivations.

Potential audiences may not be obvious. They may be 'sleeping', and you need to work out who they are and have them woken up in the appropriate manner. So 'starting from where the audience is' could mean for instance, in a campaign about genetically modified (GM) food, getting chefs to talk about food quality, taste and goodness, in order to engage with people interested in food, rather than trying to reach them by talking about agricultural policy via news coverage.

FRAMING

All our communication, particularly condensed 'snapshots' such as news or advertising, is dominated by hidden mental short cuts that we use to make sense of the world, and of new information. These are 'frames', an idea attributed by the Frameworks Institute to Walter Lippman, 'a grandfather of public affairs',[17] who said 'first we see, then we understand'.

When confronted by something unknown, we reach for established patterns (also called 'pattern matching') or experiences to say: 'Aha: it's a one-of-those.'

This largely unconscious and silent process is profoundly powerful because each frame comes with its logic, rationale and explanation as to who or what is responsible, and what a built-in solution looks like. The choice of frame determines the outcome of a debate because it sets the terms of resolution – how something will be decided.

Words can trigger frames, but, most often and most powerfully, images trigger frames. Effective campaigns trigger the 'right' frame – the one that reinforces the impression or conclusion you want – and are planned to do so again, and again, and again.

The institute gives examples from international relations to US elections and dental care at www.frameworksinstitute.org. Its Global Interdependence Study showed how Americans use the frames of neighbours and families to understand international affairs, with quite different results from Europeans, because it has different embedded assumptions. Americans also tend to see 'climate' as made by God or Nature, and hence the idea of human-made climate change (a frame) as inherently implausible, whereas reducing carbon dioxide (CO_2) pollution (a different frame) sounds more feasible to them.

During the 2000s both Vice President Al Gore[18] and the UK government fell into the trap of framing climate change as a global, intractable, frightening problem requiring international cooperation, and then proposing small domestic actions as a 'solution'. The problem and solution frames did not fit: they failed the 'jigsaw' test (see page 253). Of the three major psychologial groups – Pioneers, Prospectors and Settlers – only the first are likely to 'think globally and act locally'. The others tend to see the international framing of the problem as denoting that the solution has to be by 'international actors' like presidents and prime ministers, that is 'not people like us'. So the characterization of the problem isolated it from most of the 'public'.

> *The cognitive cultural models that are sparked by the frame allow us to forget certain information and to invent other details, because the frame is now in effect. For example, if people believe that kids are in trouble, they will be drawn to facts in a news story that reinforce this notion, and will disregard those that deny it. If the facts don't fit the frame, it's the facts that are rejected, not the frame…*
>
> *If the messenger in a TV news story is a teacher, for example, the viewer is likely to assume that this is about education or about a problem that should be solved by schools. If the visuals show people sitting around doing little, the viewer may decide this is about laziness, regardless of what the narrator is saying about unemployment statistics among rural peasants in a certain country. (The Frameworks Institute)*

So who you put up as a spokesperson can easily trigger a particular frame, as may your organization's very presence.

Triggering the frame is more important than defining a particular message or argument. Once a frame is established – for example in an interview or other communication episode – attempts to argue against it are doomed.

Frame a 'new issue' carefully. Hair-shirt climate campaigners so successfully embedded the idea that climate change is a huge, intractable problem with painful 'solutions' that contrary information is discounted. So when American climatologist Stephen Schneider and Swedish energy economist Christian Azar showed the total cost of 'fixing' global warming meant only a two-year delay in a fivefold increase in wealth over a hundred years, the response was negligible.[19] They were boxed in by conventional wisdom – their facts did not fit the frame. Contrast this with the Stern Report released in 2006. Economist Sir Nicholas Stern suggested that global warming could shrink the global economy by 20 per cent whereas the cost of action would be just one per cent of global gross domestic product. Stern was a former chief economist of the World Bank and his study was promoted by the UK government's Treasury department. Whereas Schneider was a climate scientist (what do they know about money?) and Azar a relatively obscure economist, Stern was mainstream, wrapped in all the financial authority of the World Bank and the City of London. The Stern Report was credited with helping change the minds or providing the excuse for a change of position in national capitals such as Canada and Australia.

Rhetoricians and therapists[20] trigger frames with words to redirect conversation. The outcome frame evaluates things in terms of outcomes. The ecology frame in terms of fit with what's going on around us. The evidence frame tests detail – how will we know when we have succeeded? The 'as if' frame supposes that something has happened, or not happened, in order to test how we feel about it.

The most popular book on framing is George Lakoff's *Don't Think of an Elephant* (the point being that once you hear this injunction you can't help but do so and the elephant frame is in play). His later book *The Political Mind* explores how frames can be reinforced by use because they create bespoke neural pathways in our brains. In the latter, Lakoff argues for a political 'New Enlightenment' in which we all become more aware of how most of our decision-making is not down to opinions and thoughts we are conscious of – 'reflective' thought – but the unconscious (and easily manipulated) 'reflexive' thought that is emotional and automatic.

Lakoff's favourite test case is the frame of tax, which he uses to illustrate how the political 'right' in the US came to dominate media and social debate in the 1980s and 1990s:

> On the day that George W. Bush took office, the words *tax relief* started appearing in White House communiqués to the press and in official speeches and reports by conservatives. Let us look in detail at the framing evoked by this term.
>
> The word *relief* evokes a frame in which there is a blameless Afflicted Person who we identify with and who has some Affliction, some pain or harm that is imposed by some external Cause-of-pain. Relief is the taking away of the pain or harm, and it is brought about by some Reliever-of-pain.
>
> The Relief frame is an instance of a more general Rescue scenario, in which there is a Hero (The Reliever-of-pain), a Victim (the Afflicted), a Crime (the Affliction), a Villain (the Cause-of-affliction) and a Rescue (the Pain Relief).

The Hero is inherently good, the Villain is evil, and the Victim after the Rescue owes gratitude to the Hero.

The term tax relief evokes all of this and more. Taxes, in this phrase, are the Affliction (the Crime), proponents of taxes are the Causes-of-Affliction (the Villains), the taxpayer is the Afflicted Victim, and the proponents of 'tax relief' are the Heroes who deserve the taxpayers' gratitude. Every time the phrase tax relief is used and heard or read by millions of people, the more this view of taxation as an affliction and conservatives as heroes gets reinforced.

The causes espoused by many campaigners require government spending, which in turn requires tax. So in 2009 I proposed[21] a way to 're-frame tax' from a bad to a good thing:

Let's start with the heroes of the piece: those who pay tax. Given freely, voluntarily, their sacrifice resonates with a host of positive frames. They help build communities, they invest in our children, they care for each other and care for the carers. They pay for our defence. They aid the poor and protect the weak.

Without taxpayers there would be no public schools, hospitals, roads or armies, no public broadcasting, no judiciary, nowhere for the elected representatives to meet, and precious few railways, roads or water treatment systems, not to mention overseas aid budgets, bail outs of banks, help to mortgage owners or an Apollo Programme for renewable energy.

So why not talk about these people in more positive terms? Not 'taxpayers' as if they are fined, implying bad behaviour or other victim hood, but contributors, the funders and builders of our society...

There are a host of simple ways in which this tide could be turned in a new direction. Tax contributors could be sent a thank you for, example, or a certificate to display. HMRC (UK tax) envelopes could be colour coded so that the postman or woman would know what scale of contributor he or she was delivering to and so on. Instead of a tax 'demand', government might send you your Contribution Calculation ... Presidents and prime ministers could invite high contributors to receptions – the Queen might have them to a garden party based on cumulative contributions? Accountancy or a career in the Inland Revenue could take on a whole new friendlier tone.

STRATEGY

A pattern or plan that integrates an organization's major goals, policies and action sequences into a cohesive whole. It helps marshal and allocate an organization's resources into a unique and viable posture based on its relative internal competencies and shortcomings, anticipating changes in the environment and contingent moves by intelligent opponents. (Mintzberg, Lampel et al, 1992)[22]

Strategy means changing the prevailing forces so that you can win. Strategy is your route map for change: more than a conventional navigation, one that doesn't just traverse the terrain of society but reshapes it. Your communications strategy and engagement tactics need to take supporters on a journey too.

Military planners quickly learned that the big choices, the 'first cut' among options, are those that determine much of what follows. Once a campaign starts, major changes are usually not an option. Prussian General Helmuth von Moltke said: 'A mistake in the original concentration of the armies is very difficult to rectify in the course of the campaign.'

Making strategy is followed by making plans, and that is followed by campaigning. Expect chaotic, unpredictable turns of events. The expression 'cry chaos and let loose the dogs of war' is well founded.

Rick Le Coyte, formerly a Greenpeace strategist, says:

> *If strategy involves having goals and plans to reach them, but remaining flexible about the extent that they are fixed and how exactly they are to be achieved, it means that the strategy, especially for a pressure group, is like an odyssey of ancient mythology. There is some big, over-riding purpose to the whole venture and on the way there are some tasks to perform. However, do not be surprised if the intervention of various gods, Cyclops and other mortals causes some surprises and distractions en route.* (personal communication)

Strategies differ according to your view of how change can come about. As is detailed in Appendix 1, since 1988, hundreds of organizations have run climate campaigns, and though many focused on the United Nations Framework Convention on Climate Change (UNFCCC), they vary widely, from bottom-up city campaigns, to promoting solar power, to investing in forests, to lobbying for fuel efficiency standards to promoting alternative refrigeration systems that do not use hydrofluorocarbons (HFCs).

These are not tactical differences but incompatible strategic choices. Incompatible because they require so much effort and resources that any one organization could not run both at once, or because they will impede each other, or because they compete for attention, which, like goodwill and political capital, is in short and limited supply.

Similarly, when *New Scientist* magazine gave seven leading forest conservationists a notional US$10 million to spend on protecting tropical forests, they came up with wildly varying answers – ranging from changing the global economy to educating future leaders and short-term site protection.[23]

To achieve a significant objective it is often necessary to fight shorter-term tactical battles, sometimes with different targets. In the 1980s, for example, while at Friends of the Earth, I campaigned against habitat destruction by intensive farming in the UK countryside. The prevailing 'Dan Archer'[24] myth was, however, so strong that the media and public rejected the idea that farming could be to blame (rather than, say, building development). To overcome the power of the farming lobby, we first had to weaken it. So we paused to run a campaign against straw-burning, because this was widely seen as unacceptable, and by achieving a ban we set a psychological precedent, and began the process of dismantling the public facade of industrial farming.

If there is one reliably useful rule for developing strategy and the campaign capacity of an organization (see pages 52, 215, 298) it is Sun Tzu's idea of 'a strategy of tactical positioning'.[25] Work out what your best tactic is, and define a strategy around that. Plan the strategy so that you can deploy that tactic, perhaps frequently but certainly decisively.

AIMS AND OBJECTIVES

Terms such as aims, objectives and goals are used in many ways. I find it most useful to refer to 'aims' as long-term end points.

Aims can be fulfilled, objectives achieved. Objectives are the waypoints that can be actually planned for.

Table 1.3 *Possible campaign aims and objectives*

Aim	World peace	Protect ancient forests	Save the climate
Long-term campaign objective	Nuclear disarmament	Stop destructive logging	End use of fossil fuels
Current campaign objective	Nuclear test ban treaty	Stop illegal logging in the Amazon	Stop further development of reserves
Project-level objective	Sign up country X to support it	Stop illegal mahogany exports	Stop new oil exploration
Sub-objective (project level)	Mobilize supporters of Y key politicians	Stop such exports into the US	Stop exploration at the UK Atlantic frontier

To achieve any one objective, you will normally need to achieve intermediate or sub-objectives. All can be 'campaigns': the processes of campaign planning are almost the same, from the smallest to the largest scales.

At one extreme, once a mission-level campaign is achieved, the organization itself may be no longer needed;[26] at the other, individual campaign projects or 'pushes' may be just weeks or months.

The aim is what we ultimately want. The strategic objective of the campaign is the big difference we are planning to make in order to (help) achieve that. The objective of the current campaign is what we're trying to do now, or first. The project-level campaign objective is one of the things we need to do in order to get there.

CAMPAIGN MASTERPLANNER

The campaign planning and execution tools in this book can be used together or independently of one another. For those who like to tie things up, or see how they might be used that way, these diagrams show the basic campaign planning system that I use when working with groups to plan campaigns. It's not the only way nor necessarily the best – just the one that I've found works best for me.

Here's a simple overview (Figure 1.8) that I used to use some years ago. 'Outline a strategy' corresponds roughly to the 'Planning Star' on page 124.

Figure 1.8 *Devise and test a strategy*

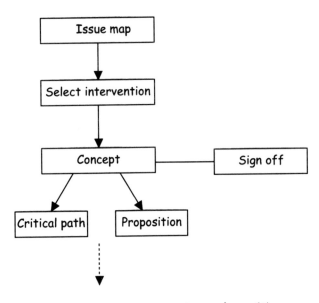

Figure 1.9 *Basic campaign pathway (1)*

Now here's a basic campaign pathway (Figure 1.9) that more closely matches the content of this book. The first part gets us as far as a campaign proposition and a critical path. (Relevant sections: Chapter 4, especially 'Issue mapping'; Chapter 5 'Making a campaign concept' and 'Making a critical path'; and Chapter 7 'Constructing RASPB propositions'.)

The rest of the basic pathway is in Figure 1.10. This level of detail may be useful in explaining to managers or colleagues that there's a system behind all those brainstorms and issue maps.

Your organization may dispense with 'sign offs' or have a different system of campaign management. Most, however, will demand some form of accountability. Few campaigns are over in 'one cycle' – for most campaigns, the planning to execution period is months or a year to 18 months (after that the landscape begins to change), and the 'live' period of a planned campaign is a few months to a year or so. Of course you can try to compress planning into a much shorter time, but if you do, the amount of guesswork involved increases rapidly. Ask yourself 'How right do we want to be?'

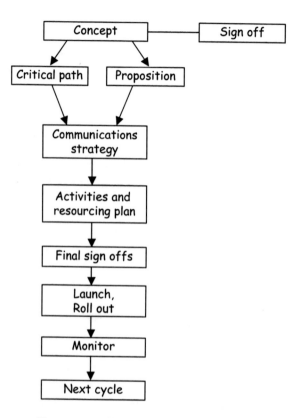

Figure 1.10 *Basic campaign pathway (2)*

Those are the main campaign development steps. Further details about key steps can be found elsewhere in the book: for communications strategy, see much of the book, but especially 'Skeleton campaign communications strategy from critical paths' in Chapter 5 (and also Chapter 20); for monitor and next cycle, see 'Evaluation' in Chapter 11 and 'Fixing a Campaign: Changing a strategy' in Chapter 9.

On the following pages, Figures 1.11 to 1.16 expand on various aspects of the steps in the alternative campaign pathways.

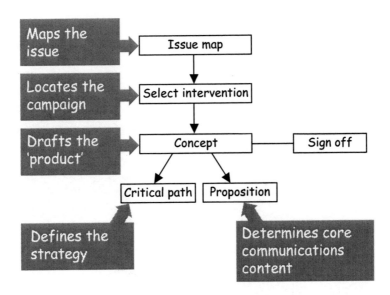

Figure 1.11 *What these steps do (1)*

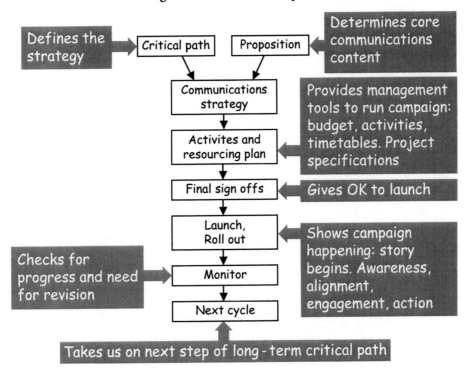

Figure 1.12 *What these steps do (2)*

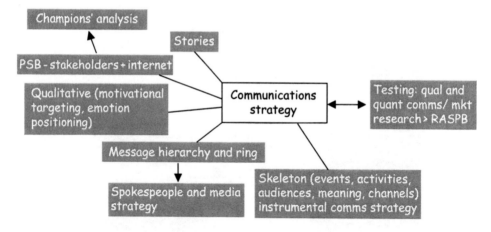

Figure 1.13 *Expansion of communications strategy (1)*

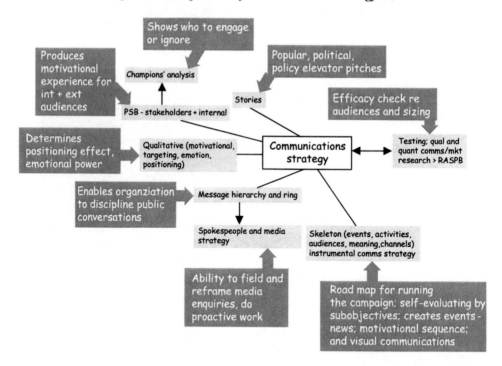

Figure 1.14 *Expansion of communications strategy (2)*

Note: PSB = problem – solution – benefit

RASPB = responsible party, action required, solution, problem, benefit

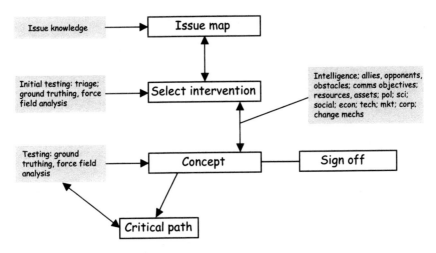

Figure 1.15 *Work needed for other steps (1)*

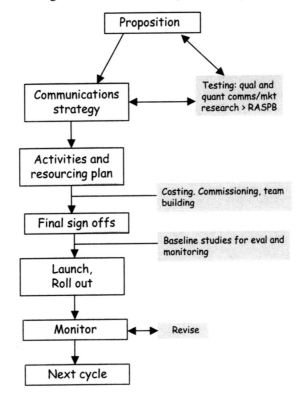

Figure 1.16 *Work needed for other steps (2)*

In management terms you may also need to consider:

- Training;
- Human resources (HR) recruitment/assignment and so on;
- Discussion, information sharing, workshops;
- Remote working;
- Coaching;
- Mentoring; and
- Project management.

Generating intelligence about allies, opponents, obstacles and so on usually merits commissioning external studies. To do proper testing to generate a proposition, you usually need to hire some external expertise for qualitative and quantitative research (see page 108). The activities and resourcing plan means using project planning and management techniques. Costing projects and creating teams often involves human resources expertise. The qualitative communications strategy demands creative skills that few organizations have in-house. Sorting out the message hierarchy and ring, and assigning and training spokespeople, is most often a role for the press office. Creating good events and direct communications may mean hiring more external input from agencies or production companies who specialize in such work, such as events and festival artists.

Basic campaign training should cover topics like issue mapping and communications strategy, while the majority of campaigners can benefit from training in project management techniques. Sectoral specialists such as political lobbyists and industry analysts can be worth hiring for champions and stakeholder analysis, while for qualitative communications, we might hire in help with visual langauge, myths and story construction.

2

COMMUNICATING
WITH HUMANS

STORIES

When a person listens to a story, both sides of the brain are working. The left brain is processing the words, while the right brain is actively filling in the gaps. This is the reason why it is so important to read to children, to allow their brains to imagine the story, rather than using television and films for all their learning.[1]

Campaign communications need to roll out before an audience like a story, from the beginning.

Figures 2.1 and 2.2 show two ways of giving the same information.

We can immediately see what's happening in Figure 2.1, because it's a story. Figure 2.2 addresses the same subject – wolves, minors and near-death experiences – but in a quite different, less memorable way.

Stories certainly pre-date writing, and probably art. Use stories wherever you can, because people remember them, and if possible use real people in stories, because we can identify with them. Save the academic report format for communicating with machines, or for professional seminars.

Figure 2.1 *A story involving a wolf, a little girl and a near-death experience*

Report on Non-accidental Wolf Related Deaths

Historical statistics showing trend in wolf-related non-accidental injuries involving minors (under the age of 16) in central regions. Daylight hours observations only. After column 3 the basis of calculation changes but the base sample remains the same. The trend is not significant but individual cases remain a cause for concern. especially in the small number that result in fatalities or close escapes. The figures speak for themselves.

Figure 2.2 *Another way of displaying the information in Figure 2.1 – but less memorable*

Stories are how we relate many important things in our lives, inside and outside organizations. They provide a free way for an idea to spread: as in urban myths, moral tales, or 'memes',[2] well beyond any paid-for communication.

Stories with human interest, based around a person, whether real or not, can move us from right-brain to left-brain communication, from facts and rationality to emotions and feelings. They take us there: 'it could be me'. Like pictures, stories don't need to argue, and you can't argue with them. Because *you* work out the meaning of a story yourself without having it thrust upon you, they can also more easily lead to that rare event, a change of mind. The deeper meaning can come to you long after you first hear a story.[3]

Using stories multiplies your options with the media: human stories are the stuff of feature pages, not news pages. That way you often get more space, and more readers, and your message is more likely to emerge intact, especially if it is embedded in the story structure.

Some say stories tap into fundamental psychology. Jan Stewart[4] points to four 'brain states': beta (awake and most active), alpha (awake but daydreaming), theta (almost asleep) and delta (sleeping). She says of stories:

> *At the second attention level, as the brain searches for a deeper meaning … the right brain is often favoured as relationships and patterns are developed. Processing … is*

an unconscious process – that is, we are not aware that we are doing it. The second attention level is where the story is reformulated to have personal relevance. Sometimes the story stays at this level and causes unconscious behavioural change, or it can rise into the first attention level through an 'A-ha!' reaction.

It is vital that the story, myth, legend or whatever is chosen is selected carefully. Ideally, the story should be easily understood at the first attention level, but stimulate a search for a deeper meaning at some time in the future.

There are said to be a number of 'basic types' of story. These structures might help tell yours. Here are examples[5] applied to opera:

1   *Cinderella* – Unrecognized virtue recognized in the end. It's the same story as the tortoise and the hare or the grasshopper and the ant. Cinderella doesn't have to be a girl, nor does the story even have to be a love story. What is essential is that the good is at first despised, but recognized in the end. Further examples are *La Cenerentola, Cendrillon* and *The Magic Flute;*

2   Achilles – the Fatal Flaw – this provides the groundwork for practically all classical tragedy, although it can be made into comedy, too – for example, *Samson et Dalila, Madame Butterfly, Falstaff;*

3   *Faust* – The debt that must be paid, the fate that catches up with all of us sooner or later – other examples include *La Bohème, Rigoletto* and *La Traviata;*

4   *Tristan and Isolde* – that standard triangular plot of two women and one man, or two men and one woman – also *The Marriage of Figaro, The Barber of Seville, Tosca* and *Lucia di Lammermoor, Carmen, L'Elisir d'Amore (The Elixir of Love), Pagliacci, Cavalleria Rusticana;*

5   *Circe* – the spider and the fly – such as *Othello, Salome;*

6   *Romeo and Juliet* – boy meets girl, boy loses girl, boy either finds or does not find girl (it doesn't matter which) – *The Merry Widow, L'italiana in Algeri (The Italian Girl in Algiers), La Bohème, Cosi fan tutte, Orpheus in the Underworld;*

7   The gift taken away. This may take two forms: either the tragedy of the loss itself, or it may be about the search that follows the loss, such as in *Orfeo, Orpheus in the Underworld, Il Trovatore;*

8   The hero who cannot be kept down. This is demonstrated in stories of perseverance and determination that result in either joy or destruction for the protagonist, as in *Turandot, Don Giovanni* and *Aida.*

The story often has a familiar pattern, 'grammar' or structure. Robert McKee[6] identifies five stages: the inciting incident – which is the primary cause of all that follows – the progressive complications, the crisis, climax and resolution. American business practice is full of stories about the importance of stories. Many of these reflect the dominance of Prospectors (see page 72) in the US culture, with an emphasis on 'me, me, me', and personal presentations. Annette Simons details 'six stories you need how to tell':[7]

1 Who I am stories;
2 Why I am here stories;
3 My vision story;
4 Teaching stories;
5 Values in action stories; and
6 'I know what you are thinking' stories.

Another good resource is the Giozueta Business Library,[8] with seven forms of organizational story telling.

Campaigns are always full of stories, but few campaigners have made enough use of them, myself included. The biggest political impact achieved by a pesticides campaign on which I worked with Friends of the Earth resulted from the public response to crop-spraying incidents, but not because we planned it that way. The campaign presented policy arguments based on detailed desk research, but we were unexpectedly contacted by large numbers of the public with their (often very distressing) stories. If we had appealed for the public to come forward with their experiences from the start, and based the campaign around those, we might have achieved more.[9]

SEEING IS BELIEVING: COMMUNICATION PREFERENCES

Of all of our inventions for mass communication, pictures still speak the most universally understood language. (Walt Disney)

Almost every campaign is best conducted visually. Visuals give reach, accessibility and impact; modern technology has created an increasingly visual media world, and seeing, generally, is believing, because most people have an inbuilt preference for receiving information visually.[10] For most people, a picture is worth a thousand words.

When we understand, we often say: 'I see'.[11] Some people's inbuilt preference is for speech – 'we sang from the same hymn sheet' – or touch – 'we clicked'.

Visuals can reach our emotions, bypassing argument. They can reinforce or change views. Research any issue and you tend to find that people's views often track back to some event, recalled as a picture. 'It was when I saw X that I realized things were serious.'

A campaign should communicate in as many dimensions as possible, but if you needed to choose one medium, and without one-to-one knowledge of your intended audience, then it should be visuals. Once there's feel-touch-and-smell media, things may change.

Being visual often means escaping institutional preferences for text. Even if they accept the need for visual communication, many organizations communicate that with a written note!

However partial, TV is still enough of a window on the world for visuals to be used as a benchmark of truth. 'I just saw that – it's true.' All reporters tend to say 'we have seen' or 'we have been shown', when introducing an element of the story that they are positioning as true. If, on the other hand, a report begins with 'we are being told', then you are immediately suspicious that a 'claim' is being offered, something open to dispute and only a varnished version of the truth. The starting point is already some way below the 'truth'. So events that can be photographed or directly witnessed or participated in are important.

However, Gardner[12] argues that schools and culture focus on linguistic and logical mathematical intelligence (measured as intelligence quotient, IQ) to the detriment of other types of intelligence and ways of learning. Institutions tend to promote people who are good at text, speech or numbers, and their preferences tend to dominate internal communications. If this then dominates campaigns, however, the consequences can be disastrous.

Gardner proposes teaching based on multiple intelligences.[13] Campaigners could profitably do the same:[14]

- words (*linguistic intelligence* – offer speech or text);[15]
- numbers or logic (*logical/mathematical* – offer numbers, classifications);
- pictures (*visual/spatial* – offer visual aids, colour, art, visual organizers);
- music (*musical* – offer music or environmental sounds, or key points in a rhythm or melody);
- self-reflection (*intrapersonal* – self-discovery, self-analysis, setting your own goals – offer choices and evoke personal feelings or memories);
- a physical experience (*bodily/kinaesthetic* – 'hands-on' – involve the whole body);
- a social experience (*interpersonal* – for example a party or exhibition – offer peer or cross-age sharing or cooperative work);
- an experience in the natural world (*naturalist* – offer ways to relate the subject to environment or ecology).

Putting on a festival complete with opportunities for reading, logic workshops, model-making, quiet contemplation and so on may be impractical. Yet reliance on words and numbers is likely to be less effective than a more holistic approach.

Most successful NGO communication has hinged on visuals. Amnesty International's candle, symbolizing its role of bringing hope and light into dark places, the guide dog of Guide Dogs for the Blind, the Worldwide Fund for Nature's (WWF) 1961 launch with pictures of doomed rhinos and its panda logo, the Cousteau Foundation's ship Calypso, Greenpeace's actions at sea, the stylish advertisements of Médecins Sans Frontières (MSF),[16] invoking the established dramatic format of the 'flying doctor'.

Face to face, our body language outweighs what we say. Although there are important cultural differences,[17] how we *look* generally says more than anything else. Psychologist Albert Mehrabian,[18] is said to have stated that when it comes to expressing feelings:[19]

- 55 per cent of the communication consists of body language;
- 38 per cent is through tone of voice;
- 7 per cent is through words.

Feelings are important in determining what we think of a person or proposal. Do we trust them? If not, we're unlikely to believe them. Emotional and psychological deficits easily overwhelm rational, scientific, economic or technical plus points. As the PR firm Burson-Marsteller states: 'You can't win an argument with someone who has more credibility than you do.'

Even if you don't bother to communicate in pictures, then visually dominated media, such as TV, much online and 'social media' or even many newspapers, will do it for you and insert images themselves. These then dominate what is communicated and received – and may not be what you had hoped for. So make sure *your* pictures tell your story.

BE INTERESTING – OR BE IGNORED

Sometimes the most basic lessons of campaign design are the most important. In 2007 Elaine Lawrence and I conducted an evaluation[20] of the Friends of the Earth campaign 'The Big Ask'.[21] As usual, we tried to look at outputs, outcomes and impacts, including through internal and external interviews. One of the most pertinent comments came from journalist Mike McCarthy, Environment Editor of UK newspaper *The Independent*:

> *Being interesting is very effective. Don't be boring. Many environment groups, in trying to win media interest, focus on the important rather than the interesting. There is a massive difference for the media. This campaign made something important interesting. What was 'The Big Ask' actually about? It took a frankly rather dull and complex public policy process about mandatory targets and made the legislative process interesting. It would have been very easy to make it boring.*

The Big Ask was certainly effective. It mobilized tens of thousands of individuals and hundreds of Friends of the Earth groups in England and Wales to lobby almost every MP to support moves for a climate change bill requiring the government to set targets for progressive reductions in CO_2 emissions. By a combination of energetic execution and good fortune in political circumstance it resulted in the government reversing its opposition and adopting the idea itself.

BBC political correspondent Nick Robinson said:

> *People often ask, 'Does anything change politics?'. Well it has here. Friends of the Earth did a rising campaign for a climate change bill. Ministers pooh-poohed the idea. What is the point of a bill they said? It wouldn't be worth the paper it is written on. Then David Cameron [then leader of the main opposition party] adopted it as his key theme. Menzies Campbell's [then leader of the second opposition party] first big policy announcement was on green taxes and ministers have gradually said, 'Oh, let's have a bill.'*

But what was the interesting bit? It was the ask itself. What *was* 'The Big Ask'? As Mike McCarthy points out, the ask was politics and policy – inherently dull stuff. But by creating a brand for the campaign that did not even appear to be Friends of the Earth unless you looked closely, using rock music figureheads such as Thom Yorke of Radiohead and giving it personality and style that was younger, cheekier and more expressive than the Friends of the Earth brand, the campaign took the organization into new social and psychological territory, reaching new types of supporter and energizing old ones.

Advertising agency CHI helped create the idea of The Big Ask (Figure 2.3), which in communications terms was effectively a 'dangle', a tease that dangled in front of the viewer, reader or listener, inviting you in to find out what it was about (the D after ABC bridging – see page 198).

Figure 2.3 *The Big Ask*

Organizations often worry (see page 251) about avoiding mixed messages and getting key messages across or getting details wrong, but a far bigger risk is being ignored. You are interested in your subject, but others are more likely to see it as important perhaps, worthy yes but quite likely not compelling. So being interesting, if not enough in itself, is vital.

For another example of 'being interesting', this time on road safety, visit the topless campaigners of the Danish Road Safety Council at www.speedbandits.dk, or the equally popular www.globalrichlist.com, a very direct way to make people in rich countries realize how much richer they are than most of the world's population.

ENGAGEMENT AND AGENCY: WHAT DIFFERENCE CAN I MAKE?

The trouble with socialism is that it would take up too many evenings.
(Oscar Wilde[22])

Many campaigns fail because they simply never gather enough support. Campaigning is a 'follow me' or 'come with us' exercise. It invites others to give up some of their time, and make your agenda theirs. So why should anyone go out of their way to support or join your campaign?

Variations in campaign support are not just due to some people being better at it than others, or some causes being inherently 'sexier' or easier. If you hear a campaigner say that, it is likely that they haven't done the necessary design work to attract support.

In assessing a campaign proposition we all ask, 'Is it worth it?' We mostly assess the proposition intuitively: 'This is for me', or not.

The cause

Do we care about the cause? Is the campaign needed? (If the audience is already aligned, the answer should be 'yes'.)

The benefit

What will the results be if the campaign succeeds – generally or personally? Does it make a worthwhile difference? What agency does it give me: how does it increase my influence over the world around me? Does it make existing mechanisms work better, or provide new ones ?

The means

Are they attractive – or do they put me off?

The prospects

Does it stand a chance of success?

Three things – the objectives, resources and activities – 'triangulate' a campaign's perceived feasibility. If they are seen to match, the campaign can look attractive, workable and credible. If they do not, the campaign will be rejected, no matter how good the cause.

The 'feasibility triangle' can be used to assess a campaign, project or an organization.

In academic circles this is described by 'Values Expectancy Theory', originated by psychologist Martin Fishbein, but we can think of the 'feasibility triangle' (Figure 2.4) like a three-legged stool – if the legs don't match in length, it will topple over.

A lack of support may be put down to 'the fact that people don't care', or the idea that 'they are ignorant of the facts'. The press can take the rationalization a step further and call it 'compassion fatigue' or announce that something is 'no longer an issue – people don't care'. Just as likely, the project doesn't look credible.

Common feasibility problems

The objective is too big
The naive NGO failure, where the ultimate aim rather than an achievable objective is stated. For example, the Lower Snoring Campaign to Change World Trade (resources: four

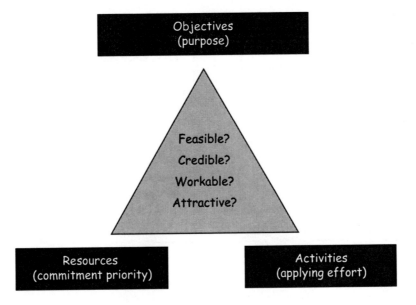

Figure 2.4 *The credibility triangle*

people and a dog). Many small groups 'taking on' big issues stay small and marginal, talking about change rather than achieving it.

A striking example arose in 2008 when a UK national 'Energy Saving Day' was reported by the BBC[23] as having had 'no impact'. People were asked to switch off appliances they were not using and national electricity consumption was monitored – with no discernible impact. The problem was that the project was far too ambitious in relation to its capacity to reach and engage the public. Of the many difficulties facing this campaign (discussed in an edition of the *Campaign Strategy Newsletter*[24]) probably the greatest was that while originally to be backed by the BBC, it was continued after the broadcasters had pulled out. It was then too small to achieve its stated objective but big enough to get noticed and reported. If you are going to mount a campaign that is a 'numbers game', you need to be sure there is a good chance of exceeding expectations (see also 'Bridging the engagement gap', page 60).

Objectives too small
1990s research on the world views of UK Greenpeace supporters and others like them revealed a motivational 'black hole' that disconnected campaigns from potential support. People sympathetic to environmental issues often did not find them at all engaging.

Recycling was among a host of 'green' activities too small to be worth discussing in public: normal to do but not worth remarking upon. Others, such as global warming, were

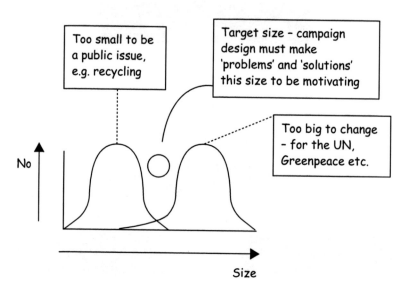

Figure 2.5 *The too-big–too-small problem*

'too large' for individuals to engage with: 'environment for environmentalists' (Figure 2.5). The answer to this is to break down big problems into smaller parts so that, for example, when Greenpeace and its supporters acted together, small efforts could add up to big results.[25]

Objective not visible

Public bodies often suffer from this when they fail to make the objective explicit, and simply announce activities or resources, leaving the audience to 'patch in' an assumed objective from rumour or what they may have heard or seen on TV. Frequently, the assumed objective is huge.

Too much time spent on the objective

Where campaigning is not the main activity of a voluntary organization, there is often too much focus on defining the objective, and too little on putting together activities and resources.

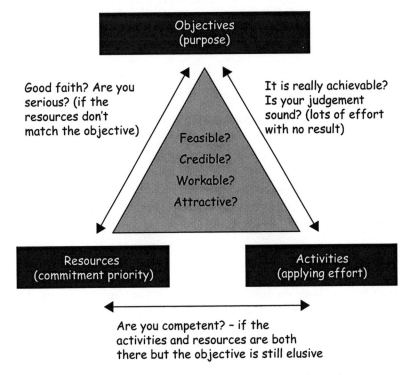

Figure 2.6 *Some of the doubts that can be raised if the objectives, activities and resources do not seem to fit*

Being vague
Companies tend to succumb to waffle outside their core business areas.

Poorly defined goals on 'difficult' issues sound good in a senior management team meeting, but look flimsy once they reach the annual report, and fall apart completely under public questioning.

Inadequate activities
Established NGOs can become too cautious to campaign effectively; too bureaucratic, with internal stakeholders defending their departmental interests or career paths, to take any serious risks. They may believe their own propaganda about being 'quietly effective' – if true, then of course there will be no need to campaign. Such groups set good objectives and have the resources, but they don't deploy them, don't invest in campaign tools, and don't involve top staff in campaigning.

LEVELS OF ENGAGEMENT

Engagement often seems to fit a four-stage pattern:[26] Do nothing; do one thing; systematic change; and lastly, wholesale change.

Stage 1: Do nothing

People may not have heard of the problem, what causes it, or the solution. Or it may not be significant or interesting to them. There may be no trigger. It might be that they have yet to see it in the right context, or hear it from the right messenger.

Perhaps you need to use a different channel. If you are trying to move people from Stage 1 to Stage 2, then try using the CAMPCAT tool (see page 25).

Because of circumstance or psychology, belief systems, social pressures or culture, some people will never be promoted from Stage 1.

Stage 2: Do one thing

Here we identify one thing we have done 'to make a difference'. People have bought the cause but not gone very far with it. In the UK, and probably many other countries, a large number of people are at this stage in relation to, say, global environmental problems: 'I buy ozone-friendly products.' Media coverage is usually enough to recruit people to Stage 2.

With established issues, these are usually the best prospects to be 'promoted' to take more action, as they have already accepted that there is a problem/solution.

Campaigners sometimes dismiss just doing one thing as 'token', but this is a mistake. Token efforts are not a sign that people don't care: it's a sign that they do. It's a rational use of time and effort: a form of bet-hedging. By doing at least something, individuals make a small contribution to what they hope is a bigger effort.

Token efforts may also be debris from some tidal wave of public concern that once swept society. Although high, dry and isolated, token gestures remind society that the problem could come again, and may be touchstones for igniting popular perception and promoting an issue to the forefront of consciousness.

Token gestures provide handles, short cuts and communication footholds, sometimes becoming icons; symbols with more than their literal meaning.

A single action may also be a response to social pressure to conform, for example around a campaign issue that has become normalized. Behaviour campaigners (see page 62) sometimes worry about 'single action bias', in which people disengage after 'doing their bit'. The answer to this is firstly to design campaigns with strategic outcomes (that is where the change is not simply at the individual level) and to organize another effort to get people engaged with your next campaign 'push'. Only a minority are likely to go on to Stages 3 and 4 below.

Stage 3: Systematic engagement

For most of us, big life changes mean working alongside others doing the same thing. This is the beauty of campaigns: they enable people to act together. They provide examples, proofs that things work, a socially acceptable or impressive explanation for taking action, and the ways, means and support to 'step out of line' without undue costs.

People at this stage frequently feel that they are not doing enough, externalize and become advocates, and consciously search for the campaign in the media. As such, they are not indicative of interest in the cause in general, but will make good use of training opportunities or campaign resources.

Table 2.1 *Levels of personal engagement*

Stage	What people say
Do nothing	'I don't need to do anything'
One thing	'This is what I do about it'
Systematic	'I do a, b and c. I try to do d and e ... I would like to do more, but ...'
Wholesale	'I have changed my life because of it'

Stage 4: Wholesale life change

Here people change their lives completely. They might:

- Give up a job to join a campaign group full-time;
- Embark on a new career;
- Stop campaigning and start a business to achieve the same ends; or
- Adopt an 'alternative' lifestyle, such as becoming a traveller or building an 'eco-home'.[27]

I met one Dutch campaigner with a conviction that nuclear power posed a serious threat to future generations. Nothing unusual in that, except that he was a rather long-term thinker. He had formed this view at school, then enrolled at university and undertaken a degree in nuclear physics, just so he could understand the industry and find ways to convince politicians that it needed to be shut down.

Another colleague was a former chief inspector of police at Scotland Yard in London: for him, coming to Greenpeace meant that he could 'do something really useful' (which had been his original motivation to join the Met), though it also meant reducing his salary by more than half.

Political institutions can show the same four-stage engagement with a campaign issue (Figure 2.7).

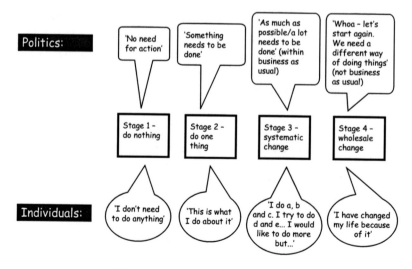

Figure 2.7 *Four-stage engagement*

ENGAGEMENT AND SHOPPING

Campaigners use engagement mechanisms lifted more or less unaltered from centuries-old political campaigning: tracts, leaflets and their cyber-equivalents, polemics and speeches. This puts them at a disadvantage in a consumer context.

Discover how to best communicate in specific environments by talking to those in the business: practitioners, suppliers and trade journalists – check for them in your supporter base. They may well save you time, money and effort with free advice. Find out how the decisions you seek are made, and present your desired decision in those terms, not yours.

The engagement mechanism needs to match the timescale and dynamic of the process being targeted. A sustainable timber campaign might ask people to exercise buying power when moving home, a time when they may buy furniture or timber. It also needs to target the key actors – in most house-buying the critical decisions are mostly made by women, not men, for instance.

Each transaction has its own culture. In some cases it may be better to enlist the shop assistants rather than the consumers – purchases of white goods, for example, are often decided by a conversation with a sales person or engineer, who is treated as an expert. For some goods or services there may be websites that are heavily used for referral or making choices; often not the same ones used to buy from.

Although shoppers may complain about supermarkets, they will be reluctant to change established habits. Context means getting both the time and place right. Potential supporters may be in supermarkets, making decisions about what products to buy – two essential factors – but that's not necessarily enough. Shoppers may be too busy. Parents of young children may be easier to reach with the same information while they are waiting to pick up the youngsters from school. Or perhaps you should go via their parents, who may have more time. Older shoppers might welcome a chat, especially if offered a cup of tea, as well. Young singles shopping in the evening might welcome an interview as a chance to meet others.

In 2000, Greenpeace UK adapted the technique known as 'accompanied shopping', in which a researcher shops with a consumer, for a genetically modified (GM) food campaign. Campaign Director Jane Wildblood explains how it worked:

> Greenpeace trained a network of volunteers and provided them with a kit to run events at supermarkets, to inform and engage shoppers. They set up information points outside supermarkets on Saturdays over a period of months. These had an eye-catching backdrop in red (the big, vegetable-head logo of the campaign) and leaflets to take away, as well as knowledgeable people to talk to. They used the interaction outside the supermarket (that is, not interfering with the actual shopping) to recruit the really interested for 'supermarket tours giving information on GM and organic food, promoted as the safe solution to GM and other concerns'. These tours

*were scheduled throughout the day with the full backing of the supermarket manag-
ers (mostly!*[28]*). This avoided haranguing or interfering with people when it would
irritate them, but enabled high-quality engagement and visibility. The feedback
mechanism was via a send-back coupon on the basic leaflet. These people were then
entered on a database and sent further information and invitations to participate
in campaign activity. At later stages, we gave people at supermarket entrances tear-
off coupons to send into the local shop manager, MP and so on. Later still, a shopper's
guide was created on the website...* (personal communication)

PERCEPTION OF CHANGE AND SIGNIFICANCE

Perception of change and significance often drives decision-making. *Relative* change may
be the most effective thing to communicate – a rate of increase or decrease, for example.
Or you may want to focus only on recruits or losses, not total amounts.

To win media attention, indeed the attention of most audiences, changes usually need
to be abrupt and discontinuous. This can be achieved by using the right scale of focus, and
looking for thresholds or discrete consequences of a trend.

Because of the dominance of economists and accountants in institutions, it's often said
that 'what counts is what's measured'. Campaigners who supply some numbers will find it
easier to get their case talked about. However, careless quantification can easily anchor
debate in the wrong place.

A list of points or reasons is usually helpful, but reliance on statistics is not advisable.
Though the press love them, the public generally does not trust statistics, at least in the UK.

He or she who chooses the measure, often determines the conclusion. 'Horse race' polls
show which political candidate is ahead: a favourite news-making device of politicians and
political commentators,[30] which also implies that things outside the focus can be disregarded.

The context affects whether something looks big or small, effective or ineffective. The
old UK Central Electricity Generating Board used a demonstration of renewable energy to
make it look small.[31] A solar panel that could illuminate one light bulb was placed outside a
vast nuclear power station. On a bright day the bulb lit. The information panel explained
words to the effect that: 'One day solar energy may have advanced to the point that we can
use it to supply our energy needs. That day has not yet arrived, and for secure supplies of
electricity, nuclear power is an essential part of a mix of reliable and proven energy sources.'

Altering perception of how to judge change may be the object of a campaign itself.
Redefining Progress[32] promotes a Genuine Progress Indicator[33] (Figure 2.8) in place of gross
domestic product, because the latter fails to measure things such as depletion of nature,
natural capital and ecological services. Here the gap between the two indicators may be the
important thing to communicate.

BOX 2.1 – UNDERSTANDING WHY PEOPLE DON'T ENGAGE: THE HIER CAMPAIGN

Psychological optouts are often of strategic importance for campaigns – the reasons why people don't engage or take action. Understanding what these are, which is best done through qualitative research (see page 108), is often the key to amending an existing strategy or creating an entirely new one. This happened in The Netherlands in the mid-2000s.

The Dutch Postcode lottery, which funds many good causes in The Netherlands, had grown frustrated with the small-scale and scattergun approach of many of the projects it financed. Apparently, with good Dutch directness, it gave notice to NGOs that they would get no more money until they came up with something strategic on which they could cooperate. After several research projects, the NGOs found that on climate change, a major obstacle was the common perception that it was a 'not-yet' and a 'not-here' issue. Their response was equally direct: they launched Hier (Dutch for 'here'), a campaign of prominently labelling impacts, responses and actions associated with climate change, involving some 40 organizations (visit www.hier.info).[29]

This approach meant that many things that were immediately understood as real and immediate, such as helping people on a one-to-one basis, or dealing with flooding, could be shown to be part of the response to climate change. It avoided the many problems with trying to 'sell' wholesale changes to society as a response to what might otherwise happen in the future as a result of continuing to pollute the atmosphere. As a result, organizations with a reach to particular constituencies that could not be engaged, or were unlikely to be engaged in the 'climate change' issue framed in terms of emissions of gases or global change, could be engaged in taking useful actions.

Hier has involved development, humanitarian and nature conservation NGOs developing projects to reduce the risks of the impacts of climate change, with a focus on safety, health, disasters, drought or desertification. These have included United Nations Children's Fund (UNICEF) teaching children how to swim in Bangladesh, where drowning is still a major cause of infant mortality; Simavi constructing so-called 'cloud catchers' in Nepal in the battle against drought conditions; the Red Cross and FreeVoice working on a disaster emergency system for hurricanes in Central America; and Natuurmonumenten, the major Dutch Nature Conservation NGO, proposing natural climate buffers as a way to improve safety against floods and sea-level rise.

Hier also links to the well-researched consumer product (TVs, computers, fridges, cars and so on) website www.topten.info, which shows the best products by carbon (the motivational purpose) rather than by price.

At an individual level, perception will be affected by unconscious ways in which we filter incoming information, some of which are genetic and others probably cultural. For example, most people in the 'West' conceive of time as going from the past, behind us, to the future ahead of us. Research suggests[34] that some cultures see 'past', 'present' and 'future' as distinct, others as overlapping, while in some, such as India and the Middle East,

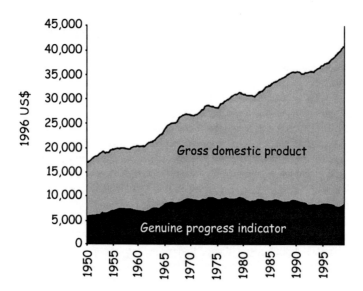

Figure 2.8 *Gross production vs genuine progress, 1950 to 1999*

there is little clear distinction between past, present and future. With the past behind you (others think of time as passing before them, as from left to right), it is easy to conceive of the future as a destination yet to be reached, its requirements not yet applicable, and the past as somewhere you cannot go back to. The directional idea of time ('time's arrow') chimes with the notion of progress, and anything framed (see page 28) in this way can render technologies and practices from 'the past' inapplicable for the future.

Some cultures (for example in Germany) are believed to see time as rare and precious, leading to propositions like 'no time to waste' (a popular slogan with Greenpeace), but elsewhere this idea may not have the resonance that its authors like to imagine. Just such an assumption seemed to lie behind the campaign www.tcktcktck.org, used by the Global Campaign for Climate Action in the run up to the Copenhagen talks in 2009.

BRIDGING THE ENGAGEMENT GAP

Annual income twenty pounds, annual expenditure nineteen nineteen six, result happiness. Annual income twenty pounds, annual expenditure twenty pounds ought and six, result misery. (Mr Micawber, in Charles Dickens's *David Copperfield*[35])

A campaign needs to be able to honestly say, and better, show, that 'without you, we will fail: with you we can succeed'. Support has to be needed.

Pick objectives you think are just possible with a reasonable degree of public engagement. Others will tend to view them as just about impossible. Engage enough support and you can bridge the gap and make the impossible possible. When a campaign bridges the gap, it succeeds. The longer the bridge, the more successful the campaign is seen to be.

This is what makes a campaign different from everyday life. It can make campaigning exciting, inspiring and motivating: the magic that helps to change the established order of things.

Without the gap, there's no need for anyone to support your campaign by joining in. It may amuse or please but it will not engage. People will not feel needed.

In campaigning, anything better than business as usual is achievement. It is the political equivalent of Mr Micawber's sixpence – result: happiness. Anything below is within expectations – result: misery. A campaigning organization is not necessarily expected to deliver huge change, but to change more than business as usual can. Normal politics is the art of the possible. Campaigning is the art of the impossible.

ALIGNMENT

Effective speakers begin by getting the attention of a group, and reminding everyone why they are there.

Generations of British children were introduced to radio stories by the BBC[36] with the question 'Are you sitting comfortably? Then we'll begin.' The injunction to 'sit comfortably and listen', helps secure audience attention (awareness) by asking a question. It focuses your mind on your body and stops you thinking about whatever you were doing or were focused on before, and it aligns the audience – concerned with the same task. But the speaker doesn't need to explain all that. Indeed if she did, then it wouldn't work – you might even end up thinking about communications processes! Nor does the campaign need to explain it but the process still has to be followed.

In the process of trying to align an audience, use as few arguments as possible. Arguments come imprinted with age-old political meaning. Words are a fast lane to prejudices and preconceived ideas. Pictures are more reliable – they exist much more in the mind of the beholder, while words tend to remain the property of the source.

The more arguments you use, the more reasons you are giving that someone can disagree with. Resist the temptation to embellish a case with extra arguments: people only need one reason to disengage, adding arguments is likely to dilute strong ones with weaker ones while creating a wider range of options for disagreement. For alignment in the campaign sequence see Chapter 1 (problem–solution).

Resist also the temptation to box in your intended audience by offering a set of choices that say in effect 'you should choose to do this or that or the other to help our cause'. A large drinks company once developed two spirit-based drinks aimed at women, with slightly different offers. Let's call them A and B. A was intended to be smooth, silky, sophsiticated. B racier, a bit naughty, daring. The company decided it lacked the money to run an ad campaign for each so it tried to run a campaign featuring both at once, asking at the end 'Are you an A-woman or a B-woman?' The result was disastrous: total failure. Women were prompted to think 'I'm neither of those', because it made them aware that the communication was attempting to play on their identity.

BEHAVIOUR CHANGE AND HEURISTICS

Almost any campaign involves a change in behaviour: inducing people to talk about something different, or attend an event, or causing a decision-maker to sign on the 'dotted line' all involve behaviour. Some campaigns are overtly designed to spread a new behaviour in society or amongst a particular group (see also 'Social marketing', page 279), and are explicitly labelled or conceived as 'behaviour change' campaigns, in which it is usually hoped that the behaviour will be repeated. Most commercial marketing and charity fund-raising falls into this category. And many campaigns stumble because they fail to achieve a desired change in behaviour.

Behaviour change is a massive academic subject but accessible best-sellers that are useful for campaigners include Robert Cialdini's *Influence: The Psychology of Persuasion*,[37] which is famous for popularizing 'heuristics' or 'rules of thumb' that apply to behaviour (below), and George Lakoff's book *The Political Mind*,[38] which explains 'framing' (see page 28) in terms of reflexive thought (unconscious 'automatic' decision-making). A useful accessible short report is *Homer Simpson For Nonprofits: The Truth About How People Really Think and What It Means for Promoting Your Cause*, from US group Network for Good.[39] A huge amount of behavioural studies are understandably about relationships and these are often hard to apply to the group and society-wide scale, while many studies of society are in terms (for example social class or wealth) that tell you little about how to influence behaviour. Of all those I've come across, by far the most useful is values analysis, which because it divides people up by how they think as a result of their experiences in life, can map motivational values from the level of the individual through to whole countries (see page 71).

Heuristics

In this context[40] 'heuristics' are rules of thumb for behaviour that are more often right than wrong. Behavioural heuristics have been derived from experiments and observation, both in the psychology laboratory and in sales and marketing. Ultimately they derive from our evolutionary hard-wiring, our culture and the interaction of these two influences in our upbringing. Here are some 'heuristics' described by Cialdini and others such as Daniel Kahneman and Amos Tversky, that can be useful in designing campaigns.

Reciprocation (or 'exchange')

Much used in marketing (for example free gifts and vouchers) and door-to-door or face-to-face fund-raising – you do something for someone, however small, and they feel the need to return the favour. Making a concession in a negotiation invokes reciprocation, for example retreating from a large demand (A) to a smaller one (B), makes it more likely that (B) is accepted than if you went straight to (B). (A), however, has to be seen to have been asked for in good faith.

Consistency and commitment

While two different heuristics, these frequently work together. Consistency means we prefer to go on doing what we are already doing (and we rationalize it as our opinions – see VBCOP, page 143). If we start out doing something because we want it to be true, we are also very likely to ignore evidence to the contrary, even if we recognize its logic is invalid. Cialdini calls this 'walls against reason' – an example might be ignoring evidence that pleasurable behaviour is risky; this could be personally as in sexual activity or drugs, or socially as in driving a gas-guzzling car that adds to climate change for example. If the emotional rewards of changing behaviour (the feel-good in various forms) do not outweigh those of retaining the behaviour, we tend to retain the behaviour.

Commitment means that once committed to a course of action we tend to continue, even if the case for it begins to collapse. Salesmen may exploit this by first gaining commitment to buy something, and then changing the terms to their benefit. People who say what they would do in certain circumstances (if asked 'Would you be likely to donate to charity X?' or 'If you knew A, would you do B?') are then more likely to actually behave that way than if they had not first been asked and responded. They behave in line with their commitment. This effect is reinforced or multiplied if the commitment is made publicly, or even if it was expected to be made publicly and then is not. Numerous community-level campaigns have made use of this to make people into energy-savers and neighbourhood advocates.[40]

So campaigns that trigger an indication of how we might respond and then create the opportunity and need to respond are likely to get a bigger result: trailer strategies. This is because we are mentally committing to be the-sort-of-person-who does this sort of thing (changing self-identity). It works even if the initial act seems very weak, such as responding to a survey.

Cialdini sites a famous study that shows how commitment and consistency can lead to small actions becoming large ones. In an American town, people were asked to display a very small notice advocating safe driving. Those who did were then much more likely to later agree to display a very large sign saying the same thing in their front garden. More surprising, the effect was independent of the message: the sign displayers became willing to undertake other 'civic' acts – they had become more 'public-minded' citizens.

Confirmation

The power of an act of alignment is considerably increased if you do something yourself, of your own 'free will', to confirm it. This is why propagandists and 'brainwashers' get their victims to write down their new 'beliefs', and why suicide bombers are induced to make their commitments to carry out an act in a video. It's also why if someone repeats or endorses the message or claim of an advertiser or cause group 'in their own words', such as 'I support X because…' or 'I like [product A] because', they are more likely to then go on and act consistently with that behaviour.

Effort

Sometimes in combination with the above (as in the case of painful or humiliating 'initiation' ceremonies giving access to a group), people tend to place more value on something that required effort to get than something that required no effort. Illogically but rationally this applies to the ultimately 'fungible' commodity of currency. A coin found in the street is more freely discarded or spent than one which you had to work for.

Social proof

Are others doing it? If so, there 'must be a reason'. So I will too. This heuristic is famously a cause of accidents and disasters. Car drivers for example sometimes cause pile-ups by copying what the car in front is doing even if there is no visible reason to do so. It is the cause of the 'bystander' effect, in which the more people are present at the scene of an accident or crime the less likely they are to intervene, unless others are doing so, in which case they will join in. Obviously it has a long evolutionary advantage for a social animal in terms of finding food or avoiding predators, but it can easily be manipulated or produce perverse results.

This has been frequently used to correct problematic behaviours. Cialdini cites an experiment in which simply showing withdrawn children a film of a similar child changing behaviour and ending up accepted and happily playing in a group was enough to change them, the more so if they saw several children doing it. The by stander effect or inaction inertia can be overcome by being specific. For example a campaign appealing for support from 'the public' makes such a general call that it has little traction with any individual, whereas a more specific appeal for the help of 'retired dentists' or 'people with a 1998 VW Golf' is more likely to produce results. If you are an accident victim, point to someone in the crowd, identify them and tell them to call the emergency services.

Similarity

Many studies show that we respond better to people like ourselves. We tend to assign them better motives and extend them kinder acts than people who do not look like us or share our origins or backgrounds. This applies to how we dress, speak and to other personal identity signals, such as club or sporting affiliations, and clearly has implications for choice of 'messenger' (see CAMPCAT, page 25).

Alarmingly it also applies to suicides and violence as seen on TV or reported in the press. After a plane crash or suicide is reported, more such events tend to occur, including ones where a pilot, train or car driver, for example, takes others to their death, and in the US the same was found to apply to black on white or white on black violence following a boxing match between a black and white opponent. What we see in the media, especially where many people are presumed to have witnessed it, can lead to emulation based on similarity.

Campaigns that *demonstrate* desired behaviours by people-like-you are therefore more likely to work than those that simply advocate behaviours, or use unlike messengers or agents.

Liking and praise

Cialdini produces the remarkable statistic that somewhere in the world a 'Tupperware party' is taking place every 2.7 seconds. Tupperware parties and their many imitations work on the 'liking' heuristic: we are much more likely to respond to a request from a friend than a stranger. We feel 'obliged'. Canny communicators therefore get their audience to like them before asking for anything. Simply saying you like the audience will help: 'I always like coming to Anytown, where the people are friendly and known to be generous' may sound crass but it will increase the giving.

Many research projects have shown that liked situations transfer to liking the content: Ciladini points out that the 'luncheon effect' was documented by Gregory Razran in the 1930s, influenced by Ivan Pavlov, the celebrated discoverer of 'Pavlovian reactions'. We feel good when eating, so we feel better about a message received while eating. We feel good when we hear a favourite tune, so we are more likely to approve a message linked to the tune. Charities that organize free concerts with popular music are 'doing the right thing'. Yet many campaigners eschew fun and enjoyment – to the detriment of their campaigns, as these 'limbic' emotional reactions apply to us all.

This transference notoriously connects content to messenger (for example the messengers in ancient Persia who brought news of defeat and were slain, and American weathermen may be attacked for 'bringing' bad weather). Cialdini quotes Shakespeare: 'The nature of bad news infects the teller.' Like politicians, therefore, campaigns need to seek to be bearers of good news, as well as of bad. An NGO that becomes associated with doomsaying is not going to be liked or welcomed and this will not help it get listened to.

Other studies show that we tend to favour attractive people. Our rational conscious brain may try to deny it, but research finds otherwise. Courts and teachers favour attractive children or adults with better treatment, and attractive politicians and staff are more likely to be elected or promoted and assumed to be more honest, trustworthy, intelligent and kind. Not just a little more likely, but hugely – one Canadian study[42] found a 250 per cent voting bias in Canada on this basis, although 73 per cent of voters denied it and only 14 per cent allowed it might be true. So put your best looking advocates to the fore.

Cooperation and groups
Anything that puts people into groups with the potential to compete leads to competition and decreasing cooperation. Anything that is perceived as a common threat promotes cooperation. A campaign that sets out to mobilize support from an audience should therefore find a common reason for cooperation. As many large-scale problems require coordination or cooperation, this is a frequent issue for campaigners. (For an exploration of cooperation, coordination and trust, see James Surowiecki's *The Wisdom of Crowds*.[43])

Authority
Most people will have heard of the experiments in which an authoritative 'white coat experimenter' leads normal volunteers to impose what they think are cruel electric shocks on a 'subject', or the students who role-played cruel guards and ended up ready to abuse people playing prisoners inhumanely. The point being that we are, as a whole, conditioned to accept authority, although the degree of deference and the forms of authority vary from one culture to another (see the work of Geert Hofstede[44] for an international system of mapping cultural values including 'power-distance'). Campaigners are often pitted against authority: quite often they need to invoke the trappings or support of authority. The mind-bending antics of the 'yes men'[45] are based almost entirely on an entertaining (liking) hijacking of authority to give space for a 'rethink' of issues.

Scarcity
The 'rule of the few' or the scarcity heuristic is often linked to social proof and competition. We see a queue to buy something and join it (contagion[46]): there must be something worth having. It's hard to resist the thought that we should get 'it' now before it runs out. Generally the less available something is, the more desirable it seems to be – from potential

partners to food or commodities. Absence makes the heart grow fonder: a survey found Florida State University students rated their cafeteria food as unsatisfactory, but after they learned part of the cafeteria had burnt down and food would be unavailable for several weeks, they rated it more highly.[47]

Linked to this is 'reactance': we learn aged about two or three to resist restrictions on our freedoms (and so want the 'forbidden fruit' or cake or toy), and campaigners who seek to stop us doing something should bear in mind that, in varying degrees, this reflex never leaves us.

Cialdini cites[48] the case of a local phosphate-detergent ban imposed in a US town (for water-purity reasons), which led to 'soap convoys' headed to nearby towns to stock up, and people accumulating a 20-year supply. Campaigns might reverse the effect with a proposition that shows the new alternative is better but hard to get. This shifts the 'problem' to whoever is responsible for the scarcity. Scarcity is more about the satisfaction of possession rather than use, and may be linked to status (Richard Layard, for example, shows in his book *Happiness*[49] that whereas being wealthy does not necessarily make people happy, what makes them unhappy is being less well off than others – relative wealth).

Tasting a better life and then having that withdrawn, or gaining something and then losing it, has also been shown to cause much greater upset (even revolution) than not having it in the first place (note that this also matches the transition from Settler to Prospector – see page 72). Campaigns that mobilize support to recover something lost or rescue it from being lost are therefore more likely to generate support than those that try to give people something they've never had.

Representativeness

First identified by Daniel Kahneman and Amos Tversky this says we tend to judge how likely something is to be true by reference to a 'comparable known' event, and then assuming that the probabilities will be similar.[50] This can often be done using just one property of the thing in question, for example an element of someone's appearance. Although this leads to many fallacies (for example misreading the probability of events), people often do it, so for campaigns it means that if you want people to adopt a cause or support a project, find a way in which it is like something they already agree with and use that 'thing in common'.

Availability

The availability heuristic is well known to exert a huge influence on beliefs in good or bad events recurring. It works because it is easier for us to recall more recent events than more distant ones, so we assume that the more recent ones are more likely to happen again. This too may have an evolutionary advantage – for example if a predator is still in the area – but it is totally useless in estimating things such as the probability of flooding. For the same reason, prominent media coverage of crimes or accidents makes us think they are more likely to occur than they actually are.

In campaigns, this will mean that people are more willing to accept arguments based on readily recalled evidence – recent or very memorable examples – than on any amount of scientifically generated 'facts'. It also means that people will extrapolate from one favourite example to the general. The allied idea of 'vividness' means that if you make the memory or description more 'real' by recalling or invoking multi-sensory properties (such as the bad smell of a flood), it becomes more real as a prospect. What 'comes to mind' most easily is treated as the most significant.

Adjustment from an anchor

In this heuristic we are prompted to define an estimate by a given starting point. We use the given fact as a reference and then are more likely to estimate close to the anchor. If asked to guess if the distance from London to New York was more or less than 2000 miles, we'd guess more or less. If then asked for the actual distance, we'd be biased to around 2000 (in reality it is 3470). This heuristic is often used in negotiation to define the general area where you want to end up by making an initial offer. It can also lead to excessive reliance on the particular factor chosen to start with, for example by asking how tall our recruits should be, or even how much over or under 1.8m. This phenomenon can clearly affect the way a campaign fares if it makes claims or calls to action in terms of how much or how something should be judged.

There are many other 'heuristics', and all of them are simply rules of thumb: they are not necessarily logical (in other words right for example in estimating probabilities) and nor do they describe how any one individual will respond, but they can be useful in formulating campaigns, especially if they involve perception and behaviour. If you compare these heuristics to the unconscious motivational influence of 'values' driven by unmet needs, you will also see that some are more likely to sway certain people than others. By their nature 'heuristics' do not separate out these differences, so they should not be taken as substitute for doing more detailed perceptual research where this is affordable.

3

MOTIVATIONAL
VALUES

Directly or indirectly, all campaigns are an exercise in motivation. If they stop and think about it, most people will acknowledge that we are 'not all the same'. For the most part, 'people' don't 'do things'; only some people do them. 'The public' is never a target group – as the public is not a single group, it is too diverse to communicate with effectively, as well as too large to engage strategically.

Whether we do a little or a lot of something, and why we do it, depends on our motivation. And just as the best spoken language to use in France would be French, the best motivational language to use to reach, interest, engage and motivate an individual is the one that they themselves use. The problem is to see this language of motivation.

'Values Modes' is a system that breaks down populations into three main 'motivational languages' and 12 distinct 'dialects' that campaigners can use to design and plan communications that are far more likely to work than if you try to match motivation to categories like age, sex, ethnicity, profession, socio-economic group, lifestyle or geodemographic tools like ACORN[1] or MOSAIC. These languages, however, are unspoken. Like other forms of reflexive thought, we are not conscious of which Values Mode we are in, although the consequent differences in how we behave and perceive the world are profound.

Values Modes, run by the UK-based company CDSM (Cultural Dynamics Strategy and Marketing, www.cultdyn.co.uk) is one of several systems[2] developed for marketing and communications strategy that categorize us by motivation rather than class or other handles. You can check your own Values Mode by visiting the website and completing the ten-point online questionaire.

These systems are based on mapping the fundamental motivational 'values' first identified[3] by Abraham Maslow, the father of 'humanistic psychology' in the 1950s. These values are ultimately driven by the developmental human requirement to meet a sequence of needs. So long as it remains unmet, a need dominates our behaviour and outlook on life, then as that need is met through our life experiences, so our dominant (but not only) need is replaced with another.

Such needs affect how we see any issue or treat any opportunity: they are overarching influences on our behaviour, much deeper, more powerful and slower to change than the ephemeral notion of 'opinion'. It is the unmet needs that drive our behaviours, and those that in turn drive our opinions (see VBCOP, page 143). The most powerful communications strategies therefore go to the mother lode of motivation, to analyse, plan and create offers and propositions, rather than dealing in the mixed alloys of behaviour or the fragmentary and unrealiable evidence of opinion as a guide to what might initiate or reinforce behaviours. At my website, www.campaignstrategy.org, there is a guide to Values Modes, 'Using Values Modes', and numerous examples of their application to campaign design (select the drop-down menu in the 'document store').

Note: This sort of 'value' is independent of character, personality or NLP preferences,[4] and has little or nothing to do with rhetorical or philosophical 'values' such as those in political theories or religious beliefs, which are put forward as reflective, conscious reasoning. Nor are they culturally determined: for an excellent system of mapping cultural differences, which any campaigners working internationally should explore, visit the 'Cultural Dimensions' work of Geert Hofstede at www.geert-hofstede.com.

THREE MASLOW GROUPS: SD, OD AND ID, OR SETTLERS, PROSPECTORS AND PIONEERS

Maslow proposed that we all start life in 'security-driven' (SD) or 'sustenance-driven' mode. We give first priority to these 'survival needs': air, water, food, safety, security and comfort, then, if we meet these, sex, belonging, love and acceptance. Cultural Dynamics terms people in this 'SD' category 'Settlers'. It then describes them, and the other two main Maslow Groups, in a hundred different ways at once, by correlating the answers to over 1000 questions from a survey of over 8000 people for the UK population. (This is how, by selecting the questions that are most effective in separating all the cross-correlated data, it can put us into one of the 12 Values Modes with over 97 per cent confidence using just ten questions).

If these needs are fully met, we will move on to meet the needs of the esteem-driven or 'outer-directed' (OD) phase: now we want to achieve the esteem of others, for example through obtaining recognition and approval, and then, if we achieve that, self-esteem or self-acceptance. Historically relatively few people would have enjoyed a fortunate enough life to move beyond meeting the SD needs. Indeed up until the mid-1980s even in the UK this was still the majority of the population, but as societies have developed, and medicine, sanitation, peace, stability, education and freedom from famine helped ensure security needs were met, more and more people began to develop the needs of Prospectors – the search for esteem.

If esteem needs are met, we move into the 'inner-directed' (ID) stage. Here our world is more determined by our own thoughts rather than the need to win approval of others (hence 'inner' rather than 'outer' directed). Now the needs to be met are aesthetic and cognitive, such as beauty, symmetry, the need to know, to understand and explore, to act ethically, bring about justice, and, ultimately, find 'self-actualization'. These have been called 'meta-needs' derived from integration and transcendence of all needs (Maslow, 1987, see note 3). Cultural Dynamics calls these people 'Pioneers'. They act as the 'scouts' for society, testing out and developing new behaviours. A dynamic of the model, which campaigners can utilize, is that new things start with the Pioneers (IDs), may be adopted by the Prospectors (ODs), and only then are likely to be taken up by the Settlers (SDs).

Pioneers, Prospectors and Settlers react very differently to campaigns, campaign propositions and campaign mechanisms:

- To be 'sure' of gaining support across a population of groups, campaigners need to communicate differently for each group (see Table 3.1). In general it is best to plan separate communication exercises for each main Maslow Group. For supporter purposes organizations may well prosper with a 'base' located in only one Maslow Group, but to put forward a policy, for example, it will usually need to 'work' across all the main Groups to be seen as politically credible.
- In analysing audiences and other CAMPCAT factors (see page 25) and in testing a critical path (see page 125), campaigners need to determine which motivations (T – trigger) are critical at which steps.
- To recruit support from each group, campaigners need to accept that motivations and appropriate engagement mechanisms differ.
- In a mixed audience addressed together, a speaker or campaigner can provide 'cues' or hit 'hot buttons' that will 'work' for each of the main Maslow Groups (for example safety [SD], success [OD] or ethics [ID], or, with a common portal such as a website, or at an event or in the course of a campaign, you can provide options tuned to each Maslow Group and people will strongly self-select and ignore the others. However, if you force or allow a debate between supporters as to *why* something they agree on should be done, you may engender what Pat Dade of CDSM calls 'the logjam of violent agreement' – they agree on the objective but disagree on how and why, and may end up doing nothing!

Figure 3.1 shows the main orientations of the three main 'Maslow Groups'. Instead of a pyramid with SD at the bottom, OD in the middle and ID at the top, as Maslow originally conceived it, CDSM uses a circular map,[5] represented by the box on the left.

New behaviours start with Pioneers and move clockwise around the map to Settlers, but human beings move, if they do, in the opposite direction. This means that while society gradually changes as the proportion of Maslow Groups varies (for example as of

Table 3.1 *A ready-reckoner for using Maslow-based value modes in campaign communications*

Segment of population	Dominant motivation	Action mode	Desire	Why they save dolphins in Seatown	I want a brand to …
Inner directed	Exploration	Do it yourself	Better questions	I feel I could be one myself – and for their own worth	Bring new possibilities
Outer directed	Status and esteem of others	Organize	Answers	Good for the town's image and economy (and my house price)	Make me look good
Security driven	Being safe and belonging	'Someone should do something about it'	Safeguard against external threat	So long as the dolphins keep coming back, Seatown will be Seatown	Make me secure
Segment of population	I like to meet	I connect through	I like to be associated with	I most respond to threats to	I
Inner directed	New, challenging and intriguing people	My own networks	Good causes that put my values into practice	Visions and causes	Am me
Outer directed	Desirable and important people	Big brands, systems and organizations	Success	What I've worked for	Am successful
Security driven	People like me and people I know	Club and family	Tradition	My way of life	Know my place

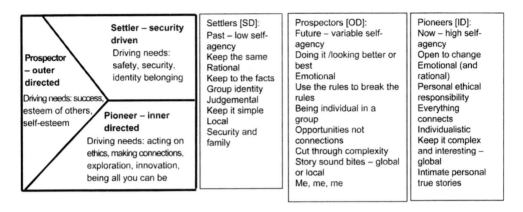

| | | Settlers [SD]: | Prospectors [OD]: | Pioneers [ID]: |

Figure 3.1 *The main orientations of the three main 'Maslow Groups'*

2008 Pioneers were the largest UK group at 41 per cent with Prospectors at 28 per cent and Settlers at 31 per cent), behaviours can spread much more quickly. Instead of trying to change people's values, therefore, which in any case requires the 'heavy-lifting' of giving them life-changing experiences, well-designed campaigns can achieve contagion and spread behaviours without needing to change values.

Figure 3.1 is highly simplified, but even a brief look at it shows that Pioneers are the 'natural' recruits to most campaigns, that is campaigns that seek to bring about something new or are 'ethically based', emphasizing things like justice, benevolence or protection of nature. Pioneers are also the only group who actually like 'issues' – they welcome the complexity and, because they are the group with the highest sense of self-agency, feel they can probably do something about them.

Settlers are the least likely group to start a campaign or to join one, unless it meets their needs for safety, security or belonging. You may, however, find large numbers of Settlers in campaigns to defend the local, stop change, resist innovation or protect traditional values, including 'family values'. For Settlers to join such an initiative, someone else has to give a lead: they follow authority rather than challenging it.

Prospectors are generally even less likely to sign up to a campaign than Settlers, as they avoid social conflict or controversy because it is a social risk (it might be seen to fail; they might 'look stupid' or 'losers') and because it takes up too much time (better spent 'getting on' or 'getting ahead'). Those campaigns that Prospectors do join in any number tend to be campaigns for the best or better, such as demanding rights or defending the chances for their children, or their property rights, or when the cause is seen as fashionable and the opportunity is fun. (See below for an example of how an inherently ethical and so Pioneer-oriented cause, international aid, gets converted to one that also has an appeal to Prospectors – the BBC telethon 'Red Nose Day').

These orientations spill over into attitudes towards politics:[6] Settlers are the bedrock of 'tribal' and identity-based politics, highly conservative and loyal in voting patterns and affiliations. Pioneers are the most 'civic minded' but also most likely to abandon, circumvent, question or subvert formal politics in favour of new forms of agency, such as campaigns. Prospectors ask 'What is in it for me?' Their approach to politics (which much of the time they tend to regard as rather boring) is the most transactional, and they are attracted to celebrity, winning, winners and political 'stars'. At an international level we have shown a correlation between the 'inner-directedness' of a country and its proclivity to give international aid.[7]

The recurrent values-failing of campaigns by NGOs is to pitch ideas and propositions that appeal only to their 'base', which tends to be Pioneer-dominated. Figure 3.2, for example, shows a CDSM scatter diagram plotting the UK supporters of an international aid charity.

The skew to Pioneers (ID – bottom right) is very clear: in fact 87 per cent of the supporters are Pioneers, whereas only about 40 per cent of the population are Pioneers; about 8 per cent of the supporters are Prospectors (OD), compared to 30 per cent in the general population; and 5 per cent of the supporters are Settlers as opposed to about 30 per cent in the population at large.

If you compare this result to the spread of Attributes on a detailed version of the same underlying statistical 'values map' in Figure 3.3, you can see why the skew occurs. Each of the Attributes represents about half a dozen similar questions in the large CDSM survey, and each is positioned at its point of maximum 'espousal', plotted relative to all the others.

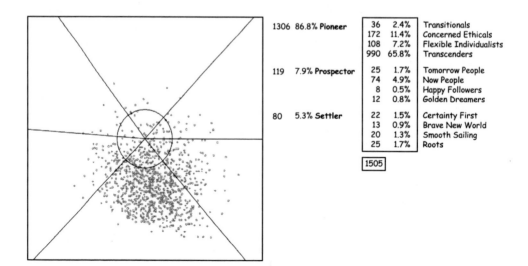

Figure 3.2 *Scatter diagram of Maslow Groups*

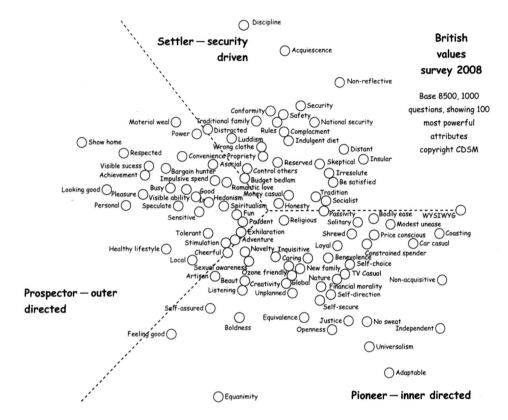

Figure 3.3 *British Values Map showing 100 most powerful Attributes*

Some of those that are strong Pioneer values and 'fit' with the idea of international charitable development work include Justice (as in social justice), Nature (as in caring for the environment), Benevolence, Universalism and Equanimity.

A person scoring high on Universalism and Equanimity would be untroubled by foreigners living next door, or finding themselves in an alien environment, and would agree that people the world over should enjoy equal rights. The polar opposite values, and the people who most espouse them, would be found at the opposite side of the map if you drew a line through the Attribute and the centre. There, in this case, you'd find people who scored much more highly on values like the importance of National Defence, the imposition of Discipline and Acquiescence, which essentially means accept things as they are, 'don't rock the boat'.

Using the same rich set of data, CDSM sorts people into 12 Values Modes, four within each of the three main Maslow Groups. Figure 3.4 shows their names and transitions. If people move between them, they move along the path shown. Not everyone does move.

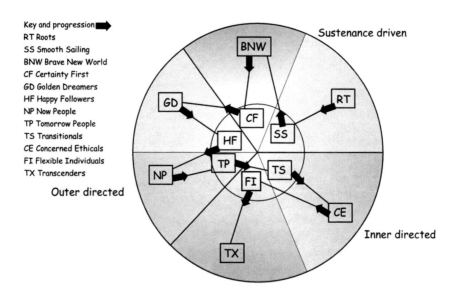

Figure 3.4 *Values Modes transitions*

A number stay all their lives in 'Roots': in a developed country with good social conditions and many material and 'post-material' opportunities, these would be few, but in a high-risk society such as with high childhood mortality and pervasive insecurity, such as Ethiopia or Afghanistan, for example, they would be many. Professor Ron Inglehart and colleagues have made very similar values measurements in dozens of countries over decades and demonstrated that over generations, societies show major values shifts. As improving conditions allow the numbers of SD people to dwindle and the number of the other Maslow Groups to increase, the number exhibiting what Inglehart terms 'self-expression values'[8] increases, and it is this that eventually brings about democracy.[9]

Unlike the major Maslow Groups, which are broad and thus if looked at in the aggregate can seem full of contradictions, the Values Modes are much more distinct and can be used to fine-tune marketing or campaign propositions. The six outer Values Modes are the most different, and people from these Modes therefore dominate most social debate (the others tend to find them a bit bothersome and even obsessive). They are therefore the ones to target or account for in most change campaigns or communications strategies.

Figure 3.5 shows the unmet needs that unconsciously drive their behaviours and outlook (and different versions of 'common sense') together with a condensed pen portrait of each. The central Modes, which have the same unmet needs as the adjacent outside groups and are mostly like a 'paler version', are not shown.

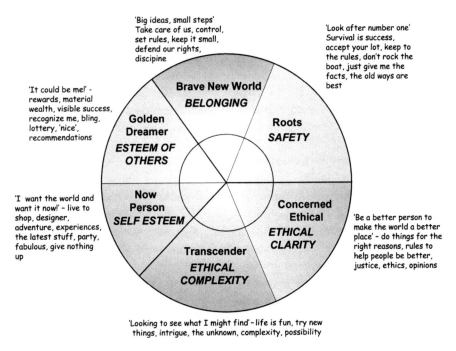

'Big ideas, small steps'
Take care of us, control,
set rules, keep it small,
defend our rights,
discipline

'Look after number one'
Survival is success,
accept your lot, keep to
the rules, don't rock the
boat, just give me the
facts, the old ways are
best

'It could be me!' -
rewards, material
wealth, visible success,
recognize me, bling,
lottery, 'nice',
recommendations

Brave New World
BELONGING

**Golden
Dreamer**
*ESTEEM OF
OTHERS*

Roots
SAFETY

'I want the world and
want it now!' – live to
shop, designer,
adventure, experiences,
the latest stuff, party,
fabulous, give nothing
up

**Now
Person**
SELF ESTEEM

**Concerned
Ethical**
*ETHICAL
CLARITY*

'Be a better person to
make the world a better
place' – do things for the
right reasons, rules to
help people be better,
justice, ethics, opinions

Transcender
*ETHICAL
COMPLEXITY*

'Looking to see what I might find'– life is fun, try new
things, intrigue, the unknown, complexity, possibility

Figure 3.5 *Unmet needs*

The six outside Values Modes, their driving unmet needs in italics, and some of their main orientations.

In research projects for campaigns and communications strategies, we have found huge differences between these groups on many issues, from fear of crime to marine landscapes (see page 303), and developed different propositions that could lead them to take actions in support of campaign objectives. For example, a project for local authorities in the west of England in 2006–2007[10] researched mechanisms to engage people with domestic actions that helped fight climate change. We showed how a solution built around the Attribute 'Showhome' (the desire for a home in which everything is just-so and worthy of display), an orientation strongly espoused by Golden Dreamers and Now People, could be used to engage Prospectors who were otherwise 'turned off' by conventional campaign 'asks'. (Mostly as these were strongly framed in 'Concerned Ethical' terms that Prospectors see as hopelessly dull, worthy and smug). That led to the '100 Ideas House', which you can still find online.[11]

A 2008 report *Who Gives a Stuff About Climate Change and Who's Taking Action?*[12] reported a range of questions put to thousands of people in the British Values Survey about many aspects of climate change and showed, in line with previous surveys, strong values-driven differences. Transcenders, for example, were the Values Mode showing the highest level of personal action in terms of changing shopping behaviours on environmental grounds, although Pioneers as a whole consistently out-scored other groups on convictions about climate change being a real present threat, and one that could be tackled. Settlers and the Values Mode Golden Dreamers were the home of climate 'scepticism', which is mainly driven by a desire not to accept change or the need for change. For instance, Settlers were many times more likely than Pioneers to agree that action on climate was best done at the 'planetary level' – not because they were global thinkers, rather the opposite: this was as far away from involving themselves in it as they could get!

Several of the findings in that survey suggested errors in the conventional wisdom on what you might get 'the public' to support in response to climate change. Overall, for example, 44 per cent opposed 'introduction of an environmental tax', while a majority (56 per cent) supported it, and the rejection was strongly concentrated just in the least influential Values Mode: Roots. Contrary to received wisdom, therefore, the political support for such moves was broad, although if you went by vox-pop surveys or phone-ins, the rejection by Settlers would seem large and more significant. When we looked at those 'open to persuasion', it took in a significant number of the Prospectors, not just the 'usual suspects'.

Similarly, while fewer were yet taking action, the great majority of Prospectors (but not Settlers) declared they 'heard the call' to change behaviours because of climate change: an example of the change dynamic in which Pioneers adopt the new behaviours first (innovators) and Prospectors follow (in conventional marketing terms, the Now People are recognized as 'early adopters'). So as of 2008 they were mostly 'behaviour contemplators'.

Motivational values surveys have not just been conducted in the UK and a few other countries but across more than a hundred. Perhaps the most useful set of data has been gathered by Israeli Professor Shalom Schwartz at the Hebrew University of Jerusalem. He has used a 21 item inventory of human values developed over 40 years and surveys of teachers across dozens of countries. Schwartz has worked with over 50 collaborators to create the 'Schwartz Value Inventory', drawing on responses from more than 60,000 people across 64 nations on all continents. CDSM has cross-correlated its model with that of Schwartz, and produced the diagram opposite, which I term the 'Schwartz Wheel'. This provides any campaigner with a quick and relatively easy way to plan or evaluate a campaign proposition, knowing that your potential audiences all will have their values located somewhere around this 'map' (see also the International Values Outline Campaign Planner at www.campaignstrategy.org).

The values marked on this 'wheel' diagram are broadly equivalent to those shown in the CDSM 'map'. The left-hand side is the OD Prospector zone, the top right the Settler SD area, and the bottom right the ID Pioneer part. The essential values problem for most campaigns is that they are conceived in terms of the bottom right – ethical, universalist and justice-oriented. This 'works' for Pioneers but not for the majority. In a country like the US, for example, the largest Maslow Group is the outer-directed Prospectors, while in a country like China or India, although the OD segment is growing fast and campaigns can

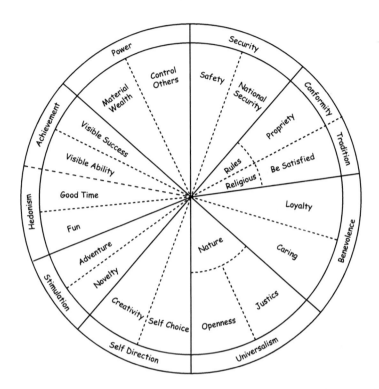

Figure 3.6 *The basic Schwartz Wheel or Schwartz in 'Maslow Space'*

Source: CDSM; see www.cultdyn.co.uk

be designed to draw support from them, the largest group is still the SD Settlers, with conformist values shown top right.

The commonest difficulty for campaign groups from developed countries is that they pitch universalist propositions at 'the public' at large and incite direct opposition (see also 'Choosing an antagonist', page 140) from the top left (in Values Mode terms, Brave New World and Golden Dreamers), and the disinterest of the Now People (lower left). They are too 'PC' for the former and too dull for the latter. This can of course be solved by better strategy and campaign design.

Figure 3.7 gives some framework ideas of what campaign propositions might look like if tuned to values.

As mentioned, a good example of a campaign that reaches across values groups is the BBC Red Nose Day (www.rednoseday.com). This is a fund-raising exercise that channels money to development and poverty relief projects in Africa. Under the TV name 'Comic Relief' it was launched on Christmas Day in 1985, live on BBC 1. At that time, a devastating famine was crippling Ethiopia.

To reach 'new' parts of society create offers (activities, asks, products, services) that resonate with the values around the map. Do not try to 'sell' opposing values! This shows a few generic examples.

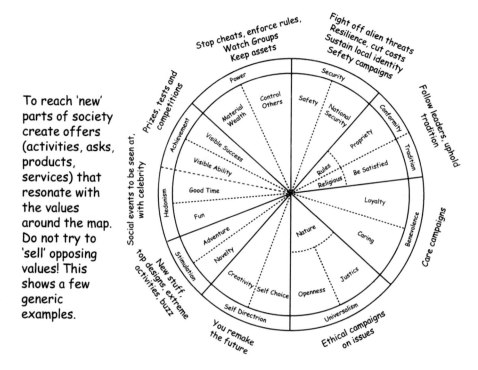

Figure 3.7 *Outline campaign planner*

The core proposition or rationale is the same as that promoted by development aid and poverty relief groups such as Oxfam or Christian Aid, whose core supporter base and values are highly Pioneer (ID). But it has a number of attributes that transfer it as a brand to encompass the OD Prospectors and some Settlers because it also:

- Is fronted by comedians (appeals to all Maslow Groups);
- Is 'about fun' (and the promise matches the offer – it is actually 'fun') not 'about the issue';
- Is on national TV (OD Prospector – high profile);
- Involves celebrities (OD Prospector);
- Allows participants to be an instant small celebrity in their own workplace, school, home or community – wear a plastic red nose and 'do something funny for money' (OD Prospector and SD Settler);
- Shows results (cuts through complexity – OD Prospector);
- Is on a very familiar channel (SD Settler) – in the UK they talk about the BBC as 'Aunty';

- Does not ask people to make a 'political' stand (SD Settler and OD Prospector);
- Has a very simple and easily actioned ask – raising money (SD and OD dislike complexity); and
- Celebrates results in real time (you are a small hero or celebrity – OD Prospector).

This is even though the 'territory' of helping foreigners in countries often seen as corrupt and dangerous (controversial and remote) on a 'political' issue (international relations, inequalities, injustice and so on) is firmly ID Pioneer. The event was also initially timed for Christmas, which is a traditional time of goodwill and giving in the UK (SD Settler).

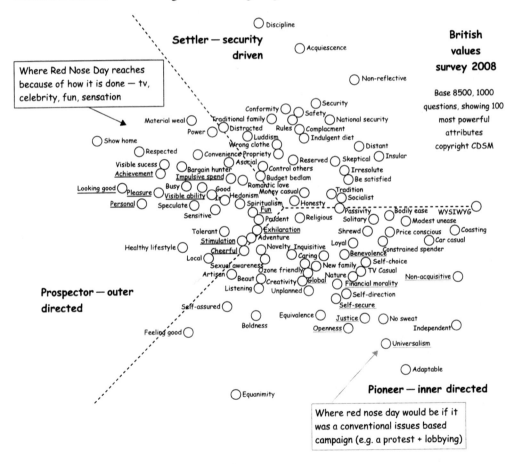

Figure 3.8 *Red Nose Day in the UK: it reaches across at least two dissimilar values groups by resonating with a wide set of attributes. The outer directed (Prospector) ones are made the most obvious in how the programme is presented.*

Although Red Nose Day/Comic Relief is a fund-raising exercise, it has also helped (since 1985) change perceptions of debt and aid issues in the UK and hence made policy space for politicians such as Gordon Brown on subjects such as official development assistance. That will have helped pave the way, for example, for campaigns such as Make Poverty History, which had a much more political proposition, but again used mass participation 'fun' events to widen its appeal beyond the ethical base. Global cool is an example of a campaign group making deliberate use of Motivational Values (see Box 3.1).

BOX 3.1 – GLOBAL COOL: TIPPING POINTS FOR BEHAVIOUR CHANGE

Global Cool is a perhaps unique example of an organizational campaign strategy (see page 261) defined by audience psychology. Global Cool (www.globalcool.org) started as a media and music industry funded charity and now targets Now People (see page 76), the 'Uber-Prospector' Values Mode. 'We are the climate change charity to get you inspired. We want you to feel good about doing good,' say Global Cool.

The Institute of Public Policy Research (IPPR) observed in a study[13] of Now People in 2009 that they have been 'underserved' by environmental campaigns and 'social marketing' in the UK, but the same can be said of other issues and countries. This unwillingness to engage Now People is a great shame as they are a social 'bridge' of strategic importance far beyond their numbers. This is because of the dynamic of behaviour change, in which new behaviours start off in Pioneer land and are then taken up, if they are, by Prospectors (and only after that by Settlers). In values terms, Now People sit next to the terminal values group the Transcenders, and although to become a Transcender they will need to make several transitions, they may adopt the behaviour of Transcenders much more quickly. If they do, other less confident Prospectors may pick up the behaviour from them. If they don't, it usually stays confined to the Pioneers. The social and political implications are obvious. Now People are the gatekeepers of widespread behaviour change, and thus can determine whether or not a behaviour reaches a 'tipping point'.

Global Cool targets the same behaviours and sources of CO_2 as many other groups but doesn't talk about 'CO_2' per se and uses social activities designed to be enjoyable, lots of entertainment and celebrities to create its campaigns, rather than protest or argument. As of 2009 it was focused on energy efficiency in the home and heating (including work with designers at fashion shows to promote looking good by wearing more clothes indoors), driving and public transport, flight-free holidays and reducing the embedded carbon in purchased products (for example by promoting 'Swishing Parties' where people swap fashion items, and reusing fabrics to create new clothes). Its core strategy, says Director Caroline Fiennes, is to 'make it cool, and make it easy'. If campaigners haven't heard of Global Cool, it's maybe because they are relatively new but also because their activities tend to get talked about on Facebook and in the pages of *OK! Magazine* and *Female First*, rather than the news pages. Pioneers can easily overlook the behaviours of Prospectors because they lead rather different lives.

COMMUNICATION BETWEEN DIFFERENT VALUES GROUPS

The principal risk for campaigners, who tend very much to be from the inner-directed Pioneers, is that they simply do not see what the Prospectors or Settlers are doing or mix with them enough to understand what they are thinking. Caroline Fiennes at Global Cool (see Box 3.1) plays a recognition game in her presentations. These presentations are usually given to audiences of decision-makers and ethical campaigners, among whom there is a high proportion of inner-directed Pioneers.

Fiennes shows her audience a range of faces, magazines and clothes. Do they recognize them? The faces are mainly from TV soaps and the clothes are the latest fashions. The magazines are those favoured by Now People. She also shows them faces of politicians and current affairs journalists. Most campaigners, officials, policy and issue experts can recognize the political journalists and government ministers but few have any idea what the latest shape of women's trousers are called, or who many of the soap stars are, and the magazines they have rarely even heard of.

This tactic usually works in making the point to the audience that the people Global Cool targets are not like them in terms of what media they consume, which things they are interested in or who they know about. Indeed CDSM (www.cultdyn.co.uk), which maps people according to these Maslowian Groups, asks dozens of questions about hobbies, past-times and media consumption. The differences it finds between the psychological groups are stark.

For example, Settlers in the UK score significantly higher than the other groups on 'doing nothing in particular'. Perhaps this explains why they tend to dominate in on-the-street media vox pops.

The esteem-driven Prospectors, in contrast, score significantly higher than the other Maslow Groups on these options: go to a wine bar or club, visit a comedy club, pamper myself with personal products, wild party, drinks and dancing, dancing at night clubs, go to a pop concert, dancing to live music, have a 'happy hour' drink, have friends round to watch sport on TV, and attend a formal party or dinner party.

Pioneers significantly opt for the following: discuss social, political or economic issues, go to exhibitions or museums, send or receive social emails, attend a meeting of any kind, visit a church, mosque, synagogue or temple, go to the theatre, ballet or concert, meet new people, go to the cinema, and have friends around for a meal.

All this means the Maslow Groups tend to spend more time with themselves than with each other. When it comes to what they look for in a newspaper, the differences are just as pronounced. For Settlers, the top choices are 'outrageous headlines and unbelievable stories'. They also rank significantly higher than the population average in selecting material such as: regular competitions and prizes, private lives of Royalty, cartoons, puzzles, emotional stories which pull at the heart strings, stories about ordinary people, crosswords, letters, and local news.

For Prospectors the equivalent results are: beauty and personal appearance, lifestyles of the rich and famous, fashion/clothes, homes and interiors, private lives of Royalty, property, scandals in high places, your stars and problem pages. Pioneers, on the other hand, significantly over-score on: features on theatre, art or classical music, in depth comment on cultural affairs, features on books, British politics, editorial opinion, features on modern music or musicians, science and new technology, social issues, and 'the environment'.

Pioneer audiences need to realize that these 'different' Now People not only consume media and live in a world very different from that of the 'political' classes, but that they

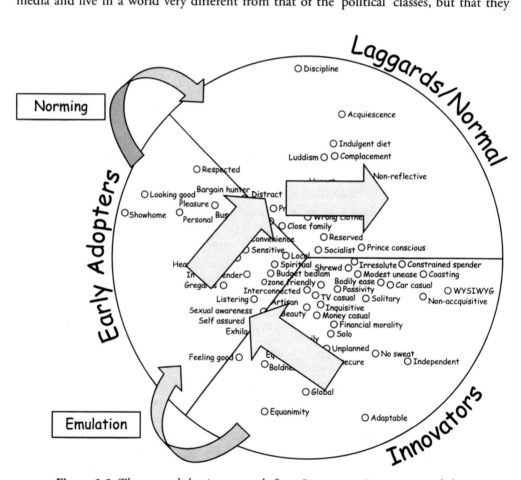

Figure 3.9 *The way a behaviour spreads from Pioneers to Prospectors and then Settlers. Emulation (fashion) and norming are two different stages and driven by different needs (to be successful, and to be normal). This corresponds to innovation, 'early adoption' and late adoption in market uptake.*

also largely ignore the ideas-driven inner-directed world altogether. That is they don't only consume additional media, or simply do more shopping, are a bit more fashion conscious and rather more socially active than the inner-directed Pioneers, but may hardly follow issues, current affairs and politics at all.

EMULATION AND NORMING

New behaviours start with the inner-directed Pioneers and, if they spread, move to Prospectors, and finally then Settlers. The step from Pioneer to Prospector occurs when the outer-directed Now People emulate the neighbouring Pioneer Values Mode 'Transcender'.

The step from Prospector to Settler is what is normally referred to as 'norming'. The desire to be normal and fit in is one that Settlers score highly on in questions asked in the CDSM Values Survey. 'Being normal' is part of Settler self-identity and consequently, if the proportion of Settlers in society is smaller than Pioneers and Prospectors combined, they will feel a strong pull to conform to anything that looks normal because both those groups are doing it. So both the emulation and norming processes can cause 'tipping points' of rapid change.[14]

This process mirrors the conventional innovation curve of market penetration (Figure 3.10).

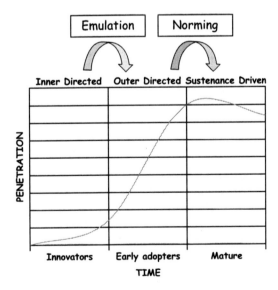

Figure 3.10 *The correspondence between uptake of a new behaviour across values groups and the conventional market penetration model*

It follows that while a new behaviour is only live amongst Pioneers, it will tend to be overlooked or discounted by Prospectors and Settlers (often dismissed as 'weird' or 'geeky' or 'trendy', depending on the subject). On the other hand, Pioneers, especially campaigners on the look out for the next battle or innovation to pursue, tend to overlook uptake by Prospectors. In the UK many 'green' behaviours are at this stage and the Pioneer tendency not to notice Prospector uptake is exacerbated by the fact that the transition often involves stripping the behaviour of its 'issue' context, as Prospectors tend to avoid what they see as 'politics'. Consequently the behaviour can spread while overt support for 'the issue' does not.

BOX 3.2 – ENTERTAINMENT FIRST: THE FAIRYLAND TRUST

The Fairyland Trust (www.fairylandtrust.org) is a UK-based conservation charity that introduces families and children to nature, through fun and magic. It is not a campaign group as such but an example of an organizational strategy designed around a psychological template for engagement. It applies the principles of communication for entertainment to a 'cause' at the brand-architecture level rather than attempting a bolt-on. One visiting father described it as 'an organic Disney'.

The underlying logic of the Trust's strategy is that experiences we have as children shape our attitudes and interests for life. There is considerable evidence that attitudes to nature are affected by whether or not children are allowed to play in nature, and that such play has become increasingly rare in countries like the UK and US. Similarly, habits of eating and exercise formed before 10 years of age are believed to influence people for the rest of their lives. Engaging children in nature is therefore a strategy of generational consequence.

Parents will do many things if they please their children, which they might not otherwise do. Because of the consistency heuristic (see page 63 and VBCOP, page 143), if an adult does something about nature for their children, and the children enjoy it (so denoting it as a good thing), the parent is then likely to transfer some of that 'goodness' to 'nature' in future. 'Being a Parent' is important to all Motivational Values groups – it is a very powerful motivating frame reaching across the public. Engaging children with nature is therefore likely to have a positive and strategically valuable effect on all motivational adult groups.

The Fairyland Trust tunes the ask and offer (the enagagement) so that it too resonates with values across the public. Instead of producing information or argument, or promoting the problems faced by natural habitats, plants and animals, the Trust creates enjoyable days out for families. The offer is a family day out with mention of fairies, in other words a 'magic' signal. The offer appeals to families across motivational groups because parents, guardians and grandparents are looking for interesting 'things to do with their children' (especially Pioneers), and displayable things they can buy for the children (especially Prospectors) and safe, heartwarming events to attend as the family (especially Settlers).

From 2001 to 2008 the Trust engaged over 40,000 children and family members. A visitor survey showed 70 per cent had no previous contact with 'conservation'.

The Trust's use of 'magic' is subtle and strongly cultural, in other words specific to Britain, although very similar resonances exist in many cultures. At a surface level pre-Christian nature-

Figure 3.11 *'Where the bee sucks, there suck I; In a cowslip's bell I lie'* (*The Tempest, Shakespeare – refers to Ariel, Prospero's fairy servant*)

Figure 3.12 *Messenger workshop leader (fairy jewels)*

based religious traditions are intermingled in sayings, customs, traditional holidays and local celebrations, sometimes securalized, sometimes Christianized, sometimes resurfaced by modern 'Pagans'.

The Trust doesn't push that level of meaning at its audiences and conservation; the programmatic cause (P in CAMPCAT) is not mentioned.

Figure 3.13 *Audience: Boy with magic wand*

Figure 3.14 *Context: Another world*

The format also allows for dressing up or for 'becoming another person', and being immersed in an environment where we are all 'different' for a time. This resonates with the outer-directed Value Attribute of 'Persona', which is closely associated with those for 'Looking Good' and having a 'Good Time'. The Trust creates an 'other-worldly' experience (semi-natural setting, no vehicles, generators, franchises and so on), in other words a transformative Context (see CAMPCAT, page 25).

The workshops are designed to use the multiple-intelligence learning styles identified by Howard Gardner (see page 47) and the 'effort' heuristic (investing worth in a thing because of the effort made). Each workshop, such as Magic Wings, Magic Wands, Fairy Gardens, Wizard Shields and Fairy Crowns (see www.fairylandtrust.org) has its own props, performance space and story. The story and the content of the item has its own embedded nature learning, for example Magic Wands teaches about native tree species. It is delivered by a leader who is 'in character', for example as The Wand Maker, with their own story. The Workshop Leaders are the Messengers (M in CAMPCAT) and, like actors, can increase the emotional power of the 'message' by the joint suspension of disbelief.

There are no images of fairies in the Trust's work – the point being to stimulate the imagination as the power of engagement at events, in a way equivalent to the inspiring power of the imagination in a child's (or adult's) exploration of nature on their own.

Tip: The Fairyland Trust was started by my partner Sarah Wise and myself and inspired by our daughter Amazon who, aged four, was asked what she wanted to do that weekend and replied, 'I want to go to the kind of places where I can look for fairies.' Many of the subsequent activities developed by the Trust have been created with her younger sister, Willow. So, start from where your audience is – if you want to engage children (as many groups do), then try to get children to help define what they want to do, and how, and get them to create the solutions. You can start with your own if you have some, then friends of friends and so on.

4

CAMPAIGN RESEARCH
AND DEVELOPMENT

ISSUE MAPPING

Issue mapping helps define the ambition, the objective (Chapter 5), who the actors are and what interests are at stake. It can:

- Illuminate the landscape of the issue;
- Identify players, processes, forces and connections;
- Show what you know and reveal what you do not know;
- Stimulate thinking about how and where to intervene with a strategy.

Issue mapping puts information out on the table – or most often up on a flip chart. It pools and shares knowledge. It acknowledges that everyone will have something to contribute, enables people to be heard, and uncovers absences and gaps in intelligence. It begins to align people internally and can unlock hidden knowledge in your organization. Initially, at least, it is also quick, dirty and cheap. Mapping may show new strategy options, potential allies or points of influence.

To begin, look at all the main processes and attitudes you have identified and then simply ask for each, 'how?' or 'why?' Do we know how or why these decisions are made? Do we understand the reason country X or politician B or civil servant Z takes the view that they do – or seem to? If something is a 'closed book' to us, then have we tried to open it? Would a new technique help? If we cannot do it, is there someone who can? Try writing up issues, causes, effects, resources, needs or processes, just to get discussion flowing.

You can also map problems and solutions, and weigh up factors with force field analysis (Chapter 5). Following lines of industrial production or political accountability can be useful. You can then identify possible areas of campaign intervention – the beginning of strategy making – and later take one of these options, focus on a single link, and work out what would be needed to affect that (which is the critical path).

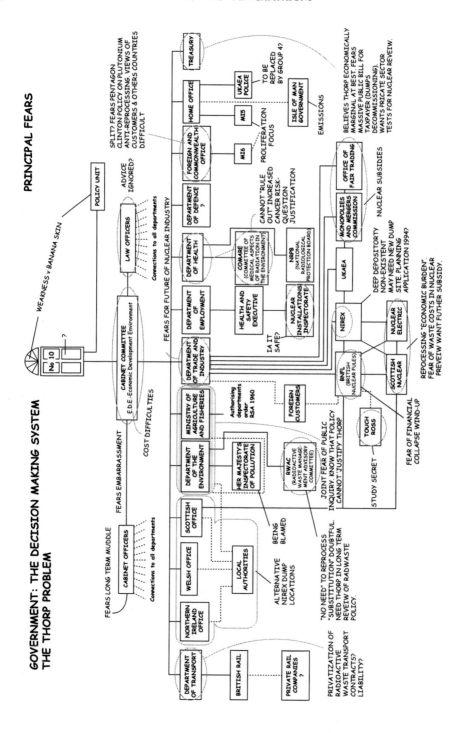

Figure 4.1 *THORP issue map*

The origin of issue mapping is said[1] to be Hans Rittel's 1970s development of Issue-Based Information Systems developed in the 1970s. The idea, says Paul Culmsee[2] is that:

> *at its heart, is a language specifically designed to break down the often convoluted and complex structure of a conversation into something much more simple to understand and digest. The premise ... is that no matter how complex or argumentative an issue is, we can break it all down to just three basic artefacts:*

- *Questions*
- *Ideas*
- *Arguments (pros and cons)*

> *There are a couple of very basic rules by which these artefacts interact (the grammar behind the language). Ideas respond to questions, offering possible solutions to the question. The arguments argue for and against the various ideas. Questions can then be expanded on or challenge other questions, ideas, or arguments.*

The relevant or most useful issue map will vary from topic to topic. In the case of the campaign against the opening of the Sellafield Thermal Oxide Reprocessing Plant (THORP), Greenpeace put a huge amount of effort into understanding the decision-making process (Figure 4.1).

WWF-UK's 'Sustainable Homes Initiative' seeking one million sustainable houses in the UK, focused on characterizing the problem (see Figure 4.2).[3] Paul King of WWF says:

> *It is important to focus on a) what is the central problem or threat you are seeking to overcome and b) what are the root causes of this problem? By stating the central problem clearly you can ask the people interested in solving it, 'why does this problem exist?' In this way it is possible to break the central problem down, bit by bit, and to map all the sub-problems that contribute to it. These 'sub-problems' can then be further broken down in the same way, until you reach the root causes.*

It is then relatively simple to turn each problem into a solution or 'desired future state' – that is, turning each negative into a positive. This will create your 'objectives tree'. There are many issue mapping type resources online, going by names such as dialogue mapping, mind mapping and concept mapping, including http://cmap.ihmc.us/conceptmap.html and www.comapping.com/. A useful online resource is 'tactical mapping' at the human rights campaign website www.newtactics.org/en/tactical-mapping.

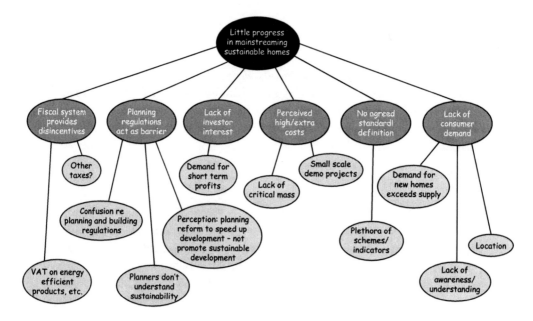

Figure 4.2 *WWF homes issue map*

TAME AND WICKED PROBLEMS

At the time of writing, the idea of 'tame' and 'wicked' problems is back in vogue with management consultants. I say 'back' because it was invented in 1972 by Professor H. Rittel,[4] who wrote: 'A tame problem can be exhaustively formulated so that it can be written down on a piece of paper which can be handed to a knowledgeable man who will eventually solve the problem without needing any additional information. This is not so with wicked problems.' These, said Rittel, 'have no definitive formulation'. Faced with a 'wicked' problem, people keep coming back for more information. As soon as you assume something about one element of the problem, it changes possible interactions of all the other parts. In short, said Rittel, with these, you can't 'understand the problem before you go on and solve it. Indeed solving the problem is the same as understanding it.' Rittel identified a number of other properties of 'wicked problems', including that 'there is no stopping rule': unlike chess, there is no formal check mate condition that ends the game.

Campaigners will recognize this: it is one of the big differences between the rule-bound world of electoral campaigns and almost any social issue campaign that is capable of mutating into something else as soon as what seemed to be a 'win' is achieved.

Sandra Batie argues that economists in particular need to understand the nature of such 'wicked problems'.[5] She points out that they also include 'issues' from terrorism to health care, poverty, crime, pandemics, trade liberalization, nanotechnology, gun control and animal welfare, as well as climate change (see below).

This is one reason why there is no definitive 'how to plan campaigns' model in this book. The 'right' way depends upon the problem, including who wants to campaign upon it. Some of the tools in this book, such as issue mapping, are steps to 'tame' problems such as climate change, and most of the campaigns that have made a difference to climate change have followed this approach. Map the issue, select an intervention ('cut the issue'), cut down the parameters involved, create and test a critical path, all informed by your knowledge of the system, and see what happens when you reach the objective.

Wicked climate

Climate Change is a classic 'wicked problem'. One of the attempts to tame its 'wickedness' is to set an end condition, such as a return of the climate to its pre-industrial condition. Although the climate would continue changing for hundreds of years because of the changes already set in motion as the atmosphere transfers heat energy to movement (weather), and raises the temperature of land and sea, if you returned the concentration of heat-capturing gases to their natural levels you should get large and beneficial changes.[6]

The authors of the UN Climate Convention adopted just such a goal. The Convention sets an ultimate objective of stabilizing greenhouse gas concentrations 'at a level that would prevent dangerous anthropogenic (human-induced) interference with the climate system'. It states that 'Such a level should be achieved within a time-frame sufficient to allow ecosystems to adapt naturally to climate change, to ensure that food production is not threatened, and to enable economic development to proceed in a sustainable manner.'[7]

'Dangerous' was not such a weasel term as it might appear, because before that was written, scientists had already tried to build something of a consensus on what 'dangerous' meant, and had done so in terms of ecosystems and rates of warming.[8] You can relate the amount of carbon in the air to the amount of warming, and so judge how much more, if any, can safely be taken from underground and put into the air.

At the other end of the scale, 'taming strategies' don't try to reduce climate change to its political elements but restrict their focus to particular behaviours, or local geography, such as the carbon budget of a community and its use of food, transport and energy.[9]

GATHERING INTELLIGENCE

To help create and test a plan, gather intelligence about the players and forces at work – how change works:

- Who takes which decision?
- Who influences them?
- What formal and informal decision-making processes are at work?
- Who owns whom?
- Who owes whom what?
- Who are enemies and allies?
- How has change happened before?
- How it all works – what the main processes are
- Which are the critical steps?
- Where the players get their information from
- Networks, associations and get-togethers
- Fears and concerns – what worries them?

Good sources may include:

- Academic studies;
- Websites and publications (it is amazing how few people actually read publicly available information they profess to be interested in);
- Your own experiences and those of colleagues;
- Professional or trade networks you have connections with;
- Supporters;
- People who work in the target institution or business;
- Rival suppliers and customers of a target company;
- Trade journalists or consultants (commission them to do a project, 'brain dump' or workshop);
- Politicians with a track record in the area concerned;
- Gossip and loose talk (not to mention the old standbys of journalists, such as dustbins[10]) – few organizations resist the temptation to treat a particular bar or café as the alternative canteen, and many people talk more freely about the office once they are outside it;
- Staff at a former advertising or PR company that has lost the account; and
- Relevant conferences, exhibitions and meetings (a good reason to accept invitations to talk at the conferences of the 'opposition').

One short cut to finding Achille's heels, metaphorical jugulars and other important pinch points, is to talk to people who have lived with the target process for a long time. They are unlikely to be able to tell you how to run a campaign (though they may be very opinionated) but will often tell you something of significance that will give you an idea of how to do it. You need not ask for 'secrets', only for what in their world 'everybody knows already': how things work and what changes them. Parting words[11] often say most: 'Of course, it's impossible, but what would really make a difference is…'

A senior executive from a leading UK retailer told me in 2005 how he has been repeatedly lobbied over GM foods by an equally well-known campaign group, which in his view had an overly optimistic belief that the current 'non-GM' policy of the British supermarkets is secure for the foreseeable future:

> *In practice a number of profound, but complex changes deep within food supply chains, particularly relating to non-GM animal feed, are conspiring to jeopardise this position, something some retailers are only to keen to use as an excuse to move away from non-GM. Its only by understanding how modern supply chains work that NGOs can anticipate these pressure points, identifying the optimum place and means to intervene to affect change.*

As an example of the type of analysis NGOs need to do, he gave the value chain of clothing, drawing up a matrix that along the top read *Fibre production, Dyeing and finishing, Garment production, Shop, Consumer use, Disposal,* and down the side read *Environmental and social issues, Supply chain challenges, Potential legal, political, voluntary and market solutions.* NGOs, he suggested, needed to analyse each cell of the matrix in order to understand where and when to campaign, what to try and change, and what needs to be changed in order to ensure the result they want. He suggested hiring people who had worked in the business, although you could also acquire the same intelligence by consultancy or other means. Among those NGOs best at this sort of analysis is the US-based Rainforest Action Network,[12] which invests heavily in detailed supply chain research for its campaigns on agribusiness and forest products.

Rely on research: once battle lines are drawn it is tempting not to venture outside even to test the basic assumptions. An easy error to make is to assume that finding the 'right answer' means choosing between known options rather than findings new things out. The Antarctic policy example (Box 4.1) shows how wrong this can be: nobody realized there was, in effect, no political oversight.

BOX 4.1 – ANTARCTICA

In the early 1990s, UK environment groups were struggling to convince the UK government to change its policy over Antarctica. Two unknowns were: why did Britain have the policy it did, and why was that policy apparently immune to public opinion?[13]

Campaigners had promoted a World Park, rather than minerals development, since the 1970s. In the 1980s WWF, Greenpeace and the Cousteau Foundation persuaded many governments to support non-development of Antarctica, but the UK remained a hold-out. It was assumed that this simply reflected ministerial views.

Research at the Public Records Office confirmed what Prime Minister Mrs Thatcher had inadvertently hinted at during the Falklands War – that Britain wanted the minerals of Antarctica. Papers dating from the time of Winston Churchill showed prime-ministerial interest in hopes of gold, uranium and especially oil, and that exploration was deliberately disguised as purely 'scientific' study.

Also significantly, enquiries among diplomats revealed that one Foreign Office official, Dr John Heap, had maintained a firm grip on key aspects of Antarctic policy and its international presentation for decades, yet he was not a diplomat himself. One well-informed journalist said later: 'The situation with John Heap was remarkable – he was a law unto himself entirely.' In other words, it seemed Dr Heap was negotiating for the UK and effectively making policy, rather than Ministers making it.

Having discovered the underlying minerals rationale and the pivotal role of Dr Heap, NGOs were able to better target lobbying of ministers who, contrary to NGO assumptions, had not, in fact, given the issue much attention. When Margaret Thatcher resigned in 1990, Environment Minister Michael Heseltine was soon convinced to quickly reverse policy and back a 50-year mining moratorium.

This is probably what US Secretary of State for Defense at the time, Donald Rumsfeld, meant to say when he famously said:

> *There are known knowns. These are things we know that we know. There are known unknowns. That is to say, there are things we know we don't know. But, there are also unknown unknowns. These are things we don't know we don't know.*

If the problem can be overcome with existing practices you do not need to campaign. So campaigns ought to innovate. As a result, expect to have to uncover something unknown, to find the best strategy.

The costliest and most arrogant form of research is to launch a campaign without doing any – that way you are allowing your prejudices free rein at the cost of your supporters.

Listen carefully to others: what leads people to take the actions they do? In constructing a campaign about chemicals, I once asked a businessman who was a major supplier to the industry what he thought the main concerns of his client companies would be. What would they see as a real threat? I had a vague idea that it might be things like government regulations or consumer behaviour. I was surprised when he said: 'Graduates – if they lose the supply of new graduates, then their business will fail.' Not knowing the sector, I failed to realize their business depended on the ability to innovate, and that relied on attracting and retaining bright young graduates. Suddenly we were no longer thinking of strategies involving politicians or voters or consumers, but chemistry students.

Beware of preconceptions. These can stop us really listening. Think how wrong people can be about your work and consider how wrong you probably are about theirs. Common misconceptions include:

- Companies only ever do things for profit. Yes, generally, but I have come across companies that take environmental or social actions because they think it is morally the right thing to do (mostly privately owned companies), or because of reputation, or in the (often small) hope of long-term advantage. All 'against' the interests of the next results.
- Politicians only do things for votes. Sometimes not – they may act because of deeply held beliefs, or internal party deals or to trade favours, or for ego, friendship or a place in the history books. The nearer to an election, and the smaller the majority, the more voter-sensitive they tend to become, unless they are not standing again, in which case they may back even electorally suicidal campaign propositions.
- The government has 'a view'. It may express a single view, but inside most governments there are a number of often conflicting opinions on the same subject. Much of the time these are suppressed by the system and only fine nuances of difference can be seen from outside, but at times they are in free flux as policies are thought out or renewed, and those are the opportunities to lobby effectively from the inside. Many political decisions are also taken for reasons of expediency, not because they fit with avowed 'policy'. In 2005, for example, UK political insiders had it that the then eternally bickering UK Chancellor (finance minister) Gordon Brown and the then Prime Minister Tony Blair agreed to pursue action on taxation of aviation fuel because it was one of the few things they could agree on (Iraq, education, health and the economy all being ruled out). Understanding very personal politics can be crucial.

BRYCESON'S POLITICAL CHECKLIST

Simon Bryceson's 'political checklist' was first published in *Campaign Strategy Newsletter*[14] in 2005. Bryceson[15] is a public affairs consultant who has also worked for NGOs and a political party. Perhaps the main thing for campaigners to note is how little weight is given to the contribution of your idea to 'the issue' (as in 'Is this the best way of achieving change?') and how much is to do with political process. It's not so much what you know about the issue, as what you know about politics that counts with politicians.

How interesting to the political process is the project on which I'm working? A checklist

- **Uniqueness**: The political process is crucially concerned with the new. If your proposal appears to be a way of doing more efficiently that which is already done, it will be an administrative rather than political issue. You may find sponsors, you won't find champions.
- **International comparisons**: The above not withstanding, politicians love to show that their radical idea works very effectively elsewhere.
- **Cost**: Is this proposal likely to be financially viable? A standard process of financial assessment, not to be confused with Treasury assessment (see below).
- **Timescale**: Are the alleged advantages of this scheme likely to appear on a timescale relevant to other factors? A project that is likely to encounter electoral opposition but not come to fruition before the next election is unlikely to be thought 'interesting'.
- **Personal advancement**: Will sponsoring this proposal benefit my personal reputation? Is it an issue I am historically and positively associated with? Can I take 'ownership' of the issue and, if so, how bad might the downside be?
- **Media-friendly**: Is this an issue that the popular press are going to like/take an interest in? No publicity is normally perceived in politics as no advantage.
- **Electorally acute or diffuse**: Niccolo Machiavelli wrote back in 1532:

> *There is nothing more difficult to take in hand, nor perilous to conduct, or more uncertain in its success, than the introduction of a new order of things, because the innovator has for enemies all those who have done well under the old conditions, and lukewarm defenders in those who may do well under the new.*

Do those likely to lose under the new scheme know? Do those likely to gain care? A small group of electors who care a lot always outweigh a large group of electors who have other things to worry about.

- **Wrongfooting the opposition**: Politicians have an inordinate interest in their continued occupation of office or the rapid acquisition of it. This, of course, is entirely a matter of the public interest since the other lot are so awful one has a duty to prevent them holding office if at all possible. If your proposal embarrasses the opposition it will have interesting aspects.

- **Treasury policy**: In most modern countries there is government policy and there is treasury policy, the trick is to be in accord with both whilst noticing that they are rarely the same.
- **Elite support**: Will a 'clever dick'[16] who knows something about the area catch me out? Have the proposers of this idea checked to see where informed opposition might come from and indicated how it might be minimized?
- **Party fund-raising**: Politics is a very expensive game; there is therefore a constant need to raise money. Can you show that your project has desirable implications for this process?

USING ISSUE MAPS

Figure 4.3 is an issue map for climate change. It's not in any way definitive – a lot of problems and opportunities are not shown. It illustrates the range of possible interventions, of which a dozen are shown. In reality, there are many more.

Some campaigns, such as the Multisectoral Initiative on Potent Industrial Greenhouse Gases (MIPIGG) and Future Forests, can be distinguished by the gases they are concerned with. Most are distinguished by how they engage with psychology and politics.

The Global Commons Institute punts its favoured *solution*, a single tool for terms of negotiation ('Contraction and Convergence') between nations. This, with WWF, Greenpeace and FoE lobbying, is designed to oil the wheels of the climate convention. The two World Resources Institute (WRI) initiatives operate outside the framework of the convention or its Kyoto Protocol – while Families Against Bush (FAB) Climate was a direct attempt to mobilize corporate pressure for the protocol.

The WRI corporate campaigns, like Greenpeace's campaigns for solar power, wind or wave energy, seek to drive progress *using* solutions. The impacts-related campaign of Clean-Air Cool-Planet is, in contrast, an awareness-raising, problem-driving strategy.

Organizations often try more than one intervention, sometimes at the same time. If you do, then be clear about which is the main 'bet' on which you wager most of your chances, resources and opportunities. The rest have to be tactical plays and 'hedges', not just in case the bet doesn't pay off, but so you are positioned for the next phase, cover exposed flanks or maintain essential contacts or roles that may be needed in the endgame.

A well-known campaign example based on mapping the *process* of an industry is the 'back-end strategy' pursued by Greenpeace and others against nuclear power. Opposition to nuclear power arises as much from its role in nuclear proliferation (creating waste from which bomb-making plutonium can be produced) as from the radiation dangers of reactors and waste. 'Reprocessing' was started in order to obtain plutonium to make bombs.

The nuclear industry is organized and sees itself as a 'cycle'. It likes to see this as an asset. Its critics tend to see it as a problem.

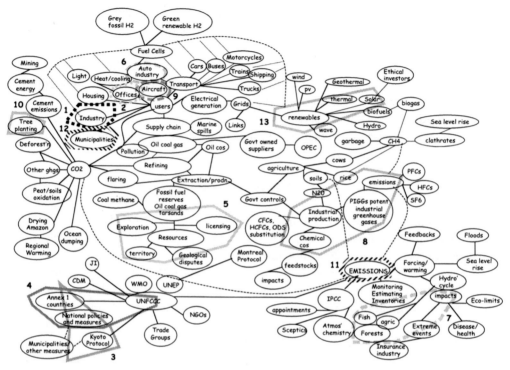

Notes

1 WRI Green power development group ■ ■ ■ ■ ■ ■
focuses on developing use of renewable power by corporates.

2 WRI, www.climatesafe.net ● ● ● ● ● ●
focuses on reducing emissions from commerce and offices.

3 Fabclimate, www.fabclimate.org ▬▬▬▬
consumer pressure on US companies to support Kyoto Protocol.

4 Climate voice, www.climatevoice.org ▬▬▬▬
Internet lobbying exercise on the Climate Convention (for the Sixth Conference of Parties at the Hague 2001), organized with coalition of 16 environmental organizations led by WWF Greenpeace FoE, also including Climate Action Network Australia (CANA), David Suzuki Foundation, German NGO Forum on Environment and Development (Forum Umwelt and Entwicklung), HELIO International, EURONATURA, Ozone Action, The Clean Air Network, Climate Solutions, The Climate Alliance of European Cities with Indigenous Rainforest Peoples (Klima-Buendnis/Alianza del Clima e.V.), The Center for International Environmental Law, Save Our World, Natural Resources Defense Council (NRDC) and National Environmental Trust. 'The first international web-based initiative to give citizens around the world a voice in demanding a halt to global warming.' Collected over 11 million 'signatures'. The website www.climatevoice.org has been launched by 16 organizations.

5 Carbon frontier campaigns ▬▬▬▬
for example in the Arctic and on the Atlantic Frontier. www.gpuk.org/atlantic/.

6 Fuel-efficient vehicle campaigns in the US ▮ ▮ ▮ ▮
Ford fuel economy campaign – US national day of action by Greenpeace, Rainforest Action Network, Public Interest Research Group, Friends of the Earth, the Sierra Student Coalition, and other groups: 'please call Ford today, 2 April 2003, and tell them it's time to increase fuel economy, for their customers' wallets, and to address global warming emissions. Just Dial 1-800-392-3673. Press 3, and at the next prompt press either 1 or 2. Once you have a customer representative on the phone, ask

them why Ford isn't using current technologies that would reduce gas consumption, and tell them that it's about time they did' (Greenpeace e-mail action alert).
Also Americans for Fuel Efficient Cars (AFEC), and the Detroit Project, a 'grass-roots project by Americans for fuel efficient cars'.
www.detroitproject.com, argues that oil dependence 'helps terrorists buy guns' ... 'Let the car corporations in Detroit know that fuel efficiency is important to our national security.'

7 www.cleanair-coolplanet.org ▬▬▬▬
regional US group that specializes in mobilizing around 'New England's dramatic ecological diversity that we risk losing as temperatures rise in our region'.

8 www.mipiggs.org ▬▬▬▬
dedicated to eliminating potent industrial greenhouse gases.

9 Friends of the Earth (in the UK) ▬ ▬ ▬
www.foe.co.uk/campaigns/transport, opposing a new London airport on climate grounds.

10 Tree planting to try and compensate for fossil fuel emissions ▬▬▬▬
www.stichtingface.nl/ and www.futureforests.com.

11 Global commons Institute ///////////
www.gci.org.uk/. promotes the emissions scenario of contraction and convergence – as a negotiation strategy.

12 Energy conservation ///////////
Association for the Conservation of Energy (UK). www.ukace.org.

13 Many organizations simply promote renewable energy ▬▬▬▬
for example Montana Renewable Energy Association, www.montanagreenpower.com/mrea, and Friends of the Earth in the UK, which has an online comparator of energy companies, www.foe.co.uk/campaigns/climate/press_for_change/choose_green_energy, and at the time of writing promotes good energy, www.good.energy.co.uk.

Figure 4.3 *Issue map for climate change with interventions*

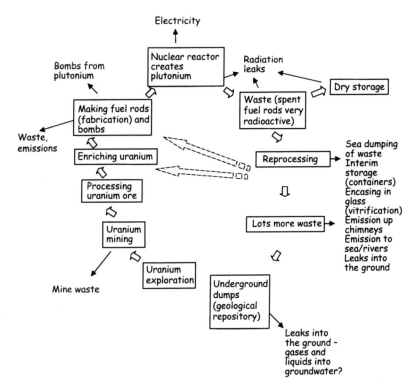

Figure 4.4 *Nuclear power issue map*

If 'Fast Breeder' reactors were used they could make more radioactive fuel in the form of plutonium than they started with, so generating a 'plutonium economy' but the cycle has been used to run logic in reverse. For example, to keep reprocessing going to 'handle' waste when in fact, it increases waste, and to create new types of 'fuel'[17] when there is no shortage of uranium, while justifying it as a way to get rid of plutonium, when plutonium is only produced in reactors – you get the idea.[18]

Instead of attacking nuclear electricity, which is exactly like any other electricity once it is 'downstream', anti-nuclear campaigns have focused on the 'back end': nuclear waste and its human and environmental costs. When householders and citizens have to live with waste, they rightly want to ask hard questions and have guarantees. When you disperse it into the sea or air,[19] the opportunity to ask useful questions is lost. Back-end strategy gets questions about risk asked now, before the risks are commissioned, rather than years – maybe hundreds or thousands of years – into the future. With dwindling options to dispose of nuclear waste, the industry has had to curb expansion and justify itself to the public in a way that it could always formerly avoid, as long as waste was dumped in the Atlantic Ocean.[20]

QUANTITATIVE RESEARCH

Quantitative market research, often called 'polling', tells you how many people say they think something. Popular with politicians and the news media, it makes it easy to tell stories that appear to have authority because they are quantified. This is often taken to be more 'objective' and 'scientific' than qualitative research, but this is largely false. Indeed, polling is sometimes argued to be an ideological rather than a 'scientific' instrument.[21] By determining what is discussed in the news through commissioning and releasing a poll, as well as deciding the questions, those who can afford to buy polling are able to frame what is important to society.

A more respectable use of quantitative research is a 'before-and-after' study to help evaluate a campaign or in communicating with key audiences – for instance, by showing how many other people think something.

Polling can be very persuasive in private lobbying, such as when you have data that relate to the customers of retailers that you want to influence. In 1987, for example, I was working for WWF International, and we were able to provide people close to the owners of the *Daily Mail* with unpublished MORI[22] survey results that showed 26 per cent of the newspaper's readers wanted more coverage of conservation issues. This figure was higher than that of any of its competitors, and this helped persuade the *Daily Mail* to start campaigning on the environment.[23]

Quantified data are useful in lobbying, because numbers can be passed around as a fixed 'fact' in conversation. Qualitative research is unlikely to make much of an impact in private lobbying unless the target is familiar with the methods, as its results sound like a matter of opinion.

Quantitative research is also useful for broad comparisons within an issue. For instance, Eurobarometer surveys commissioned by the European Commission, and global polls by Environics,[24] based in Canada, reveal something about levels of environmental concern. In each year since 1997, Environics International's *Environmental Monitor* has reported the views of randomly selected 'average citizens' from over 25 countries (it shows, for instance – and contrary to popular assumptions about motivation in the North – that concern is as high if not higher in most developing countries).

QUALITATIVE RESEARCH

This sets out to understand how and *why* people think the way they do. It can appear as 'soft' research, but you should resist the idea that qualitative research is less objective because it lacks numbers: quantification often lends a wholly spurious air of objectivity. Qualitative research may also inconveniently reveal that people don't think the way we'd like them to, and this may become a reason to resist doing it. Reject this idea!

At its simplest, qualitative research could mean conducting your own straw poll or, like Mass Observation of the 1950s, eavesdropping on the bus. Talking to colleagues, friends or relatives is, however, a very unreliable way of discerning motivations. Answers are heavily coloured by who is asking the question, and the respondents' relationship with the questioner.

Done well by experienced moderators, qualitative research is expensive but well worth it. Cheap qualitative research, however, tends to be useless or, worse, misleading. Before embarking on buying qualitative research it's a good idea to read up on the subject, look on the web[25] and take recommendations from people in your line of work.

Here's a list of why it's hard to understand motivation, from George Silverman and Eve Zukergood of Market Navigation:[26]

- People often do not understand why they are doing the things they are doing, and therefore can't tell you;
- Even when they do understand why they are doing things, they don't want to tell you;
- When they do tell you, they often don't tell you the truth, or the whole truth. Or, they tell you more than the truth;
- It is more important for most people to preserve their view of themselves than tell you why they are doing what they are doing;
- There is rarely a single reason why a given person does something. Any simple, single act of behaviour is usually the result of many complex forces from inside and outside the individual;
- The same act of behaviour can be motivated by different things in different people. Members of the same group, performing the same task at the same time, may have vastly different motivations;
- The same person will do the same thing at different times for different motivations;
- Some motivations, even if you find them out, are often irrelevant to marketing, in that you can do little, if anything, about them. These may involve motivations based upon deep fears, pathology or illegal activities;
- Yet motivations are extremely important for the marketer to understand, particularly those centring around fundamental beliefs, values, tastes and emotions.

'The best way,' they say, 'to find out about motivation is by inferring the causes of behaviour from people's thoughts and actions. The worst way, often, is to ask them, "Why did you do it?"'

Take a product such as fish fingers. If you ask men why they buy fish fingers they may say that they are convenient, easy to cook, nutritious, covered in breadcrumbs and so on. But the real reason,[27] which you need a deeper method of study to uncover, might be that it gives them social 'permission' to sit down with their kids to eat – in other words, to be a child again.

When my Greenpeace team was researching a campaign on ozone depletion in the 1990s, we found that, while people were quite prepared to accept that it was a serious problem and believed there might be evidence of a link to skin cancer, many were less willing to accept that commercial chemicals had to be banned as a result. Activists strongly agreed that ICI, a major British chemical company, was to blame,[28] but more typical public groups were reluctant to consider measures that might damage ICI, which was seen as a rare example of British industrial achievement.

Greenpeace tested different ways of talking about chemicals – about 'holes in the sky' or 'pepperpots' (lots of small holes), or edges of holes or expanding holes (all versions of reality). What finally turned out to motivate many of the younger women in the test groups was the threat to their holidays. The idea that ICI might be endangering their chance to sunbathe for two weeks was enough to blow away any concerns they might have for the profitability of the chemicals giant.

Research also showed that people were not surprised that solar electricity could power light bulbs (the standard demonstration used by campaigners), but believed that for 'hard work', such as washing clothes, other forms of electricity would be needed. So Greenpeace built a solar-powered kitchen containing a washing machine and cooker and toured it around shopping centres on the back of a truck.

Silverman and Zukergood emphasize the need for research within 'an atmosphere of psychological safety, about what [people] do – not why they do it – and how they feel about what they do'. Conventionally, the best way to do this is in a focus group[29] moderated by a psychologist. They noted: 'People get caught up in the spirit of the group' and when they discover others who are sympathetic, 'these other people quickly cease to be strangers, yet they aren't friends, family or co-workers. They begin to pour out information, opinions and feelings that they would not ordinarily share with most other people.'

Investing in qualitative research is one of the most valuable things a campaign can do. Whereas polling exercises tend to reinforce what you already think, qualitative research can give you important insights that would otherwise remain unknown. For example in 2006 the EU planned a £10m 'public awareness' campaign to promote conservation of 'biodiversity' and used a Eurobarometer Poll to convince itself that:

> The term 'biodiversity' is known by more than 60 per cent of Europe's general public and accepted amongst all stakeholder groups. The campaign should thus not replace the word, but should establish a catchy way of communicating the subject of biodiversity loss and its consequences.

This claim, however, rested on sand.[30] The poll had first told people what biodiversity meant and then asked them to explain its loss. In contrast, a qualitative study conducted in north-east England by MarketWise Strategies in 2007 found only 9 per cent of people 'got it right' when asked what biodiversity meant without first prompting them. Because it is an obscure elite term, people did what they always do in such circumstances and used a heuristic (see page 62) as a guide to guessing. In this case representativeness – 'biodiversity' had 'bio' and a 'd' sound and was vaguely to do with environment, so the most popular guess was that it meant 'biodegradable' (33 per cent). Because biodegradable washing up liquid is also heavily advertised, this would have also ticked the box for the 'availability' heuristic – it was easily recalled.

INVESTIGATING CONVERSATION POTENTIAL

To reach 'cross-over', where new audiences discuss new ideas, and for campaign propositions to acquire the velocity to escape from old assumptions, campaigns need to become a lively 'conversation in society'. Doing that is hard if people are disinterested, and a potent new form of disinterest is the instant opinion. In a world where everyone begins to deconstruct messages – to ask 'Who is behind it?', 'How was it put together?', 'How did it get here and why?' – having an instant view about any proposition short-circuits most attempts to stimulate that conversation in society (witness the failures of politicians' attempts to launch 'big conversations' or stir up 'national debates').

This is bad news for campaigns. People have an increasing number of mental off-switches they can use to disengage with. Yet some things still bother them enough to form the conversation 'everyone is talking about', on the bus, at the rail station in phone-ins and, as qualitative researcher John Scott notes, in the queue at the chip shop.

So an important test for a campaign proposition (see Chapter 7) is whether or not it passes the chip shop queue test – does it stimulate that conversation? The magic ingredient, says Scott, is dilemmas: hard-to-resolve things that nag at us and we can't put down – hence they keep the conversation (read, campaign) going.

'Campaigns work,' he says,[31] 'according to the number of discussions they generate by two people who have nothing to do with it. In such moments people say things like "it's brilliant someone's doing that", or they pass on a factoid; they share something they didn't realize about the world. This is when campaigns achieve leverage: because things become currency. This effect is usually much bigger than a few people taking a lot of action.'

Rather than trying to test campaign propositions, Scott argues that campaigners would do better to use qualitative research to create an 'atlas of understanding' for an issue, and then look for and test out dilemmas. To do this he uses 'constructor groups', in which people are encouraged to effectively take on the role of researchers themselves by being given a brief and sent out to solve a communications problem, test it with friends and relations, amend and present it back.

'Get people to create something and sell it to you – that way you can challenge them, they challenge each other and you can better understand what they really think about something,' Scott says. 'As a result, they are confident enough to give you access to things that are not resolvable. Otherwise, they feel they must give you answers that add up.'

So don't try to shut down all uncertainty and ambiguity in campaign propositions, but stimulate the need for action despite paradoxes and ethical options that cannot be weighed or equated, even while uncertainties cannot be resolved. The UK government 'drink-driving' (anti-alcohol) campaigns are interesting, observes Scott, because 'they make people disapprove of each other'. They make it impossible to think 'the government's to blame': a thought that 'insulates people from dilemmas and irreconcilable things'.

He believes that one reason the Brent Spar issue resonated for so long is that it 'stimulated ongoing debate about whether Greenpeace should even have done it'. Something, as he points out, 'that you were unlikely to have ever discovered by research based on the campaign structure (the campaign plan)'. But, he suggests, if you had asked about dumping waste at sea and about corporate responsibility, then your atlas might have showed a potential for powerful ambivalences to collide. 'It's the gossip in the chip shop queue effect: the issue of whether the government is lying is actually more interesting to discuss than whether sea-dumping is a good idea.'

In the 2000s a good example of a dilemma that passed the 'chip shop queue' test was air travel. Surveys found[32] that increasing numbers of people were giving up flying: in values terms most were clearly Pioneer Transcenders or Concerned Ethicals (see page 80). They were also those most likely to agree[33] that flying was too cheap – yet these the very groups that fly most. Settlers, who fly least, were also least disposed to agree that air travel was too cheap, and were more likely than Pioneers to agree that 'quite a lot' of climate changing pollution came from aircraft'. Thus 'paradoxically' the greatest support for raising air ticket prices came from the more frequent fliers who also least believed that it was an important source of pollution. Not surprising then that the air travel conundrum generated a lot of very confused discussion.

USING NETWORKS

A few years ago, statisticians worked out that we were 'just six handshakes' away from anyone in the world. Some say it's only four handshakes.[34] Studies of the internet and many other networks show the number of links needed tends to be even lower. This so-called 'small-world' effect may be bad news for disease transmission, but it helps explain how the public affairs industry works. Once you are in contact with a few people in an industry or political system, they are likely to be able to reach everyone else in it rather easily.

Add human chemistry, and networks can deliver real punch. This is one reason why experienced international lobbyists go to such lengths to 'network' and press for changes in national policy positions even right down to the wire, hoping that personal pressure will win some shift in position at the last minute. Sometimes it works; most delegations have some scope for concessions, and many ministers can call on favours with their political bosses if they really need to get out of a situation they feel personally uncomfortable with. Many love the dramas of last-minute deals.

Supporters are often undervalued by NGOs. Chances are that most of the connections you need are closer at hand than you might think. Campaigns tend to be networks, with a disproportionate number of links to others. Many of the targets you may be after will tend to be in the minority of highly connected nodes that are over-influential in 'scale-free' networks.[35] Simply checking around your own network may uncover many useful links, and contacts of colleagues and supporters will reach into entirely new ones.

Families, too, are an important factor. Being lobbied by your sons or daughters is far more uncomfortable than being got at on a nine-to-five basis by professional pressure groups, PR agencies or political opponents. You may not know the chief executive officer (CEO) or brand manager or a minister, but do you know someone who does, or someone who might know someone who does? Use networks to their full advantage, but never 'hostage' private relationships and intrude unfairly.

QUALITATIVE EVIDENCES

It is often more useful to show presence – or absence – from visual evidence rather than resorting to statistics. 'Evidences' are things people take as signs of something being true, or being the case. An egg frying on a pavement, for example – 'it's very hot'.

In one campaign, research[36] showed that segments of the UK public were aware of the depletion of the ozone layer and the link to ultraviolet light and skin cancer, but this information was beginning to lose its effect because it was 'not of their world', and nobody they knew was getting skin cancer. These would have been 'evidences' that warnings about the risks were indeed valid. Similarly, at that time the ice caps weren't seen to be melting; hence people were ambivalent about global warming. In another study, one person cited seeing Antarctic cod in a supermarket as evidence of globalization being real.

The important point is that these perceptions reflect the issue as constructed from existing perceptions, not from the viewpoint of campaigners or experts.

What's the expectation; what's understood as evidence that something is getting worse or could improve? How can you make sure that the relevant audience sees that evidence, maybe not just once but in a series of 'evidences'? Find out through research.

CHOOSING MEDIA AND COMMUNICATION CHANNELS

Different types of media are best used for different aspects of communication. Table 4.1 is based on my own experience.

Table 4.1 *Using different types of media for different aspects of communication*

Medium	Best uses	Less good for
Film/video (i.e. commissioned video) non-broadcast	Persuasion, emotions, feelings and stories, speaker support and group discussion	Information
Reportage (being reported by the media)	Endorsement	Engagement, recruitment
Newspaper reports	Establishing a campaign or project – matter of record, logging milestones, reaching political and corporate decision-makers	Persuasion
News websites	A record and archive (if maintained long term, e.g. BBC)	Social intrusion
TV news	Events, awareness, reaching status conscious decision-makers, internal communication	Information, sensitive topics, reflection or messages that should be segmented
TV documentaries	Depth treatment, stories	Time-critical work
Local newspapers	How-to information for the home Case studies and human interest stories that people can believe	Reaching young people (in most cases)
Advertisements, e.g. posters	Reinforcement, awareness	Information, persuasion
Advertisements in special interest magazines including women's etc.	Reinforcement, awareness, cross-support to editorial or features, segmented messaging	Reaching wider audiences
Text – print	Information, reference, stories	Persuasion
Radio news	Breaking news (i.e. urgent)	A record
Radio general	Human interest, stories, reflection	Launches, events
Radio strand or specialist programmes	Segmented messaging and discussion of problems and opportunities	Reaching wider audiences
Radio advertising	Reinforcement (very cheap and can be targeted for certain audiences or localities by listenership)	Reaching 'decision-makers'

Medium	Best uses	Less good for
Human interaction, face to face (PR)	Persuasion, changing views	Large-scale recruitment
Events (to which people are invited or can attend)	Inspiration, integration (multimedia)	Reaching disinterested audiences
Tailored briefings by invitation or side meetings at conferences etc.	Informing professionals and stakeholders, persuasion	Anything else (high cost)
Exhibitions and receptions	Introductions, making new contacts	Information
3 D	Reinforcement, events	Information
Entertainment activities, e.g. sports events, concerts	Awareness of an issue in new specific audience	Information, persuasion
Websites	Reference information, narrow-casting, network building	Endorsement
Microblogging (e.g. Twitter)	News, network building	Information
Email (interactive)	Data, network updating, mobilizing existing contacts; networks	Persuasion Establishment Networking
Texting (interactive)	Updating, awareness Prompting immediate action	Information
Ambient	Awareness for groups that do not use other media, media-wary, or media-saturated	Networking Information
Stories, written or verbal	Changing minds	Information, pressure
Showbooks and laptop computer presentations	Small group persuasion, training, speaker support with small groups	Anything else

Media such as advertising can reach a mass audience but carry only simple information. At the other extreme, face to face such as at public events can reach a relatively small audience but can handle greater complexity, while direct marketing and editorial are intermediate.[37]

The immediate impact (remember of course this is not the same as long-term influence) of different media is probably something like this (in descending order):

- Face to face (the 'sender' communicates with you direct);
- Group (the 'sender' communicates with a group direct);

- An event that 'just happens';
- A clearly organized public event/meeting;
- Interactive online, for example email from a friend or other online personal contact;
- Cinema or virtual reality;
- TV;
- Photography (still pictures or large images/objects such as art installations);
- Internet (with a degree of interactivity);
- Radio (but it can be extremely powerful as a form of one on one, especially when the content is an issue that requires reflection or is very personal; radio is generally the most underrated medium);
- Print (not enough thought usually goes into using print – magazines that end up lying around in waiting rooms, for instance, have a valuable staying power if they contain interesting features); and
- Internet (non-interactive).

As well as media that can't be purchased, such as news or features, campaigns may want to use media that can be bought. Some may be glamorous and worth doing as a morale booster (high production-values film for example) to increase the 'presence' of the campaign. Few are as effective as face-to-face or edited communication (for example magazines and radio). This is why commercial PR (designed mostly to stimulate press coverage) has undergone a boom at the expense of advertising. The more 'paid-for' a message is, and the less unsupported by surrounding and reinforcing free messages, the less it will be trusted.

'Ambient' means 'around you' and is an attempt to get 'messages' out of obviously paid-for slots and onto 'the street' or any other public space, bodies or any place that can be used. It works best while it's new.

ALLIES, DECISION-MAKERS AND OPPONENTS

Who's who, and what's what? Checking through the opponents, decision-makers and allies helps identify key audiences. A campaign might come down to wanting to know how to influence one individual, or even to influence one individual to influence another.

- Mapping individual contacts – a PR company favourite. Who knows who, and in what circumstances do they meet? Draw in your target person and then draw connections to those she or he knows, and who they know, and so on. Often you need to reach a series of 'audiences' to secure a chain of events.
- Winners and losers – as it stands now, and as it will if your campaign succeeds – make a list; brainstorm; be prepared for strange bedfellows.

- Where do costs and benefits fall and how might that be changed? For example, a well-known problem arises in energy efficiency if home owners benefit from installing insulation (lower bills) but landlords have to pay for it.
- Where is value added and profit made in a production chain?
- Don't assume beneficiaries will understand the campaign. They probably won't be expecting it – approach them directly or indirectly.
- Potential allies may want to remain hidden. Possible exposure may shift them from complete inaction to giving private help or useful intelligence.
- Don't demand a lot at first – some will be quite happy to be counted as supporting you – for example in letter writing to newspapers – but are unlikely to do more. However, even that much may convert an invisible majority into a visible one.
- Political, social or commercial competitors are potential allies. Credit-takers are another. Politicians who may finally put their imprint on the decision, even if they do little or nothing to force it to happen, and journalists who may 'discover' the issue with information you have fed to them, are also beneficiaries. Don't forget that there may also be people riding on their coat-tails, who may be even more ambitious for their success.

BRAINSTORMING

Any campaign tends to generate demands for 'brainstorms'. Done well, they can break stalemates or 'campaigner's block' and generate great new ideas. Done badly they descend into a rehash of old debates, arguments and become simply 'another meeting'. My favourite tip for avoiding group-think and dullness came from Martin Scott at Ashridge Management College. It may help to explain this to reluctant participants who start out regarding a brainstorm as a 'waste of time'.

Martin drew a line on a flip chart.

Too wacky -- Too dull

Somewhere along this line lies the great idea. At point X. The right idea. But we can't see it because we haven't had the idea yet.

Too wacky --------X--- Too dull

Here's the catch. In almost every organization, discussion is pushed along by a current. This current flows towards the 'Too dull' end.

Too wacky --------X--- Too dull

---------------------------the current---------------------➤

The current is driven by 'being realistic'. As in 'that would be nice, but let's be realistic'. Waves of 'being realistic' ripple around every suggestion, causing the whole raft of new ideas to drift imperceptibly towards too dull. (One client of mine tried to tell his team to be 'realistic' before they even started the 'brainstorm'.) Then, whether the ideas are simply discarded, or worse, acted on, whether by reaching consensus about the 'best' or by someone just picking the best, you end up with an idea that's too dull to work once it gets out in the real world.

If you start off on the dull side of X, you never bump into X.

And until we find X, we don't know where it lies. So the only way to find X is to start as far up the wacky end as you can get.

So the first rule is to encourage all and any ideas, however 'wacky' they may seem. Other tips might include:

- No debate of ideas – just generate them (cuts off the current of dullness) – no arguing with an idea;
- Capture every idea, however weird or fragmentary;
- Allow and encourage everyone to immediately write down their own idea and stick them all up on the wall (you can sift them later – this stops a dominant participant being, well, dominant);
- Start with a very narrow brief – the narrower and smaller the subject, the more creative the ideas will be. For example starting from where your audience is (see page 27) or exploring any one of the CAMPCAT factors (see page 25). It's best to brief so that you change only one factor in a campaign, as otherwise ideas won't throw up synergies or be comparable;
- Build on ideas – encourage people to build on what the previous person said or put up – that's how ideas develop because people have different ways of thinking;
- Make sure everyone understands the brief before you start so there is absolutely no information-giving in the brainstorm;
- Maximum of one hour, preferably 40 minutes or less;
- Limit numbers to a maximum of seven, and try to select people who haven't been working together on the problem (with bigger groups split into teams – if people have arrived and sat down the best way is to go around the room 1, 2, 3 etc. – in the case of three teams – so that they end up in a different mix from the self-selection they'd otherwise make);
- Lubricate with drink and food (if it's the right time of day);
- Get well away from other work, and no phones, laptops etc.

Beyond these basics, many creative agencies use rapid simple techniques to turn the initial ideas towards concepts that can be taken away for further testing or development. Obvious ones include getting one or two people to cluster your ideas into groups, say over a coffee break, and then discuss or do more work on them. This can help identify new connections or possibilities that hadn't occurred to you at the start – some 'lateral thinking'.

Ways to take it further or pre-structure the tasks might include taking the germ of an idea from this 'idea-generation' and then trying to turn it into a campaign proposition using RASPB (see page 175) or a campaign concept in terms of the 'planning star' (see page 124).

If you are way back at the stage of trying to define what the problem is or seeking common ground on what the organizational strategy should be (see page 261), you might want to start with a 'heaven and hell' exercise, in which everyone privately writes down a series of would-be-great-ifs and would-be-awful-ifs, for example on Post-it notes, and these are then put up on a wall and then clustered. That's useful if you have a mess, for example a programme-based organization where there is little buy-in or understanding of campaigns. Type 'idea generation' into any internet search engine and you will come up with dozens of techniques.[38]

Brainstorming for idea generation is useful when you need ideas. It is not appropriate, however, if you need first to explore what is known or exchange information. If that's the case, you should perhaps first do some issue mapping and run a few seminars or information sessions. These you can obviously do remotely online, but brainstorming is much harder to do that way.

5

CAMPAIGN PLANS

GENERATING A CAMPAIGN PLAN

Campaign planning should find what will make a strategic difference, and then find a way to make that happen. There are many ways to do it.[1] Here's one in six main steps:

1. Make a campaign concept: a vision of what you want to achieve, and how you'll do it;
2. From the concept, make a critical path plan;
3. Test it and revise it;
4. Define the campaign proposition;
5. Draw up the skeleton communications strategy;
6. Before finally committing yourself to action, check that you or your organization is ready for the consequences of both success and failure.

The last stage is where the board or senior managers should give their final sign off. They may also be involved right at the start in setting high-level priorities, but probably shouldn't be involved[2] in details along the way.

MAKING A CAMPAIGN CONCEPT

There's no escaping the need to consider a lot of factors together and come to a judgement. Campaigning can have method with 'scientific' inputs, but it's also an art, a craft. The 'planning star' (Figure 5.1) gathers inputs from five main points:

1   Ambition: what we want to achieve in terms of change (both to the problem directly, and in terms of changing potentials, or the context, to increase the possibility of longer-term change). Analysing the significance of possible objectives.

Figure 5.1 *Campaign planning star*

2 Actors, obstacles and players: the who's who and what's what of the issue. Current situation analysis.
3 Social weather conditions: how things change in our society today, and how we think they're going to change in future, the means of change and agency. Reading the tea leaves.
4 Communication desires: what we want to communicate as an individual or, more likely, as an organization. This may exist quite independently of the need to achieve the immediate objective.
5 Campaign assets: the tools for the job. Social, material, financial, intellectual and other resources, including intelligence capacities and special campaigning tools.

The decision to start a campaign can be driven from any one of these points. A change in who's involved in an issue, or a new resource becoming available, is just as legitimate in determining that now is the moment to campaign, as is a study of objectives or the issue.

Each organization will have its own priorities and ways of making plans, and there's no way to convert these inputs into a numerical process so the right answer can be arrived at by calculation: it's always a question of judgement.

The concept needs to include a draft campaign proposition, any internal requirements or objectives, and an idea of key assumptions about why it ought to work. Most organizations need something like this in order to give a go-ahead to a campaign idea.

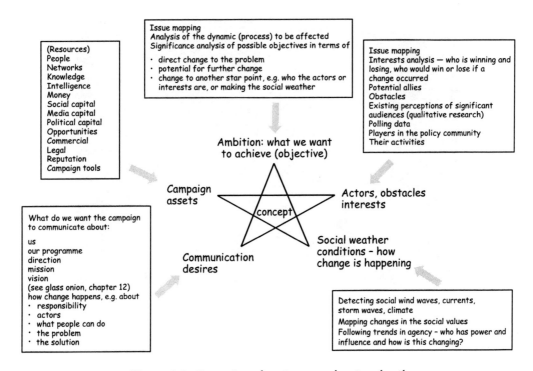

Figure 5.2 *Campaign planning star, showing details*

MAKING A CRITICAL PATH

A critical path is a series of steps in which achieving one is necessary in order to move onto the next one, as with a series of dominoes set up to fall over, one onto another (Figure 5.3). It is best planned backwards from the chosen objective. Each step is essential for achieving the end objective and is then a sub-objective.

The critical path converts a concept into a do able mechanism, a series of events linked by campaign activities. These in turn roll out as a story visible in the outside world.

There are two key parts to this: first, using your existing knowledge, work out a path that would, if achieved, arrive at your chosen objective. This also generates a skeletal communications strategy as a series of activities and events. Second, go out and test this critical path plan by doing some more research, to see if it looks viable.

Such planning[3] hinges on knowing the causal relationship between each component: *how* one leads to another, or *why* one has to happen before another. It's not just a 'time line' or 'plan' of things that someone has decided ought to happen on particular dates. Critical path planning can be used at the 'mission' level (or 'aim'), the 'campaign' level and the 'project' level. Figure 5.4 is a hypothetical anti-smoking campaign.

Figure 5.3 *A critical path is like a set of dominoes set up to fall*

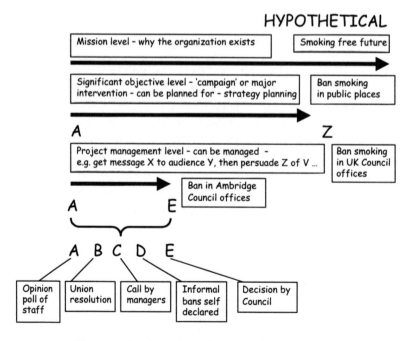

Figure 5.4 *A hypothetical anti-smoking campaign*

In this campaign, suppose that research – intelligence gathering – revealed that while a council decision was needed to deliver the desired final objective, politicians would only act if they felt the organization was ready. So an intermediate objective became informal, self-declared bans. To get those, the support of managers was key. But managers in turn were unlikely to act without both an informal signal of staff opinion, and formal pressure from the trade union. So achieving these became prior requirements. Finally, because the union was most likely to act if it began to look out of step with popular concerns, organizing an opinion poll became Step (objective) 1.

Simply going straight for the final objective would have resulted in failure – maybe sustained failure. Note also that planning required working backwards from the final objective and figuring out what the preceding objectives had to be.

Moving down a level, each step would require micro-campaigning, identifying likely champions, working out who could be brought on side, and who to ignore, and so on. The campaign sequence (awareness → alignment → engagement → action) would be needed at each. Moving up a level, achieving the ban in Ambridge would help in a bigger critical path (not shown here) of council decisions across the UK.

So the project-level objective, a ban in Ambridge Council offices, might be followed by projects to secure bans in other government offices. Then this might be followed (E–Z) by a series of other campaigns to stop smoking in all other offices, and wider public places.

A key part of a really good critical path is an 'inevitable consequence', that is a step, which if achieved, makes the final desired outcome inevitable. Many campaigns have to be run without knowing this but a good enough understanding of the internal dynamics of the system you are trying to change may reveal it. A forensic analysis of a campaign that works will usually reveal one – the point at which winning became inevitable.

The case of the Brent Spar

The Brent Spar campaign, detailed in *The Turning of the Spar*,[4] was a real strategy with critical paths at all the above three levels. It came some decades into a long-running Greenpeace campaign[5] against ocean dumping. More recently, Greenpeace has focused on space junk, sea disposal of the Mir space station, and carbon dioxide emissions, but it began with sea dumping of nuclear waste.[6]

The focus on stopping the dumping of radioactive waste at sea was not because this was the worst or biggest part of marine pollution. You can't sensibly compare, say, nutrients, persistent organic pollutants (POPs), sewage or radiation. The topic was selected because it could be done, and because it was the least acceptable, most awful[7] treatment of the sea, and particularly reckless.

Greenpeace eventually got nuclear waste dumping ended, and moved to stop the dumping of industrial wastes at sea, securing a ban by the Oslo Commission in 1990[8] and worldwide under the London Convention in 1993. After that, it stopped the less obvious problem of incineration (such as toxic solvents) at sea, and won a prohibition on the dumping of nuclear submarines in 1989, and sewage sludge dumping in European waters in the 1990s,[9] while POPs were progressively restricted. These fell under the Oslo and Paris Commission regulating the disposal of wastes in the North East Atlantic (OSPAR) convention. Greenpeace political director Remi Parmentier[10] saw it as the progressive elimination of the philosophy of 'out of sight, out of mind'. At the largest political scale, Greenpeace sought to use the North East Atlantic, and OSPAR to set a precedent for how the seas ought to be treated worldwide.

In 1994, campaigners were told that the oil industry was about to test-drive a loophole that oil lobbyists had secured within OSPAR, which allowed sea disposal of obsolete offshore installations. This was despite the 1958 Geneva Convention 'Law of the Sea', which said that any offshore installations being abandoned should be entirely removed, and a political commitment to do so made when the North Sea fields were first developed.

As the oldest installation in the oldest field in the North Sea,[11] the Spar was a test case for the legal and industrial processes that would be used to dump much of the rest of the oil industry's major waste problem.

So at the next scale down, stopping governments and the oil industry from taking the Brent Spar on a test drive through the loophole became the objective of the campaign. Greenpeace determined that if political lobbying failed, it would use non-violent direct action to try and force the issue.

Industry sources said Shell planned to tow the Spar from its mid-sea moorings near the border of Norwegian–UK waters, to a deep-water Atlantic dump site west of Scotland, in the summer of 1995. The 'weather window' would open around May and close again by October. Accordingly, the Greenpeace strategy was to occupy the Spar, on the assumption that if people were on it, then it could not be sunk.

Greenpeace had been invited to participate in preparatory meetings for a North Sea Ministers Conference.[12] There it raised the anomaly of the oil industry exemption, and the Brent Spar.[13] In autumn 1995 it published a detailed policy paper by Simon Reddy, *No Grounds for Dumping*, making a call for oil installations not to be dumped. Greenpeace expected it to be ignored, and it was.

At international meetings, the Spar case met no interest from any government. As late as March 1995, at an OSPAR meeting, UK civil servant Alan Simcock announced that he did not feel the need to answer questions from Greenpeace as it wasn't a nation state. In February 1995, Greenpeace objected to the granting of the dumping licence, again expecting to be ignored by the UK government, which it was. Inside Shell, the head of public affairs circulated a self-congratulatory memo on how a potentially difficult exercise had been successfully negotiated. Later she recovered all but one of the memos and presumably shredded them.

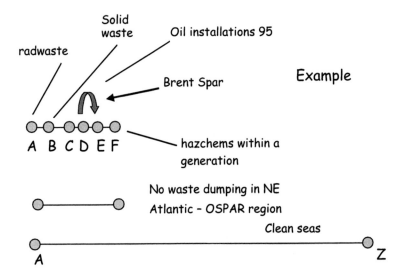

Figure 5.5 *Evolution of Greenpeace anti-dumping strategy*

At the end of April 1995, Greenpeace occupied the Spar,[14] under the bemused gaze of oil workers on nearby platforms.

Greenpeace's favoured alternative was to scrap the Spar at the Norwegian fjord where it had been assembled. That had been the original plan[15] of Shell/Esso, the owners, and that was what eventually happened.

The Greenpeace plan was to use the occupied Spar as a platform for pirate radio, with which to broadcast to Europe about environmental issues during the North Sea Ministers Conference in Esjberg. By making the source dramatic, they hoped to make the message much more interesting. The radio station never came about, but the dramatization worked better than anyone expected.

The occupation escalated into a major physical, legal and political confrontation, culminating in the removal of dozens of protestors over a period of several days. Then Shell blew the anchor chains and tried to start towing the Spar towards its dumping ground, just as the North Sea Ministers Conference was about to begin. By this time, German church groups had spontaneously started a boycott of Shell petrol, soon supported by many newspapers, radio stations and millions of consumers all over Europe. Many governments called on Shell to change its plans.

Greenpeace re-boarded the Spar, were removed and re-boarded it. From 30 April to 20 June the campaign involved more or less continuous, very visual direct actions, backed up by political lobbying, media furore and consumer boycott. One UK newspaper described it as the 'mother of all environmental battles'.

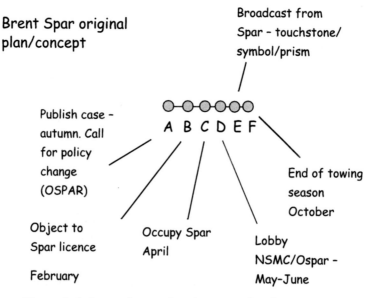

Figure 5.6 *Original critical path project plan for Brent Spar*

In terms of a critical path, the Spar campaign was planned as a series of events, working around three key points in time: when towing could begin, when it had to end by, and in between, the political meeting of North Sea ministers.

SKELETON CAMPAIGN COMMUNICATIONS STRATEGY FROM CRITICAL PATHS

The event that takes place at each objective (how that objective is finally achieved) is the switch from the pre-campaign to the post-campaign condition, like flicking a switch from off to on. This is what can be photographed (see photo test, this chapter) and experienced. It automatically generates a communications strategy.

The stage-by-stage changes from 'off' to 'on' or wrong to right are objectives that, as they are achieved, can be communicated, preferably visually.

The *activities* that drive this process – which might be petitioning, direct action, public speaking, voting, buying, selling or a host of other things – can also be filmed, photographed, experienced or described.

So the two communications outputs that a critical path-based campaign generates are *state changes* in the target, the sub-objectives or waypoints (for example, when a pen is put

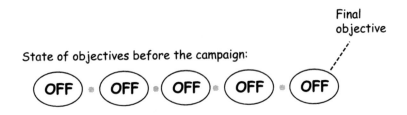

State of objectives before the campaign:

State of objectives after the campaign:

Figure 5.7 *Stage-by-stage objectives towards a communications strategy*

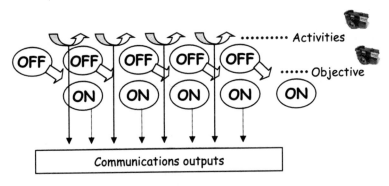

Figure 5.8 *Outputs to which you should apply the CAMPCAT grid*

to paper, a prisoner is released, a waste pipe is blocked), and the *campaigning activities* that the campaigners or their supporters do in order to make that happen. These are all events: activity (an event) → objective being achieved (an event) → activity (an event) → objective being achieved (an event), and so on.

For each of these outputs you need to apply the CAMPCAT factors (see Chapter 1). This creates a communications planning grid (Figure 5.9).

Start at the top with the images created by doing the activities and achieving the objectives.

Then decide who (which audiences) they need to be shown to, based on what effect you want to have. Knowing that, you can decide what meaning to give the 'message' – what action you say it calls for, what motivation or trigger needs to accompany it.

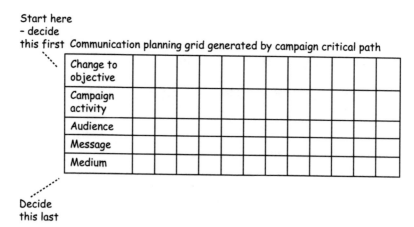

Figure 5.9 *Communications planning grid*

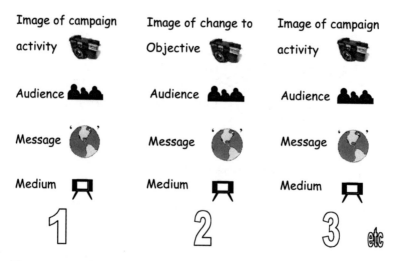

Figure 5.10 *The campaign communicates an image of activity, followed by image of change, followed by image of activity, et seq*

Having decided, that will, in turn, help tell you which channels, context and media to use (choice of TV, video, radio, exhibition, face to face, direct-mail, newspapers, and so on). This has to be the final step, not the first one.

Never start by saying 'let's have a video', or 'so we need a press release', or commissioning a report, and then trying to construct the campaign to make use of it. This is a classic 'communications amateur' error, and can be very expensive – and you may need a warehouse to store the unusable results.

TESTING A CRITICAL PATH

You can't discover *exactly* what will happen if you do run a campaign, but you can find pitfalls to avoid, and research almost always uncovers some hitherto unknown opportunities.

For a significant campaign, this stage can take quite a while. It's a process of research and revision – which can go on as long as you have time, patience and resources – although generally, the 80:20 rule will apply. The bulk of useful insights (80 per cent) will be gathered in the first few (20 per cent) trawls of research or testing.

It's effort well spent, because it's your prototype-testing, research and development phase. Pennies spent here will save you pounds later on. It's also where you let the cold light of reality in on the ideas from the hothouse, and check external perceptions against internal assumptions.

Most of the research usually consists of checking assumptions, using the sorts of tools and processes described in this book, to 'ground-truth' the plan.

FINDING THE RED THREAD: ACHIEVING SIMPLICITY

In Germany, campaigners speak of 'finding the red thread', the vital line that runs through an issue. Defining this and discarding other possibilities is one of the hardest and most pivotal steps in organizing a campaign concept. It is about achieving simplicity, not simplification.

Simplification would take the whole issue and try to reduce it to a simple explanation – but as such, it would be a misrepresentation, a deception or self-deception or a bland précis. Simplicity is achieved by understanding the complexity, identifying the key part that can be changed to strategic advantage, and making a campaign that deals *only* with that single, pure element.

A common difficulty is knowing far too much about the subject you wish to campaign on. Any campaign organization will rapidly accumulate a huge store of knowledge. It will probably find it very hard to sort out which bits are relevant, and which of those illuminate a potential battle-winning strategy.

The best way to make the choice easier is to produce concepts, then test them as critical paths for feasibility, so eliminating possibilities. Another is to ensure that most of the inputs to a campaign discussion are about how to change the issue, and not the issue itself.

IS AN OBJECTIVE REAL? USING THE PHOTO TEST

If you can't photograph the objective, or at least *imagine* photographing it – a fly-on-the-wall test – it's probably not much use, and quite likely not real.

The photo test avoids ambiguity. A good campaign objective often involves something happening, or no longer happening – stopping or starting. For example:

- A political agreement – the objective should not just be to 'get the agreement'; it needs to be the relevant act. This might be a vote – the moment when enough people put up their hands in a parliament.
- A corporate decision – similar to the above, except it might be a board decision, or a decision by a brand manger. Who knows? You really need to know, if only to make sure you are pushing or pulling at the right part of the organization.
- Public awareness. Of what? Rarely an objective worth having in itself. As you can't see inside people's heads, this sort of objective needs to employ a proxy; such as a before-and-after survey, or an action that from research you know people will take once they are 'aware'; or some sort of self-declaration by those who do become aware. In which case, one of those, not awareness itself, becomes the objective.
- Stopping a process. A negative or absence can be converted into a positive that can be photographed – whaling ships staying in port, for example.
- A solution. Can you photograph it being put in place? Can it be inserted into the problem, like a plug in a plughole, or by direct substitution? Examples are renewable energy being plugged in, or Forest Stewardship Council (FSC)-certified doors being installed at the UK Cabinet Office, in place of forest-damaging ones, in a Greenpeace action in 2002.

The photo test focuses the mind and forces you to cut away vague concepts:

- It can be communicated in pictures;
- It leads you to discover exactly what the delivery mechanism is for a change – how it comes about, who does it;
- It can be inspiring, because it shows that the objective is real, concrete, achievable and understandable;
- It helps resolve internal debate and progress planning; and
- It can be detected, and so evaluated. It is often said that it's important to have 'quantifiable' objectives, but this is not as important as being *detectable*.

THE AMBITION BOX

Picking the right objective means considering:

- Your ambition for changing the overall problem;
- Resources and activities;
- Organizational strategy – on a revolutionary–managerialist spectrum.

These translate into three dimensions, creating the 'ambition box' of possible objectives:

- Size – how much of the overall problem does it represent (immediate yield)?
- Toughness – how hard do you have to try to achieve it?
- Significance – what consequential effect results from achieving the objective (longer-term yield)?

For a government agency or an organization charged with doing something about a problem in the most cost-effective way, the rational place to start is with the low-hanging fruit. For a campaign organization, the targets are likely to be tougher. After all, the low-hanging fruit has probably already been picked by someone else.

If you want a strategic effect, it is no use picking a target simply because it is 'relevant' or 'connected' to the problem. It might be a brick at the top of the wall. Pull it out, or if it's tough, chisel it out, and the result is maybe not much. If, however, it is the keystone brick in an arch, then it may bring the whole thing down. This quality is not to do with the immediate 'toughness' or size of the target, but its *significance*, another dimension making up the 3D 'objectives box'.

For example, in the Florida Everglades, the alligator acts as a 'keystone species' by creating dry-season ponds, which also allow a host of other species to survive. In *The Tipping Point*, Malcolm Gladwell gives numerous examples of how specific social dynamics can lead the spread of ideas to have big effects.[16]

Campaign groups may deliberately pick 'hard nuts' in order to draw attention to a problem. Exxon, for example, is unlikely to succumb to pressure from www.stopesso.com

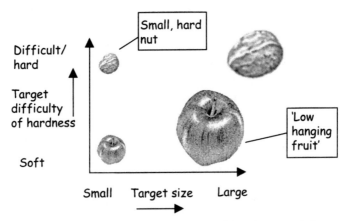

Figure 5.11 *Immediate target in terms of hardness and size*

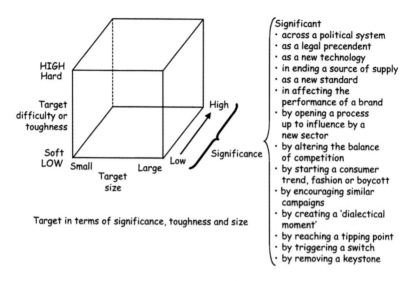

Figure 5.12 *Target in terms of significance, toughness and size*

but is likely to remain deserving as a climate campaign target with huge political resonance. Greenpeace's tryst with the PVC industry, eminently logical (PVC being a linchpin of chemical pollution), has proved a war of attrition because of communication problems – a less-resonant tough nut.

The Californian car market has proved itself to be a political–industrial keystone of great significance, from catalytic converters in the 1970s to electric vehicles in the 2000s. Eron Shosteck, spokesman for the Alliance of Automobile Manufacturers, said in 2002: 'You can't make one car for California and another car for Washington, DC.'

In the Brent Spar campaign the target was known to be:

- Of strategic importance to the oil *industry* – as an industrial test case for a waste disposal option (sea dumping) for all North Sea 'brownfielding';
- A *political* precedent (within OSPAR) regulating the disposal of wastes in the North East Atlantic; and
- A *legal* precedent within the same framework.

Quite unexpectedly, it also became of strategic significance:

- As a symbol and trigger for change within Shell, including its view of its future as an energy company, rather than simply an oil company;

- As a touchstone and jumping-off point for a lot of corporate thinking about corporate social responsibility (CSR) – some, such as Stephen Colegreave, business development director at McCann-Erickson, say it is where the notion came from;[17]
- As a demonstration of what 'new politics' might achieve – consumers, businesses and NGOs negotiating an outcome, independent of government.

Disputes over which is the 'right' objective can often be resolved if the three dimensions are teased out and discussed separately.

FORCE FIELD ANALYSIS

This is a fancy name for identifying and weighing up the factors acting for and against the change you want to achieve, at any stage of planning. It involves identifying each component of change and then assessing the factors acting for and against it. Usually, it's possible to assign scores to most factors just from a discussion among colleagues – for example low, medium or high intensity.

Force field analysis[18] is a useful way to hit upon less-obvious factors that may provide the most fruitful avenues for change. The media will tend to focus on the points in your issue at which there are powerful forces opposing each other. These will generate a lot of sound, fury and heat, but may also involve a stalemate. Doing the obvious and adding your weight here may not be very cost-effective. If you can find a factor where there are few or no forces in opposing what you want, and only a small force already acting *for* what you want, then this may be where you can make a significant difference.

In Figure 5.13, above the point circled by the hatched line, rather than the more obvious solid circle, is the best place to intervene and add extra force. The objective is to bridge the 'change gap'. Each set of arrows represents a line of conflict or point of dispute within the issue.

As well as finding the best place to add weight to 'pro' factors, force field analysis can help spot opportunities to reduce the impact of opposition.

Reviewing the factors acting for and against what you wish to achieve should be part of any periodic re-evaluation of a campaign. The failure to persist is relatively easy to identify as a cause of failure. Campaigners may be unrealistic about how hard it is to shift behaviours, for example, or what it would take to do so when faced with major interests and behaviours. A classic example is smoking and the once hugely powerful tobacco lobby. NCVO quote[19] Wyn Grant, Professor of Politics and International Studies, University of Warwick: 'Opposition to smoking used to be seen as eccentric; it's taken 40 years or so for that to change.' The London smoking ban strategy described in Box 5.1 could not have been deployed 20 or even 10 years earlier.

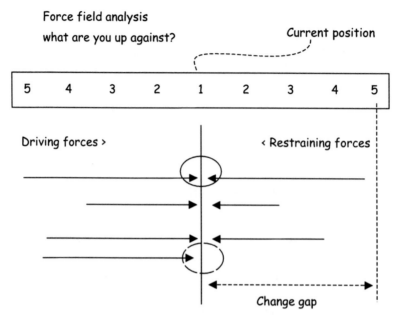

Figure 5.13 *Force field analysis*

BOX 5.1 – A BAN ON SMOKING IN PUBLIC PLACES

In 2006 the health group Ash (Anti Smoking for Health) achieved a significant breakthrough in their long running anti-smoking campaign, through a campaign to ban smoking in public places in London.[20] In a conventional but well-planned and executed lobbying effort, Deborah Arnott and Ian Willmore set out to 'reframe' the issue as one of health and safety for workers in pubs, cafes and clubs rather than health in general. Their long-term aim was obviously to end smoking, but they knew that a significant way to reduce the amount that people smoke would be to restrict the opportunity.

When Ash began campaigning for smoke-free legislation in 2003, they were 'told by politicians, civil servants and commentators that there was no chance'. An official of the governing Labour Party called it 'an extreme solution', but within three years it led to a national legal ban that a government minister hailed as a 'historic piece of legislation'.

Ash focused not on personal consequences for smokers, which frames the question as one of personal rights and responsibilities for one's own health (the frame used by pro-smoking groups such as Forest[21]) but in the consequences for those subjected to other people's smoke (starting with bar staff and so on). Thus the campaign defined a category of blameless and unjustly treated victims (see 'Motivational campaign sequence', page 19), and shifted the debate from voluntary measures and smokers' rights, to one of 'health and safety', which had long enjoyed official endorsement.

The well established 'health and safety' context helped Ash form an alliance of local government officers, health institutes and trade unions to each push forward towards a common goal. Effectively Ash set up a swarm of campaigners, each using their initiative to push towards the same target, rather than itself engaging in gladiatorial debate with the pro-smoking lobby.

The next step was to split the opposition – identified by campaign analysis not as the tobacco industry but the hospitality trade (see 'Issue mapping', page 95). They did this by using the spectre of local political action leading to a multiplicity of laws (a case of identifying and playing on different interests, see this chapter). The final moves were mainly a case of exploiting splits within the government – notably between Health Secretary John Reid and the Chief Medical Officer – and conveying that there would be some votes in the issue.

Pivotal in the process – which took several years – was the 'Big Smoke Debate' engineered by Ash and its allies in London. As the national capital, a global media and financial centre, and with more change-orientated Pioneers (see page 72) than in almost anywhere else in the country, London was a strategic social bell wether. Initially Ken Livingstone, Mayor of London, was not interested, he but became a campaign champion after public affairs firm Munro and Forster (M+F) helped Ash show that public opinion was on side.

M+F worked with 'SmokeFree London' and the London Health Commission to put the issue of smoke free public places on the capital's agenda through the Big Smoke Debate consultation. 'An exclusive was given to the London newspaper the *Evening Standard*, and Londoners' views were captured on a website questionnaire. They were asked if they thought seven different types of venues, from taxis to pubs, should be smoke free,' said M+F. About 40,000 Londoners responded, with 78 per cent in support of a ban on smoking in public places.

So the campaign used 'salami' tactics to chop the problem up into slices, such as smoking in cabs, cafes and pubs, rather than smoking in general. The results of surveys persuaded Livingstone that he should write to the national government supporting legislation, thereby making Livingstone, a political heavyweight, into a campaign messenger. Ash was able to surmount obstacles such as John Reid's advisers by showing the effect that similar policies had achieved in Scotland, Ireland and New York – not in terms of health but in terms of public opinion.

In the final stretches, the campaign benefited from what another PR, Simon Bryceson, has called the 'law of anticipated consequences', that is, politicians usually react to the threat of what might happen, rather than just the impact of what has already been achieved. This campaign 'ticked the boxes' in much of 'Bryceson's political checklist' (see page 103).

Persistent one-man-band campaigners are often celebrated in the media, but usually only after they succeed, and that after a long wildnerness period where the media ignored them. In 2001 Phil Thornhill started a one man vigil outside the London US Embassy when G. W. Bush rejected the Kyoto climate Protocol. By November 2006 he was joined by 19,999 others.[22] Phil also started the now global Campaign Against Climate

Change,[23] which is primarily an old-style demonstration group. The Protocol entered into force in 2005, and although the US never signed up, Thornhill's vigil was one of the campaigns that maintained the will of other campaigners and their allies not to give up the struggle.

Georgina Downs, author of www.pesticidescampaign.co.uk, is another who stands out by her unflagging commitment and her success, waging a more-or-less one woman project that used personally collected evidence, the media and the law, to challenge government rules about how farm chemicals can be applied close to homes.

Such campaigners win awards (unlike most of those whose profile is subsumed in larger organizations), but those you don't hear about are the ones who persist with a strategy that does not work. Persistence in itself is not enough.

THE IGNORANCE GAP

In most campaign planning, there's a lot we don't know. We usually cannot wait until all unknowns are resolved or uncertainties are reduced before proceeding – it's urgent or else we wouldn't be campaigning.

Risk analyst Christopher Tchen[24] identifies two important effects in dealing with the unknown that can lead to failures in any 'risk'-related planning. First, to overestimate the total risk. This, he says, is typically done by senior management. They imagine things like upsetting stakeholders or other high consequence but low probability events, culled from years of experience. Consequently their accumulated perception of risk is high.

They might, in a commercial situation, say things like: 'We can't get into consumers' business', 'We must not upset our partners' and 'We should concentrate at home'. The net effect is 'Uninformed Pessimism'.

Second, and in effect the opposite, is to underestimate specific risks. This is typically done by middle managers or project staff, who are naive about what can be achieved. In campaign planning they might mistake Level 2 (see page 9) for Level 3: seeing a route that could indeed lead to the desired result but not actually testing for its doability.

In the commercial world they might be saying things like: 'And then we'll develop and run a joint venture with Microsoft' or 'And then we'll get a permit from the Chinese government, and then we'll recruit some local management talent'. This easier-said-than-done effect amounts to 'Uninformed Optimism'.

A task in campaign planning is, therefore, to be aware of these dangers and to maximize communication between the two groups, and to test, test and retest your assumptions.

CHOOSING AN ANTAGONIST

How a campaign opens is all-important. Who is it against? All campaigns have an opponent: the antagonist, to you, as the protagonist in your story.

Like a tennis player, you may serve for the first point. Where you place the ball will play a part in determining what happens next. Unlike tennis, the campaign game may be joined by any number of other players, including the spectators. It's more like the original versions of football, played between villages, in which the whole community could participate if it felt like it.

The campaigning dialogue is with society, your opponent, your supporters and, sometimes, between them all. The starting conditions help determine the future route of the 'conversations' just as surely as if you stood on a watershed and dropped a toy boat into one headwater or another.

So try to think several steps ahead: use 'what if' scenarios. 'If I communicate this, then what will the reaction be?' Then 'what will I do next – and what will be the response to that?' And so on, as far ahead as you can envisage. Then try another sequence and another.

To pick an opponent, examine the chain of responsibility – from who or what you think is ultimately responsible, to who is immediately responsible. Decide where in that chain to start. Consider:

- How the buck-passing will work.
- Public motivation – how do people feel about blaming a potential target (demonology)?
- Likely response – can you ignite a conversation?
- Are some ostensible opponents actually closet supporters, who'd welcome pressure?

Companies, encouraged by their PR companies and some journalists, tend to assume that the main factor in deciding a target is demonology – how big and bad the reputation is. Effective campaign planners, in fact, spend much more time thinking through the dynamics – the buck-passing and interests at play.

To make these choices is very hard if you haven't worked out a critical path. Tip: this is the part of campaign planning that politicians tend to be very good at, so involve them if they are available.

Lastly, be sure to choose your antagonist – don't let values choose them for you. As you can see from the 'Schwartz Wheel' (see page 81), each Schwartz values dimension has opposing values at either end. Vigorous general promotion of one set of values is almost certain to arouse opposition from people who share the opposite values orientation. The most likely one for campaigners to encounter is power versus universalism, but others can also set up an unhelpful see-saw effect in which a polarized debate swings back and forth. This is not what you want to happen unless you simply want a perpetual debate, so think about how to avoid it, for example by finding ways to satisfy, sideline, outweigh or work around opponents with diametrically opposed values sets (Figure 5.14).

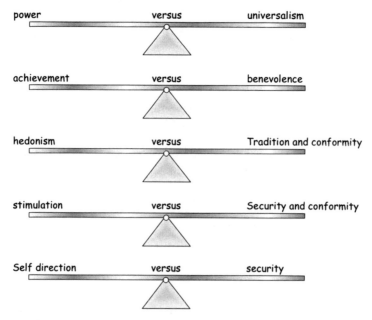

Figure 5.14 *Debates to avoid – Opposed values sets can set up unhelpful polarized debates if the campaign involves a simple head-on assault against diamterically opposed values*

Source: Values dimension antagonisms identified by Shalom Schwartz of Hebrew University of Jerusalem (Pat Dade, personal communication)

CHECK FOR CONSEQUENCES

Do you really want to do this? Before lighting the blue touchpaper, get everyone to buy in to the plan. Success can have consequences as well as failure. There may be a backlash, or expectations will be created. You need to know what you'll do next, and what to do with enthusiastic supporters or allies. Have you thought through the effects on losers?

Of course, your decision-makers should have given an in-principle 'OK' long before this, but it's good to make sure that any unpleasant surprises generated by the campaign arise on the outside, not within your organization.

Before targeting any individual or indeed institution with a campaign, you need to be sure that what you are doing is needed and justified. Here's a list of consequences as might be perceived by a politician thinking 'Do I need to respond, how should I treat this campaign?'. Not to be taken too literally and British examples, but it might be worth making a similar list of your own. The trick is to make the threat your campaign credibly poses just as serious as it needs to be to get the result, and no more.

worst

could end my career

could lose us the next election

could precipitate an election

could bring down the Prime Minister (PM) (requiring a new leader)

I could have to resign (as Minister)

I could lose a Minister (beneath me)

another Minister might have to resign

officials might have to go/be moved

could damage our popularity (party) long term

could embarrass/damage reputation of PM

could affect my promotion chances

could stop me achieving major departmental plan/objective

could embarrass me/damage my reputation

could upset powerful business interests/ other important stakeholders

could show I am wrong

could show my department is wrong

could lose us a vote

could mean I go before Select Committee

could take up a lot of media time (on someone else's agenda)

could take up a lot of media time

least bad

VBCOP – DRIVING POLITICS WITH BEHAVIOUR

Influencing policy is perhaps the commonest desire of social campaigners, even ahead of opinion and behaviour. Endeavours to change policy and change behaviour are often executed separately. VBCOP[25] is a way of bringing them together in a single strategy, and a very different way of influencing politicians from the conventional approach of making argument or providing facts to mobilize opinion, and then trying to use that to convince politicians. It can be used 'from the start' in a campaign or where the making of arguments has already been tried, has exerted what effect it is going to have and where that is not enough.

VBCOP stands for Values, Consistency, Behaviour, Opinion, Politics, V>B>C>O>P, and the model is basically this:

Define an action that resonates with the values of a target audience [V]

↓

Secure the behaviour [B]

↓

Utilize consistency heuristic (i.e. my opinions adjust to match my behaviour) [C]

↓

Reveal the resulting opinion (what I believe in or am in favour of) [O]

↓

Deploy that to change politics [P]

As such, VBCOP utilizes the 'consistency heuristic' (see page 63) – we adjust our opinions to fit what we do, because we'd otherwise be going around saying one thing and doing another, and it is simply too mentally uncomfortable to speak against our own behaviour.

In common with the conventional approach of making arguments to change opinions, and hoping that this in turn has a political impact, VBCOP utilizes the political interest in expressed 'opinion'. Indeed today's politicians are often accused of paralysis or slavishly following public whims because of their ever greater sensitivity to the need to 'stay in step' with public opinion,[26] usually manifest through proxies like media phone-ins, online petitions and blogs, Twitter and structured opinion polls. The difference is that to generate the opinion, it changes behaviour (or samples opinion from those who are undertaking a consistent behaviour), rather than making arguments.

The 'consistency heuristic' is an example of unconscious, reflexive thought. It's not something we often realize we are doing. The same goes for values that drive the behaviour: we adopt behaviours that help us meet needs of which we are unconscious (see page 62). So this is a strategy based on reflexive thought. It is also what actually happens, whether planned or not. Politicians are regularly in thrall to 'interest groups' whose opinions are driven by their behaviours – 'motorists' on the question of transport options, for instance, and gun owners in America on the question of 'rights' to carry firearms.

We can see the 'consistency effect' in changing views about the efficacy of environmental actions. A 2005 UK survey found 70% of people saw 'recycling as the solution to environmental deterioration, compared to 46% in 1999'.[27] Was this rapid increase of belief in the efficacy of recycling the result of systematic analysis by the public? Unlikely. More probable is that it was the result of the 'consistency heuristic'. More people were recycling, so more people ranked recycling as effective: 'I do it, therefore it makes sense': behaviour leading opinion.

Using VBCOP

To use VBCOP, campaign planners should start by determining what 'opinion' they need to deliver to politicians (although this approach could apply to any other target, such as a company, if it considered opinion to be important), and then working back through opinion, to behaviours to values. This means using your knowledge of the dynamics of the issue and the state of politics to identify the sort of 'opinion' required, in terms of authors (*whose* opinion) and in terms of the ways it should be measured, and in terms of which channels, contexts and messengers are most likely to relay it to the intended political target.

Ideally the behaviour will be one that is also desirable 'in itself' (in other words it contributes incrementally to a solution), but it is more important that the behaviour is strategic: it might have an indirect effect rather than any additive direct solution effect. Its key role is to generate the opinion.

Knowing whose opinion is required means you can then use values analysis to work out how to generate the desired behaviour, using values mapping systems such as those of Cultural Dynamics Strategy and Marketing, Y and R's 4cs, or Environics Social Values Groups. This approach may sound like hard work, and it is more difficult than simply generating expressions of your own opinions in terms of arguments or advocacy that is delivered to politicians or audiences you hope will act as intermediaries. On the other hand, many campaigns remain 'treading water' for years because they keep generating demands, often louder and more shrill, from the same small group of the 'usual suspects'.

A good starting point for this approach would be to find out from politicians who they think are the 'missing voice' or the missing signal in terms of segments of public opinion, and use VBCOP to activate them. Bear in mind too that politicians will find it easiest to recall those who have actively opposed opinions. It may be that the best prospects are people who currently are saying nothing and have not thought about the subject, but who could be moved to undertake a relevant behaviour much more easily than those who have declared a relevant position.

This can therefore be used to secure opinion changes where argument or information is not going to work – which is in many cases,[28] and in nearly all where an 'issue' is 'mature' and so people have adopted 'positions' on it that they are conscious of. Indeed because of the consistency effect, if you go to someone with an established 'bad' behaviour and *tell* them to change it, their reasoned opinion is quickly accessible to them to explain why your view does not make sense. So the trick is first to get them to do the behaviour, not to develop the opinion.

Survey the behaviours

Another starting point is to survey *helpful* behaviours that are already out there and available to be sampled and communicated but where they have yet to have an effect on the perceptions of your target audience (for example politicians). This is especially if they are new and therefore unfamiliar.

Take, for example, politicians' perception of how hard or easy it might be to get people to invest in domestic renewable energy systems. The conventional political view is that outside a small number of 'deep greens', 'normal people won't pay'.

In the UK, where domestic heating has long relied mainly on gas, coal, oil or electricity, the late 2000s saw a growing trend to use wood. The conservative *Daily Telegraph* reported in 2008:[29] 'Sales of wood-burning stoves have risen every year since 2005 to 140,000 last year, according to manufacturers, as electricity bills have increased along with the cost of oil.'

Some of these consumers were Settlers, the most socially conservative (security-driven) Maslow Group and normally last in line to take up any new behaviour. They were buying quite expensive wood burners and some of them solar water heating. (Solar water heating sales increased 90 per cent in 2007–2008, despite the 'credit crunch'.[30])

The reason they gave, though, is entirely in tune with their values – safety and security: a defence against uncertainty of power supplies and rising costs. It was not to help 'the planet' (the typical inner-directed Pioneer values-driven reasoning for the same behaviour). In one focus group conducted in the west of England in 2006,[31] researchers KSBR found a rich Settler woman who had equipped her home with a comprehensive array of solar technologies – her logic though was pure security-driven. She wanted to be safeguarded against 'them'. When asked who 'they' might be, it encompassed Tony Blair (the Prime Minister) and all those in control: the government and big world events. She was making her home her self-sufficient castle.

Some campaigners might see this as the right thing for the wrong reason. But if you surveyed the opinion of that lady and others who had done like her on the subject of solar power – 'Should there be more done to encourage it?' or 'Does it work?' – she'd be likely to say 'yes'. And if a politician met her, she'd be likely to stand out as somehow different and unexpected, and therefore signify wider and more important support than another ten who seemed like the 'usual suspects'.

Making opinion count

Opinions do not count unless they are seen or heard, and this usually means measuring them. The obvious thing to do is to run surveys to show the types and numbers of people who think that X or Y is 'effective' or a good thing or 'should be encouraged' by asking those who are undertaking a behaviour that is consistent with this opinion.

Obviously a poll with a baseline and a time series is more convincing than a one-off snapshot, but campaigners generally should avoid acting like academics. The purpose of all this is to make your case and bring about change. It is not to show how few people are doing the right thing or holding the right opinion, it's not a description of the problem: it's to demonstrate the solution. If everyone was already doing the 'right' behaviour and politicians held the 'right' views, you wouldn't need to be running the campaign. Like the great majority of polls commissioned from polling firms by government or commercial companies, therefore, yours is to help make a case.

Of course its message needs to be borne out on enquiry. What lies behind it? This is the real purpose: to show that a real group of people exist who hold these views and, in this case, that they are undertaking relevant behaviours. That is, to show change is possible. On many issues politicians do not act because they think it is not feasible to persuade the public to accept a policy with behavioural implications (see the credibility triangle, page 51, and feasibility element of problems and solutions, page 162). There's little more convincing than seeing that people are undertaking a behaviour.

If you can't afford to commission a commercial poll, then at the start, a straw poll will do, and if you put that online and network it, that can help start the ball rolling. The behaviours themselves can also be made more visible – if products or services are involved, suppliers may help because promotion is in their interest. At a community level you might find ways to get people to attend a gathering or talk to their neighbours, family or friends or display something such as a badge or sign. It all says 'this is happening'.

So create these manifestations of opinion, involve third parties in doing so, and then find ways to incite conversations with them – face to face, online and in other ways – and draw in the media and politicians. Start conversations of cause and effect, build the constituency and repeat the cycle.

6

ORGANIZING CAMPAIGN
COMMUNICATIONS

VISUAL LANGUAGE

Few campaigners are unaware of the general importance of visual communication, yet often it is not used effectively. Frequently, it's an afterthought. Using visual language often involves taking existing icons, symbols, objects or styles with an established meaning, and constructing a message from them. It doesn't just mean arranging for things to be filmed or photographed.

The classic example is the launch of a report. Many times, organizations hold a press conference or even a photocall, when all there is to film or photograph is the report itself, and the proud authors. A campaigner waving a report looks only as if they are trying to sell it or swat a fly. 'Tarting up' the image with a few props, or a corporate backdrop is usually an expensive waste of money unless the important audience is the organization's own senior managers.

Even the viewpoint may have meaning. A film director told me for example, that if he wanted someone to be believed, he shot the discussion with them on the right of the screen, and if he wanted them to be doubted, he arranged it so they were on the left. Apparently, in many Christian religious stories and in many traditional plays, the left is the 'sinister' side: bad characters apparently tend to enter stage left; good ones occupy the right-hand side. Other things are more obvious – the way the camera may be used to suggest nervousness or lying, by close-ups of fidgeting fingers, for example.

Visual language is *independent* of written or spoken words. It is *not* a visualization of words or slogans. When that happens, the result is usually an unhappy one. In 2003, for example, the excellent organization Common Ground[1] wanted to celebrate and encourage care of trees. Its thought was 'every tree counts', and campaigners visualized this with a group of trees in London's Shaftsbury Avenue, decorated in numbers. What did it say visually – an odd piece of art, perhaps? A Christmas tree, on the other hand, says 'Christmas'. The intention behind 'every tree counts' might have been better expressed with some sort of caring for trees – hugging even the smallest or ugliest tree, perhaps.

Figure 6.1 *Boy throwing stone at a tank: David and Goliath*

Figure 6.2 *David and Goliath*

Belgian Amnesty International leaves thousands of empty shoes on the pavement outside a government building. In Argentina, the 'Mothers of the Disappeared' hold up framed photographs of loved ones whose whereabouts are unknown. Former US President Bill Clinton stands on the lawn of the White House with an Israeli and Palestinian leader, and as they shake hands, doves are released. Teddy bears hang on the wire of a nuclear military base. Flags are raised, half-raised or burned. Emperors wear purple, protestors don white suits, pilots and admirals have navy blue and gold stripes on their jackets, Greenpeace ventures out in a small inflatable to confront a vast ship. All of these show effective use of visual language. It's not simply a question of producing images, but of using visual cues, norms, traditions, cultural references and icons to give added value to communications. These are 'magic-bullet' communications because they slip in under our conscious radar. Often they have profound results. The colour red, for example,[2] has been shown to sway judges awarding points in sport (red denotes winners) by a significant amount. It has a similar effect in team games and intimidates people.

Figures 6.1 to 6.3 are three David-and-Goliath images that chime subconsciously. Figure 6.3 says 'Greenpeace', and is immediately recognizable as something small and good versus something big and bad: David and Goliath again.

The Brent Spar image is elemental, reduced to uncluttered essentials. The Spar, a vast lump of industrial junk (bad). Greenpeace, small good thing. The sea, the waiting victim, metaphor for all nature. The fire hoses are the hand of Shell reaching out to try and stop

Figure 6.3 *Greenpeace at Brent Spar: David and Goliath at sea*

Greenpeace. The absence of any headland, another ship or other geographic reference renders the image placeless, timeless, undiluted. You can apply the same principle in any interview or event: eliminate everything that muddies or clutters the visual message; say only one thing.

CONSTRUCTING VISUAL ECHOES

One trick of effective visual language is to make people respond to an image without considering whether they have seen it before. Find something powerful and then create a visual echo of it.

In spring 1995, Greenpeace 'invaded' the Sellafield nuclear plant, and blocked various parts to try and stop the separation of plutonium. The action was timed to coincide with talks about to be held in New York on the Nuclear Non-Proliferation Treaty. Greenpeace was concerned to make the Sellafield 'invasion' look interesting, and like an *invading* swarm of people rather than just another white-suit protest.

Sarah Wise, one of the organizers of the campaign, had just seen the Japanese film *Ran*. This featured a battle with hundreds of warriors carrying orange banners streaming across the screen. It enjoyed cult status with TV professionals because of its cinematography.

If they could make the Greenpeace action look like that, she reasoned, TV news editors might say 'I have to have those pictures', rather than waiting (it was on Easter Bank Holiday Monday at 0600 hours) for the skeleton staff in the newsroom to find time to haul

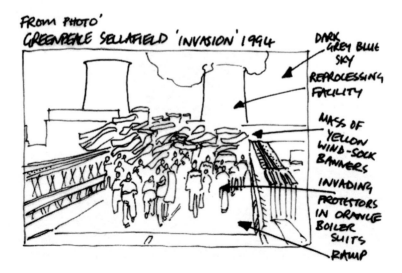

Figure 6.4 *Representation of Greenpeace Sellafield 'invasion', 1994*

Figure 6.5 *Still from Ran, redrawn*

some energy or nuclear journalist out of bed to pronounce on whether the story was newsworthy, and trying to describe the footage to them over the phone. So Greenpeace put hundreds of its local group activists in orange boiler suits and gave them pole banners, echoing the troops in *Ran*.

Wise says: 'It worked so well because the sky was indigo blue in the film, and the scenery was a dark green – not unlike the hills around Sellafield. We considered using smoke bombs to ensure the dark-sky effect, but decided they would be a choking hazard. As it was, the morning was dark and rain-filled, just like in the movie.' The film ran extensively on TV.

Caution: watch out for inadvertent echoes. Google for images on the web, and you may find a PR event in WWF-UK's (quite successful) wildlife-trade campaign, with a man holding a skull. It is a striking image, but for theatrical rather than ecological reasons, because it echoes a famous scene from Shakespeare's *Hamlet*. It says theatre, not save animals.

VISUAL NARRATIVES

At the zenith of the 2008 'credit crunch' panic, *The Times* of London had a front page picture of a man wheeling a private wall safe out of the front door of a shop, ostensibly on his way home to stash away his cash, having lost confidence in stocks and shares. It was an image quite likely to precipitate a further squirrelling away of funds, and like photos of bank customers queuing to withdraw their deposits, sent the exact opposite of the message that governments needed to communicate. Outside Wall Street offices, TV crews captured and relayed images of newly redundant bank workers carrying away their possessions in cardboard boxes. They provided what newsman Roby Burke once explained to me that TV needed above all else: 'moments'.

Politicians and many campaigns often fail to dominate TV and other visual media because they do not provide such visual 'moments', and more so, don't weave them into a series that tells a story: a visual narrative. The search for 'narratives' has become a preoccupation of many political parties and other organizations – over arching stories of why and wherefore, that make an ongoing connection with the audiences who matter most.

At one level you need to deploy and develop recognizable actors and symbols, and then you need to storyboard and use them, not to illustrate a story but to compose it like a film. All too often the culture of government and large institutions is word- and text-focused, as betrayed by the importance accorded to discussions about 'the line to take'. Then pictures overwhelm the words. In 2001 Britain's meat exports were banned from other nations as the country was swept by an outbreak of foot and mouth disease. Hapless ministers tried to reassure the public that it was under control but did so against against a backdrop of burning pyres of cows that said almost the exact opposite. It was only when the government called in the army, and the craggy General Sir Mike Jackson began to prowl the fields in combat kit, that the visuals began to say 'control'.[3]

Visuals don't work if they don't resonate with substance and intent (the activities and resources of the credibility triangle, see page 51). The narrative has to be composed of real deeds, not 'messages' you'd like an audience to adopt.

If, for example, climate negotiators planning the 2009 'crisis' Copenhagen climate talks had wanted to send a really effective signal that the threat was real, hugely significant and immediate (see 'It's an emergency', page 171), then they could have cancelled all but a few of their climate-polluting flights and changed the way international get-togethers were conducted, by requiring 90 per cent of the communication to be done by telepresence or other remote technologies, and allowed only less polluting travel such as by train. That would have created a long running story well before, during and after the event, with an immediate narrative and a bigger picture out-take that was all about our lives, into the future. Actions speak louder than words.

Less dramatically, a government can often get more effect for its euro if it only changes the way it spends money. Campaigners promoting a policy should remember that how it is delivered in terms of mindspace impact may be just as important as the outcome measured in other ways. For example, in the 2000s the UK government was a leader in climate-saving ambitions, but its *actions* did not help create an effective visual narrative at home, as it favoured largely *in*visible accounting solutions such as tweaking the terms of the electricity trading pool, or 'emissions trading' to deliver change to the energy mix. These measures meant and signalled nothing in every day life. In contrast, with its more engineering-oriented political culture, Germany's solar programme[4] put solar panels on 100,000 roofs by 2002. So in Germany, renewables became a *visible reality*, and one experienced by thousands of homeowners who therefore knew first-hand that *renewables work*, while society saw climate action was a here-and-now reality. This said cooperation, collaboration and coordination, whereas in Britain many people still saw 'renewables' as experimental and something for others or the future.

BE MULTIDIMENSIONAL

A campaign has more chance of success if it communicates in many dimensions. Ideally, each of the points on a critical path should register in each dimension.

In terms of argument and the research needed for it, this means being able to *make a case* in each. In terms of perception, the campaign should be *visible* in each dimension. Ask yourself what the picture would be, what you would be doing at each point (the photo test).

For example, there might be scientific, technical, political, economic and emotional dimensions, and maybe ethical, moral, historical, cultural or others (Figure 6.6).

Atlantic Frontier

The Greenpeace Atlantic Frontier campaign[5] was deliberately designed to communicate in a number of dimensions:

*   Scientific/logical – it opposed development of more fossil fuel resources, intervening at the point of political responsibility (licensing development), based on the 'carbon

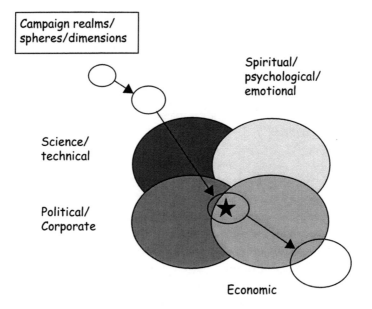

Figure 6.6 *Critical path passing through multiple dimensions*

logic',[6] which shows that burning available oil, coal and gas in the atmosphere will cause catastrophic climate change (so don't develop new reserves).

- Political – it drew a line in the sand at the Atlantic Frontier oil field of West Scotland, and at specific development blocks within that. It contrasted UK climate rhetoric with fossil fuel in practice. It planned to make the contrast between Tony Blair's oil policy at home with his climate rhetoric at the UN.[7]
- Ethical/political – it challenged the UK's right to take the oil beneath the Atlantic based on its claim to the remote islet of Rockall – and, likewise, that of Iceland, Ireland and Denmark, by occupying the rock for a record time. It called for establishment of a world park.
- Ethical/emotional – it communicated (with surveys and information) the wildlife of St Kilda, and the Rockall Trough, known as a 'motorway' for migrating whales. It also raised the case against destructive deep-sea fishing to support the world park set-aside case.
- Legal/ethical – it challenged[8] oil development in court on grounds of damage to ancient cold-water corals and other species (resulting in a successful ruling to greatly extend application of the European Union Habitats Directive).
- Economic/political – it argued for conversion of oil fabrication yards to wave- and wind-power manufacturing (with some success). It also challenged BP over its internal allocation of funds to renewables as opposed to new oil, for example with shareholder actions.

The campaign was also designed[9] to take place in a national theatre of great romance, mystery and physical security and drama – an inspirational setting of epic scale – making it more natural to raise fundamental questions about the future direction of society. This context (see CAMPCAT, Chapter 1) also helped increase the possibility of making some sort of progress, because the immediate target was a 'tough nut' (see page 134), on the grounds that if you wanted to initiate a campaign to stop littering, then the easiest place to start might be a cathedral.

THINKING IN PICTURES

You can control things to change visuals. An invisible process can be made visible. Changing the colour or clothes or equipment, or the size of something might suddenly make the 'point' of the picture more obvious. For example, a magazine carried a photograph of a large 'fossil fish' from an exhibition at the London Natural History Museum. Not a memorable picture – until the photographer took the scientist-curator onto the roof and got him to hold up the fish nose to nose – then it was an arresting picture, made that way by changing the context.

Tips for communicating visually:

- Decide the most important thing (one thing only) that you want to communicate.
- Work out how to make a picture show that one thing (without words) – do a storyboard, step by step.
- Invest in visual communication. For example, building a 3D realization of what you want to say, or organizing a day-long event that says it, may cost thousands of pounds, but it may save you from having to produce a printed report of equal cost, and be more effective.
- Think about what message the context sends. An office interview says 'bureaucrat'. If your work or project is about people, be with people. If it is about a community, be there to be interviewed. If there is a victim, show the victim. If a solution, show the solution. Check with the campaign motivational sequence. If it's an engagement opportunity, be hands-on, demonstrate it.
- Itemize success. Map out processes stage by stage until you can identify the moment or step where success occurs. Which ones can you photograph?
- If you have trouble brainstorming but have a friendly or commissioned advertising agency, then get their creatives to take part.
- Research what the target audience think success (or a problem, or whatever is relevant) would look like. Then think how to play that back in communication when success occurs, so that it gets noticed.
- Remember that TV needs movement. Only huge stories are covered by a reporter standing outside a closed door.

Check and test intended and unintended 'take-out'. A demonstration, for example, is a visual manifestation of support for a cause, but what does it say about that level? Do you engender the thought that: 'there's a lot more than we expected, and there's a lot more still at home' or, conversely: 'there's less than we expected, is this all there is?'[10]

ICONS

Things become icons when they gain meaning beyond their literal meaning. A white dove is more than just a white dove. Coke is more than a brown, fizzy drink: it's America. Friends of the Earth's bottle dump became an environmental icon – despite the campaign's failure to encourage reuse of bottles.

Images can be used to prompt thoughts and anticipation. 'The Earth seen from space', an image from Apollo 11, deeply affected a generation for whom it was a revelation. *Spaceship Earth*, by the environmentalist Barbara Ward, was in press around that time.[11]

The National Aeronautics and Space Administration (NASA)'s images took a metaphor and made it real (Figure 6.7).

Astronauts then added to its power by creating environmental parables, becoming witnesses – almost disciples – to environmental concern, deeply affected by what they had seen humankind doing to the planet, as viewed from space.

NASA and other space-related agencies developed an environmental subtext to their mission. Was this not helped by the fact that astronauts looked down upon the Earth like angels and flew silently above it in white suits with gold visors (Figure 6.8)?[12] Astronauts and cosmonauts acquired an unusual status as bringers of honest environmental wisdom, as privileged, disinterested witnesses bearing testimony to the condition of Planet Earth. Their role echoed a religious frame of belief and authority.

While it's not difficult to construct events that draw on the power of established visual language, overuse creates a cliché: 'We've seen this before.' White-suited protestors, for example, have lost all the wit and chill that they once had. White, paper suits were once only associated with 'ultra-clean high-tech' and high-hazard environments. Their transfer to another environment had some shock value. Friends

Figure 6.7 *The Earth viewed from Apollo 11*

Figure 6.8 *An angel?*

of the Earth produced a striking anti-nuclear poster in which cricketers wore such suits and gas masks, instead of cricketing whites, playing on the expression: 'It's not cricket' (meaning, it's not fair).

The unconscious visual impact of 9/11, an horrific event that had people looking at the images again and again, is explored in a brilliant essay: 'September 11, 2001, the power of the images' by Professor George Lakoff.[13]

The images we see and recall interact with our system of metaphors. The results can be powerful. There are a number of metaphors for buildings.

Children's drawings often depict houses and buildings as people, with the door as a mouth or nose and the windows as eyes. For many people, this metaphor interacted with the image of a plane going into South Tower of the World Trade Center, producing, via visual metaphor, the unconscious, but powerful image of a bullet going through someone's head, the flame pouring from the other side representing blood spurting out.

This, in turn, echoed the famous Vietnam war image of a Vietcong suspect being executed by being shot through the head. Tall buildings also represent power, control, sexuality.

PROBLEM PHASE AND SOLUTION PHASE

All campaigns need to exist in two modes: problem-driving, and solution-driving. Change tends to be alternately driven by the problem and the solution. This is how the media helps us all make sense of change, and lack of change. In a problem-driven phase, lack of change is explained by 'if enough people care'. In a solution- or feasibility-driven phase, change is halted if 'it's not economic' or 'no solution exists', or 'it's not possible'.

Overall change can be thought of as the resolution of two forces in the public consciousness: perceived urgency and perceived feasibility. Campaigners need to think about which phase their campaign is in now, or will be in next.

The conversation with society (or here, typically, with politicians in the news media) that this leads to, is something like Figure 6.9.

Psychologically and physiologically we are hard-wired to pay attention to problems first, with fright, flight and fear. 'Look at how they sell pain-relief headache pills,' a colleague pointed out some years ago. 'It's 80 per cent problem, 20 per cent solution.' Fire (see Chapter 1) is news: urgent life-threatening problems get our attention.

At a deep level, the most urgent, most important news is always the bad news, the immediate problems. For security-driven people this is usually the only important news (see Chapter 1) and studies for the BBC, for example, show that they dominate regular news watchers, looking out for the next bad thing.

The public relations industry has become adept at using this to sell 'solutions' by wrapping them in a problem. PR director Ed Gyde[14] says: 'We call these "negative–positive stories". Say you have a drugs information leaflet to promote to local parents. In itself that's not news: it is boring. But if you survey parents and find that 70 per cent of them are

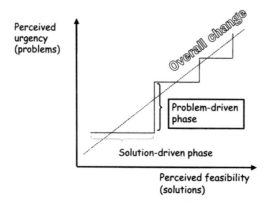

Figure 6.9 *The two forces that resolve to bring about change*

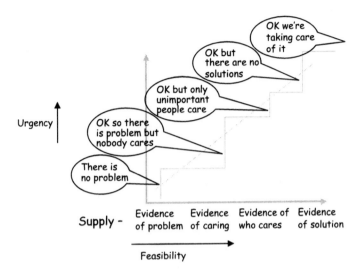

Figure 6.10 *The dialogue that often results from problem and solution phases*

worried that they don't have enough information about drugs their children may use – then that's local news. Suddenly your leaflet, a "solution", is newsworthy.'

Problems alone soon become demotivating (see communications sequence, Chapter 1). So any campaign design needs to paint the issue in characters of light and darkness, of solution and problem.

If we engage people with a problem and then abandon them without a solution, we've 'led them up the garden path' – and next time they won't come. While working with Media Natura[15] I saw one study after another in which we interviewed people who had ended their subscriptions to campaigning NGOs or who were aware of the 'issues' and the problems, but who were 'turned off'. Usually, their decision to leave or not to connect wasn't because they disagreed with the cause, or, as was often assumed, due to dissatisfaction with the efforts of the group, but because they wanted to 'stop the flow of bad news' and felt they 'couldn't do enough to help'.

Without an opportunity to take action, sympathetic people feel guilty, overwhelmed by the tragedy of the situation. In the end they have to disengage for their own protection. This is a good reason to start campaign planning with an opportunity to take action and work back from it.

For others, the lack of a feasible alternative is the watertight excuse they need not to take part. For those who don't want to *appear* unsympathetic or uncaring, the fact that 'nothing can be done' is the most comfortable excuse, maintaining self-esteem while providing a moral hand-wash.

The speech bubbles in Figure 6.10 show what politicians say. Between each horizontal 'step' the campaign reverts to 'problem-driving'. How the problem is framed changes at each step. Surmounting each step will be a project or a campaign in itself. This process is 'scale free' – it can apply from the level of the conversation between two individuals up to a wholesale revolution in national consciousness or behaviour. The role of the campaign has to change from supplying evidence of the problem to caring, to who cares, to the solution. It's no use sticking with showing how many people care, if the 'debate' moves on to *who* cares, or beyond that, to solutions. After these steps, the issue becomes one of enforcement and delivery.

Lastly, present only one problem at a time. Too many injustices at one time are indigestible. They can induce a state of denial, a mental and moral retreat not because of the impossibility of taking action on them but because there are so many that appear impossible to deal with.[16] In fund-raising, the usual rule is only to offer one action, at several different levels: typically three ways of doing the same thing. Too many options can induce indecision.

Some campaigners love to point to linkages, but too many problems all linked together are hard to take in: 'What am I supposed to do?' It's the woolly blanket problem. 'There's a problem in there somewhere – I can see the shape of it, or I thought I could – but now there's another, and two more, and they're moving about, and as it twists and turns and gets more complicated, it gets snagged on one thing and then another until the original thing I was fixed on is lost, somewhere in a huge woolly bundle of smothering evidence and other problems.' In the end, all it says is: 'There's definitely a problem in here somewhere, but it's surrounded by complications.'

SOLUTIONS IN ENVIRONMENTAL CAMPAIGNS

Originally, environmental campaigns were all about pressing for problems to be recognized. Once politicians accepted these, however, people wanted solutions to be delivered.[17] The conventional campaign format was to promote policy formulae: lists for an enlightened government. But by the 1990s, government was in full-tilt mode away from 'doing things' and business was stepping into the breach. Moreover, solutions and 'progress' had for centuries been provided by business, coupled to science and technology: progress and technology were synonymous. So Greenpeace, led by its German section, set out to take the technological initiative; changing campaigns from 'they said there was no problem' to 'they said it couldn't be done'.

Chlorine-free paper

Christoph Thies, toxics campaigner, knew a small Swedish pulp manufacturer, Aspa Bruk, had made the first totally chlorine-free (TCF) paper (bleached without chlorine, so with none of the dioxins and other toxins associated with that). Aspa Bruk was followed by larger producer Sodra-Cell. German printers and publishers resisted using new sorts of paper, and paper makers were even less keen on making it.

Eventually, Greenpeace found a supplier willing to try. Together they produced *Der Plagiat* (the plagiary), a spoof of the leading magazine *Der Spiegel*, using TCF (*Der Spiegel* had pointedly refused to countenance TCF, citing technical impossibility). Greenpeace delivered a giant roll of printing paper to *Der Spiegel*'s offices as a 'gift', and somehow managed to obtain the magazine's mailing list. Campaigners then mailed the magazine's readers with evidence that what the management had been saying – that TCF was unavailable and of low quality – was unfounded.

Confronted by this evidence, and criticism from its readers, *Der Spiegel* changed over to being printed on TCF paper in the autumn of 1992. Other German periodicals followed suit.[18]

Greenfreeze solution

In 2000, UK Prime Minister Tony Blair said:

> *Eight years ago, Greenpeace began research on greenfreeze refrigeration technology to reduce the destruction of the ozone layer. It is now a highly successful example of green organization and industry working together for the benefit of the ozone layer. Coca Cola and Unilever have just announced they will move towards such alternative refrigerants such as greenfreeze by 2005.*[19]

'Greenfreeze' is the name given to non-fluorocarbon refrigeration technology – used in fridges, chillers and air conditioning (Figure 6.11). It's energy-efficient, used by all major European refrigeration manufacturers, and is in large-scale production in countries such as China. It avoids 'fluorocarbons' such as chloroflurocarbons (CFCs), hydrofluoro carbons (HFCs) or hydrochlorofluorocarbons (HCFCs).

Yet if it had been left to governments and business, all those millions of fridges would have been using (and leaking) CFCs and their descendants, HCFCs and HFCs.

In the early 1990s, the government parties to the Montreal Protocol were accepting chemical industry claims that the only way to get rid of CFCs was to replace them with another of their products, HCFCs (still damaging to the ozone layer but less so), and then yet another; HFCs (not damaging to ozone but with a very bad impact on climate).

Two technologists approached Greenpeace to propose using an 'old' alternative technology based on the more-or-less benign and cheap 'natural' hydrocarbons such as propane. Next, Greenpeace rescued an ailing East German fridge company, secured finance and marketing, generated thousands of orders from the public, and 'greenfreeze' technologies were born.

Figure 6.11 *Greenfreeze is highly efficient, is now used by all major European refrigeration manufacturers, and is in production on a large scale in countries such as China*

After a long struggle in the market and in the secretive world of industrial product standards, most nations have now taken up the 'greenfreeze' technology in domestic refrigeration.[20]

These principles can be applied to almost any campaign. There are times when change, and making the case for change, is best achieved through proving the feasibility of solutions.

THE DIVISION BELL

The call to action is the point at which you 'cash in your chips' and see whether or not you can win this round or battle. It acts like a division bell, the sound that signals the call to vote in the old-fashioned UK Parliament.

At this point, your campaign tries to force a taking of sides for the reckoning. It's therefore important that you go at the right moment. Too late and your support may have dissipated. People may burn out from the commitment, lose interest or be depressed by the problem and turn off.

More often, campaigners call the division too soon. Force a division among the audience too early and you are unlikely to have accumulated enough committed support to win. So try to show your audience a story using the sequence (Chapter 1) and let them make their discoveries, reflect and get angry – don't try to force them along by telling them what to think.

MAKE CAMPAIGNS FROM 'DOING'

For events, news and visual language we need doing, not arguments or talking, ask 'What's the verb? What's the "doing" bit in this campaign?'

Many classic direct-action tactics come from this approach: asking what the problem is, then how can it be reversed. 'Return to sender', for example, involves taking waste or other immorally dumped material and returning it.

In 1992, Greenpeace campaigners discovered 2000 tonnes of German chemical pesticide wastes, all with deficient paperwork. For months, the German government resisted calls from Greenpeace and Romania to take them back. Then, in February 1993, a letter from the German government announced it would accept the poison barrels. On 11 March 1993, the returns began, and Environment Minister Claus Toepfer apologized to the Romanian population. In May, all the still-discoverable German poison barrels – 450 tonnes – were returned by a 1.3km-long train to Germany.

The first campaign with a 'return-to-sender' objective that I am aware of was by Friends of the Earth in its historic 1971 bottles action.

Of course, Greenpeace did not invent non-violent direct action (NVDA). Before the *Phyllis Cormack*[21] sailed to the Aleutian Islands, the Quakers had sailed, to 'bear witness' against nuclear testing. They, too, were confronted by the military, only few knew about it. The Quaker *Golden Rule* was impounded near Bikini Atoll in Hawaii in 1958 – that gave Jim Bohlen the idea to take a ship to Amchitka, and that led to the formation of Greenpeace.[22] The difference with Greenpeace was the pictures[23] that gave supporters a way of 'being there', too. Actions are one way of composing campaigns by 'doing' (see Box 6.1).

BOX 6.1 – WHY WE DO ACTIONS: THEIR IMPORTANCE FOR GREENPEACE

AN EXTRACT FROM A MEMO I WROTE FOR INCOMING CAMPAIGNERS IN GREENPEACE

Fundamentals

Founding proposition – Greenpeace started with action
    Founding principles – non-violent direct action (NVDA), bearing witness, Quaker inspiration (see below)
    Action motivates and communicates
    Action demands decisiveness and honesty of purpose
    Action is just a stunt if it is just for an image, action has to be real:

- stopping the problem;
- inserting the solution;
- challenging what is wrong;
- voicing the public conscience.

Communication and action strategy

Our communication strategy
    1st   action
    2nd   image
    3rd   information
    Action-led
    Creates image which communicates
    Supported and explained with information

Not

    1st   information
    2nd   image
    3rd   action

Where stunts are used to create images in order to draw attention to a campaign or issue pursued through information

Campaign benefits/properties of actions

Convert diffuse (grey) issues to acute ones (black/white)
So converts unclear to clear responsibility

So converts not urgent to urgent political problems
Represented by pictures of an event
Not an argument – an action is done
Cannot be questioned or interrogated
Not communicated in ideological terms
Represented by anonymous individuals
Supporters can 'be there': supporters share through anonymity
Not individual named heroes
Converts public support to public action
Enables people to connect values and actions
Makes Greenpeace a bargaining rather than influencing group
'argument is constructed in one way: politics in quite another'
Politics is about events; news is about events; actions are events
Issues may be defined as ideas but are changed by events

Greenpeace campaign strategies and action

Greenpeace campaigns in three realms:

- political (government/industry);
- emotional/values;
- technical/scientific.

Actions must be done at the point of intersection of all three; this is often uncomfortable
Campaigns are planned as a process of changing power along a critical pathway
Actions and other campaign work help progress along these long-term pathways
Successful actions in themselves cause change that leads directly, in the long term, to major change: the 'inevitable consequence'

HEARTS AND MINDS

To succeed you usually need to win hearts as well as minds. The usual failure is not winning hearts. Many campaigns about the ethics of public goods are disabled by a common strategy of the public affairs industry, which is to invoke the 'rational-not-emotional' frame, and so avoid the 'ethical-or-unethical' frame.

This trick works because journalists, public debaters, politicians and even campaigners frequently equate 'emotional' and 'ethical'. Those in power – usually governments or corporations – will often respond to any criticism by labelling it 'emotional', and then try to confine debate to the emotional-or-rational frame, which is usually accepted without question by the media and many professional politicians. This enables them to avoid having to justify their actions in ethical terms – a frame in which they are far more likely to lose a debate.

Campaigners have three issues to deal with. First, how to avoid the trap above. Do so by explicitly raising an *ethical* challenge – for example, in terms of responsibility. Call out the opponent in those terms.

Second, how to avoid opponents or third parties suggesting that your 'rational case' rests on emotional power. Separate communication events in the different dimensions and make sure you get your rationalistic case out first, early in the campaign, in a non-emotive context – for example, scientific, economic, legal. Make sure that it evokes a response. Get it on the record. Then work through your ethical challenge, and after that, move on to trigger emotion. This won't stop opponents trying to imply your case is 'only emotional' but it will prevent that becoming a winning strategy.

Third, how to introduce emotion. It all depends on the circumstance, but it may be best done through images rather than words, and through human interest – the struggle or plight of individuals. If your campaign intervenes to help others who are less powerful, and they convey emotion, that may help most. Remember that the public will sense natural justice or injustices.

Finally, don't forget that, although the left side of the brain is said to be the seat of language and processes in a logical and sequential order, and the right side is said to work more visually, and processes intuitively, holistically, and randomly,[25] in the real world, the right side is just as important in making decisions. Its significance is widely denied, even when your opponents concede.

Faced with a successful campaign, conventional Anglo politicians/businesses generally accede on 'rational' or quasi-scientific or other 'professional' or 'objective' grounds that do not threaten their self-image or intrude on their personal ethics. Here, for example, is Heinz Rothermund, one of Shell's most intelligent board directors, on the subject of the Atlantic Frontier campaign:

> *The specific attack, by Greenpeace in particular, on oil and gas developments in the Atlantic margin, accompanied by the usual exaggerated claims about last wilderness and environmental devastation, with emotional references to whales and endangered species, also raises a key question: in how far is it sensible to explore for and develop new hydrocarbon reserves, given that the atmosphere may not be able to cope with the greenhouse gases that will emanate from the utilization of the hydrocarbon reserves discovered already?[26]*

Note how Rothermund divides the description of the campaign into the 'emotional' (assumed to be synonymous with 'exaggerated') which can be discounted, and the 'rational' part, which is (this time) worth a response.[27]

IT'S AN EMERGENCY!

If we've campaigned, we've probably all 'been there'. Seized by the problem when all around others do not seem to be, it is natural to turn to 'sounding the alarm' as perhaps the most basic strategy of all. For instance, in the run-up to the 2009 Copenhagen 'climate summit' the UK Climate Change Campaign planned a Climate Emergency Rally,[28] US Avaaz called for a global 'wake up', and the 'emergency' frame is regularly deployed in campaigns from Los Angeles housing[29] to church roof fund-raising[30] to nuclear non-profileration[31].

Activists may respond, but are others convinced? And what makes alarms work anyway? There is a large body of research on why alarms do and don't achieve their intended purpose, most of which comes from the 'alarm industry'.

Marc Green writes:[32]

> *Effective warning design depends as much on the contents of the viewer's head as on the contents of the warning's message. People who see a warning must decide whether or not to comply. However, 'warning viewers' ... are not blank slates but rather start with a mental model containing three components. First, the viewer has general knowledge about the world and how it works. Second, s/he has a set of beliefs and expectations based on experience with the same or similar environment, product or technology. Lastly, the viewer enters the situation with a goal and strategy for achieving that goal. The goal can be specific ('I want to arrive at my destination as soon as possible') or more diffuse ('I want to feel good about myself'). Understanding what the viewer 'brings to the table' is critical for creating effective warnings.*

Or in other words, start from where your audience is (see page 27).

Dennis Mileti and Lori Peek[33] note that 'the perceptions that are formed in emergencies follow the same processes as those formed in response to any other social event': 'hear–perceive–understand–believe and personalize–respond–decide about alternative protective actions and perform them'. If campaigners are to use the 'Wake Up' or 'Emergency' 'Alarm' frame then their communication has to pass the tests of the frame (see 'Framing', page 28).

As Mileti and Peek point out:

> *The risk information must be understood [that is] the attachment of meaning to the information. Those meanings can vary among people and may or may not conform to the understandings intended. A 50 per cent probability may be interpreted as almost certain by some or relatively unlikely by others. In this sense, understanding includes the perception of risk.*

When confronted with something we don't understand, we use 'Heuristics' (see page 62), that is rules of thumb, such as 'it's from a source I like so I'll take it as true', only we usually do this unconsciously. For 'alarms', the signs and signals are all important. Mileti and Peek cite 'environmental cues' – it is more difficult to get a public to believe a flood warning on a sunny day – and the social proof heuristic: 'if neighbours are not seen leaving in concert with receiving evacuation instructions', then the alarm may be ignored. Geographical proximity (relevance), imminence and personalization (it will hit me) are also tests. Numerous studies of floods, for example, show that people tend to move towards, not away from the source of the hazard, in order to assess it. Broadly speaking if a warning is sounded people ask themselves 'Is it for real/genuine?' (messenger or source test), 'Will it affect me?' and 'Is it immediate?' You can see this behaviour every time an office fire alarm sounds.

For these reasons attempts to sound emergency warnings in campaigns can easily fall foul of the Level 2–3 problem. If people were to responded (Level 2) to such a call then that might indeed solve a problem, but it's hard to in fact get them to do so (Level 3).

To engage and potentially mobilize others, campaigners bent on using the 'emergency' frame need to supply 'evidences' and 'proofs' that an emergency is real, applicable to the audience and ongoing. Where, for example, are the blue flashing lights or their equivalent? If a campaign can't match the expectations for a real 'emergency', then don't call one. The 'emergency' frame cannot be used simply to inject a sense of importance of urgency.

7

CONSTRUCTING
CAMPAIGN PROPOSITIONS

Constructing **RASPB** propositions

The proposition sums up what the campaign is about. A helpful starting point is the popular radio news format of PSB – Problem, Solution, Benefit.[1]

> *'Well, good morning Mrs Campaigner for X, welcome to Wake Up With Borset. Now, you're concerned about X and are holding a press conference later this morning – tell us, what's the problem?'*
>
> … first answer
>
> *'So what's the solution?'*
>
> … second answer
>
> *'Well, that's all very well Mrs Campaigner, but how will it benefit the people of Borsetshire?'*
>
> … third answer
>
> *'Well, thanks for coming in… Now here's Sophie with the traffic'.*

If your campaign proposition can meet this format, you're off to a head start. The proposition usually needs to include RASPBerry:

- Responsible party (the enemy – who's to blame);
- Action – the action you want people (who?) to take;
- Solution;
- Problem;
- Benefit.

For example:

> *Illegal loggers are felling valuable timber and wrecking this ancient forest*
>
> > *(Problem)*

> *Effective policing and certification of timber has stopped this elsewhere*
>
> > *(Solution)*

> *Wildlife and communities benefit from sustainable management*
>
> > *(Benefit)*

> *The government of X is to blame because it's not enforcing the law*
>
> > *(Responsible party)*

> *We want people to call their MP/Senator to lobby the government*
>
> > *(Action)*

A real campaign should be more excitingly worded!

So this is *your* 'government lobbying campaign to save ancient forest from illegal logging' or 'the campaign against illegal logging to help communities in ancient forest'.

You may be able to then reduce this proposition to a much simpler rallying call.

The campaign 'proposition' contains the implicit promise that if you do certain things, then others will follow – such as 'sign the online petition to call on Pharmaceutical International to supply river-blindness drugs at cost in Africa'.

The 'proposition' isn't just about the cause or even the objective – it is also about how the campaign works, and what role the supporter has.

It normally helps to have the problem and the solution well up at the front of your communication, and to be able to start either from the general or from the particular – with both the big picture and the specific example readily available. Some people will like to start from one place, others insist on another, depending on their communication preferences. Relevant preferences for constructing propositions include the following.[2]

Away from/towards

The towards person stays focused on his/her own goals and is motivated by achievement. The away person focuses on problems to be avoided rather than goals to be achieved.

Internal/external

The internal person has internal standards and decides for him/herself. The external person takes standards from outside and needs direction and instruction to come from others.

Small chunk/big chunk

Big-chunk people are most comfortable dealing with large chunks of information. They do not pay attention to details. Small-chunk people pay attention to details and need small chunks to make sense of a larger picture.

Match/mismatch

People who match will mostly notice points of similarity in a comparison. People who mismatch will notice differences when making a comparison.

We all have these preferences to different degrees. Campaign planners need to ask themselves if they are simply designing a campaign that fits *their* preferences. This is a good reason to do research, and test out what works. To do that you need to know *who* you want to convince. A focus on 'problems to be avoided rather than goals to be achieved' (towards/away – the half-full/half-empty axis) obviously has immediate relevance to campaigning on problems or solutions, or how those are spoken of.

What's unlikely to ring any bells with anyone is a bland process description, as in 'our campaign addresses legal and other issues around certain forests and the political measures needed to encourage conditions of sustainability'.

Agency New Oceans[3] says:

> *Remember the old argument in business, education and parenting: whether to use the carrot or the stick approach? In other words, is it better to offer people incentives or threats? The answer of course is: it all depends who you want to motivate. 'Towards' people are energized by goals and rewards. 'Away' people are motivated to avoid problems and punishment.*

Knowing what motivates a target group or institution would be very useful. If you don't know that, you can at least consciously hedge your bets.

Many 'campaigns of transition' utilize standard-setting as their intervention: WWF's Forest Stewardship Council, for example. The Internal-External filter describes *where* people find their standards. If people have an internal reference, says Oceans, they 'instinctively know if they have done a good job'. On the other hand, 'people with an external reference need someone else to tell them. Successful entrepreneurs are extremely internally referenced – they know when they have made a good or a bad decision. Many people in organizations are externally referenced and need a management structure to give them feedback on the standard of their work.'

So if you are campaigning to introduce a standard with an entrepreneur, you might want to start with his or her work as the benchmark, but for a large institution, you might better use evidence of good practice by others.

As we noted in the section on 'framing', so-called 'emotional' or unconscious (reflexive) thought often over powers or precedes conscious analytical thinking. Researchers spend a lot of time trying to disentangle the two. For example Michel Handgraf of the University of Amsterdam has used[4] observation of the words employed in conversations about an issue (in this case wind turbines) to distinguish between times when his subjects were using analytical reasoning (when they'd say things like 'This has so-and-so effect over so many years') from moments when they were reasoning emotionally (e.g. 'but I feel' this or that). For campaign propositions the rule is to design and communicate them so that you provide an emotional driver (so people want to agree to it), and a rational case (so that they are equipped to explain it in those terms).

THE SELF-VALIDATING PROPOSITION

We most trust information from sources we know most – hence, the power of introductions from friends. Most of all, we trust ourselves – and are most easily convinced when we draw our own conclusions. Drawing on our own experience, we think we can hold a conversation in our own heads, which nobody can spin, argue with or interfere in.

No campaigner should try to 'sell' a proposition or message that will be negated or gainsaid by the experience of the audience. This may seem blindingly obvious advice, but it's often not followed. Politicians trying to warn children from using illegal drugs, for example, may tell them that a particular drug 'kills' or 'can be fatal' and should therefore be avoided. But if young people see others using it and they don't see anyone dying, then the experience will undermine the message, and, by association, this can undermine everything else on that subject that comes from the same source.

There's one type of proposition that I call 'self-righting' or 'self-validating'. Like a lifeboat with built-in buoyancy, it stays upright no matter which way you start it off. You can look at it starting from either end, and it will always appear validated. Here, two or more pieces of 'evidence' have a link that can be discovered to be true. They are like the buoyancy tanks. Many are in the form: 'X is true because all As are B', in which the A–B relationship is true, but the connection to X may not be.

For example:

> *All environmental campaigners are just after publicity: (because) all campaigns involve publicity – they're always trying to get on the news, the only time you ever see them is when they're doing some sort of stunt (and so on).*

Test:

Do all campaigns involve publicity? 'They appear to do so.'

Are they always trying to get on the news? 'Seems like it to me.'

Is the only time you ever see them is when they're doing some sort of stunt? 'Yes, every time they're on TV.'

So it's true, then? 'Guess so.'

If you examine this proposition by starting either from who campaigners are, or what's on the news, it seems valid. It works because the audience either draws on his or her very limited existing experience (mainly gleaned from the 'news' anyway) or they check it out by watching the news. The person who wants to use this approach to mislead will be careful to pitch it so that the evidence, likely to be to hand, will validate the proposition. The fact that the audience actually adds it up from their own first-hand experience adds to its veracity: 'Now you come to mention it, that's exactly what I found.'

Mrs Thatcher's appeal to the simple homilies of home economics – the money in your handbag, that you can't spend if you haven't got it, seemed instantly verifiable by anyone with a handbag. She used it to dismiss ideas of government spending and borrowing, thereby obscuring the fact that countries are quite *unlike* individuals with handbags because, for one thing, they have future generations that reap the benefits of investment made with borrowed money, for instance in public infrastructure. Thatcher was a brilliant communicator who exploited the difference between popular and elite understanding, which, in the case of routine media debate of economics, was an unbridgeable crevasse. So she successfully marginalized her critics, who were left stranded and inaudible on the elite side, waving detailed reports and textbooks, not handbags.

Saying 'go test it yourself, next time you are…' can be much more powerful than trying to lead a person through a version of your own experience.

More subtle versions of this in spin and propaganda work by use of association and loose ends, laid out like bait. Over a period of time it can be given the *form* of a discovery, the search for truth, and by suggestion, implies that it is the truth.

The net effect can be that the audience falls back on things that it already feels to be true, and judges any new information with those things. By giving cues and prompts, the orchestrators can ensure the 'right' things get used as evidence and so the 'right' conclusions are drawn.

A similar technique is to ask 'how good' something was or 'how much' of it there was, so implying that the thing you are measuring is relevant or really 'the issue'. This works on the basis that attention fertilizes belief. Simply discussing a possibility a lot makes it seem more likely.

A variation is the search for the 'smoking gun'. If expanded to become a mainstream quest, it implies that the connection must exist, simply because of the psychology of group belief or action. Most of us don't like to feel that we're wrong by being out of step.

This is similar to framing (see Chapter 1). The selection of the initial frame largely determines conclusions. For example:

'These new car technologies are unproven – they may be good for the environment but they can be expensive – don't we all pay quite enough for petrol already? Who here wants to pay more?'

Triggering a cost framework rapidly leads to the established thought: 'Yes, I pay too much already.' Anything new is equated with 'maybe more expensive' and so rejected unless it is proven cheaper. Then arguing with cost is a dead end. The choice of frame is all important.

Any attempt to argue against the frame will fail. Respond for example: 'Yes, it will initially be slightly more expensive, but…' and you've just confirmed it's 'too expensive'.

Rationalists and people who are unused to being in a confrontational situation may tend to try and find middle ground by agreeing with part of a proposition and then arguing their case. This ploy is usually doomed.

In the car-engine case, by choosing an element such as cost, which they know can lead an audience to a rapid rejection, the critics successfully invoke a fatal frame for the public view of the proposal.

If instead one had started with:

> 'These engines can bring harmful emissions below the level known to trigger childhood asthma,'

then the benefit and test would be in a quite different frame. Do you know any children with asthma? Is it true that these emissions are that low? (Yes.) Is it true that this level exists? (Yes.) Well, we must have that then. Is there a price increase? Yes, but it's only very small and there won't be by the time it's commercialized. OK, then.

A self-validating proposition can then be used to further dismiss critics with a vested interest. For example:

Interviewer: 'But Mrs Campaigner, some people are saying that these new engines are much more expensive…'
Mrs Campaigner: 'They are saying that and if you check you will find that those people represent the car industry who are making significant profits from the current grossly polluting engines, whose emissions as we all know cause asthma.'

Or she might have added:
'As anyone who's seen the prices of new cars will know, there's a lot of money being made somewhere. Have you seen the prices?'
'Gosh, yes, now you come to mention it.'

MAKE THE ISSUE AN 'EITHER/OR'

A yes/no, 'binary', presence/absence, black/white, either/or type of proposition is more compelling than a matter of degree, such as a how-much or a bit-less. It is more useful and robust, invulnerable to differing perceptions of 'how much is enough'. Monitoring, evaluation and accountability are easier. It allows for 'closure': a supporter can see there can be a clear end point.

To reduce a campaign proposition to an elemental level, map out your issue in all its complexity. Like an aerial photograph of a great city, from high up it looks grey. Zoom in to any part, however, and eventually it resolves itself into black and white. At this point, the difference between the two parts is absolute, incapable of further reduction.

Find the 'point of irreducibility' where the two adjacent bits of the issue are differentiated by a single simple difference: one is what you want, and is right, the other is not what you want, and is wrong. Here's your objective.

For example, the UK campaigns against the sale of school playing fields for development can be boiled down to 'for-sale' or 'not-for-sale' propositions. Somewhere, in an office or in a school, there will be an individual whose pen will or won't be poised to sign the order to sell. It can be photographed; you can go there.

ADVANTAGES OF IRREDUCIBLE PROPOSITIONS

Propositions and objectives around elemental, irreducible differences have five advantages:

1   They pass what communicator John Wyatt[5] calls the 'dinner party test'. You can pass these propositions around and they come back to you the same as they set out. They cannot be unpicked or unravelled, and as such, they travel without losing their meaning. They can 'go viral' without mutating in the process.

2   They are also news-proof. News polarizes, reduces, clarifies, crystallizes, sensationalizes. Remember the old news dictum: first simplify, then exaggerate. Put grey stuff into the news machine and it comes out black and white. Put a qualified, gradualist or multi-component campaign proposition into news and it will be converted into a black-and-white something (probably a something-else). So don't do it. Only put yes/no, present/absent, black/white, 0/1-type campaign propositions into the news system. They can't be simplified, and are hard to exaggerate.

3   They set up a moral line of absolute right and wrong. This, in turn, can plumb the depths and heights of emotional and spiritual engagement, which is hard – if not impossible – with a 'matter of degree'. Take transport, a subject that many people feel

strongly about and which is notoriously a tangle of issues, perceptions and motivations. If, for some reason, it is morally wrong to allow traffic down a street, we may block its path with our bodies – a classic non-violent direct action. If, however, we want a one-third reduction in traffic, then blocking every third car fails all the tests of natural justice.

4   They are unambiguous. Creative ambiguity may help align more people initially, but a campaign is a journey, and if it becomes apparent that you meant one thing and followers thought you meant another, it's a recipe for defections.

5   They make it easy to apply the reversibility test. If a proposition is sound, it gets you what you really want when the objective is achieved. If you will still not be satisfied when the objective is achieved, the campaign will irritate sympathizers and disappoint supporters. Trust and support are quickly lost. So try reversing the problem statement – does it become the solution? If not, rethink it until it does.

FOCUS ON THE UNACCEPTABLE

Some campaigns only need to reawaken interest. Most have to mobilize new and additional support, and need a target that motivates a large enough number of people. Focus on a small part of the problem that is unacceptable to a large part of the population, rather than a large part of the problem that is unacceptable to a tiny part of the population.

The Campaign for Lead-free Air (CLEAR) against lead in petrol visibly focused on the most motivating part of the problem – lead's impact on the brains of children – by conducting a survey of street dust, targeting primary school playgrounds by busy roads, using a clearly labelled white van.

German and Austrian traffic pollution campaigners achieved a similar result by taking air samples at children's nose-height, instead of the usual sampling points employed by local authorities, which were typically high up on buildings.

CONVERT THE DIFFUSE TO THE ACUTE

Political reflexes are stimulated by acute problems, not diffuse ones. The former threaten careers, reputations and interests. The latter can be more safely ignored, not because they are not serious problems, but because watchdogs such as voters, the media and campaigners have a hard time showing that they are there and needing attention now. In this way, 'soft disasters' creep up on us undetected or ignored by political systems.

So, for example, climate change is accepted as the single greatest problem facing humanity, but safeguarding jobs at a car plant, or responding to a fuel-price protest, is often a greater political priority. On the other hand, the ozone hole over Antarctica was an acute political problem – almost all the ozone had disappeared in one place – while moderate ozone depletion across a much larger areas was not.

Events, physics, ecology, nature or human affairs can all convert the diffuse to the acute or vice versa, but so can campaigners. In 2002, for example, the Dutch section of Greenpeace vacuumed homes to convert the hard-to-see, hard-to-evaluate problem of chemical toxins in household dust into a campaign tool that could be used in engaging celebrities and the public. By concentrating the dust, it became possible to analyse its contents, and work out which household products – such as paints, TV sets, carpets, plastics – had contributed which chemicals.[6] Being able to collect such evidence paved the way to strategies to confront those responsible. What 'vacuum cleaner' opportunities does your issue offer?

Other ways to convert a diffuse to an acute problem can include bringing victims together, closing the distance between the commissioning of a problem and its consequences, or altering timings.

BEWARE OF SLOGANS!

A slogan is not the same as a proposition. It doesn't usually propose much; it just expresses an attitude. Memorable and short is good, but they often say more about the source than they do to persuade the audience. Being handy and familiar, slogans are often a substitute for thought about how to communicate effectively If you hear the word 'slogan', reach for the CAMPCAT checklist (Chapter 1).

As slogans are fixed, they can easily turn into liabilities when context changes. Before the 2003 Iraq War, some UK organizations banded together as the Stop the War coalition. Before the war started, the majority of people in the UK opposed it. After it started, however, the majority supported it, or so it appeared from the way polls were conducted and reported. The media often represented this as a 'change of mind' by the public. It was implied that those who had spoken against the war,[7] were 'wrong' now that they were out of step.

They had trouble dealing with these questions because the literal meaning of the slogan 'Stop the War' meant one thing *before* any war started (don't start it, stop it from starting), and another (don't finish it, or don't win it), once it was underway. Yet the statement itself had remained the same. 'Stop the War' was insensitive to this difference.

Many people took the view that the war was wrong and should not start, but once it had begun, the least-bad option available was to continue and win it. Their view could not, however, be differentiated within the 'Stop the War' formula. Consequently, the groups also failed to take control of the agenda on issues such as the nature of the peace, because they were stuck with 'unfinished business'.

THE GROSS FACTOR

Does your campaign include something gross? Something that reaches you in the heart or the guts and makes you feel sick, angry or revolted? If not, what motivates you to work on the 'issue'? Try redrafting your plan to include it.

If your critical path intersects with something gross – a huge injustice, an intolerable act of selfishness, a stomach-turning consequence, an event that moves you to tears – it will have power that any amount of argument or design can never bring.

Good campaigning means getting your emotional hands dirty. Polite hand-washing classes may enjoy 'expert' status in policy circles, and discuss a problem knowledgeably while allowing it to continue, but effective campaigns can't run on reasonableness. When you are retired, or on your deathbed, they should be things that you feel glad you did, not ashamed that you left aside to maintain credibility with experts who stress facts but whose real motivation is to not rock the boat.

In this case of the Brent Spar, the gross factor was supplied by the world's biggest piece of litter, by one of the world's biggest corporations, in the backyard of one of the world's richest countries.

After the campaign, I developed the 'Brent Spar Scale' (Figure 7.1) to try and explain how the public seemed to see things.

Corporate and government issue specialists often live in a world where 'good practices' are defined between themselves or policy benchmarks and professional consensus. They may regard these norms as more objective and superior to opinions of outsiders. They may be concerned to meet internal performance targets. This objectified world view focuses on the bottom levels of the Brent Spar Scale.

Figure 7.1 *The Brent Spar Scale*

Many bosses and managers used to (and some still) resort to the 'bottom line' of legality as the first response to external challenge. 'We're going about our business, and this is legal.' If that failed, their focus slid up to relative performance – are we better or worse than others? – and output failures (was there something we failed to deliver?). Yet the things that count for more – complacency, incompetence, deceit, and grossness – they tended to dismiss as 'soft' issues. Institutions doing this are continually frustrated by the 'wrong' perceptions of the public.

The public doesn't know about things like best practice. If we are not involved in a 'professional' world, we assess the actions of organizations as we see and judge individuals. We say: 'Switzerland did this', or 'Shell thinks…', or 'Greenpeace has said…'.

Second worst behind gross acts come deceitful acts. Exxon did this when it tried to fix climate science by evicting Bob Watson from his job at the Intergovernmental Panel on Climate Change (IPCC), and Pfizer when it continued to sell hip-replacement joints it knew to be faulty.[8] After that comes uncaring complacency, as Dow[9] appeared to be over Bhopal, and that is less forgivable than being incompetent. Just being legal is not impressive – decades of commercial lobbying have ensured that most laws to protect the public interest are as weak as possible.

So with the Spar, Greenpeace said it was gross, and Shell said it was legal. Arguably, both were correct. Greenpeace won, however, because the public felt Shell was in the wrong.

ELIMINATION AND SACRIFICE

A big outcome grabs the attention much more than a small one. The technology that, at a stroke, can eliminate a whole factory's worth of pollution, is dramatic.

Stopping all the traffic in a city has an audacious 'make-another-world-possible' appeal. Hence the initial adrenaline-spiked attraction of the group Reclaim the Streets. To leave your car at home on 'Car-Free Day', however, when you know that everyone else in the street will probably drive as normal, is less attractive because it seems futile.

In the words of eco-philosopher Theodore Roszak:

> *Prudence is such a lacklustre virtue. It does not match the exhilaration of the heroic exploits to which the myth of limitless progress summons us. If ecological wisdom cannot be made as engaging as the reshaping of continents, the harvesting of the seas, the exploration of space, if it cannot compete with the material gratifications of industrial growth, it will run a poor second to those who appeal to stronger emotions.*[10]

Propositions to eliminate a problem are stronger than those that merely mitigate it.

Campaigns that promise entry to a new world where anything is possible may inspire support, despite considerable sacrifice or discomfort. Those that leave all the underlying causes and constraints in place simply offer major re-adjustments, rather than fundamental realignments: benefits that may only prove temporary. Why sacrifice anything for that?

INSPIRATION AND DRAMA

Campaigners can take to heart the admonishments of Theodore Roszak. Once your attention is captured, it's a lot more fun to run a campaign composed of positive, exciting, 'doing' things rather than one that makes people feel guilty and just asks them to do less. Roszak quotes Earth Island Journal,[11] which stated: 'It is not enough to find "50 simple things you can do to save the Earth". We need *50 difficult* things.' The list begins:

1   dismantle your car;
2   become a total vegetarian;
3   grow your own vegetables;
4   have your power lines disconnected;
5   don't have children…

Says Roszak:

> *Habitual reliance on gloom, apocalyptic panic, and the psychology of shame takes a heavy toll in public confidence. In part, the problem arises from the way the environment movement has come to be organized. The pattern resembles the telethon disease-of-the-month approach…*
>
> *Like all political activists busy with their mission, environmentalists often work from poor and short-sighted ideas about human motivation; they overlook the unreason, the perversity, the sick desire that lie at the core of the psyche. Their strategy is to shock and shame. But it is one thing to have the Good clearly in view; it is another to find ways to make people want the Good…*
>
> *Are dread and desperation the only motivations we have to play on? What are we connecting with in people that is generous, joyous, freely given – perhaps heroic?*

Benny Haerlin is a former German MEP and, most recently, anti-GM campaigner. I asked him why the Brent Spar campaign attracted such public attention. He pointed out something that, in retrospect was obvious: 'It was a drama. There was a struggle and the outcome was unknown, right up until the very last moment. It lasted for weeks, and many people thought it was over many times. It was not until the very last second that we knew the outcome.'

Drama holds our attention. We want to know the outcome of the struggle. Drama could arise through a parliamentary vote if enough hangs on it, or a protestor in hiding, such as the English anti-roads tunneller 'Swampy'.

Yet so many campaigns are quite unlike that. Many seem unambitious, or simply an extended form of complaint: unexciting, uninspiring. Does your campaign excite you? If not, stop it and rework it until it does. Select your campaign from among the things that excite you, not the ones that you feel you ought to be seen to work on. Plan for drama by embarking on adventures where you do not know the outcome yourself. As a friend once said to me: 'Have a nice adventure.'

BOX 7.1 – SUPPLY CHAIN TARGETING: DEFORESTATION IN THE AMAZON

In October 2009 Greenpeace announced that four of the largest players in the global cattle industry had made a collective agreement to zero deforestation in the Amazon. 'This means,' said Campaign Director Sarah North, 'they will stop purchasing cattle from newly deforested areas of the Brazilian Amazon. They will also register and map all cattle ranches which supply their business to ensure their commitment is upheld.'

Cattle ranching, said Greenpeace, was 'the single largest cause of deforestation in the world'. The Greenpeace Amazon campaign is an example of a campaign based on supply chain targeting (as opposed, for example, to starting by looking at consumers, or laws, government policies or forest management). The overall logic is simple: identify the largest causes of the problem, find those that are susceptible to leverage that can be exerted by the organization, and build a critical path to stop that part of the problem. In most of its Amazon campaigns, Greenpeace has used its pulling power with European consumers, and alliance building by its Brazilian-led team in the Amazon, to exert pressure on corporates, with Brazilian government action following along.

In this respect the logic of the cattle ranching campaign followed several previous Greenpeace campaigns in the Amazon, which had targeted mahogany logging and the clearance of forest land for soya production. That included a specific campaign push against McDonald's, which has, unusually, been written up by both sides.[12] McDonald's not only stopped using Amazon soya to feed its chickens, but joined Greenpeace in a campaign that led to a moratorium on further forest clearance for soya (for more details of Greenpeace's Amazon campaigns, see extended case study at www.earthscan.co.uk/onlineresources).

Greenpeace made its case for targeting the cattle trade companies with evidence-gathering investigations. In media analysis terms, this made Greenpeace into 'primary providers' of information. The importance of this for any campaigner is that if you are a 'primary provider', your information has more impact than if you were relying on material already published or gathered by others, and if this is visual and first-hand rather than simple statistical, its power is increased. This applies to any campaign, whether the evidence is gathered in a high-tech way or simply testimony from local video interviews, collected on a mobile phone. Of course your evidence will be tested for 'uniqueness', representativeness and so on, but it almost invariably gives you some licence for advocacy and political capital.

As *Greenpeace Business* magazine recorded, in this case 'Greenpeace tracked the trade in cattle products back from the export-orientated processing facilities of Bertin, JBS and Marfrig in the south of Brazil to three frontiers of deforestation in the Amazon'. Undercover investigations identified hundreds of ranches within the rainforest supplying cattle to slaughterhouses in the Amazon region belonging to these companies. Where mapped ranch boundaries were available, satellite analysis showed significant supplies of cattle come from ranches active in recent and illegal deforestation. One Bertin slaughterhouse was receiving supplies of cattle from an illegal ranch occupying land belonging to indigenous peoples.

Evidence showed these slaughterhouses then shipped beef or hides to company facilities thousands of kilometres away for further processing before export. In effect, illegal cattle were laundered through the supply chain to an unwitting global market.

That market included the three biggest supermarket chains in Brazil – Wal-Mart (parent company of Asda in the UK), Carrefour and Pão de Açúcar. When after a three-year investigation, Greenpeace released a report[14] 'Slaughtering the Amazon' in 2009, the Federal Prosecutor in Pará state filed a billion dollar lawsuit against Bertin, based on evidence that the company's slaughterhouses were buying cattle from illegally deforested areas. The Prosecutor's Office issued letters to 69 other companies, including Carrefour and Wal-Mart, which announced that they would cancel contracts with ranches facing prosecution.

Downstream pressure from Greenpeace and Bertin's key customers, including show companies Clarks, Nike, Adidas, Timberland and Geox, prompted the company to expand an official agreement signed with the Brazilian Federal Prosecution Office and the government of Pará state in Amazonia a few months earlier, to include any ranch involved in new rainforest destruction. Pressure from Princes, a customer of JBS for canned beef products, led that company to join the agreement and join the others in a commitment to register and map all cattle ranches that directly supply them with cattle, and join a traceability system from farms to slaughterhouses and processing facilities by 2011.[15]

WORKING WITH
NEWS MEDIA

USING THE MEDIA

It's natural for campaigners and journalists to develop a close relationship. Too much focus on news though, is a bad thing. News can report conflict beautifully, but it isn't a very good tool to help *promote* change.

Nevertheless, almost every campaign is likely to involve substantial media work, so it pays to discover how to deal with the media machine. The news media[1] presents a version of reality. From within, it is a machine and a community. Once you learn how to gain access, it can be entrancing, flattering and addictive[2] so be careful.

Friends of the Earth (FoE)[3] answers the question 'Why do press work?' in this way:

- Profile – making sure people know you exist, what kind of organization you are and what you do;
- Specific publicity – the fastest and most effective way to reach a wide audience;
- Leverage – targets (for example, local authorities, industries) are more likely to get a move on and change their ways if they know that the debate is visible and very public.

To which I would add third-party endorsement. Being reported by someone else implies that someone has evaluated and tested a version of events, and found it true enough to be worth passing on.

FoE's 20 ways to get into the news (with my comments):

1 Launch a campaign (make sure there are activities to report, as well as objectives);
2 Hold a public meeting (see www.campaignstrategy.org);
3 Mark an anniversary (this can be the anniversary of a related event, even a setback);
4 Hold an annual general meeting (AGM) (only likely to excite core followers, unless dramatized, for example with a vote);

5 Announce formation of a new group (if true!);
6 Welcome new proposals (in media-speak this is 'giving reaction');
7 Condemn new proposals (as above);
8 Call for a public inquiry;
9 Give evidence to a public inquiry;
10 Lobby someone else's meeting;
11 Publish findings of a survey or opinion poll – public (these can be very simple and cheap – they don't have to be the best possible, only better than anything else around that day);
12 The same for trade/industry;
13 Involve a local celebrity;
14 Invite a local dignitary to an event – they don't have to accept for this to be press-worthy. (The media then goes to them for 'reaction' – often it's best to leave a story as an open invitation for the media to complete it – an unfinished story has more 'legs');
15 Send a letter to someone important (be sure to hand deliver or courier it, or confirm a fax: if the press will want a reaction from them, they must have it!);
16 Present a petition;
17 Quiz election candidates (council, parliamentary or European Commission (EC));
18 Hold a vigil (looks much better at night);
19 Direct action (follow the principles of non-violence);
20 Stunts/dressing up/build a display (use visual language – see Chapter 6).

ELEVEN THINGS TO KNOW ABOUT THE MEDIA

1 Create your own events and public conversations (such as using face-to-face approaches, email, internet) and then get the media to cover that – create the reality, don't let the media become the reality – they will turn on you.
2 News is not the only media – features pages/programmes and magazines are often better read and remembered – news polarizes but features don't. Only use news for irreducible either/or stories; use other media channels for more complex stories.
3 News media needs events and people – provide both.
4 Local media are (in the UK) more trusted than national media – it's more important to correct inaccuracies in local media.
5 News has the absolution of time. Each day begins anew. A good letter or the story of your own event is better than a small comment embedded in a story framed by an opponent.

6 Find out about timing and markets (listeners, readers, viewers) for each outlet – they determine what's covered. Even news is in the entertainment business.

7 Invest in contacts – get to know journalists and help them.

8 News is about a change to something already understood. Don't use it to explain something completely new. For that, first carry it to the social mainstream and then into local or specialist press.

9 Find out which media your audience consume and target those. First though, check you can't go direct – which may be more effective.

10 Don't count publicity as success – plan, and look for effect.

11 Don't waste time arguing with the media unless it becomes unavoidable. Don't 'have a pissing match with a skunk'.

> *Pure opposition ... is the force behind much radio and television journalism. Broadcasters change the subject whenever they are proved wrong. They show irresponsibility in its purest form because they are not required to defend the stands they take. What works well for the BBC, however, is fatal for the politically committed, [who] are meant to understand the world and show how their principles could improve it.* (Nick Cohen[4])

'NEWS VALUES'

> *News is history in its first and best form, its vivid and fascinating form, and ... history is the pale and tranquil reflection of it.* (Mark Twain)

News in the end is what we think it is and say it is. News is what people talk about – gossip, scandal and events that matter, shock or surprise.

Key factors making something newsworthy are 'news values'. For years, I thought these were a set of values in the sense of moral principles, but no: they are factors that make a story valuable – that is, useful – to news outlets. They develop sales and egos, not ethics. In 1965, Johan Galtung and Marie Holmboe Ruge compiled a much-quoted list of 'news values' based on coverage of international events:

- Frequency: Timing and how it fits news schedules and deadlines. 'On this basis,' says media researcher Mick Underwood,[5] 'motorway pile-ups, murders, plane crashes will qualify, as they are all of short duration and therefore nearly always fit into the schedule. Such events are also unambiguous, their meaning is quickly arrived at.' Trends and complex processes are generally ruled out unless they can be told through one-off events such as trade figures – hence the importance of indices such as the Financial Times Stock Exchange 500 (FTSE500) as a way of covering things deemed important but difficult.

- Threshold: Is it big enough to count?
- Clarity: Underwood says: 'The mass media generally tend to go for closure, unlike literature, where the ambiguity of meaning of events is exploited and explored.' He cites[6] a US survey that revealed that 'the most regular reason why stories don't appear is that they are too complicated'. So only ever ask news to cover things that are unambiguous. An action, or a criticism, or a call for a resignation, can be the 'news', while the reasons for it may contain too many unknowns or ambiguities to be reported.
- Meaningfulness: Will readers or viewers see it as relevant to them? The media reflect popular culture.
- Consonance: Does the event match the media's expectations? An early warning sign can be unexpected media wanting to come to cover your event or taking an unusual interest: they will probably be using it for some other news purpose. Find out what it is!
- Unexpectedness: Classically, 'man bites dog' is news, vice versa is not. Hence, skateboarding ducks are news. Unexpected success can be news – a positive story!
- Continuity: This is a question of convenience. It's why the media loves anniversaries as 'pegs'. Don't let its 'no brainer' nature put you off. Campaigners often try to be too clever. PR agencies, on the other hand, go for the easiest option. It enables TV to pull out some old footage – no cost involved. TV news budgets have plummeted, and cost is a major reason why news coverage is increasingly spasmodic, cheap and shallow. The BBC has a website devoted to anniversaries of events 'on this day'.
- News context and competition: Is it a heavy news day or not? Is there a lot of news? If so, of course your story stands less chance.
- Important or elite nations: 'People like us' get most coverage in our media – similar nations, for instance. Local media often demand that someone 'local' features in the story. The adage 'every name mentioned is a copy sold' is true – only it ought to be 'every name mentioned is probably several copies sold' once relatives are taken into account. 'Aberdeen Man Lost At Sea' was allegedly the headline in the *Aberdeen Journal* in 1912, on the occasion of the sinking of the *Titanic*, which also killed 2223 other people (not from Aberdeen).
- Reference to elite persons: Anything done by the most powerful people is news. The US President having a cold, for instance. Campaigners can add important people to make an issue media-friendly. In May 2003, Christian Aid published a report on oil wealth, which, it argued, often caused inequality, conflict and poverty rather than sustainable forms of development. Not an easy sell to the mainstream news media, but Christian Aid also sent actor and sympathetic supporter Joseph Fiennes (of the movie *Shakespeare in Love*), to Angola. Fiennes came back to give a first-hand report of what he saw, which was covered along with a Christian Aid spokesman in a studio discussion on BBC Radio 4's *Today* programme.[7]

- Personalization: Politics is often presented as a tussle between two party leaders. Campaigns can do this – for example by focusing on the personal responsibility of a World Trade Organization (WTO) official over globalization.
- Negativity: most news is bad. Fiske[8] refers to a US journalist arriving in the war-torn Belgian Congo, running up to a group of white women waiting for a plane to leave, and shouting out: 'Has anyone here been raped and speaks English?'

Then there are other professed news values – educational value for instance, and some that just seem self-evident, such as stories involving money or sex.

PRESS RELEASES

A press release is simply a written statement that aims to entice the media into covering an issue you want to communicate. FoE quotes journalist and politician Denis McShane in his book *Using the Media*,[9] describing it as:

> *A partially digested helping of news which can then be made into the real thing by the journalists in the newsroom.*

- One side of A4, double-spaced, is ideal;
- Use descriptive, not clever, headings, with an active verb;
- No jargon or professional speak;
- Check that a 14-year-old understands it;
- Keep a hard-copy archive and one online, if you have a website;
- Use email – most journalists now write from their desk;
- Allow three days for hard-copy material to be opened and reach them;
- If justified, use an 'embargo' – which means it should not be used before a particular time and date. It allows journalists time to investigate and prepare. Embargoes are, however, informal and rely on neither side abusing the system. Don't try to embargo news that has already broken in order to control it or break an embargo you have set;
- Make a follow-up phone call, to find out if it has been received, who is handling it, and whether you can help at all;
- To simply notify an upcoming event, make it a press *notice;*
- If it's immediate reaction write 'For Immediate Release' with time, place and date.

The first paragraph is the most important part of a press release and should contain the most interesting point of the issue, using the four Ws: Who? What? Where? and When? – Why? and How? can follow. For example:

Ambridge group launches drive to save hedges

In a year-long project starting today, the Ambridge Tree Team plans to save hedges in three ways:

- *Mapping all the ancient hedges in Borsetshire with a metre-by-metre field survey*
- *Running 'Project Hedge', a new grant scheme to help with management costs*
- *Hedgeline – communities whistle-blowing if valuable hedges are being cut down, with a free-phone number and website.*

The project follows last year's council survey showing a 20 per cent increase in the rate of loss of hedges in the county. 'It's time to stop the rot,' said Cindy Thaxter, project coordinator.

If there are a lot of points, use bullets. Helpful background information should go under 'Notes to editors' after 24/7 phone and email contacts at the end of a release. Where the actual press release finishes, write 'Ends'.

PRESS CONFERENCES

Press conferences appear on TV, so they look important. They can be useful, but backfire badly if used without real justification. Meeting people is key – if it's just you and a pack that could be posted, then don't bother.

Checklist[10]

- Define the story and your key messages;
- Decide who are the best/appropriate people to speak (ideally no more than three);
- Identify key media and send them an invitation;
- Decide on a time that suits key media you want to reach (10.30am or 11.30am is usually good). To catch the breakfast broadcast media you will need to have a breakfast briefing at 7.30am/8.00am – a high-risk time!;
- Remind news desks by phone the day before (expect a high drop-out, even so);
- Brief all speakers, and any other people who might be interviewed (case histories) beforehand. Have bullet points for each speaker;
- Rehearse the conference the day before: key points and the possible problem questions, rehearsing answers – time well spent;
- Check the room, ensure all equipment works and provide simple visual backdrops that add to the story;

- Provide coffee and tea on tap and take the names of all journalists attending;
- Issue journalists with a press pack on arrival – including the press release (with pre-formatted quotes from the speakers) and any other useful background material (research synopsis, background information about your agency and what it has achieved, facts and figures, and so on);
- Start and end on time;
- Ask the chairman to welcome and introduce speakers, and briefly review the issue;
- Each speaker should have a different role and subject area. They should talk for a maximum of five minutes, clearly and concisely;
- Have a balance of 'experts' and 'real people';
- Chairman should invite questions;
- Remember all that is said is 'on the record' – but remember that there is no such thing as 'off the record';
- Offer interviews afterwards – usually for radio and TV. But stick to the key messages laid out in the conference;
- Send the press release out by fax or email to journalists who didn't attend;
- Evaluate the media coverage gained.

Disadvantages of a press conference include journalists getting ideas and 'hunting in a pack', and speakers who start arguing or contradicting each other. Preparation and control are key. Advantages are that it can help journalists enlarge a story from a news piece into a longer feature with visuals, because they can meet a lot of different characters in one place.

The environment should reinforce the content and tone of what is said.

THE INTERVIEW SUITCASE

Only do interviews or media appearances if you have something to say – something that you *want* to say. Have some communication points – write them down – and pack your 'suitcase', including:

- A headline: the *main* thing you want to say. Whatever happens, say this! It's your 'jacket';
- Three reasons supporting the headline (for example: 'Save this forest for its beauty, its genetic resources and because it safeguards a clean water supply for 10,000 people'). Journalists won't just accept your headline point, they'll ask 'W' 'why?'. These are the 'shirts' or proofs;
- One fact to go with each reason[11] – preferably a number. Many news stories have one number. This is the 'skirt' or 'trousers';

- Lastly, anecdotes, the 'socks and underwear': an anecdote converts a view into a story and brings an interview to life – 'Let me tell you about a little girl I met only the other day, whose life has been so improved by... ' Have one in mind that you will try to bring in if you get the chance. Few interviewers will cut off a short story in mid-flow, but all will feel entitled to cut short a list of 'points'. To begin with an anecdote is high risk, as people will weigh up all the issues in their head against your example, and one example is unlikely to be generally applicable. It's best to start with the big picture and introduce examples later.

BRIDGING

In any interview, the journalist will have his or her agenda and you yours (communication points). A struggle ensues as to what gets recorded. You can't trick the press into reporting what you want, so seek the best in the relationship.

Remember, their task is to sell newspapers, keep viewers watching and stop listeners switching to another station. Journalists need you to fill their airtime or column inches, so cooperate by being as interesting as possible.

Ed Gyde says:

> In the 'battle of agendas', you need to follow very different rules from a conversation with a friend whom you might meet in the pub or in the office. An interview is not like a normal chat – it may look like one, but it's run on quite different lines. 'Bridging' is the way you can get back from the journalist's agenda to your communication points. Used properly, it is very useful and wholly legitimate. Used badly, it's annoying to all concerned. It follows the sequence A-B-C. A stands for acknowledge; B stands for bridge; C for your communication points.

Don't ignore questions, but don't be led by them unless they lead to your communication points. Instead, acknowledge them, and bridge away to what you want to say. This needs practising – preferably with a media trainer – as it's not a natural way to talk, but it sounds fine in a media interview.

The reason you need to do this is that very few, if any, questions will either be open – 'So tell us all about it' – or appropriate to your communication points. If you are asked nine questions and only one naturally leads to your points, and you answer them directly, the other eight answers will dominate and the audience won't remember your points at all. If you manage to repeat them nine times, they probably will get at least one of them. Bridges are verbal invitations to yourself to make your points.

Some bridges:

- 'That's an issue, but *what the public are most concerned about* is…';
- 'Some say that, but *what our research shows* is…';
- 'Yes that debate will run and run, and *today we are focused on…*';
- 'An important point and *I'd like to answer it in three ways, if I may…*' (high risk, as it requires style and confidence, but used to great effect by elder statesman who, of course, never do answer);
- 'I agree that needs answering and *I will in a moment, if I may*, but first I would just like to say…' (using politesse to take control of the interview agenda);
- 'That is an issue but *the important thing to focus on…*' (very popular but patently judgemental and thus rather obvious);
- 'Well I think *the three main things to focus on* are' (double bridge, only viable if the question wasn't very clear);
- 'Let me *be absolutely clear*' (not a bridge at all, a smokescreen favourite of UK Prime Minister Tony Blair, which everyone takes as 'I'm not answering that');
- 'But what *we know works* in this field is…' (useful, as long as you really do know);
- 'That's a possibility but what *we're calling for* is…' (likewise);
- 'That's one view, but we need to look at *how this fits into the bigger picture.*'

Don't be like politicians and push past the question without acknowledging it, from A to C without B – that's rude.

The temptation may be to bridge everything and never to answer any question directly. That is a mistake. If you get questions that can be answered with a yes or no, do so, and add your key points. If it's reasonable, there's nothing wrong with saying: 'I don't know, but I'll find out and get back to you/the listeners' – in fact, come to think of it, that can also be a bridge.

Lastly, advanced users can try to add 'D' to the ABC – the Dangle. Expert interviewees can start an entire new conversation by judiciously inserting a 'dangle' that the interviewer can't resist, something that sounds so good that the listeners or viewers would be 'robbed' if they didn't give it time. In the case of the successful Friends of the Earth 2005–2006 campaign 'The Big Ask',[12] ad agency CHI and Friends of the Earth created a D right up front in their campaign title – what was The Big Ask anyway? That is a high risk strategy, but using a dangle in an interview can be a good idea if you've made sure you got in your C points first.

BE PREPARED

Before agreeing to do an interview, find out who else is going to be there, who listens to the programme (is it drivers, teenagers, grannies?), and what the story is (why they want you). Make sure to know if it is live or recorded, and whether (especially TV) there's a studio audience. (Live is actually easier, though beginners find it more worrying. The thing is to have your points in your head, so they just come out naturally. Having 'time to think' in an interview doesn't help because you're likely to think of something new to say that isn't one of your key points!)

Be prepared: don't do interviews 'on the hoof'. Take time to think. Paint a picture with your words – particularly for radio. Media trainer Angela Coles lists five Ps:

1   people (name or describe);
2   pictures;
3   passion;
4   plain language;
5   preparation.

She stresses PEP – point (make it), evidence (give it), point (repetition), and thinking about who your audience is, what language to use and what examples to give.

Stick to the points you've carefully prepared. Avoid last-minute brainwaves. As Alan Watson of Burson Marsteller says, 'the TV studio is no place for original thought'.

Finally, avoid unnecessary clarification. Don't focus on misconceptions, however annoying they may be – there isn't time to educate people in an interview. Make your points, not just once, but as many times as possible.

IT'S A SCANDAL

Many news stories are driven by 'scandal'.[13] Obviously, a scandal revolving around a terrible problem is bigger than one that's only slight, but there's more to it than this. My scandal formula is:

$$\text{Scandal} = \text{Awfulness} \times \frac{\text{What can be done}}{\text{What is being done}} \times \text{immoral profit from it}$$

'Awfulness' is often the first port of call for a news report. 'Just how bad is it?' Like most useful news story constructions, 'just how bad is it?' is a question that can be asked with an air of authority but without any knowledge of the subject matter.

Most scandals start with some sort of damage report. The 'immoral profit' factor is where the media go next, if there is the slightest hint that malpractice was involved. A favourite line of enquiry after a disaster is whether safety measures were compromised to save money. After the Potters Bar rail crash in the UK in 2002, where maintenance was seen to be at fault, there were accusations that 'insecure freelancers were cutting corners to meet the demands of cheese-paring managers'.[14]

Immoral profit is the reason, for instance, why deaths from illegal drugs are more scandalous than deaths from substances whose sale was legal. Paracetemol, for example, kills around 200 people each year in the UK through accidents or suicide. Few of those make headlines, whereas ecstasy deaths (27 in 2000[15]), cocaine (57) or amphetamines (19) are more likely to be reported.

Implicit in the media construction of a scandal is that it was *avoidable*. If there's no solution, if nothing can be done, then there is no scandal, only a tragedy. The world is full of problems, but there are far fewer clearly avoidable ones.

If alternatives are overlooked – or stronger still, neglected or *suppressed* – then a problem builds into a scandal. In this way, a solution-driven campaign can become highly newsworthy.

Check if:

- A solution to an accepted problem is being suppressed;
- A solution to an accepted problem is being neglected;
- If someone is doing something awful (check also for grossness – see Chapter 7);
- If an immoral profit is being made from a problem continuing;
- If an immoral profit is being made from a solution going unused; and
- If those responsible could do more.

Journalistically, scandals can be just awfulness × repression or secrecy. Newspaper proprietor Lord Northcliffe once said: 'News is what somebody, somewhere, wants to suppress; everything else is advertising.'

CONFLICT MAKES NEWS

In May 1981, we were organizing the launch of the London Wildlife Group[16] with a conference. To help publicize this, I thought it would be a good idea to plant some primroses (wild ones rescued from a road development) on London's Primrose Hill, symbolizing an intent to return nature to the city. Equipped with primroses and photogenic local schoolchildren – even armed with the memories of an old lady who lived nearby and remembered picking primroses there as a child – I thought we had 'a package'. On 13 May, I embarked on a final 'ring-round', trying to interest news desks, and in particular, photo desks. Harassed photo editors answered with the question: 'You do know what's happened, don't you?' The Pope had just been shot. 'Yes, but there must still be *something* else going in the papers', I found myself saying plaintively, but without much hope.

Then we were rescued for the following Sunday newspapers by the inadvertent assistance of the government. The press were not very interested in planting wild flowers – until, that is, the Royal Parks unexpectedly refused us permission. Here was a story the press could handle – bureaucracy versus the little people trying to do the right thing. The official at the end of the phone even thought a primrose was a tree, and asked: 'How tall is it?' It got on the front page of the national newspaper *The Observer*.[17]

The primrose campaign taught me two things: first there was a conflict, along with the helpful ingredients of easy access for photographers and 'human interest'. Second, while newness is a news value, it was not entirely new. It was a formula that the newspaper had run many times before.

If you have a campaign it will be in conflict with someone somewhere. That is probably your most newsworthy opportunity.

The first thing a news journalist does when faced with a possible 'story' is often to look for the conflict, The culture of news is to require the two sides, the dialectical struggle. Usually the more dramatic, the better, and the less competent the journalist is, the more obvious this process becomes.

Having decided where the line of conflict it is, they then tend to go on to test 'how good' the story is by checking it against other 'news values' (see above). Because news does this, if you don't do it, the media will do it anyway and then make you 'fit' into that story. At this point you have lost control of the framing (see page 28). Therefore you must have a problem/solution, winner/loser, right/wrong line in your version of the story, or your 'position'. Test it out in your head or with colleagues before going public, think where it leads. If you don't have such a dividing line, then the best that can happen when you engage the media is that they find 'no story' and disengage. The worst is that you are trapped in a bad story you can't get out of.

9

KEEPING A
CAMPAIGN GOING

STAYING ON THE SIDE OF THE VICTIMS

A constant media reprise is that the 'real victims deserve our sympathy' (their case is implicitly right). Make sure that the most empathetic figure in the story is you, or on your side. Don't let the media fall out of love with your campaign through the natural tendency for it to dry out and become an elite dialogue.

- Causes start their lives as 'left-field', driven from the heart and over simple instances of injustice or abuse, expressed in everyday language.
- As time goes by, progress brings calls for systematic evaluation, qualification, objectivity, dispassionate analysis. 'Expert' dialogue develops: this is harder to understand, less public.
- Knowledge of problems and solutions progresses; the campaign pushes for further change; perhaps losers start to fight back. For example, polluting industries see costs rise and markets shrink as policies favour cleaner technologies. They are self-interested, yes; but what they now kick against is an abstraction, a bureaucratic policy, an esoteric issue and statistics, maybe about risks yet to arise or problems that seem far away.

Now flesh-and-blood 'victims' are appealing for 'fairness'. The woeful business person finds a sympathetic hearing in an economics report on TV, positioned against 'bleeding-heart liberals', 'rules' or 'the interests of frogs'.[1] The campaign 'no longer deserves sympathy' and the media positions the campaigners as the ones to blame.

Avoid this roll-back in two ways: First, don't let it happen.

- Keep the victims' reality locked into the heart of the campaign, be they coral reefs succumbing to climate change, victims of chemical poisoning, cancer patients, or slum-dwellers thousands of miles away;
- Make them the channels or messengers, or get as close as you can;

- Keep experts on tap, not on top.

Second, lead renewed calls for progress with evidence of the victims in terms that make them the *most empathetic* characters in the story – not, say, the latest results of a computer model – unless a victim is also the messenger.

Left to drift, campaigns tend to dry out, become status conscious and accumulate experts – scientists, lobbyists, policy workers and others. It's cheap, too – expert chats have no need of costly mobilization, communications staffs, political theatre, legal, marketing, protest, action or other elements of the campaign army. Most experts like to talk to experts, not to the public. That is no way to run campaigns.

A good example is the role of Handicap International Belgium in the Cluster Munitions Coalition, which campaigns to influence international negotiations on banning cluster bombs. 'Ban Advocates', who have themselves suffered from such devices, play an active part in lobbying officials and politicians for a ban on cluster munitions and for the rights of survivors and affected communities. Handicap International Belgium gives them practical support and, where necessary, interpreters, training, briefing reports and support networks (www.banadvocates.org). NCVO[2] points to the following advice:

> *Go at people's own pace, take the time to explain the project and build relationships with your beneficiaries based on mutual trust; help build confidence, through training, briefings and support networks; help foster a group dynamic for people to exchange experiences and help each other; and, most importantly leave the Advocates to speak in their own words.*

I came across similar sensibilities working on communicating drugs treatment. Many drugs workers did not want to expose people with stories to tell to the media (for fear of what they might say about their own theories of 'what worked' as well as for their own well-being), but without stories, claims that drugs treatment was a worthwhile public investment were treated with scepticism. The best compromise was to start small and local, and only to use those people who had already 'gone public' with their stories in their own terms.

FISH AND SYMPATHY

A classic dried-out campaign problem is the annual crisis over fishing quotas in the European Union Common Fisheries Policy.

The problem starts because there's no news from the fish. As victims, fish don't take part in the media directly. Then it's generally a matter of degree – not an either/or problem (see Chapter 7). A bulging net can be visual evidence of either a 'good' or a 'bad' fishery: a victim problem, right away.

Pressure groups, and most of all governments, take advice on stock and fishing levels from fisheries scientists. The debate is elite, technical, inaccessible. Then officials set quotas – politics supplies the event – and fishing activity gets cut.

Now the 'issue' is the cuts, and fishermen, who are at least part of the problem, become 'the victims'. The media then reports *this* as the problem.

Politicians grandstand against their own conservation policy to play national interests. Campaigners see fishing in the news: talks are in 'crisis'. A 'solution' is urgently needed, but it's just political theatre. The media waits to see which Member State (in the case of the European Union fisheries policy debates) is going to come out on top. So the real players and victims are not fish, but politicians. Environment groups are largely irrelevant except for providing some pictures.[3]

The best campaign opportunity is outside such a forum and well before the endgame begins, in the stacking of odds and setting of terms. Politics then plays the cards that you have helped to mark. Make the fish the victims earlier on, and keep them there with visuals (for example, underwater visuals) and spokespeople, such as concerned field biologists and fishermen, throughout.

Not surprisingly, successful fisheries campaigns are almost as rare as hens' teeth. Witness the miniscule number of fisheries certified by the Marine Stewardship Council (MSC – see www.msc.org).

> *Severe cuts in white fish quotas will 'decimate' Scotland's fishing communities, it has been warned... In Brussels, an agreement was reached which will limit fishing vessels to 15 days at sea. There will also be a 45 per cent cut in cod quotas, a 50 per cent reduction in haddock catches, and 60 per cent cut in whiting catches.[4]*
>
> *For the World Wildlife Fund, Julie Cator also said that it falls far short of the cuts that environmentalists said were necessary to prevent the further decline of fish stocks. The deal came late on Friday after UK Prime Minister Tony Blair had made a telephone call to his Danish counterpart, Anders Fogh Rasmussen, in an attempt to end the deadlock...[5]*

Either/or campaigns to set aside no-take zones (in effect, nature reserves) or to stop fishing of one species altogether, are more winnable.

WHO'S TO BLAME NOW?

When starting a campaign, analyse who has the power to stop the problem; the capacity to cause change. The appropriate campaign target is usually the one with greatest direct culpability and capacity to act. Often, a major player will argue that the link from themselves to the problem is not clear. Multinational logging companies blame peasants for forest destruction. Chemical companies blame farmers for not following the instructions on pesticide packets. Oil companies blame car owners for burning fossil fuels.

A favourite tactic of governments or corporations that don't want to act is to assign culpability to everyone, or to an abstract.

What are companies doing when they use methyl-bromide to fumigate cut flowers or vegetables, and in so doing, knock a massive whole in the ozone layer? They are 'meeting a need'. What's Irish businessman Kevin McHugh doing when he builds and launches the UK£50 million *Atlantic Dawn*, the world's largest trawler, able to fish as much from the waters of impoverished Mauritania as 7000 local artisan fishermen can in a year, and acquires permission to fish there?[6] He's meeting market demand. What's the answer to the problem of climate change? For us all to change our 'habits', or to 'end our love affair with the car'. Yes, it is true; to 'save the climate', we could all take to bicycles, buses and trains instead of cars. We could all go into our garden sheds and invent alternative technologies. We *could*, in theory, but we would find it rather difficult.

Campaigns become vulnerable to this dialogue when they are stuck in the problem-driving phase and need to shift to solution-driving.

Try turning the question upside down. Ask who's responsible for *not* implementing the solution, rather than just who's responsible for causing the problem. Whether it's through suppressing a solution or denying a problem, any party with the power to solve this is the problem-holder or problem-owner.

Fixing a campaign: Changing a strategy

A campaign can become tired or stuck, or both, or need a change. Here's one way to stimulate thinking on changing a strategy.

The main areas in which it's usually worth thinking about change are resources, objective, and activities as perceived by supporters (including engagement opportunities).

The principal options for change are to become more (or less) popular, or more or less ambitious or to give greater agency. An example of popularization, cited by Gerd Leipold, is the involvement of Diana, the Princess of Wales in the campaign to ban landmines.[7] Change in effective resources could involve converting invisible or visible support. Change in the objective might be from one that is too large or too small to stimulate engagement, to a 'bite-sized' objective. New forms of involvement might bring in whole new constituencies.

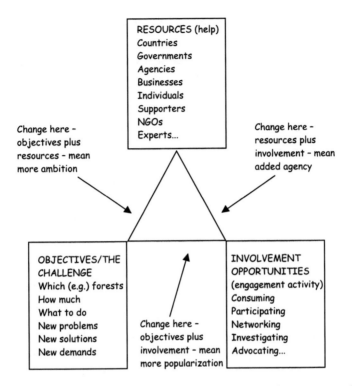

Figure 9.1 *Fixing a campaign that is drying up or becoming tired*

A useful technique can be to step up or down strategy levels. Consider if your campaign would do better if its proposition changed focus from one of those levels to another.

Thus using climate change as an example:

(Up)
- future of society;
- industrial future;
- energy future;
- fossil fuels future;
- oil company future;
- future of a site/technology;
- attribute of a site/component/brand.

(Down)

How to Tell When You Are Winning

It is remarkable how difficult it can be to tell if you are winning a campaign, or even to know when you've won it. Most campaigns are subtler and more multidimensional than the sorts of see-the-hill-take-the-hill projects favoured in media depictions of 'campaigns'. They are often 'wicked' (see page 98) in the sense that even if you have a well-founded critical path, the very act of progressing along it causes things around you to go into a state of flux. Instead of falling, the dominoes have an Alice in Wonderland-style habit of getting up and walking about.

Nevertheless the best way of knowing remains to have a tight and well verified critical path, so you know where you want to go and the unambiguous stepping stones along the way. The very best indicator is if you know the change that makes winning the 'inevitable consequence'. There always is one but it's often a development or decision so deeply buried in processes not accessible to campaigners that it only becomes obvious years afterwards.

The two other principal indicators are the state of play in the issue around you and the audiences and 'stakeholders' directly or indirectly engaged by your campaign, and the actions of your opponent (the antagonist, page 140). Sadly, because it would be convenient if it were not so, what the media say about you is generally not a good indicator. The news media in particular is more interested in the degree of conflict than in the outcome.

For example, in the 1990s, with colleague Steve Shallhorn, I visited campaigners in British Columbia (BC) who had been waging a long and pretty desperate struggle against clear-cutting and destructive logging in the temperate rainforest. Sitting in a small house whose owner showed us photos of black bears raiding the kitchen, we worked through the status of the campaign.

Things, they told us, were pretty bad. In the past the major timber companies had pretty much ignored them in the media and political circles and relied on brutal action by logging gangs, 'security' and the police against roadblocks and tree blockades in the forest. Now they also had the personal attacks, campaigns of vilification in the media, the hiring of major American PR companies and an advertising offensive to contend with, as well as attempts by the industry to wrong-foot them by wheeling out its own ecological 'experts', set up dialogue groups and woo politicians and the public not just in BC but in the end-markets of Europe and elsewhere. The counter-campaign they faced had grown like topsy.

We listened and talked, and enumerated the changes one by one. Soon we concluded that these were signs of success, not of failure. End buyers and pulp processors in European markets were up in arms about the impact of clear-cutting, and demanding alternative supplies. Major companies such as MacMillan Bloedel were heading for a reversal of key policies. The BC government was coming to a realization that damage to its international image – and industries such as tourism – was more costly than the gain to be made by continuing to prioritize 'strip mining' of forests. While the battle was at its most intense, it was now being won by being fought both in the forests and along the whole supply chain – territory where the 'forest' industry was socially and politically vulnerable.

That campaign (around Clayoquot Sound) scored major – though by no means complete – successes. In the closing stages, companies such as Macmillan Bloedell made FSC standards their own. The FSC (Forest Stewardship Council) had been invented and nurtured by WWF as a forest certification process. Without the FSC it is hard to see how these timber companies would have been able to make the necessary U-turn: it gave them the marketing foundation for a new business case. Later, in the US, Home Depot adopted a similar approach. When the opposition starts engaging with third-party initiatives that have a different logic from their previous positions, you know you have probably won, even if by doing so they manage to avoid actually having to hoist a white flag.

Do not try to humiliate your opponent: it will probably be counter-productive, because you will no longer be the empathetic figure in 'the story' (see page 43), and it delays the time when you can turn an old opponent into a new ally.

Similarly, in 2005, at a time when many American environmentalists in particular were engaged in unsubtle heart-searching and rancorous debate about whether 'environmentalism' was 'dead',[8] and when the Administration of G. W. Bush remained implacably opposed to the Kyoto Protocol, it was possible to see quite clear signs of 'winning' on climate. It was not that the 'issue' was being won – on most measures the problem was getting worse but the campaigns were working. In July 2005 I wrote:[9]

> *The battle is gradually being won. Not the war but at least the battle to break the logjam in which the US is the biggest plug in the pile. Consider this: the US is isolated over Kyoto, and Kyoto exists – it was not replaced by some US-led alternative and nor did it die from lack of ratification. A growing network of both American States and American Cities are taking unilateral action 'in line with Kyoto' (at least in sympathy with it – action to reduce emissions), effectively starting to do global politics despite and in opposition to the US Federal Administration. Car companies are rushing to produce hybrids – still a small part of the market but a rapidly growing one, and hybrids are being developed across all the main market segments, socially, psychologically and technically. Climate-induced actions are becoming the norm in many industrialized countries: in the UK, for example, with acceptance of wind power.*
>
> *This is a very different picture from a world successfully locked into inaction by a G. W. Bush White House controlled by Exxon. On top of this, Bush's ratings are plumbing new depths, and the Iraq war, inextricably associated with oil, is unpopular in the States.*
>
> *Hybrids are also particularly favoured by the American Washington right wing. Their reasoning is not climate but energy independence. The formula*

espoused by the Detroit Project for some years (www.detroitproject.com) and picked up by Kerry in his campaign has become mainstream. We are seeing what is so often seen in the execution of a U-turn: the opposition is embracing the substance without the rationale. That will eventually come later, once there's no face to be lost. An acceptable American will discover that human-made climate change exists and action is needed.

That American turned out to be Barack Obama. Even then, though, you could see that the opposition knew they were going to lose. The highly intelligent Frank Luntz, widely loathed by American 'progressives' as a Republican pollster, wrote in a leaked and widely circulated memo:

The environment is probably the single issue on which the Republicans in general – and President Bush in particular – are most vulnerable. A caricature has taken hold in the public imagination: Republicans seemingly in the pockets of corporate fat cats who rub their hands together and chuckle maniacally as they plot to pollute America for fun and profit…
The fundamental problem for Republicans when it comes to the environment is that whatever you say is viewed through the prism of suspicion.

When inside information shows your opponent is clearly on the defensive, when potential influential allies that would be important in their winning are joining the other side, and when their proactive strategies are failing, then you know you are winning. The final U-turn often involves them becoming quiet or silent on the topic, talking to others, and agreeing about the problem but not your solution, or accepting the solution but for different reasons (especially if there is a difference of values – see Chapter 3).

STICK TO YOUR ROUTE

Once a campaign starts, chaos and enthusiasm can easily pull it off course. Any issue will offer multiple diversions and 'opportunities' that must be resisted if they take you away from your critical path.

Take the metaphorical campaign route through London using the 'Tube'. The London Underground is large and complex. It offers many possible journeys between its 272 stations – probably too many to even start thinking about.[10] A real issue would offer even more possibilities. The 'red thread' is your path, threaded through 'the issue map'. This is what everyone involved in the campaign has to stick to. Don't spend time in other parts of the 'issue' – they may be relevant, but that's unlikely to help achieve your objective.

Imagine a journey from, say, West Ruislip in north-west London to Borough in central south London. That is the red thread through the map. You have plotted it one step at a time and there are a number of critical steps in this journey. They would include:

- find the station;
- go in;
- buy a ticket;
- board the (right) train;
- change at Bond Street onto the southbound Jubilee Line;
- change at London Bridge onto the southbound Northern Line;
- get off at Borough;
- go upstairs.

Fail at any of these stages and you won't arrive at the objective.

Other trains will come and go and fellow passengers may invite you to join them, say to discuss issues at Swiss Cottage. This could be interesting but, hopefully, you won't go. Journalists may board the train at Green Park and try to ask you about the controversy at Westminster – but London Bridge will still be your focus.

Other routes are possible to the same destination, but you've already researched this as the best. Stick to it. Transport issues extend beyond the Underground, but that is not relevant to this journey.

ORGANIZING MESSAGES: A MESSAGE HIERARCHY

A 'message hierarchy' or ring (Figure 9.2) can be a useful tool to help organize and prioritize conversations and reactive press work. However, it is not a replacement for making a communications strategy from a critical path. Brainstorm strategies – not messages alone (see also CAMPCAT, Chapter 1).

A message 'ring' and hierarchy can:

- Help people who deal with incoming queries to get back to the issue you want most to talk about;
- Acknowledge to allies that their issues are relevant, without losing focus;
- Help in phone-ins, debates or other discussions where you need to show how your work is relevant to other issues, but where you still want to get back to your priority communication points.

It is an internal guide – not something that needs to be published. Construct it from your strategy messages, plus anything you think is likely to come up from the surrounding issue.

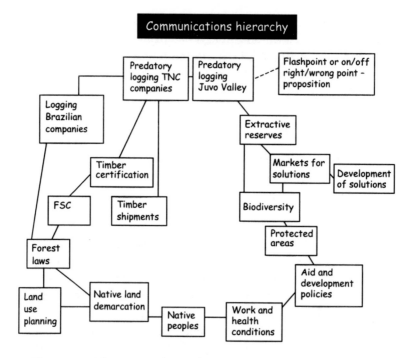

Figure 9.2 *The message hierarchy used in a hypothetical campaign*

If you start from anywhere else, then before you can get there, journalists will have tried to define the issue by dividing it at that point, and you may never make it. Journalists will normally try to cast any issue in the starkest available terms, with the greatest contrast and drama. However unfounded, they will tend to play devil's advocate and can adopt wildly contradictory positions on the same subject in the course of one interview, or a series, or in a series of articles or even editorials.

Put your point of action, your central irreducible proposition, at the top. This is like the keystone, the summit to which you want to always steer the conversation back.

That is one reason why it's important to choose a proposition that really does draw the right/wrong line in exactly where you want to be, at the point of what is/what ought to be, the right-state/wrong-state.

ASSETS AND RESOURCES

A well-planned campaign should start with adequate resources to achieve the objective – if it succeeds in engaging the public. Time or success can enlarge the task so that the campaign, while better established, no longer has the right resources. Some campaigners respond to this by becoming shrill and trying to do more with what they have – a better move is often to analyse what's needed and find a way to expand the resources available.

So conduct a periodic inventory of the resources and assets available to your campaign, and think what can be done with them, but don't accept the status quo as inevitable.

US President Theodore Roosevelt once told Americans: 'Do what you can with what you have, where you are.' Good advice to those who can do nothing strategic, but not good advice to anyone who intends to run a campaign. Think more about what you can do *if* you *change* where you are, or change what you face, or change when things happen – or even, who 'you' are, and what your assets are. To plan solely for targets that are already within reach can lead to failure due to lack of imagination.

Roosevelt also said: 'A man who has never gone to school may steal from a freight car, but if he has a university education, he may steal from the whole railroad.' Transport campaigners note: before trying to change the system it may be necessary to change your assets.

A common failing of 'mature' NGOs is the failure to invest in logistical capacity. They may try, for example, to campaign on marine issues with no ships. Others fail to develop intelligence networks and end up talking to trade bodies or other front organizations instead of getting inside an industry or institution they want to change. Small groups grown larger tend not to invest in the necessary engagement mechanisms, such as direct-marketing capabilities. Intellectual ones used to communicating via publications are likely to need street capacity, such as touring buses, street theatre or other assets to create an intrusive visual presence necessary to set an agenda with events. Most now invest in 'e' or cyber-campaigning but many fail to connect it to what they do in the physical world – one needs to reinforce the other in real time.

WHEN PUBLICITY IS GOOD

Publicity is a good thing when it moves you along your critical path, when it helps persuade or motivate your intended audience. Otherwise, it is bad because it will be wasting resources, taking up an opportunity that could be more usefully used for something else, and, most probably, helping an opponent.

Publicity is good when it results from triggering or reinforcing a frame (see Chapter 1) that leads to your conclusion. It's a bad thing – pushing you backwards – when it supports someone else's framing! So taking part in debates initiated by others may be unavoidable, but it should be minimized and its effect outweighed by events created by you, at a time and place and with a visual message of your own choosing.

It's easy for a media-oriented campaign group to become very busy debating 'the issue' in the media while still being driven backwards, or at least being held stationary. This is especially the case if they are not investing much time and effort in creating events that set the pace or agenda (itself encouraged by under-investment in logistics and or working on too many issues at once), and if they don't have a campaign that is real outside the media.

UNDERSTANDING 'SUPPORT'

The level of support can become a vexed question, but 'support' has many different meanings. In 1990–2003, research[11] showed around 10 per cent of the UK population were committed enough to environmental issues to be prepared to 'stand out' for it. A great majority considered themselves in some way 'environmentally aware' (ranging up to 90 per cent), only about 10 per cent were 'browns' and around 30 per cent were 'environmentally sensitive' or 'persuadable'. This last group generally did not want to be seen to join 'pressure-group activities' unless they were fashionable, but might join effective lobbying, or make significant lifestyle purchases.[12]

How did this landscape of feelings towards the environment translate into other forms of support? By the end of the period, the National Trust had about 3,000,000 members (around 1 in 20) and the RSPB 1,000,000. More activist organizations had smaller engaged support bases.[13]

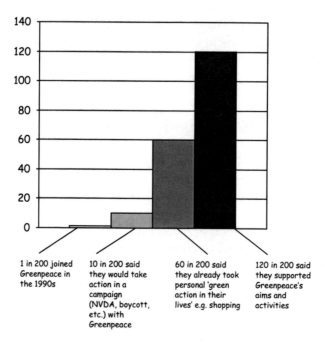

Figure 9.3 *Greenpeace supporter numbers*

In the case of Greenpeace, around 6 in 10 people – 120 out of every 200 – said they 'supported' its aims. They tended to indicate similar agreement with the aims of other well-known environmental groups. This sensitivity was rarely mobilized unless they were confronted with a request that reinforced, rather than challenged, their lifestyle. Around 3 in 10 (60 in every 200) claimed to take some personal environmental action, such as shopping for green products. About 1 in 20 (10 in 200) said they would be prepared to take part in a Greenpeace campaign. Only 1 in 200, however, actually joined Greenpeace as subscribing supporters (see Figure 9.3).

Within the 1 in 200, a minority were 'dug in', fully expecting a pitched struggle with the forces of politics and big business who could be relied on to destroy much that was good about the planet. A majority had reached the same conclusions but more reluctantly. They still hoped that reason, democratic processes and decency would prevail, but believed that experience showed that vigorous campaigns were usually necessary.

This shows that the simple 'supporter' category is of limited use in communications. Many supportive people are outside the 'subscribing membership', and within it, there are significant differences. Campaign designers need to be aware of this – and to think about how to engage all those supportive people beyond the paying membership. The internet, for example, makes it almost free to maintain and service a list for an electronic newsletter.

Lastly, don't let critics talk down your support, especially in terms of legitimacy, and don't let enthusiasts run away with the idea that agreement automatically translates into activism.

DEALING WITH DISASTERS

Disasters generally come to the attention of campaign groups for one of two reasons. The first and commonest are disasters seen as 'issue opportunities'. The second are those that strike the organization itself.

External disasters

External disasters, especially 'acts of God' with no attribution of human failings, are not usually good 'opportunities', but they may change the picture (see 'Reading the weather and the tea leaves', page 276), and the task then becomes one of rapidly understanding what it means in terms of strategy. As a rule, I would advise against being the first to say what it means in 'issue terms'. A rain-induced mudslide engulfing people in their homes is probably not a good time or place to start making points about climate change or settlement planning, while the human misery and the rescue effort are still ongoing. Relevance is not, on its own, a sufficient justification. Similarly, if you have the assets to help, then help but do not seek to exploit it – otherwise you may fall foul of the 'scandal equation' (see page 200).

When Hurricane Katrina devastated New Orleans in 2005, it was an event long anticipated by climate campaigners – a climatic disaster in the Continental United States – as likely to change American views of 'global warming'. In an edition of the *Campaign Strategy Newsletter*,[14] I argued 'groups who spend a lot of time "problem-driving" would be wise to be cautious and stay out of the frame'. I advised letting others raise links to climate change and if groups were unavoidably asked for their views, then consider these guidelines, which would also apply to other issues:

- If there's an attribution issue (in this case, was it something to do with climate change?), it's best to stick to one unassailable – or at least the strongest – link of evidence and avoid mentioning anything weaker or more disputed.
- Ask questions, seek answers. This is very hard to rebut and aligns the campaigners with the media, because it's what the media are partly there to do themselves.
- Be seen to help – if you really can help – preferably visually. But don't make a big issue about it. Let it be discovered. You have to mean it – the people you meet on the ground are your real reward. Any media it creates has to be a secondary benefit.
- Remember that your finely divided policy world is not like the public conversation triggered by a disaster like Katrina.
- Lastly, if there are things that society is thinking but aren't being said, it may be a rare occasion where simply making a statement is the right thing to do. This is where banner hanging on national monuments or advertisements and so on (or an online petition) can come into their own. Speak directly, not through the media. It is vital, though, that it gives a voice to a common feeling. Shrill statements from the margins just remind people that a marginal concern is marginal.

As it was, Katrina did have significant consequences for politics of the climate in America, and these came from a rather unexpected quarter. While the public agencies struggled with Katrina, Wal-Mart used its stores and logistics capacity to give significant and much praised help. Numerous authors later described the 'personal epiphany' of Wal-Mart CEO Lee Scott, who turned the company in a greener direction in late 2005. For him, Hurricane Katrina was 'a key personal moment'.

The online business magazine *ClimateChangeCorp* reported[15] that he had:

> *Done an about-face on what he says was initial 'scepticism of the company's environmental critics'. The idea of a Wal-Mart environment programme, he says, had sounded 'more like a public relations campaign than substance'. Scott has taken strong stances in his new commitment, even directing his new zeal against*

critics of climate change science. 'This used to be controversial, but the science is in and it's overwhelming,' he insists, in stark contrast to the Bush administration's continued position that the evidence behind global warming predictions is weak.

Disasters of the other kind

The biggest disaster for any not-for-profit cause group is not a setback, or even getting something wrong, but an act of hypocrisy or one against its values (see the 'glass onion', page 262). In 2006 Campaign Strategy Ltd conducted a survey of 25 leading NGOs and allied organizations active on climate change and asked them about their policies and practices on air travel.[16] They nearly all responded and the (very variable) results were posted online.[17] This is an example of an issue where some NGOs are very vulnerable to being perceived as 'do what we say, not what we do' organizations.

If your organization is hit by a real 'reputational' disaster, the best advice is to follow the PR staple of C-A-R: Concern, Action, Reassurance. Here's an account from Jeff Randall in the *Daily Telegraph*:

> *In Britain, the classic lesson in how to handle a catastrophe was given by Sir Michael Bishop, British Midland's chairman, in January 1989, after his airline's flight 092, a Boeing 737 jet, had ploughed into an embankment of the M1 in Leicestershire, killing 47 people and injuring 74.*
>
> *Bishop went immediately to the scene, took personal responsibility (it later emerged that the accident was caused by mechanical failure and pilot error) and dealt with the media. He was reassuring and authoritative. A weaker man might have hidden behind the need for an official inquiry. Instead, Bishop displayed a masterful understanding of adversity leadership: sympathetic, transparent and helpful. Despite the enormity of the disaster, public confidence in British Midland was retained'.[18]*

As Nathan Skinner points out[19] on the website Strategic Risk:

> *The response was quick and Bishop offered himself up to the media inquiries. He filled the information void with his own feelings of compassion for the victims and he accepted personal responsibility and told the press what he was going to do about it. His emotional TV interviews from the scene of the crash were accepted as genuine and he received the sympathy of the media and public.*

Skinner and Randall also give some examples of how not to do it, such as the Tylenol case and Trafigura and toxic waste.

The point is that even before Bishop knew the facts he went to the scene and was on the phone to radio stations acknowledging a disaster and expressing sympathy: concern. He was at the scene (action) and committed the company to further actions. Only then could it be time to give reassurance, such as the fact that such air accidents are rare. Whatever you do, don't make the 'experts' mistake' of starting with 'reassurance' as in 'of course we are sympathetic but these things are very rare and people shouldn't worry': you will seem evasive, uncaring and arguing against legitimate emotion.

NGOs are unlikely to face such a dramatic disaster, but if you do have a problem, don't try to suppress it. Admit it as soon as you can, be open and honest and take responsibility, express appropriate concern and say what you are going to do about it, starting today. Once that is accepted, you can reassure.

Lastly, if in any doubt, before reacting as if something is a disaster, check with someone outside the organization. Campaigners strongly committed to their issue can easily lose perspective and see a major setback as cause for organizational self-flagellation. If you are the only victims, then it's really a solely internal disaster, and you are not under the same expectation to explain it in public. On the other hand, as a friend of mine in PR says: 'I know when we're really in trouble when I hear the client saying something like "let's keep this in perspective".'

SEEING CHANGE

Change is the name of the game for all campaigns, but it can be harder to see than one might imagine. For example the change leading to the 'inevitable consequence' (see page 127) in a critical path may not be very noticeable but is the most significant development.

In the case of the famous Kyoto Protocol of the Climate Convention, Russia's agreement to sign up in 2004 was a critical change. It meant that the main attempt of the nay sayers in the US to wreck the international process by keeping the US out of the Protocol would be defeated. Because there was a formal set rule for ratification (by country's share of emissions), in this case campaigners knew the significance of getting Russia on board. Typically, however, this attracted little media attention because it was undramatic and hit few 'news values' (see page 193). It was reported in a UK broadsheet newspaper under 'In Brief' in just 50 words.

In the case of non-institutional changes, it can be even harder to see change. In their huge study[20] of long-term values shifts in many countries, Inglehart and Welzel show that values shifts that make other changes inevitable may precede institutional change by a considerable time. Exactly how long that lag is is dependent on many factors particular to the country, its culture and the dynamics of the institutions. For instance legalization of gay marriages in The Netherlands did not come until 2000, by which time disapproval of homosexuality had fallen to half its 1981 level. Care therefore needs to be taken when drawing inferences about values, attitudes or beliefs from the sort of institutional changes, such as new laws, which get written down in history books.

Perhaps of more practical importance is the failure to notice change across values groups, or to imagine that it is possible.

The case of Britain and 4 × 4s

Less than a decade ago, 4 × 4s (sports utility vehicles (SUVs)) were riding high on British streets and prominent in the lexicon of aspirational goods. In 2004 an article entitled 'The 4 × 4 is here to stay – On and off-road'[21] appeared on the Society of Motor Manufacturers and Traders website.

It stated:

> *Sales of 4 × 4 vehicles are rising. Last year six per cent of the new car market were 4 × 4 off-roaders … the market for Sports Utility Vehicles and large 4 × 4s has more than doubled in ten years.*

In such circumstances it is hard to imagine that large-scale change in the opposite direction can possibly come quickly, but 4 × 4s had become the accessible Demon No 1 for climate campaigners, so they began to campaign against them. In 2004 the tiny but creative British group Alliance Against Urban 4 × 4s (www.stopurban4x4s.org.uk) copied a tactic from anti-SUV campaigns in New York and began putting what looked just like parking tickets (infringement notices) on the windscreens of 4 × 4s declaring 'Poor Vehicle Choice'. Within a few years a wave of derision hit 4 × 4s in the UK, and they became déclassé, at the same time as the government started to raise road tax on 4 × 4s and fuel prices rose.

By 2007 the *Daily Mail* reported:[22]

> *Sales of 4 × 4 'Chelsea Tractors' have plummeted by a fifth as fuel prices soar and motorists are hit by hefty gas-guzzler taxes. New registrations of 4 × 4s last month dropped by more than 18 per cent compared with May 2007.*

By 2009 Richard Headland, the editor of *Which? Car* stated[23]:

> *A previously healthy market for 4 × 4s has virtually collapsed and some people have finally realized that an off-roader isn't the perfect car for the school run. Expensive, gas-guzzling cars like 4 × 4s are becoming socially unacceptable – unless you're a farmer.*

As of June 2009, sales of new 4 × 4s were down by nearly a third on 2008. 4 × 4 maker Dodge sold 91 per cent fewer vehicles, Jeep 79 per cent less, Chrysler 77 per cent less and

Land Rover 50 per cent less. The desocialization of 4 × 4s began well before the UK government hiked taxes on them, before fuel price rises and well before the recession struck, but all these factors probably combined to drive down sales. It is the speed with which this happened, though, that is remarkable – remarkable because it only took a few years, while many policymakers and almost all pundits seem to assume any significant change in social behaviours is going to take generations. (In the US, the Hummer went out of production in 2010.)

The case of England and recycling

In a country like the UK, household recycling is now utterly 'normal', but it was not always the case.[24] Throughout the 1980s and 1990s Britain recycled far less domestic waste than many comparable northern European countries and politicians and officials got used to assuming this would always be the case. Examples of higher rates elsewhere were dismissed on the logic that these people were different: you'd never get the British to do what the Dutch, Swedes or Germans did for example.

Assuming that we now lived permanently in a 'throwaway society', government planned accordingly. The English government committed itself to using incineration to burn waste in 2004. It then erected a policy stockade around its decision under the banner 'Energy from Waste'. The then Environment Minister Elliot Morley urged councils to 'press ahead urgently' with the task of approving planning applications for new facilities.[25] Government produced a study rubbishing concerns that incinerators might be bad for health, and later put out a tender for PR companies to build public support for the 'energy from waste' policy. Companies saw a new market in becoming 'energy from waste' firms.

Yet by 2010 there were cases across England of councils finding that recycling rates achieved by householders so far exceeded what government had assumed possible that costly waste incinerators planned on those assumptions were no longer needed. Surrey abandoned plans for two such plants, and in other places councils were searching around for waste to import in order to keep existing incinerators in operation.[26] What had happened was simply that increased local authority efforts at promoting household recycling had paid off in behaviour change.[27]

Friends of the Earth, which has long warned of a waste-creating 'lock-in' tied to 'public–private finance' contracts that make it very costly or 'impossible' to escape from the policy, could be permitted a quiet 'told you so'. All campaigners, however, should look at such examples and consider the implications for their issues.

What should alarm campaigners is that even as late as 2009, the Department of Environment, Food and Rural Affairs (DEFRA – the English government's environment department) looked ahead to 2020 and still assumed a one per cent annual increase in 'waste arisings' (that is 'residual' waste left over after some has been recycled or otherwise dealt with). DEFRA consultants imagined that recycling rates would not go above 50 per cent.[28] In reality, rates of recycling now often easily exceeded 50 per cent and the total waste arisings were falling, not increasing.

Even after these events, the Environment Agency for England and Wales still declared on its website: 'We live in a throw-away society.' The mental lock-in of framing and group think is an even more powerful effect than the institutional one of misjudged contracts and investments.

All this is important because politics is 'the art of the possible', and what politicians and their adviser imagine is possible often becomes reality because they adopt policies calibrated by that level of imagination.

There are other cases where change has been dramatic. From 2006 to 2009, for example, there was a 48 per cent reduction in the number of plastic bags given out in England, following voluntary action by retailers to make it harder to obtain them, which itself followed campaigns against plastic bags. Similarly, compliance with smoking bans has been so great that the practice is now almost extinct in indoor public places in the UK, after only a few years. The strident debates over 'freedoms' and anticipation that smokers would simply refuse to change their behaviour, which for years accompanied any discussion of a ban, all dispersed like yesterday's smoke.

How we misread change

As well as false frames sustained by 'group think', we may misread change because we don't see it, and we imagine that what we are seeing is representative. One reason for this is that people from the different motivational values groups (see Chapter 3) tend to mix, socialize and discuss things much more with their own group than with others. Hence the 'well everyone *I* know thinks' or 'I don't know *anyone* who...' and '*everyone* these days is saying...' school of argument. As described in Chapter 3, campaigners tend to be from the inner-directed Pioneers, and they simply do not see what the Prospectors or Settlers are doing, or mix with them enough to understand what they are thinking. This can mean that they do not see the changes happening in other groups, and what seems incredibly important to campaigners, news journalists and the political classes, therefore, is really only of great interest to the Pioneers. 'Issues' exist mostly in a Pioneer bubble. It seems likely that this massively skews the perspective of campaigners about what is going on in society, and is even causing them to overlook the potential of change they have initiated themselves.

If campaigners exist mostly inside a Pioneer bubble, then the news media and particularly political commentators exist in a bubble inside a bubble, one that feeds on opinion polls rather than measures of behaviour, and treats political debate as if it writes the route-plan for society. In reality, politics as reported in the news is not most people's reality. In 2010 BBC's Radio 5 demonstrated this when it despatched reporter Stephen

Chittenden to spend a week without papers, TV, radio or website news, relying instead on social media to find out what was going on (Twitter was most informative, Facebook least so).

Emulation and norming

The rapidity of desocialization of 4 × 4s in the UK was almost certainly down to them falling out of fashion with Prospectors. The 'unexpected' totality of recycling behaviour was probably due to a spread from Pioneers (who have long adopted it as 'ethical') to both Prospectors and Settlers, prompted by new visual cues and signs (provision of separate recycling bins for kerbside collection) and the advent of rules from authority (possible fines if you did not use the right bin and so on).

As described in Chapter 3, new behaviours (such as avoiding 4 × 4s or doing recycling) start with the inner-directed Pioneers (see page 72) and, if they spread, move to Prospectors and finally then Settlers. This change can be difficult for campaigners to see, because it is the behaviour that is spreading while overt support for 'the issue' does not.

10

OLD MEDIA

NEW MEDIA

THE CHANGING NEWS CHANNELS

Campaigners tend to be news watchers. So are politicians and journalists. But most people aren't, and only a few read the 'serious' newspapers. In 2001[1] only 16 per cent of UK people regarded themselves as 'regular current affairs watchers'.

When this is overlooked in planning communication strategies, failure often follows – the rest of the population is better reached by using 'non-news' media. Overall, campaigners would do well to put less emphasis on national broadcast news or newspapers, and more on features, magazines, entertainment broadcasting, internet, texting and direct communications.

Conventional TV, radio and newspaper news remains important to the world of decision-makers – it's effectively their local media – but it's not a very good way to reach the 'public'. So to influence them and to influence events, it's generally better to use other channels to engage audiences, and then use the mainstream news media to alert politicians to the issue if you need to.

For decades, fewer and fewer people have watched mainstream broadcast news or read daily newspapers. A 2001 survey[2] by Ian Hargreaves and James Thomas showed that national newspaper readership had fallen to 31.6 million in the UK (68 per cent of adults). UK regional press readership increased to 39.4 million, 85 per cent coverage of all adults, of whom nearly half do not read a national daily newspaper.[3]

The Newspaper Association of America reports[4] adult readership of daily newspapers (at least once-weekly) fell from 80 per cent in 1964 to 55 per cent in 1997. In 1996, newspaper readership was falling in 10 of the 15 EU countries. In that year UK newspaper readership fell by 3.8 per cent, while Irish readership declined by 4.4 per cent.[5]

The British National Readership Survey showed that in the 12 months to June 2009, only 42 per cent of people over 15 read a national daily newspaper, compared with 72 per cent of people in the 12 months to June 1978.[6]

Newspaper organizations point out that in the UK, with its national distribution system able to reach more-or-less the whole population next day, and with 75 per cent of adults reading at least one paper a week, newspapers remain a potent way to communicate. Newspapers claim to be the only medium that can both achieve such a reach and be open for new 'campaign' ideas as late as the evening before – they are, however, referring to buying advertising, which is rarely affordable for NGOs. At the time of writing, newspapers are in general decline, and it remains to be seen whether they will make a post-paper format pay.

Sixty-five per cent of those in the Hargreaves–Thomas survey said their main source of news was TV, compared with 16 per cent for radio, 15 per cent for newspapers and 2 per cent for the internet. In 2009 the Office of National Statistics reported that 'news was the most popular type of television programme viewed in England in 2007–2008, watched by 72 per cent of adults aged 16 and over'. The internet was the preferred news medium, however, among younger ethnic minority groups. In 2009 the Pew Research Center found[7] 'the internet' had overtaken newspapers as American's source of national and international news (with much higher internet usage amongst the young – see Figure 10.1.)

The Iraq war brought 'blogging' into the mainstream, with hundreds of thousands of visitors to *Dear Raed*, a personal account of life in Baghdad. Under-represented in 'mainstream' US news but over-represented in the military, black Americans have increasingly used the internet for news since the 2003 Iraq war.

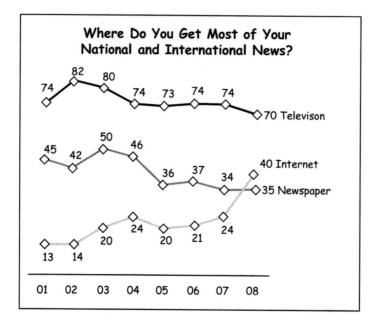

Figure 10.1 *Changing news sources in the US, 2001–2008*

Source: Pew Research Center

In Britain young adults (16–24) have been termed 'digital natives' by the government's Department of Culture, and show quite different patterns of media usage from older generations. Here's how the report[8] 'Digital Britain' described it:

- *Young adults prize above all communication (instant, personal, reciprocal) with their peers, which leads to greater use of mobiles (text, voice) and the internet (emailing, instant messaging, social networking) more than other demos. Their consumption of lean-back TV and radio is declining. Few young adults read newspapers because interest in news is low and supplied by the internet.*

- *Young adults are the earliest adopters of new technology but only if it is free or very cheap to use. An example is watching TV on mobiles: the technology ticks all the behavioural boxes (it is personalized, it can be accessed anytime, it can be meshed with other media consumption), but cost is cited as the biggest barrier by young adults (45 per cent say it's too expensive, 37 per cent simply have no interest in it, 39 per cent say their handset is not compatible and 32 per cent say their screen is too small).*

- *Social networking, used by 70 per cent of young adults compared to 41 per cent generally, exemplifies the media consumption of young adults: free to use, creating an online presence on Facebook, MySpace or Bebo makes the self public in order to connect to friends.*

- *Media-meshing is evidence of the interest in communicating and socialising by a lean-forward rather than lean-back generation, rather than of a low attention span.*

Unmediated 'own news' use of the internet by campaigners – such as www.indymedia.org and and www.webactive.com – has developed alongside social networking. The UK site www.fairsay.com was founded by Duane Raymond, previously an 'ecampaigner' with Oxfam, in 2004 and is a mine of information about how campaigners make use of 'online' for disseminating news, and organizing and building support.

Web-only commercial magazines and news sites such as www.salon.com may more readily publish information that major political or corporate interests would prefer not to see the light of day. Independent web-based news networks that challenge the old tend to have specialist agendas, such as www.opendemocracy.net.

Sites devoted to publishing what others would like to suppress include www.wikileaks. org and Information Clearing House, at www.informationclearinghouse.info. See also www.alternet.org, Index On Censorship at www.indexonline.org and News Alternative at www.asia-stat.com.

Campaigners need to be aware of:

- Changes in news consumption, including the growth of web-based and other new media news sourcing;
- The democratization of news-generation through blogging, social networks such as twitter and Facebook and 'indymedia';
- The growth of participation-news, where the boundaries between journalist and audience break down; and
- An increase in 'news' outlets prepared to publish rumour or reports that authority would rather suppress, making verification easier and total suppression much more difficult (against this, mainstream media is increasingly dominated by corporate interests and ownership is more and more concentrated).

Taken together, the last three factors bode well for bringing things to public attention, but do not make it easier to bring them to *wide* public attention unless campaigners can break these stories into more mainstream media, and into large-scale networks.

News generation has been 'democratized' in the sense that the system is now more porous, but as Nick Davies has argued in *Flat Earth News*, the content of news has narrowed, making 'news' as a whole a less and less representative window on the world. In part this is because a downside of the growth of online communications has been the decline in resources available to newspapers, and to some extent radio and TV, due to the general failure to capture advertising revenue. This has led to fewer journalists investigating and checking stories. In 2009, The Investigation Fund, set up to promote investigative reporting, stated[9] that some 60 British local newspapers had closed in the previous 12 months, and over 4,000 jobs in the UK media had been lost between July 2008 and January 2009, including at least 1000 journalists. According to the Fund, 'The average Fleet Street journalist now fills three times as much editorial space as he or she did in 1985.' It pointed to research commissioned for Nick Davies' book *Flat Earth News*,[10] which found 'only 12 per cent of stories in Britain's quality newspapers show evidence that they have been thoroughly checked' and '54 per cent of stories in Britain's quality newspapers are wholly or mainly constructed from PR material'. While some of these will be 'feeds' from campaigners, many more, of course, come from the press offices of government and business, whether they arrive as an old-fashioned press release, or filtering through paid bloggers and other participants in social networks.

On the other side of the equation, some newspapers and news groups have managed to build considerable and even profitable 'communities' of users online, and sometimes these have led to campaigns where the boundaries between media and public, campaigners and reporters blur into what some call 'disintermediation'. Strategist Rick Le Coyte says, 'A trend is developing for the more hungry news consumers to blend traditional and newer sources of news.'[11] In the Trafigura case, *The Guardian* played the role of victim, with protest from traditional and new forms of media amplifying each other to force a change by the company's lawyers.

The 2009 Trafigura waste-dumping case involved readers of the London-based *Guardian* newspaper who used Twitter, Google's SideWiki and Wikileaks to side-step repressive use of legal injunctions by UK lawyers, which had initially prevented *The Guardian* from reporting a scientific study (the Minton Report) into the consequences of European oil waste dumped in Africa.[12] The case went back to at least 2006 and involved investigations by Greenpeace and the BBC.[13]

The 2010 version of the annual Edelman Trust Baromoter[14] reported:

> *Overall the only institution to lose trust around the globe is media. Over the last three years, trust in media has fallen from 48 to 45 per cent among older informed publics. With the dispersion of traditional media's authority and the rise of opinion journalism, trust in the institution as a whole has waned.*

The good news for NGO campaigners is that trust in NGOs to do what has right has gradually climbed since 2001, lying around 55 per cent in US, UK, Germany, France, India and China. The most fundamental rule for campaigners therefore remains to tell the truth.

CODING AND HOW TO AVOID IT

When hearing a story on the radio or watching a report on the TV, people often say: 'We've heard all this before.' Often, they haven't, but think they have because it *sounds* the same as previous stories. It has the same tune and the same phrases because of editing and formatting.

Studies by Jacquie Burgess[15] showed the format of environmental news created a weary sense of 'we've heard it all before' and then a feeling of powerlessness, cynicism and a distrust of news sources.

Coding is the construction of stories, especially news, according to a series of clichés or set formulae. Examples are equating environmentalists with protesting, no matter what they do; 'wrapping' disasters with a sign off about exaggerated claims; or referring to any hazard as a 'scare'.

These codes not only make everything sound familiar but also, when added together, suggest that problems are either insoluble or certainly out of reach for ordinary people. Interview people who are actually members of pressure groups,[16] who have heard from the organization how campaigning can work, and you find that they are much more positive about the possibility of change than are otherwise similar non-members.

Messages run through the same channels tend to adopt the familiar cadences and tones of those channels. For example, steps in publicizing a report might be:

- Campaigner gets the idea;
- Consultant researches and writes a report;
- Project group discusses it and writes its own version for public consumption (recoding);
- Press office asks for a summary and bullet points (recoding);
- Press office writes press release, anticipates the principal target news outlet and their interests (for example, women's angles) and negotiates it with campaigner (recoding);
- Press conference – the campaign director presents it and gives own spin (recoding);
- Reporters take notes, get reaction from other parties, write story (recoding);
- Editor cuts down the story, changes the lead to fit in with another story and writes a headline (recoding);
- Newspaper publishes story;
- Radio editor reads story;
- Radio news carries its own version of the story (recoding);
- Listener hears it, thinks 'I've heard that before.'

Ways to avoid recoding:

- Communicate directly wherever possible;
- Communicate in pictures – they are less susceptible to recoding: let the picture tell the story;
- Create *events* that are reported or shown, not arguments, which are most vulnerable to reframing.

AMBIENT MEDIA AND NETWORKING

As people have increasingly 'switched off' to paid-for media, advertising has crept onto all sorts of unconventional surfaces. Many techniques have been borrowed from campaigning or art. Campaigners spent the 1980s projecting laser messages onto the sides of ships and nuclear power stations, but by the 1990s it had become an advertising staple. Cliff- and island-wrapping artists such as Christo were co-opted into advertising, along with the natural environment itself. Advertisers went back to earlier eras by painting large parts of buildings – even entire streets – with slogans, in what Naomi Klein describes as 'building takeover'.[17] Invasion of the civic or public space by corporate messaging is now an issue worldwide.

Social networking sites are the most obvious 'off the shelf' channels available for campaigners to use in networking, but don't be misled that being signed up to a social networking site like Facebook (400 million users in 2010) or Myspace (100 million) means that you are well connected. Large networks like these are of course made up of small networks each having differing demographics, interests and motivations. Effective use of social networks like these still largely depends on what else campaigns do, away from the social network channel itself, to make a presence there interesting. Although the picture changes rapidly, Duane Raymond at Fairsay.com and others have found that while email has remained the most effective online way to mobilize support (for example www.moveon. org and www.avaaz.org) and help focus attention for a short while (for example interacting with 'news'), social networks like Facebook have been most effective at helping build and sustain interest among supporters.

After Barack Obama was elected US president, a torrent of books and media analyses highlighted the 'use of the internet' in his strategy.[18] In reality Obama's election strategy (see also case study, page 311) involved a lot of old school community mobilization ('organizing' in America) facilitated by online networking tools to encourage real world political activities targeted at specific groups.[19] Obama had a presence on the other major networking sites and on sites that served to network particular audiences, for example Black Planet.[20] The Obama campaign also managed to cut out much of the 'framing' power of TV news by making more of its communication direct, in a combination of offline and online (some call the successful resonance of online and offline attention or behaviours 'inline').

'Ambient' media simply means carrying messages with everyday things around you. It stems from the same thought as word-of-mouth communication now popular in mainstream advertising. For example, attractive actors are paid to go into bars and talk loudly about the virtues of particular drinks.

Marketing consultant Sean Larkins[21] cites the use of London taxi drivers by the South African Tourist Authority. Rather than spend a limited budget on high-cost advertising, the South Africans took a group of these inveterate professional gossips on holiday to South Africa, then sent them home again. Of course, they talked about it to passengers in their cabs – again, and again and again. With a final twist, the drivers picked were those mainly working the route to London Heathrow, whose passengers were likely to be frequent fliers.

In *The Tipping Point*,[22] Malcolm Gladwell writes about the horse ride of Paul Revere, who alerted American colonists to the oncoming British Army with a dramatic 'ride through the night'. Two key factors in his effectiveness were drama (it was done at dead of night) and his role in the community – Gladwell says he was the man with the 'biggest Rolodex' – a networker extraordinaire, and a helping maven (expert). Revere was a member of all the relevant social groups – one of the very few super-connected people in the social network:

This is surely part of the explanation for why Paul Revere's message was so powerful on the night of his midnight ride. News of the British march did not come by fax, or by means of a group email. It wasn't broadcast on the nightly news, surrounded by commercials. It was carried by a man, a volunteer, riding on a cold night with no personal agenda other than a concern for the liberty of his peers.

The less well-known William Dawes also made a ride at the same time as Revere, but without as much success. He was a less well-connected person, not as sociable, not a networker, and he rode in the afternoon (a bad move, since most of the people were out working in the fields). A ride in the afternoon also lacked drama.

ORGANIZED GOSSIP

As publics have trusted government and business less, and at the same time have become more aware that most 'messages' have a purpose behind them, suspicion of paid-for 'communication' of any type, increases. Consequently, there's more and more commercial interest in PR and 'word-of-mouth' communication.

Enticing the media to cover an issue in a particular way has long been a delicate speciality of campaign groups – the mainstream media industry is now having to catch up in order to reach a wised-up general public.

A 1990 case involved an illustrated toilet roll (subject: Britain – Dirty Man of Europe) and two reports. The toilet rolls were designed to stimulate gossip.

Green NGOs approached Media Natura to puncture UK government PR around a forthcoming environment White Paper, '*This Common Inheritance*'. In 1989 the Government had proposed a programme of eco-taxes, to fight the next election on 'the quality of life in the broadest sense',[23] which would be 'the big issue of the next decade'.[24] Minister Chris Patten said his White Paper would 'set out our environmental agenda for the rest of this century'.

By February 1990, however, the idea of legislation was dropped until after the next election,[25] and by July the *Daily Telegraph*[26] declared the draft content a 'damp squib'. Amid worsening economic news, it had been subject to a thousand cuts by government departments such as energy, transport and industry. Having been loudly talked up, the White Paper was very quietly talked down. The general impression of sweeping change created in the first wave of publicity was still likely to frame public perceptions.

To ensure that it got a far more critical reception, Media Natura produced three pieces of communication aimed at different audiences.[27] To stimulate gossip, the 'chattering classes' were targeted using colour-illustrated toilet rolls, printed with '17 reasons why Britain is still the Dirty Man Of Europe'. These used the very 1980s 'hook' of 'Britain – Dirty Man of Europe', to reawaken an established framing and anchor the debate to actual environmental performance rather than political spin. The rolls were distributed by hand, to executive media offices, politicians, journalists, socialites and gossip mongers. Some were delivered with a neat label to the front desk, others were smuggled into Ministerial toilets or boardrooms and left to be discovered. The objective was to stimulate conversation. As they were carefully packaged in a colourful design of European flags with a message that invited unwrapping, it was unlikely that anyone would simply throw them away.

Next a plain unpublicized report, published without a press release, entitled *The Great Car Economy and the Quality of Life* was distributed to political correspondents and editorial writers. It attempted an elite 'framing' in terms of the Conservative Party's own policy choices. It made no claims but simply introduced an angle that, when the time came, might be echoed in media comment.

Lastly, published on the day before the White Paper so that it was in the press on the day, and to provide ammunition for questioning of the government by journalists, came a very detailed report fleshing out the 17 reasons in some 60 pages *'Why Britain Remains The Dirty Man of Europe'.*[28] A subsequent newspaper cartoon showed a man hesitating in front of a recycling bin, in which there were three slots: 'white paper', 'green paper' and 'government White Paper'.

The power of word-of-mouth or face-to-face communication lies in trust: people are more likely to value the opinions of people they know. With the arrival of the internet, particularly social networking sites like Facebook, MySpace and Twitter that are built around the concept of 'friends' (but also message boards and sites that offer consumer reviews), the volume of gossip has been turned up to 11.

The potential reach and relative novelty of exploiting social media grapevines for campaigns is significant but they are not easy to organize. Furthermore, and perhaps partly as a result of increased online noise but also because the public are aware of the encroachment of commercial interests into their conversations between friends, trust in 'friends and peers', as measured by 2010 Edelman Trust Barometer (www.edelman.com/trust/2010/) has recently declined.

On the other hand, trust in NGOs – already strong in regions such as the UK and Latin America – has grown, while that of government and business has declined. So campaign organizations are in a strong position to exploit new media gossip if they remain mindful of communications strategy basics: an understanding of audience motivations, respecting existing conversations and an appreciation of the way these channels work.

MONITORING TRUTH AND BIAS IN THE MEDIA

Organizations that specifically set out to counteract media bias and to monitor standards include Fairness and Accuracy in Reporting (FAIR) and the Center for Public Integrity (both US) (www.publicintegrity.org), and Flat Earth News (www.flatearthnews.net) and Media Lens (both UK).

Started in 1986, FAIR (www.fair.org) works with activists and journalists and says it maintains 'a regular dialogue with reporters at news outlets across the country ... to encourage the public to contact media with their concerns, to become media activists rather than passive consumers of news'.

FAIR aims to 'expose neglected news stories and defend working journalists when they are muzzled'. It believes that 'structural reform is ultimately needed to break up the dominant media conglomerates'.CounterSpin[29] is FAIR's weekly radio show, broadcast on over 125 commercial radio stations across the US and Canada, and on the internet. The Center for Public Integrity aims to 'produce original investigative journalism about significant public issues to make institutional power more transparent and accountable'. It raises donations to make itself financially independent and generates 'high-quality, accessible investigative reports, databases, and contextual analysis on issues of public importance'.

UK-based Media Lens – 'correcting for the distorted vision of the corporate media' – is at www.medialens.org. It pursues specific instances of what it sees as incomplete or inaccurate broadcasting and frequently engages in public email exchanges with media editors.

Historically many news 'sources' were controlled by wealthy individuals and some still are – Rupert Murdoch's News Corporation' being the obvious example – but increasingly they are business consortia, and their editorial content and news agenda broadly reflect their political and business interests, or simply reflect the prejudices of their readers. Among UK newspapers, the only one owned by anything remotely similar to its readers is *The Guardian*, which is owned by a trust.

One of the best-known UK media studies team is probably the Glasgow University Media Group.[30] It takes issue with theoretical post-modernist communications studies that focus on how people 'construct their own meaning' for media. As a result of these ideas, say Greg Philo and David Miller, 'there can be no assessments on grounds of accuracy/truth'.[31] They say:

> *There is a silence in most media and cultural studies about the consequences of popular culture and the media. There are very few analyses of the content of the press or television, and of the influence which these can have on public belief and understanding.*

Their own work has examined the influence of media on understanding of breast cancer, food hazards, bovine spongiform encephalitis (BSE), migration and race. The less academic (although penetrating) analysis by Nick Davies in *Flat Earth News*[32] should be on the reading list of any campaigner. It exposes the 'perfect storm' in which the rise of the internet, changing management values and business strategies have created a culture of low budget 'churnalism' in which accuracy, checking and often the truth have been sacrificed in favour of a narrowing and increasingly conservative news agenda based increasingly on 'feeds' from official and other sources rather than first-hand investigation. His website carries updates.

NEW MEDIA

Digital media and interactivity[33] are fracturing audiences as they globalize. In the early 1990s, the average momentary audience per UK TV channel was 350,000, but by 2003 it was 23,000, and heading lower,[34] a tenfold reduction.

The network, or new, economy (originally called the information economy) refers to value created in trade of goods or services because they are networked – that is, connected together – or because of what is known rather than used up.

In a network economy, potential value increases with the network, the resource becoming both more valuable and cheaper the more it gets used; the reverse of non-networked resources. Business strategies differ from those for non-networked economies. Networks are not new, but information technology coupled with dematerialization[35] may transform much economic activity into a network economy. Thinking this would happen almost overnight promoted the dot.com bubble, but it would be a mistake to conclude from that that new media or the network economy will not happen.

In the past, most campaigns have conformed to the old industrial design model of design > build > sell (that is, design, build and launch). The newer 'info-com' model is sell > build > redesign. The best-known example is software floated onto the web in 'beta' form, for users to work with and redesign.

The classic engagement sequence is broadly: awareness > engagement > action. Direct action by groups such as Greenpeace and Earth First! broke with this format by making *action* the starting point. The internet now offers *engagement* as a starting point. This works where knowledge of cause and problem are saturated, but opportunity to take effective action is limited.

The channel primarily gives agency rather than information. This invites a completely different and non-linear style of campaign design. In the end, it changes most campaign communication from 'we've been' ('we did it, look what we achieved, give us your backing') to 'let's go together'. The immediacy, intimacy and interactivity of media such as email invite a rethink of the temporal nature of campaigns – how they are planned and conducted in real time.

The Yes Men (www.theyesmen.org) and Stop Esso (www.stopesso.com) both provide extensive campaign toolkits, and then show the results. Helping supporters to participate as campaigners begins to turn the old closed-box, office-based model of campaign organization inside out. The Yes Men also enable supporters to colonize web space and spoof major corporations, supplying tailor-made software at www.reamweaver.com.

There are a plethora of social media tools – many captured in one remarkable diagram at http://the conversationprism.com/ (listing tools for collaboration, blog platforms, blog conversations, blog communities, micromedia, Twitter 'ecosystems', lifestreams, Short Message Service (SMS)/voice, forums, social networks, interest and curated networks, reviews and ratings, location, video, customer service, documents and content, events, music, wiki, livecasting video or audio, pictures, social bookmarks, comment and reputation, and crowd-sourced content.

New media's significance

'New media' is significant for campaigns because:

- It is often global – switch on the old TV and you saw local TV. A local phone call was normal, a call to the other side of the world, a novelty. Now with one click you are anywhere. (Although note that while the internet has had a globalizing effect, much use is very non-global. For example mapping Facebook usage in the US shows clustering by region, culture and lifestyle.[36])
- It is cheap and almost instant. Email and website interactions have reduced transaction costs to almost nothing. Newsletters, virtual communities and clubs can communicate at almost no cost.
- It's interactive. Digital TV for example allows more interaction than analogue TV.
- It shrinks distance and equalizes time. Videoconferencing can eliminate some travel needs and email exchanges across a wakingday. It can include friends in other time zones without the dislocating effect of someone talking from a working morning perspective to someone about to go to bed.
- It is accessible. The technology needed to act as a source, as a sort of broadcaster, is now widespread and affordable by many people.
- It is more transferable – what works on one platform can often easily cross to another, hence all forms of convergence.
- It enables all information, libraries, databases to be shared globally.
- It makes some previously specialist information or knowledge widely available.
- Social media have made brands more exposed as control of communications and potential scale have changed: the public conversation – complaining or recommending – can

potentially be very large and will take place whether organizations engage in it themselves or shy away.
- New media dialogue depends on having something interesting to say. Communities engaged in campaigns will generally have better stories to tell than the decision-makers the campaigns seek to influence.
- Communication tools are changing all the time. With a well-defined strategy, adaptable campaigns can exploit new communications tools effectively to reach specific audiences early on.

All this has implications for campaigns because they are an exercise in communication.

NEW RULES FOR CAMPAIGNS

Many of the 'rules for the new economy'[37] popularized by writer Kevin Kelly, designed to describe economic transactions, also apply to campaigns. Indeed, in many ways it seems they apply better to campaigning than to business. They are at least useful in thinking about how to design network-based campaigns.

Here, paraphrased, are some of Kelly's 'Dependable principles for thriving in a turbulent world', with my ideas of possible applications shown as bullet points (reproduced with permission from Kevin Kelly; see also www.kk.org/newrules/blog).

1 The law of connection

Embrace dumb power. Dumb parts, properly connected, yield smart results (for example, embedded microchips networked together).

- Many supporters each taking small actions.

2 The law of plentitude

More gives more. The first fax machine cost millions but was worth nothing, as you could not communicate with it. The second one made the first one worth something, and each additional fax machine increases the value of all the ones operating before it. So strong is this network value that anyone purchasing a fax machine becomes an evangelist for the fax network. 'Do you have a fax?' fax-owners ask you. 'You should get one.'

- Establish campaign networks where there is an incentive for members to recruit others because each new one makes it work better.

3 The law of exponential value

Success is non-linear. For 20 years, fax machines spread slowly, and then, in the mid-1980s, they crossed a point of no return and 'the next thing you know, they are irreversibly everywhere'.

- Solution technologies.

4 The law of tipping points

Significance precedes momentum. The moment where contagion's momentum 'has tipped from pushing uphill against all odds to rolling downhill with all odds behind it'. Technologies are being taken seriously much earlier in their development.

- Trail the long-term consequences of achieving your campaign objective, or better still, get a third party to do so.

5 The law of increasing returns

Make virtuous circles. Value increases with membership of networks much quicker (exponentially) than the old economies of scale (linear). Hence, Microsoft is tolerated despite its huge profits because there are so many on-sellers.

- Ethically based NGOs could create large networks, giving political and social agency to participants.

6 The law of inverse pricing

Anticipate the cheap. The best things get cheaper each year. Computer chips have halved in price, doubling in power, every 18 months (Moore's Law).

- To lever changes in commercial systems, find ways to influence consumers rather than producers to pull development.

7 The law of generosity

Follow the free. Where services become more valuable the more plentiful they are, and if they cost less, the better and the more valuable they become, then the most valuable things of all should be those that are given away. For example, Microsoft gives away its web browser, Internet Explorer.

- Externalize some of your campaign tools and know-how and make your network accessible, for example the tools and website of www.stopesso.com.

8 The law of the allegiance

Feed the web first. The distinguishing characteristic of networks is that they have no clear centre and no clear outer boundaries. The vital distinction between the self (us) and the non-self (them) – once exemplified by the allegiance of the industrial-era organization man – becomes less meaningful in a network economy. Standard-setting becomes important.

A network is like a country but with three important differences:

1 No geographical or temporal boundaries exist – relations flow 24 by 7 by 365;
2 Relations in the network economy are more tightly coupled, more intense, more persistent, and more intimate in many ways than those in a country;
3 Multiple overlapping networks exist, with multiple overlapping allegiances.
   - Ethically driven NGOs could create a global virtual country and thereby create a significant counterweight voice and alternative channel to profit-driven systems and profit-driven politics.

9 The law of devolution

Let go at the top. All organizations face two problems as they attempt to find their peak of optimal fit.

First, unlike the industrial arc's relatively simple environment, where it was fairly clear what an optimal product looked like and where on the slow-moving horizon a company should place itself, it is increasingly difficult in the network economy to discern which hills are highest and which summits are false.

You can easily get stuck on a local peak. There is only one way out: devolve – to go from one high peak to another, go downhill first and cross a valley before climbing uphill again. The company must reverse itself and become less adapted, less fit, less optimal.

The second problem is that organizations, like living beings, are hard-wired to optimize what they know and to not throw success away. Companies find devolving (a) unthinkable and (b) impossible. There is simply no room in the enterprise for the concept of letting go, – let alone the skill to let go – of something that is working, and trudge downhill toward chaos.

In the network economy, the ability to relinquish a product, occupation or industry at its peak will be priceless. Let go at the top.

• Big-brand NGOs that developed an effective strategy based on mass media are threatened unless they re-evolve, but start-ups may, in any case, take over.

10 The law of churn

Seek sustainable disequilibrium. Companies come and go quickly, careers are patchworks of vocations, industries are indefinite groupings of fluctuating firms. The network economy has moved from change to churn. Churn is more a creative force of destruction and genesis.

• Potential problems, solutions and allies are in constant flux, while campaign organization needs to be constantly reinventing itself.

11 The law of inefficiencies

Don't solve problems. In a paradox, increasing technology has not led to measurable increases in productivity.

Productivity is exactly the wrong thing to care about. The only ones who should worry about productivity are robots. In the network economy, where machines do most of the inhumane work of manufacturing, the task for each worker is not 'how to do this job right' but 'what is the right job to do?' Wasting time and being inefficient are the way to discovery. In the words of Peter Drucker, 'Don't solve problems: seek opportunities.'

• Ethically driven organizations should question 'conventional' ideas of what useful work is, and propose new definitions as a way of targeting objectives – more on work objectives than policy objectives.

THE MEDIA DAY

Marketing strategist Sean Larkins says: 'Media can be looked at according to share of display advertising by medium – for example, in March 2001, in the UK, TV accounted for around 40 per cent by value of all display advertising, radio 6 per cent, newspapers just under a third, magazines 15 per cent and outdoor the rest – which was about 8 per cent.'

In terms of the average 'media day', or share of media consumption by time of day, says Larkins, 'TV advertising is dominant at over half, with internet at a few per cent but rapidly rising, magazines at 2 per cent, newspapers at 7 per cent, and radio very much larger than in terms of spend, at 31 per cent. Video is a 4 per cent'.[38] This means every other ad we are exposed to comes from TV – but that doesn't necessarily mean they are the effective ones.

So, in terms of time, radio is the dominant morning medium, TV dominates the evening, and newspapers are mostly consumed between breakfast and lunchtime. Until mid-afternoon, radio listening exceeds TV viewing among Britons.

Radio advertising is less 'avoided' than advertising in print or on TV. People may switch off or get up to make a coffee or tea when expensive ads run on TV (obvious exceptions are 'cult ads' that spill over into a real-life existence, such as GAP's khaki campaign run in 1999 and described in Naomi Klein's *No Logo*) but they tend not to react when radio ads are on. Sean Larkins says that responding to adverts follows the scheme below:

- First hearing – miss it altogether;
- Second hearing – pick up the message;
- Third hearing – take in the detail;
- Fourth hearing pick up address/phone/internet address.

Nobody listens all day every day, so ads are usually played 30–40 times each week, or at least four times a day. The usual minimum length of a radio 'campaign' is one month.

Evening newspapers are, unsurprisingly, particularly read by home-bound (train or bus) commuters, while drive-time radio reaches motorists. The internet occupies its largest proportionate share at night, though within that generalization, there are many niche audiences, such as students and retired people. For global internet data, see www.glreach.com/globstats and the authoritative www.nua.com.

In the UK, more people listen to local than to national radio. Local radio reaches very specific audiences. These range station-by-station and, to a lesser extent, programme-to-programme, from hip hop to easy listening, and sometimes both. Local radio is good for both editorial and advertising. Being helpful to local radio will pay dividends, as they are very short of resources. This applies as much to offering news as to taking out paid advertising.

WHICH MEDIA WORK FOR WHICH PEOPLE

It pays to research your audience in terms of the media they consume. In the UK, for example, studies segment TV advertisement viewers into the following groups:

- Acceptors (22 per cent) – I find TV advertising interesting and quite often it gives me something to talk about;
- Rejectors (20 per cent) – Nearly all TV advertising annoys me;

- Players (35 per cent) – I find some TV advertising is OK, but I think quite a lot of it is devious;
- Uninvolved (22 per cent) – Quite often I find TV advertising more entertaining than the programmes.[39]

Audiences segment in their media consumption according to social, psychological, lifestyle and other factors, and this area is heavily researched by commercial agencies. For most NGOs the best way to access such information is probably via a friendly contact in an advertising or PR agency, or a marketing department of a large company.

Young people may adopt completely different channels from their parents. Text messaging (SMS) became increasingly popular in many countries in the 1990s and 2000s, (and the main source of profit on the telephone network, exceeding internet usage in its penetration), first among the young. It was popularized by a role-playing game 'the Nokia game' invented by Finnish youth after Nokia introduced texting in 1992.[40]

Commercial and BBC local radio split the audience about evenly, but commercial radio mainly reaches younger people (an obvious national exception being stations such as Classic FM or Saga Radio[41].

Beware though, of making generalizations such as 'young people use the internet'. In Britain this disguises the fact, for instance, that socially disadvantaged young people are disproportionately unlikely to use the internet,[42] and for many social issues they are the very people who need to be reached. Better channels for reaching them in the early 2000s included cheap video rental stores and the boxes of videos, as they frequently hire and watch a video in a group. Often, campaigns need to invent their own tailor-made communication channels.

BE SIMPLE: AVOID 'THE ISSUE'

Campaign groups often organize 'by issue'. This feeds the illusion that you can campaign 'on issues'. In reality, a campaign has to change an issue by rearranging its political landscape just one step at a time.

Few campaigns of any significance are achieved quickly. Most entail many steps, each a campaign in itself, often taking decades. Any that succeeds does so in jumps forward or single blows like a lapidary cutting a diamond. A perfect, multifaceted jewel cannot be created in one step.

Issue mapping inevitably reveals, once you have a good look at it, that almost any issue is a complex beast. Its entrails will be a labyrinth with appendices that lead nowhere, and branches that split into too many choices to handle. Debate explores mature issues and expands them to fill the available space.

The complexity must be overcome or avoided, for a campaign to be planned. Issue 'experts' may misunderstand this. They know a lot about their subject – too much. They often know much less, however, about how it may be changed. If they cannot imagine how big changes could be brought about except by processes they know – which depend very much on knowing more than the next person – they assume this is how change must come. They then cannot imagine how anyone who does not 'grasp the complexity' of the issue, can work on it effectively. As for making progress by simplification; that is surely wrong.

In truth, every issue is complex. 'Drugs' (as in not taking illegal drugs) is a simple issue to anyone who abhors and abstains from them. Nancy Reagan's wonderfully simple 'Just Say No' crusade is a famous example of a strategic communications failure – not just with the wrong messenger for the intended audience, but with a naive, presumably unresearched, if memorable, message.[1]

In practice, the reasons people do or don't use drugs are diverse and very complex, as anyone who has worked in that field knows. Yet to a drugs worker, something else will seem just as simple as drugs seemingly did to Mrs Reagan. A ballpoint pen, for example, might seem a very simple beast. But try standing up at the 15th Biennial International Pen and Writing Implement Conference and saying that the pen issue is simple. The delegates will laugh scornfully. Ask them what they think of the 'drugs' issue and they will probably not want to give it the time of day – 'it's simple – just say no – I don't take drugs – why should they?'

This is why you cannot campaign 'on an issue' or 'about an issue', only to *change* the issue.

Avoid black holes and elephants

Communication 'black holes' are issue tarpits into which your campaign can fall and never escape. If you are starting a new campaign or trying to change an issue where previous campaigns have become bogged down, then these are things to steer clear of.

This is not as easy as it sounds, because established contentious 'frames' are the obvious place to go. After all, everyone else is there already. As Rick Le Coyte has put it, these are 'congested roundabouts', better avoided by breaking out across country. These are contemporary points of struggle between conflicting interests. They act like a honeypot for journalists and 'passing trade', because that's where the arguments are going on. But often it's where there isn't much scope for real movement.

Communicators also refer to the problem of 'pattern-matching', as in people thinking 'I know what this is; it looks/feels/sounds like a so-and-so', and 'I know what I think of it'. If this happens, your opportunity to frame understanding or begin a new, preconception-free conversation is lost. When Greenpeace researched an expanded campaign on genetic engineering, we found several possible 'pattern-matching' problems that could have diverted the campaign into one of these tarpits:

- Animal testing (cued through the appearance of laboratories, with barbed wire fencing, lights, testing cages, white-coated scientists);
- E-numbers and additives (prompted by any reference to food labels);
- Food technology (yeast in vats or yoghurt) – the reason that the GM industry subsequently tried to call itself 'biotechnology', avoiding 'genetic engineering').

Other tarpits can be ideological disputes – in transport, for example, the public–private ownership issue, or the car-good/car-bad debate: these are so well rehearsed, and positions are so polarized and familiar, that any strategy that stumbles across them tends to get stuck there.

Lastly, to change minds or establish a new frame, don't trigger existing ones. This is the elephant problem (see George Lakoff's book, *Don't Think of an Elephant,* in 'Framing' on page 28): a speaker tries to explain what a giraffe is. Unfortunately, he tells the audience about elephants – 'it's not an elephant' – and because they know something about elephants, they then focus on that and never do get a mental picture of a giraffe. If instead he had avoided mention of elephants and sketched a mental picture of a giraffe, its surrounding and activities, adding detail and colour in layers, they could have got there.

DON'T BE LED BY THE PRESS AGENDA

Journalists may have strong views, about 'what the issue is'. News likes to move along established tracks: use this but do not become trapped by it.

The best way to break *new* things into the news system is not by trying to make them 'news' but to get them into the work and social world of professional communicators. Then they can discover it for themselves.

Features pages are a good route, but one of the best is children's media, which comes with a helpful nag-factor. To get there, start from the real world, in public events, networks and direct person-to-person communication.

News mainly reflects the doings of the rich and powerful, such as politicians. Campaigners should be wary of following the agenda of day-to-day politics, both of government departments and of members of the legislature. As Andrew Marr wrote of the activities of MPs in the UK: 'The excitement is febrile – what seems at first sight to be important, is revealed, at second glance, to be merely self-important.'[2] The test should be, 'by doing this will we best progress our campaign plan – is it on our critical path?'

The media itself should not be the objective or the target for a campaign, unless it is a campaign about the media.

A few years ago, when asked 'where environmental problems exist', people had started to see them as 'on TV'. Environment and campaigning were becoming unreal media creatures, disconnected from real life. People would see a street scene on TV with children suffering asthma apparently associated with car fumes, and say 'how terrible', but not associate it with their own street. As a result, campaigns did not engage effectively and people did not see the need or opportunity for them to demand political action. Overemphasis on communicating through the mass media was also leading critics of environmental campaigns to blame the media for them, and encouraging a backlash against campaigners within the media establishment.

One response adopted by Greenpeace was to put effort into 'direct communication', in other words not simply relying on the press to do the campaigning communication.

EVALUATION

However beautiful the strategy, you should occasionally look at the results.
(Winston Churchill)

Table 11.1 *How to evaluate a campaign's success*

Stage	Output	Intended impact	Unintended impact
Awareness	Output achieved (yes/no)	Objective achieved (yes/no)	Unintended impact
Alignment	Output achieved (yes/no)	Objective achieved (yes/no)	Unintended impact
Engagement	Output achieved (yes/no)	Objective achieved (yes/no)	Unintended impact
Action	Output achieved (yes/no)	Objective achieved (yes/no)	Unintended impact

If you find yourself thinking 'we don't have the money for evaluation', start planning again. Without evaluation, success or failure can't be understood.

Formative evaluation involves doing research and testing ideas at the design stage. Professionals such as Pat Branigan[3] recommend three rounds of pre-planning and testing. Katie Aston,[4] an expert in public health campaigns, recommends setting aside 10–15 per cent of the budget for testing and evaluation, depending on the complexity of the communications.

Basic evaluation can consist of looking at a campaign's success (Table 11.1). Making such an evaluation requires a before and after assessment. A campaign project may only have an objective at one stage – say, awareness.

Too many campaign groups analyse 'process' and outputs, rather than the impacts of the campaign. It's important to evaluate whether the campaign achieved its objectives, but also what other impact it had. Looking only at the objectives may miss the most important effects.

Judging the size of effect to look for is vital. Campaigners sometimes phrase objectives in terms of aims, if they haven't thought them through properly. It's important to assess change around an objective that is actually attainable, and to measure the activities it is hoped an intended audience will take, which actually make a direct contribution to that.

DON'T BELIEVE YOUR DETRACTORS

It's always a mistake to believe your own propaganda, if you have any. Equally, it's a mistake to believe that of your critics. There is an old parable about the devil that goes something like this:

A man is walking down the road. He meets another man – handsome, charming, well read. They talk. The first asks the second who he is. 'I am the devil,' comes the reply. 'But you can't be,' protests the first. 'I have heard about the devil, and he is ugly, stupid and offensive.' 'Aha,' says the devil, 'you have been listening to my detractors.'

Don't volunteer yourself into this position. Don't believe the demonization of opponents by ill-informed supporters, or of yourself by opponents.

If your campaign suffers a loss of public support, for example, or a supporter leaves your organization, don't assume that this is because, as some critics have it, your campaign is 'wrong', or as others might say, 'badly targeted', 'this will lose you public support', or any other criticism. Don't accept the validity of widely or loudly expressed criticisms that predict a problem, just because some part of that problem seems to be occurring. Use objective research to find what is really going on.

WORRY ABOUT THE RIGHT THINGS

Organizations focused on not making mistakes with factual details and 'the line to take', are unlikely to succeed in visual communication. Yet this is often what will make all the difference. The most common causes of communications failure are not mistakes of fact, but communicating completely the wrong thing because of poor visuals, or simply being ignored altogether.

Worry most about the impact of your communication – which will be mostly visual – in target audiences, not the opinions of colleagues.

Of course, getting the words wrong can also have dire consequences. If you regularly address the same public groups, it is worth investing in the time of specialist writers, such as agencies that develop specific dictionaries – language that works for an audience – so you use words and terms that have the right effect. Internal language and jargon will never be the right language to use for an external audience. See www.burton-morris.com for an example of a word-based communications agency that offers a free trial of writing for tone and style. *The Invisible Grail* by John Simmons[5] makes the case for developing effective brands using written language.

Other things that are easily forgotten in the hurly-burly of running campaigns and demands for accountability (which can easily become accounting), include:

- The spirit of what you are trying to do – what keeps supporters loyal, what stops staff from leaving – each campaign should light that touchpaper, at least for a moment;
- The community – an effective campaign organization is usually also a family, a conspiracy, a ruse, an adventure, not just a job;
- Attitude – you can teach method, you can pick people with any number of qualifications, but as a friend of mine[6] once put it: 'To be any good as a campaigner, they need to want to act up.' If you're ever in any doubt about recruiting staff, follow your heart and instincts, and pick the person with the right attitude and track record over qualifications any day;

- Who you are trying to influence – you can design a great tactic that is just so beautiful, you really want to use it – and forget that it won't do the job you have in hand;
- Of the two main ways campaigns affect politics – through changing values and altering the balance of interests – values are softer and harder to evaluate, but are far more significant.

COMMON FAILURES IN CHOOSING MEDIA

These include:

- Overemphasis of news media for persuasion, at the expense of human-interest stories on features pages;
- Too much reliance on the media and publicity at the expense of business-to-business techniques and direct communication, especially face to face;
- A too-academic or 'professional/policy community' approach – too many data and too much information, not enough empathy and emotion;
- Trying to argue rather than to show: it is far better to set things up so people draw their own conclusions;
- Website fixation (a problem in 2003, giving way to texting – before that it was video, but now video is underused, while soon it will be some other new medium) – trying to make websites do too many things;
- Failing to think through the particular needs of TV – it must have *moving* pictures – a static event is really useless. The Pope is news if he just appears and stands there; you are almost certainly not;
- Failing to think through the particular needs of radio – must have *sounds* – a silent event is really useless – best to have sounds of a *process* ('that's the sound of...') and various voices;
- Failing to be visual – for example, so pictures can accompany a newspaper story;
- Targeting media that the staff of the organization read or watch or listen to, rather than those that the supposed target audience do.

DON'T ASSUME WE NEED TO CHANGE MINDS

Most campaigns succeed by mobilization, rather than changing beliefs or convictions. To change minds and *then* mobilize people is a two-stage process. If you only need to mobilize them, you don't need the mind-changing step: it's simpler. Not only that, but changing minds is hard. After we reach our early 20s, big changes in perspective generally come with major life stages, such as having children, and other instances are rare.

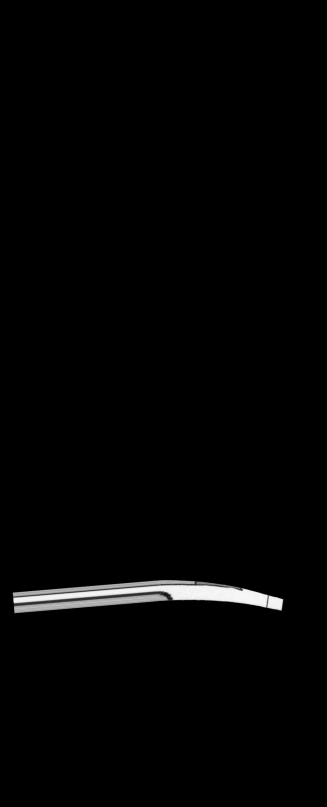

So beware the trap of analysing a problem and concluding that, because the problem would be solved if people 'changed their minds', that is what the campaign should do. Even worse is to make a hidden, embedded assumption that the campaign will do this, without knowing how.

You *can* set out to 'change minds' in a campaign, but to do so you must first understand views and motivations very well, and then set an achievable objective[7] – probably only a very small change of view.

Even if you do intend to change minds, then getting people's *attention* will probably involve starting from where they are. Using *channels* they use for instance, and *messengers* they like to hear from, and a *context* they are comfortable in – face to face perhaps – for example, a talk by a wine expert at a wine tasting. Generally, if you can get to people 'where they are', physically, emotionally and intellectually, and then *show* them something or even better involve them in something that is a life-changing or world view-changing experience, you will have the best chance of changing minds.

EXAMPLES OF JIGSAW PROBLEMS

Fuel taxes and protests

If communication jumps straight to the 'solution', without successfully selling the idea of the problem, it will be met with disinterest, blank puzzlement or polite but unengaged tolerance ('it's interesting you are doing that, but it's nothing to do with me'). Politicians in power often make this mistake. In many political systems, once elected they can introduce policies or measures that may have little specific backing. This doesn't become apparent until they hit an obstacle and try to appeal for public support.

In the 1990s, the UK government introduced a rising tax on petrol prices.[8] Ministers justified it (solution) on grounds that it would reduce climate-changing CO_2 emissions from road transport (problem). The public, however, didn't buy the connection – the pieces of jigsaw didn't fit. They suspected that a moral cause was being hijacked to justify taxes that would be used for other purposes. Environmentalists didn't feel they 'owned' the measure. When truckers later organized fuel-price protests, the public remained ambivalent. The government tried to play the climate card, and vented its frustration on environmentalists: 'Where were you?' MPs cried when news pictures remained dominated by the protests.

Eventually, the truckers were bought off by concessions,[9] deprived of their organizational spine, and with fuel prices once again dropping,[10] the protests died. In fact, all the major groups active on climate *had* supported the government, and some went much further. Greenpeace, for example, went to meet protestors face to face, and showed what it thought the real 'solution' was by giving away free biofuel (biodiesel). Nevertheless, these activities couldn't compete with the visual power of the protests, and did little to reframe the debate (see 'Framing', Chapter 1).

What does this tell us? That the 'solution' hadn't been sold to or bought by the public, so they weren't interested in defending it,[11] and that to really counter the price protests campaigners would need a solution that had a more convincing fit to the problem (in this case defined as cost).

UK backing for the 2003 US–Iraq war

In 2003, the UK went to war in Iraq, with the majority of its people unconvinced of the justification.[12] From late 2002 to early 2003, Tony Blair deployed a series of different rationales (problem), all designed to arrive at the same 'solution' (war). Here, the war was a pre-made solution. The problem for Mr Blair was the problem – there wasn't one. Or rather it kept changing[13] when it seemed that the public didn't buy it.

Changing your claims about which problems fit the solution, is as implausible as changing your mind about which solutions fit the problem, especially where the subsequent call to action has such drastic consequences. So the mistake in communication terms was to start from the 'solution' and then have to try and sell the problem. The difficulty for Blair was that he had hitched his policy to that of George Bush, who had much less need of justification.[14]

The chlorine campaign

In the 1980s and 1990s, Greenpeace conducted a lengthy war of attrition against the global chlorine (chemicals) industry. Some of this involved very direct and transparent action, such as stopping particular pollution streams leading into the Great Lakes or the Rhine. Some involved pulp and paper bleaching, or chemical plants themselves, or incineration of plastic wastes or solvents, or PVC manufacture.

The campaign secured bans and controls specific to industries, such as timber treatment, and waterway 'clean-ups'. In some cases, workers and communities had benefited, and a community understood why. In other cases, the specific role of chlorine, or chlorinated compounds, would not have been understood by the public, which just saw 'pollution' and maybe specific victims, ranging from pregnant mothers or babies to fish, where the visual 'fit' to chlorine was loose, at best.[15]

The campaign succeeded in mobilizing international bodies and governments to introduce controls on emission, production and disposal. The discussions involved were highly technical and almost totally outside the public realm. With a political appetite to do more for the environment all was fine, but when environment slipped down the scale of political priorities, problems arose. Industries organized and lobbied heavily to roll back controls.

Companies funded 'Astroturf' (artificial grass-roots) groups to campaign for the chlorine industry. Concrete job benefits were positioned against hard-to-understand environmental restrictions. Politicians faced a mobilized constituency against chlorine controls and almost no public understanding of the benefits of eliminating chlorine (for example to reduce the body burden of dioxins). 'Solutions' had been advanced too far ahead of public understanding, and without lock-ins to hold the policies in place.

Subsequent 'toxics' campaigns are now building the public engagement and understanding that some of the earlier advances lacked. Greenpeace Netherlands has sampled rainwater, and dust in homes, while in the UK, WWF has sampled blood from members of the public and analysed for over 70 chemicals.[16]

The earlier weakness of the chlorine campaign stemmed from taking a perfectly sound academic analysis of the problem – that chlorine chemistry and the organic chlorine industry was at the root of a vast swathe of the worst toxics problems – and transferring that analysis into the public domain as a broad, problem-led campaign. A series of narrower but more intelligible campaigns with the same industrial and environmental consequences might have proved more durable.

CONSIDER FAILURE

Campaign directors and boards should study failures, not look for blame. Failures usually provide the clearest lessons. The history of success, on the other hand, gets clouded by swarms of people claiming the credit. 'I was at the meeting where ...', 'I remember taking the call that ...', 'of course, what people don't realize, is that if it had not been for the work we did five years previously in ...'.

Blame prevents learning, and it only encourages the ingenious rewriting of objectives, post hoc. To get maximum value from failure you need to persist. All good campaign groups don't give up, but adapt and try again. As Winston Churchill put it: 'Success consists of going from failure to failure without loss of enthusiasm.'

As campaigning is a form of public politics, failure may be widely noticed, though really miserable failure usually just goes quietly 'phut'. So try to design the campaign so that failure will not discourage key followers or allies in the medium term. With the right qualities, a deserving or particularly poignant campaign effort can not only fail and be forgiven, but actually succeed by changing the climate around what is at stake.

When the *explicit* message is failure, the *implicit* message has to be the hope or promise of greater success. A lower-league soccer team may have its fortunes transformed by reaching the quarter finals of an important competition and being beaten by Manchester United. To get so far and to be positioned alongside such a great team may change perceptions and exceed expectations.

The unintended message of failure may, however, be less helpful – incompetence or naivety, for example. One test of a strategy should be to ask: 'What are the consequences of failure in terms of support, allies and opponents?' It should at least meet, if not exceed expectations. This argues strongly for picking objectives that you think are just possible, and which others view as just about impossible. Engage enough support and you can bridge the gap.

SHOULD WE USE CELEBRITIES?

I am often asked by campaigners if they should 'use celebrities' in a campaign. The answer for most is 'only sometimes' and, if you do, 'carefully'.

Remember the differences between Settlers, Prospectors and Pioneers in Chapter 3? That gives you one general answer. If you particularly need to reach one or another of these groups, then what type of 'celebrity' you use, how you use them and whether you ought to involve them at all will vary accordingly.

It's really only Prospectors who are whole heartedly and unquestioningly happy to see a campaign feature, even be led by, a celebrity, and this is the only psychological segment who will also accept 'celebrity' as meaning famous for just being famous. Prospectors espouse fun, hedonism, winning, visible ability and visible success, so at a broad brush level, it's a 'yes' to involving celebrities. Indeed the lack of these qualities in campaigns, and a deficit of 'stars', is one of the reasons why many campaigns fail to engage Prospectors.

If you do want to use 'celebs' to engage Prospectors, you also need to use the channels and contexts (see CAMPCAT, page 25) they are attracted to. A short piece in a celebrity magazine featuring your 'celeb' is likely to be better than a longer piece in a 'more serious' publication. Participative and social networking media like Facebook and Twitter also allow followers of celebs to share in the celebrity – so organize things to let them.

Settlers are not 'show-offs' but they too follow 'celebrities' in the sense that there are people they want to be like or be with (one of their drivers is 'belonging' – identity and affinity). To involve someone notable in a campaign aimed at engaging Settlers, or at least reassuring them that 'people like them' are 'onside', look at their values. Safety, conformity, discipline and security are Settler values, so a military general or an authoritative religious leader or a sports club icon might be a suitable Settler 'celebrity' if they identify with them. Media figures need to be very familiar and 'much loved'.

One such case occurred in Britain in 2009[17] when actress Joanna Lumley, star of several long-running TV series, successfully fronted a campaign on behalf of the Gurkha Justice Campaign, promoting the right of Nepalese Gurkhas who had served in the British Army Brigade of Gurkhas to reside in Britain. Because of the 'justice' aspect, the campaign would have resonated with Pioneers, and her celebrity would have been noticed by Prospectors, but the main resonance was with Settlers, involving as it did, qualities such as national defence and security, service and discipline, modesty and bravery, and the national flag.

As we've seen most campaigns are, however, conceived and led by Pioneers, the sort of people who most like complexity, issues and innovation. This is the audience most likely to be actively critical of your choice of celebrities. It's icons not celebrities that they want.

In 2005 a series of celebrity-led concerts were staged in London, New York, other G8 states and South Africa, under the banner 'Live 8'. These events supported campaigns on international debt cancellation, prosecuted by the alliance of development charities and other groups under the banner 'Make Poverty History'. The most prominent celebrity leaders of the campaign were Bob Geldof, who had also led Live Aid in 1985, and Bono of U2.

Bono and Geldof were not 'just celebrities', they were icons – that is symbols with a deeper meaning (deeper in this case than just being famous musicians). Years of campaigning had given them an authentic track record and personal credibility on matters such as Africa, development, environment and aid, at least as great as any Organisation for Economic Co-operation and Development (OECD) Minister but with few of the disadvantages of holding office or compromises made in getting elected. They were acceptable to Pioneers in a way that other 'celebrities' such as David Beckham or Kylie Minogue would not have been.

THREE STORIES

Distinct from the campaign 'messages' intended to do work to achieve your objective, most campaigns also need to be able to talk about themselves. That is the story-of-your-campaign, the 'why we are doing it', and 'what it's all about'. This is part of the P (Programme) of CAMPCAT (see page 25).

It useful for each campaign to have the following three stories to hand:

1. The *popular* story. The main one to use with the press and public. Written in language your mum, dad, brother, sister, son, daughter and so on would use and understand. Saying what it means for us. No jargon. Test: interests your mum/daughter/sister.
2. The *professional* story. To be used with stakeholders who understand about environment, conservation work, government delivery and so on – jargon is OK here but not in the others. Test: interests a professional.
3. The *political* story. Written in terms of where the campaign(s) sits in political initiatives, tackling policy objectives and so on – the world as seen by and debated between politicians, officials and so on – things like budgets and policies are important here. Sometimes the right thing for the press – depends on context. Test: interests a politician.

The key point is obviously to use the appropriate story for appropriate contexts and audiences. If in doubt *always* use the popular story. You can always switch to one of the others if audience response shows you need to do so.

Never use the professional story for a public or political audience: it confuses the 'public' and annoys politicians. This is the main danger, as it's the world you probably dwell in – in other words the familiar policy-wonk language emerges where it shouldn't, especially in the stress of an interview or when you don't stop to think differently.

Remember that *if someone cannot understand you then they cannot agree with you.* Then they will not support you or take up your 'asks'. Campaign staff and spokespeople must be trained in at least the popular story and do media training on it.

Your website should have the popular and the professional ones but separated so that the professional one is in a different section, flagged up as for professionals.

CAMPAIGNS AT ORGANIZATIONAL LEVEL

E ach organization has a way of doing things,[1] a purpose in life (aka 'mission' or *raison d'etre*) and hopefully, a vision (the difference it's going to make). The 'organizational strategy' is the way of doing things – style, method and route.

Such strategy does not change easily or often. It's too fundamental for that – for example, The Sierra Club's strategy for *being* the Sierra Club and for being an environmental organization. It's mind, body and soul.

Organization-level strategy decides how the organization develops, retains and deploys its assets and resources, and the big choices about core business. It sets the tone, attracts or repels partners, stakeholders and supporters; and determines whether the organization acts alone or with others. All this is communicated.

Many NGOs and even some public bodies and companies include 'campaigns' but how? Is it recognizably, say, a WWF campaign, or a Save the Children Campaign? What are the consistent features that mark out your way of campaigning?

Possible functional organizational campaign strategies:

- problem-driver;
- solution-driver;
- advocate;
- catalyst;
- convenor;
- witness;
- investigator;
- intelligencer;
- inspirer;
- enforcer;
- whistle-blower;
- provider;

- fixer or deal-maker;
- instigator of discussions;
- researcher – primary provider of knowledge;
- editor – sifter of knowledge;
- network-maker;
- fund-raiser;
- organizer of people;
- standard-setter;
- standard-bearer;
- insider;
- outsider;
- dialoguer;
- adjudicator.

Campaign strategy should fit with, or 'resonate' with, organizational strategy. Dissonance makes the organization 'unhappy in its skin' with:

- disputes over 'whether we should be campaigning at all';
- fears that 'you are trying to turn us into something else';
- internal conflict between campaigns and other parts of the organization (attack from the organizational immune system);
- planning fever and evaluation mania;
- objective congestion – trying to 'fix' an uncomfortable campaign by bolting on lots of comforting objectives;
- under-resourcing by activities and resources, in relation to the objectives;
- limited participation across the organization;
- fears among the board and senior managers that things are 'out of hand';
- resentment among campaigners: 'we're not allowed to campaign';
- high turnover in campaign staff;
- failure to capitalize on successes;
- usually, low visibility or public recognition of campaign efforts (as the organizational brand negates campaign communication);
- feeling 'it's not us – we shouldn't be doing this'.

ORGANIZATIONAL COMMUNICATIONS: THE GLASS ONION

In the 'glass onion' brand metaphor, the organization is like a glass onion, arranged in layers, through which an outside observer can see to the core (Figure 12.1). If a campaign expresses the deeper layers, it's more likely to inspire supporters.

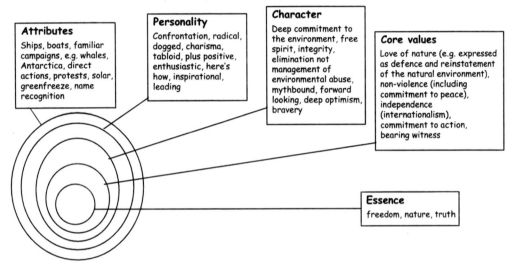

THE GLASS ONION MODEL – it is see-through and cut in half – the uppermost layers are the most obvious things about Greenpeace – attributes. Then comes personality, which you'll see next. Then, in more telling circumstances, the underlying character emerges. And if you really get to know it – core values. Then eventually you get to where words will not really do – the essence. A strength of Greenpeace is its ability to project all of this through its work and particularly its actions, visually.

Attributes
Ships, boats, familiar campaigns, e.g. whales, Antarctica, direct actions, protests, solar, greenfreeze, name recognition

Personality
Confrontation, radical, dogged, charisma, tabloid, plus positive, enthusiastic, here's how, inspirational, leading

Character
Deep commitment to the environment, free spirit, integrity, elimination not management of environmental abuse, mythbound, forward looking, deep optimism, bravery

Core values
Love of nature (e.g. expressed as defence and reinstatement of the natural environment), non-violence (including commitment to peace), independence (internationalism), commitment to action, bearing witness

Essence
freedom, nature, truth

Figure 12.1 *The glass onion model*

From outside...

- Attributes – obvious things, surface appearances, tangible assets, activities;
- Personality – its way of doing things – you find that out as you get to know it;
- Character – what only becomes apparent when the organization is tested;
- Values – beliefs that drive the organization;
- Essence – hard to put into words, but you know it when you see it – almost indefinable, largely intuitive, paradoxical, not capable of rational analysis or reductionist dissection.

...to centre

To develop a 'glass onion' model for an organization, you need to know it well. Here's one we invented for Greenpeace UK in the mid-1990s:[2]

- Attributes – ships, boats, familiar campaigns (for example, whales, Antarctica), direct actions, protests, solar, greenfreeze, name recognition;
- Personality – confrontation, radical, dogged, charisma, tabloid, plus positive, enthusiastic, here's how, inspirational, leading;

- Character – deep commitment to the environment, free spirit, integrity, elimination not management of environmental abuse, mythbound, forward looking, deep optimism, bravery;
- Core values – love of nature (for example, expressed as defence and reinstatement of the natural environment), non-violence (including commitment to peace), independence (internationalism), commitment to action, bearing witness;
- Essence – freedom, nature, truth (this could only be a stab at 'essence' – it's something like that but not literally these three things).

An example of organization-level communication was the design of a 1980s membership leaflet used by Greenpeace UK. The organization's communications guru Nick Gallie found from research that supporters and potential supporters saw the organization as a 'light in the darkness'. It was an era when UK Prime Minister Mrs Thatcher and her policies made many people feel fearful, depressed and powerless.

The Greenpeace leaflet didn't address itself to these feelings directly – it talked about the organization, its values, its work. It used the strapline 'Against All Odds', under a picture of a breaching humpback whale in Antarctica.

On the surface, the image was about well-known campaigns, but its impact stemmed from the way it resonated with both the deepest values and 'essence' of Greenpeace, and subtly identified with how many of the public felt: that they faced impossible odds. The breaching whale invoked freedom, optimism, nature. Because there was nothing else in the picture, it was pure and elemental – it could be about 'essence'. And 'against all odds' was an implicit promise, as well as an alignment of the organization with the mood of the time.

Any campaign organization can do this sort of exercise. A word of warning though – don't try to communicate the communications strategy. It's best kept as a reference – not on a shelf, but as a working tool to plan and test your work but not projected at 'audiences'. Your work should tell the story and that should express values, character, and so on.

AVOIDING THE SHOPPING TROLLEY COMMUNICATIONS STRATEGY

Organizations often want to develop a campaign 'as part of a communications strategy'. Frequently organizations see a 'campaign' as a sort of weapons platform or shopping trolley that they want to load with as many 'messages' or 'communications objectives' as they can think of. Some already have a matrix of policies, programmes and audiences that they want to promote by sending 'messages'. As you will have seen, this is not the approach advocated in this book. Any 'campaign' run through such a system is unlikely to be either visible or coherent.

My overall advice on communications strategies for groups who want to campaign is normally:

- Work out which of your most important objectives you can only pursue by campaigns (in other words where you *need* a campaign – otherwise use other means).
- Develop an instrumental campaign (using the sort of tools shown in this book – research, issue mapping, critical paths and so on), and run one campaign at a time (an organization that does nothing but campaign might run more than one but, even then, only one can be the priority at any one time – have others prepared 'ready to go'). Devote at lest half your communications resources to the priority campaign.
- Have an organizational, qualitative communications strategy (see above – this is the realm of marketing, positioning, brand expression through your core business and so on – the campaign should be consonant with this but generally should not do this work).
- Have a plan for reactive communications – the 'messages' you will use in a range of circumstances (brainstorm them, run scenarios training, identify your spokespeople matched to key audiences, do media training – with clear pre-set responsibilities – the 'red light' cases below).
- Allocate your remaining resources against other communications activities where you are not running a campaign as such but where you can have proactive communications objectives and deploy many of the tools used in this book (for example CAMPCAT). For these purposes you can also deploy the 'traffic light' system used by Sean Larkins at the UK Central Office of Information:
  - Red – media to prepare for (potentially problematic stories, enquiries, disasters and so on);
  - Amber – media you can influence (by cultivating relationships, providing information and so on: print, websites, blogs, TV, radio, stakeholders, delivery partners, professional networks);
  - Green – media you control (your own materials and publications, spokespeople, your own events, conferences, online, shared and paid for media and so on).

CHANGING DYNAMICS OF AWARENESS AND ACTION

The Values Mode model (see Chapter 3) developed by Pat Dade of Cultural Dynamics[3] reveals significant changes in how 'environment' has changed as an issue, becoming news-worthy then 'credible', then 'not an issue' as it has normed. The communication, organizational and political implications of this for 'green' groups are profound, and may be a model for any other issue undergoing similar changes. Dade recognizes three stages.

Late 1960s to early 1980s – Environmental concern (Stage 1)

- Pioneer issue – Very minority in uptake, but growing every year; not a fad, but a trend in society;
- Typified as younger in age profile;
- More educated than their age cohort and society in general;
- Aware of unsatisfactory immediate consequences of economic growth on some localities and regions;
- Aware of probable global long-term damage;
- Favoured solution – Taking personal responsibility for not further harming the environment;
- Secondary solution – Discover and practise methods of sustainably changing their own behaviour to enhance the environment.

Early 1980s to early 1990s – Environmental action (Stage 2)

- Led by Pioneers and attracting Prospectors, becoming more mainstream, 'mainstream alternative';
- Still younger and more educated than society as a whole;
- Explosive growth in the awareness of worldwide inter relationships that seemed to be creating problems – for example, aerosols and ozone-layer depletion, or fossil fuel usage and global warming;
- Favoured solution – Join together in groups that would highlight the problem;
- Secondary solution – Take indirect or direct action against the despoilers of the environment.

Early 1990s to date – Ozone-friendly (Stage 3)

- All groups – Pioneer, Prospector and Settler – agree on the need to protect the environment from further damage. Accepted as a mainstream concern;
- All ages agree (the 20-year-olds of 1970 are now the 50 year olds of the 21st century!);
- Levels of education still have an element of discrimination, but not nearly to the same extent as 30 years ago. Dozens of TV channels and 30 years of news and documentaries have created much of the increased awareness of the world as a set of worldwide inter-relationships;
- Favoured solution – No longer a clear answer, as different value modes are often 'violently agreeing' with each other;
- Secondary solution – The Settlers have introduced a new dynamic into the mix of personal and group responsibility. This is to make governments, rather than individuals or corporations, responsible for the protection of the environment.

Dade says: 'As this awareness has increased over the last 30 years, the range of options for changing the "problems" that are attractive to those who are "aware" has changed in nature and increased in number.':

- 1960s/1970s – Pioneer-only answer. Simple. Personal responsibility.
- 1980s/early 1990s – Pioneer answer *and* Prospector answer. Both simple. Prospector answer was about group responsibility.
- 1990s to date – Pioneer, Prospector and Settler answers. All simple. Settler answer was about making government responsible.

He adds:

> *Over time, we have seen an increased set of simple solutions, which has lead to the complex set of responses we see to each issue today. As more people become aware of issues, the more different value sets will begin to generate solutions to the issues.*

Ironically, as the dynamic changes, with the range of options increasing, the consensus among 'aware people' becomes less. All may agree as to the problem, but a lack of consensus exists as to the solution.

This is confusing to all but the most committed activists and creates the situation we have today, where the old adage 'knowledge is power' is almost 100 per cent wrong. With data and information at personal overload levels, the 'simple' answers of the past decades are less and less clear and empowering.

In fact, it isn't just the number of simple solutions that is presenting the problem, it is the nature of the people coming into awareness of the issues and their psychological predisposition to generate their own simple solutions that is creating a complexity to the solutions process that wasn't there in previous stages of development (see above).

As the Settlers perceive the issues and generate solutions they will not do so from the psychological space of the Pioneers and Prospectors, who are more about personally taking responsibility, or being members of groups that take direct or indirect action. The Settlers are happier to hand over 'power' to those who wish to exercise it, rather than use it themselves. In terms of awareness or concern about the environment, they are happy to hand over responsibility to their representatives, the governments of the countries they inhabit.

This passing of responsibility has many effects on the dynamics of people or groups taking responsibility for changing circumstances relating to the environment. The immediate effect is that new recruits are no longer available as activists. The newly aware will delegate this responsibility to a government department.

Another immediate effect is that there is no immediate effect! When Pioneers and Prospectors come to awareness they will tend to change behaviours. When the Settlers come to awareness they abrogate the need for any self-responsibility and expect 'someone' to 'do something' about the issue. This 'someone' is usually defined as the government. Observation of the workings of the government both here and abroad, suggests that often governments will then work together with existing, or form new, NGOs to provide solutions to the issues raised. This dramatically increases the time to 'effect'.

This leads, says Dade, 'to a situation where one of the biggest drivers of social consciousness-raising in centuries, which has driven worldwide changes in perceptions and behaviours, (the "green movement"), has created a dynamic that will rob it of its energy as it becomes more successful at raising awareness of issues'.

Campaigners may recognize some of these consequences:

- Groups start off dominated by activists (inner-directeds) but as they succeed, the managers arrive and want structure, organization and 'credibility' (esteem-drivens), compartmentalizing and controlling action, and looking for signs (and measures) of success. Activism becomes more difficult.
- The cause, once wacky, becomes newsworthy (rapidly changing and expanding relevance) and fashionable (attracting the esteem-driven, such as green consumers) and then normal (everyone agrees with it), not radical and not newsworthy.
- The news media, seeing that it's not newsworthy any more, and that activism has declined, pronounce the issue dead and conclude that 'nobody cares' any longer – in fact, the opposite is true; everyone cares.
- Once an issue is normed, only major aberrations are intrinsically newsworthy (for example, the Brent Spar). General concern is normal. In February 2004, UK Prime Minister Tony Blair said he thought climate change was the greatest problem facing the world. It got one sentence in a long press report on his views in *The Independent*.
- Campaigns tend first to be inspirational, then aspirational, and finally normal – that is, not an issue at all.

Many environment groups have yet to adapt their strategies to take account of these changes. In recent years, a number have used values analysis to plan which segment of society to focus on for recruitment and fund-raising purposes (for example the RSPB, which has systematically tuned its communications to appeal more to Pioneers, and the UK National Trust (aiming to engage younger 'self exploring' families, who tend to be younger Transcenders and Now People – see page 78). Campaigners have been slower to exploit the potential of values analysis but one group, Global Cool, bases its entire strategy on targeting Now People as the gatekeepers of behaviours between Pioneers and the rest of society (see www.globalcool.org and Box 3.1 on page 84).

WHY CAMPAIGNS NEED BRANDS, ORGANIZATION
AND PROPOSITIONS

The ad hoc group adopted the plan. Typical of those days, the anti-war crowd parted with the V-sign, saying 'peace'. A quiet 23-year-old Canadian carpenter, union organizer and ecologist, Bill Darnell, who rarely spoke at the meetings, added sheepishly, 'Make it a green peace.'

'The term had a nice ring to it,' recalls Bob Hunter, one of the founders of Greenpeace. 'It worked better in a headline than The Don't-Make-a-Wave Committee. We decided to find a boat and call it Greenpeace.'

(Rex Weyler, Waves of Compassion[4])

A brand – such as 'Oxfam' – acts as a rallying point, a flag hoist on the social battlefield. It is recognizable from a distance, it identifies whose side you are on.

A brand can help with trust. If I am an Oxfam supporter, I do not need to see the plan for its new campaign on fishing communities to know I will probably support it. A brand is a short cut to public engagement.

Brand[5] plus organization creates a mechanism for individuals to support campaigns without the campaign relying for its impact solely on the incremental effect of the actions of individuals. Instead, if they are well judged, campaigns exert leverage[6] – the brand acts as a multiplier.

If the brand says who we are, and organization makes it possible to sustain participation, the proposition gives supporters the reason to stay engaged, and offers opponents the terms on which to concede.

One of the best political campaign propositions comes from businessmen who supported free trade, so long as it suited their interests.[7] 'No taxation without representation' was a neat battle cry for the American colonists wanting to throw off the yoke of British colonial powers.

'No taxation' would have had far less traction. Even in the lightly taxed 18th century, no taxation might have seemed Utopian. How would essential public things get paid for?

Of course, 'give us representation' may be what you want, but it invites the response: 'Why should I?' The proposition 'no taxation without representation' answers that point. Provided a plausible tax revolt could be organized, it's a negotiating position.

Conventional campaigns have organization, a proposition and a brand. So far, attempts to run campaigns without these have only illustrated their value (but who knows how things may change in future?).

Winning and losing the roads campaign, with no brand and no organization

With hallmark mass treetop or rooftop occupations and tunnelling, the UK 'roads protests' from Twyford Down (1992) through Newbury (1996) and maybe beyond, were run as networked gatherings.[8] Facilitated by mobile phones and email – both new – they had no easily discernible leadership or structure. Partly this was tactical – to avoid punitive legal injunctions that could be served on conventional groups – and partly ideological – a rejection of brands, logos, and anything 'corporate'.

The 'movement' helped surface and then rode a breaking wave of public anxiety at the way society was going, with the roads programme, sold by the government as 'biggest since the Romans', a hubristic icon of much that was wrong. All party political pressure led the Major Conservative government to downsize the programme twice. The Blair Labour government came to power in 1997, claiming to be anti-road and pro-public transport. Battered by five years of intense conflict and with victory declared, the roads movement dissolved. Veterans got jobs or went gardening, neophytes moved to the anti-globalization agenda. Transport campaigning was once again the preserve of earnest but unexciting enthusiasts.

By 2000, however, Blair's Labour had planned 360 miles of new motorway and industry demanded 465 new bypasses. The great victory was swiftly reversed with hardly a murmur.

With few exceptions,[9] Britain was back on the road to road building. In 2003, Roger Higman of FoE, said:[10]

> Following the big road protests of the early- to mid-1990s, the Tories reviewed the roads programme and cut 49 schemes in 1994, 77 schemes in 1995 and 110 schemes in 1996.
>
> Labour came into power in 1997, carried out a rapid review of 18 schemes (of which they dropped three and gave the go ahead to, I think, seven). They carried out a broader review, gave the go-ahead to 37 and put another 150 or so on hold pending the results of multi-modal studies.
>
> Since then, things have been harder. The 37 schemes have largely been built and the multi-modal studies are beginning to report. So far they have tended to recommend roads get built. Ministers have also tended to confirm the recommendations.

The failure of the roads 'movement' is not down to a single factor, but lack of organization meant it had no staying power. Its considerable energy was easily lost. It depended for its effect on the collective impact of many individual commitments and was thus vulnerable to every whim, pressure or fashion affecting individual members. It had no collective memory,[11] little means of speaking to the media when there was no action going on, and perhaps above all, no mechanism to convert the sympathy and admiration of what were probably many millions of people who had seen the protests on television, into resources that could be used to sustain a campaign.

With no brand,[12] there was no mechanism for vicarious involvement – no emotional equivalent of the card-carrying party member out there in Middle England to carry on the fight. There was no 'organizational weapon'.[13] Once gone, the activism was, in effect, impossible to recall.

A CAMPAIGN WITHOUT A PROPOSITION: GLOBALIZATION

The 'anti-globalization' movement of the late 1990s and early 2000s shared some roots with the roads protests. Although most easily identified by set-piece protests – such as Seattle in 1999 – it was primarily intellectual, even narcissistically so, rather than activist like the roads movement. Like Greenpeace, the roads campaigners used direct action as a bargaining tool, as well as an influencing one: if they stayed up the trees long enough, if the M11 campaigners could have stayed on the roof in Claremont Road until the bulldozers went away, they would have won.

The protests of the anti-globalization movement, on the other hand, were merely that – protests. The 'problem' of globalization could not be stopped by the protests at Genoa or other gatherings of the G8 by a direct power grab or physical action, only by persuasion (and that is debatable) of the G8 leaders.

The anti-globalization movement has been dominated by writers and would-be politicians, keen to put their name to tracts, with even the celebrated Subcomandante Marcos enjoying high-profile anonymity. It has promoted the idea that its ideas will change the world, or are changing the world.

It succeeded in creating powerful events that generated news. It struck on a weakness in the opposition – the G8 and their ilk have a very weak case when the benefits of untrammelled marketization, globalization, privatization and other aspects of neoliberal economics or the 'Washington consensus' are weighed against results. But as a campaign it failed to push home its advantage – it failed to supplant conventional political economic thinking with its ideas in the mainstream, it failed to engage the non-protesting public, it failed to pose a question that the G8 had to answer. It failed the chip shop queue test and failed to set a directional agenda.

If the 'movement', which has now 'moved on' to social justice, was a 'campaign', then it failed. If it was simply a seedbed for political ideas, then its significance has yet to be felt.

As a campaign it failed because it had no proposition. Paul Kingsnorth titles his account of the movement 'One No, Many Yeses',[14] but in reality, it had many different nos and many yeses. It had no proposition, and as a result could not split the opposition or call a division for supporters to rally behind. It generated a lot of talk and very little effect – which is fine for a political nursery but is no use for a campaign.

The causes of this were mainly cultural. First, many in the movement distrusted the mainstream media and they left others to provide commentary and explanation at major events they organized. One US commentator[15] called it a 'reverse Jesse Jackson phenomenon'. It allowed Tony Blair and the G8 to dismiss the movement's case, reversing it as an attack on democracy by invoking the frame of meaningless violence and anarchy. Second, as Kingsnorth relates, the movement talked mainly to itself, celebrated diversity, and was generally reluctant to propose a 'big yes' or a single answer – consequently, it had no answer, and not even a coherent view of what the problem was.

Lacking a RASPB proposition (see Chapter 7), there was nothing consistent for the media or public to hold politicians to, or debate among themselves. There was no equivalent for globalization of the qualified proposition 'no taxation without representation'.

CONSEQUENCES OF WINNING: THE BRENT SPAR CAMPAIGN

In June 1995, the oil company Shell was towing the redundant 14,000-tonne oil storage buoy the Brent Spar towards a watery grave in the Atlantic, off Scotland. Backed strongly by the UK government, Shell had stuck by its plan to dump the Spar, despite a prolonged struggle with Greenpeace and massive opposition of European petrol consumers. Then, on 20 June, hours away from the intended sinking ground, Shell gave in, and turned the Spar around.

When at less than the 11th hour, Shell abandoned dumping, it handed Greenpeace one of its most spectacular and decisive campaign victories. As a director of campaigns sitting in a London office, I remember telling my staff to wait until it was formally confirmed before giving any media reaction, and having a considerable sense of foreboding. A 'radical' pressure group doesn't do that sort of thing and get off 'scot-free'.

With the benefit of hindsight, the Brent Spar clash, with its extraordinary volte-face by Shell, and the consequent humiliation of much of the UK political class and official scientific establishment, was a punishment by citizens (as consumers especially) for violating a social norm (don't litter, or dump in the sea). By turning normal power relations upside down, it provoked a two-year government-led backlash against Greenpeace that effectively ended only with the demise of the Conservative government of John Major in 1997.[16]

Vitriolic denunciation by the government and many press commentators began immediately. In a faithful pre-echo of the 2003 Iraq War affair over Dr David Kelly, enraged Ministers deployed the old trick of attacking the messenger, and in particular the BBC, for its part in 'supplying publicity'. Scientists from the official establishment joined the attack, not least because if public opinion decided issues like the Spar on ethical grounds, their established monopoly as bureaucratic arbiters of what was right or wrong for the environment would be eroded. Similar dynamics returned in the 2000s over the public rejection of GM foods: again a class of politicized scientists claimed to know better.

The propaganda onslaught against Greenpeace received a significant boost in September 1995 when the organization apologized to Shell over a mistaken estimate about how much oil might remain in the Spar. A loosely worded BBC report said Greenpeace had 'apologized for the campaign', and within hours that was the story worldwide. For years Greenpeace's critics then tried to rerun the campaign as 'Greenpeace were wrong – the campaign was wrong'. Even today, there are plenty who cling happily to this version of events.

In fact, the estimate played no part in mobilizing the public (being released only three days before the reversal) and got almost no press coverage. It wasn't even mentioned in the 37 major UK press stories about the Spar from 17–20 June. Neither did Greenpeace lie: it told the truth. Nonetheless, the BBC ran a series of knocking commentaries and programmes, ending only when the BBC itself had to issue an apology to Greenpeace, in 1999, over its broadcast of a claim by former Conservative Environment Minister John Gummer that Greenpeace had 'lied'.[17]

Apart from the obvious point 'don't make mistakes', there are at least two fundamental lessons in this for campaigns.

First, Greenpeace could have avoided the impact of the error if it had never allowed the toxicity of the Spar's contents[18] to become an issue, and had disciplined its communications better and stuck to dumping/littering. It now seems to me though, that this plurality was part of the price of scale – it brought campaigners 'on board' and made the Spar relevant to international processes, which helped the campaign develop. Big campaigns – like wars – have a lot of chaos within them.

Second, if your campaign succeeds massively and suddenly, it's unlikely that the losers will have time to save face, so expect them to seek revenge. Shell decided to do a U-turn, but the UK government didn't. Shell learned a lesson and modernized – it found a new way to listen to the public and consumers. The longer-term damage to the UK government and its system was greater. They learned few lessons and committed many of the same errors – remaining out of step with public values, not putting environmental rhetoric into practice, not standing by promises, not protecting public goods in the public interest, hiding political decisions behind a debased use of science, and denying the politics of risk – over issues such as GM foods.

RISK POLITICS

More and more campaigns revolve around issues of risk, particularly the types of hard-to-define risks, such as those from novel processes, which will come about in the future or where you need science to detect them. Writer Ulrick Beck has described how having moved beyond the simple risks of agricultural and industrial societies, the controversial creation and distribution of *new* risks is a defining condition of materially well-off societies.[19]

Yet, especially it seems in the UK, many professional politicians have a hard time dealing with risk. The old left–right culture omits risk and science, and is based on competing ideologies about economic production. Many politicians and journalists are lawyers, who notoriously tend to believe that risk is a technical issue that can be quantified, whereas, in fact, many significant risks are indeterminate.

'Science' has been comprehensively co-opted to legitimize and mystify technological development, and help dismiss public concerns about risk as irrational and unfounded 'anxieties'.

In an increasingly scientifically literate world, the public does not buy this line, and it leads to repeated bruising encounters between officialdom and the citizens (in the UK for example, over GM foods, BSE, foot and mouth disease, Measles, mumps and rubella vaccine (MMR) and the Brent Spar). Science writer Colin Tudge lists five reasons why the UK public now tends to distrust scientists or 'experts'.[20]

Risk, and particularly the creation and distribution of risk, is a political issue, including one of distributive justice, in the same way that creation and distribution of wealth is. A useful guide to the types of risk and appropriate ways to make public decisions about them, and hence how to frame risk-based campaigns, is given in Andrew Stirling's 1999 study *On Science and Precaution in the Management of Technological Risk.*[21] (See also Figure 12.3.)

HOW CAMPAIGNS BECAME POLITICS

Since the 1990s, campaigns have developed as a form of politics. There were five main steps in this process:

1   New concerns were politically excluded;
2   The mass media developed dominance;
3   Government retreated from leadership;
4   Business advanced into the vacuum;
5   Politics developed without politicians – involving NGOs, citizens (often as consumers), and other social actors, such as supermarket retailers.

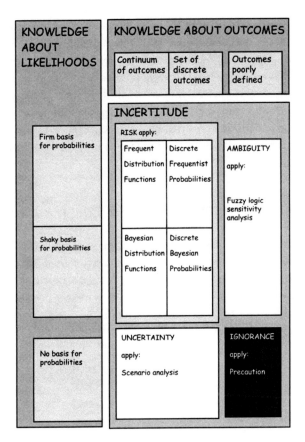

Figure 12.3 *The concepts of 'incertitude', 'risk', 'uncertainty' and 'ignorance' (after Stirling)*

Campaigns defined new concerns, but politicians, from the conventional right and left, often resisted them. Examples include sexual equality, environmentalism, human rights, animal rights and globalization. In the case of the environment, science – particularly the 'new' science of ecology – provided a new language, completely independent of established political ideology. Political parties called these 'fringe' or 'single-issue' concerns.

Governments reluctantly had to accommodate them, but they have mostly remained marginal, often treated with lip service, rather than becoming organizing ideas. However, they laid the first foundation for the rise of campaigns as a political force.

TV brought occasional power to the excluded campaigners in the 1960s, 1970s and 1980s. Then, from the 1980s, governments began to retreat from *doing* things. Privatization, liberalization, tax cuts, 'less government' and replacement of the public with the private sector, came into political fashion. One writer said in 2003 that, in the US, political liberalism and collective action have 'declined into oblivion'.[22]

The response to the Brent Spar and GM shows that, in Europe, this is far from the case, though politics now sometimes takes new forms, which professional politicians veer between denying, decrying and following. At Greenpeace in the 1990s, we called it 'unpolitics', and others have called it 'New Politics'[23] or simply, 'politics without politicians'.[24]

Politicians in power worry themselves over dwindling voter participation, and focus on spin or engagement mechanism such as easier voting, but the root problem is that they have failed to respond to public concerns, abandoned defence of the public interest, and made government less and less useful. It's only logical in these circumstances for people to seek agency elsewhere.

READING THE WEATHER AND THE TEA LEAVES

To plan or run a campaign you need to read the social 'weather conditions'. A drop of rain lands on your window pane. Does it presage a squall, a day rained off, or a storm that could wash your foundations away? Or even a long-term shift in the climate? If your campaign is surrounded by waves of controversy, hit by unanticipated pressures, or comes across unforeseen opportunities, are these temporary, short term or significant?

Campaigners may distinguish:

- Social climate change – a complete transformation of societies;
- Major currents – significant structural trends in society;
- Storm waves – social upheavals;
- Wind waves – controversies.

Climate change is a change from these long-term conditions. Naturally, you cannot see it easily – we need measurements or indicators. Social equivalents are the underlying conditions of society. Some are so slow that they are like continental drift; others are fast enough to have identifiable effects on institutions, companies, states or inter-generational perceptions. A change may involve sudden earth-shaking realignments after a long build-up of pressure.

Possible examples of social change on the scale of 'climate' are:

- Getting materially richer – in absolute terms in almost all societies;
- Ending the Cold War;
- Living longer;
- Industrialization;
- Post-industrialization;
- Seeing the Earth as limited in space (triggered by 'going to the moon' – the one event, some say, that the 20th century will be remembered for);

- Secularization;
- The global network economy

In no case can you do anything about these things, though it may well be that your entire organization's existence be down to one of them.

Major currents are frequently caused by the interaction of ideas, technologies and interests.[25]

In the physical world, such huge currents include the global conveyor by which the oceans recirculate water. Major currents that dominate society might include:

- The spread and then fracturing of mass media;
- The development of environmentalism;
- The growth of NGOs and civil society;
- Economic refugees;
- Questioning of global free market capitalism;
- The shrinking of state functionality and ceding power to business;
- Shrinking numbers of 'security-driven' people and growth in esteem-seekers and inner-directed types;
- Development of the US as a super-rich, super-power society (and then its decline relative to Asia?);
- Corresponding political intolerance of inequity and US cultural hegemony, including 'culture wars' or unconventional post-geo politics (state versus non-state etc.);
- Biotechnologies, artificial intelligence and nanotechnologies?
- The spread of numeracy.

With increasing material well-being, most societies have a shrinking population of the security-driven (see Chapter 3) and a growing number of inner-directeds.[26] The strain this places on social assumptions and institutions are at the root of many campaigns and many forced political adjustments.[27]

A campaign may ride such currents or push things into them to demonstrate that they are there. More likely, it will *use* them to try and redirect events, but it certainly shouldn't ignore them.

Campaigns and 'movements' can make waves. Very successful ones may start or redirect a current in society.

Storm waves

A really big campaign success can create formative 'events': things people will recall as a way to remember what they think about an issue.

By and large, though, it's not campaigns that cause such perception-changing events. Some may occur as a result of currents coming up against some notable obstacle and suddenly toppling it. The collapse of the Berlin Wall is perhaps the best example. At the time of writing, the jury is out on the many meanings of September 11, 2001, but it was definitely such an event.

Such signal events are usually much more important as icons or reference points that can be *used* in communication.

Campaigns that might have a claim to having provided such pivotal moments include:

- Martin Luther King's speech 'I have a dream', delivered on the steps at the Lincoln Memorial in Washington DC on 28 August 1963;
- The New York march of Earth Day, 1970;
- David McTaggart's 1972 'voyage into the bomb' in the Pacific on the Greenpeace yacht *Vega* to oppose atmospheric nuclear tests, during which he was beaten up by the French military – and the pictures smuggled out and televised;[28]
- The Green Party's electoral success in Germany in 1981, triggered by forest decline or 'Waldsterben', because of the number of small, private forest owners;
- Jubilee 2000's campaign for debt cancellation from 1996 to 2000;[29]
- The campaign to have the Antarctic declared a world park (ending 1991 with the 50-year mining moratorium);
- The Brent Spar campaign of 1995, which many say 'rewrote the rule book' on corporate accountability,[30] together with the simultaneous campaign against Shell over the Ogoni of Nigeria, and the execution of writer Ken Saro-Wiwa;
- 'Save The Whale' – the campaign to end commercial exploitation of the great whales, culminating in the 1983 moratorium by the International Whaling Commission;
- The Daintree rainforest campaign in Tasmania – Franklin River Dam halted in 1983 after a blockade, during which 1400 people were arrested and many jailed;
- Chico Mendes – shot by hired killers in 1988, Xapuri, Acre, a rubber tapper who fought for the Amazon forest and the people who used it sustainably;
- Chipko Movement – Hindi for 'tree-huggers'. The Chipko Movement of 1973 was the most famous of several similar campaigns, along with Himalayan community resistance movement against state-condoned logging;[31]
- The McLibel campaign against McDonald's, which became a trial of corporate values and accountability and changed the McDonald's brand into a political cipher;[32]
- The anti-apartheid campaign of the 1970s and 1980s, including the boycott of Barclays Bank by the National Union of Students, culminating in the release of Nelson Mandela, symbolically converted from a 'terrorist' into a global statesman.

It is said that there are three steps in creating a norm: First it's like a benchmark, a positive standard. Second, social pressure is applied to violations. Third, it is accepted and becomes the normal thing to do. Look at civil rights, sexual rights or health and safety – achieving such 'norms' took decades. Environment as a global concern was accepted by leaders of countries such as Sweden in 1972, but it took the 1985 hole in the ozone layer and the announcement of global warming in 1988 to swing laggards like Margaret Thatcher in the UK.

Wind waves

> *News is history shot on the wing. The huntsmen from the Fourth Estate seek to bag only the peacock or the eagle of the swifting day.* (Gene Fowler)

The same cannot be said of 'wind waves', the product of tempests that blow up 'out of nowhere' and often die down just as quickly. Campaigners must not mistake news squalls for major events, and end up dealing with the urgent rather than the significant. Wind waves are driven by argument, not commitments. Without the 'oxygen of publicity', they die.

The daily manoeuvrings of politics are in close synergy with the short-term requirements of news. Even in democracies, and especially in highly centralized ones,[33] a huge amount of press coverage consists of political gossip dressed up as significant developments. Much of it relates to what politicians are interested in; who is going up or down the 'greasy pole' and who will get which job, or lose a job. In such countries politics is mainly reported as a sort of blood sport, based on personalities and power, rather than 'issues'. This is one reason why the electorate takes less and less interest in politics.

SOCIAL MARKETING AND CAMPAIGNS

As campaigns succeed in 'mainstreaming' issues, many organizations, particularly in the public sector, turn to the techniques of 'social marketing' to achieve 'behaviour change' by individuals. They do this to try and secure behavioural compliance in line with policy objectives (implementation) or as a form of advocacy to try and create 'political space'. Many of the tools of 'social marketing' are captured in the acronym CAMPCAT (see page 25), which was derived from reviewing communications research, including 'social marketing'.

Social marketing, which mainly originates in the public health field, has been defined as 'the systematic application of marketing concepts and techniques to achieve specific behavioural goals, for a social or public good'. It can seem very similar to campaigning, but there are important differences. Social marketing usually makes the implicit assumption that the level to focus change efforts is at the individual, and its impact, if it has one, usually ends there. While this may be reasonable in the case of 'health', where individual free choice is hugely important, for many issues individuals acting alone can have little effect over the state of a social, economic or political system. So if campaigners equate social marketing with campaigns the dangers are multiple.

Social marketing does not usually seek to target or change power, organize group or networked action, or achieve any objectives above the personal level. While there is no doubt that 'social marketing' techniques and strategies can work – for example publicly funded campaigns to discourage smoking and drink-driving, often executed over decades and with huge public expenditure – many evaluations of social marketing also identify factors well external to the individual as important in fulfilling final aims, such as the presence or absence of regulation.

It therefore usually makes little sense for NGOs to adopt the same approach as government agencies in embracing 'social marketing', as they, more than governments, are truly free to be strategic: to go for big targets, or to try and change the system. For many issues of concern, there is a deficit of effort to change the system. In contrast to an individual-by-individual approach, strategic analysis usually identifies concentrations of power lying with institutions rather than with individuals.

To influence those institutions or concentrations of power, we usually have to come together in groups or, increasingly, through networks (an example being the Trafigura case in 2009, in which networking on Twitter and other online tools led the lawyers Carter Ruck to abandon their attempt to gag both the media and British Parliament).

The more power and problems are concentrated, the more important and fewer in number 'gatekeepers' are and the higher thresholds to influence are, the less significant the overall additive effect of individual action will be, and the more important it will be to run instrumental campaigns and/or find ways to achieve synergies between individual actions.

Given that social marketing campaigns *will* be run, especially by governments, and as a result many individuals may undertake a new behaviour, the question arises 'Can these be enhanced or exploited to create a bigger and maybe more strategic impact?' One way to do this is the VBCOP model of strategy (see page 143), which combines the use of values to drive behaviour, with the 'consistency heuristic' that in turn makes us change our opinions consistent with the behaviour, and then takes that opinion and turns it to strategic ends (P stands for politics but it could also, for instance, be impact on a company).

Another way to enhance the impact of changing *n* number of individuals is to analyse and target on the basis of values dynamics – the way one set of individuals influences another (see 'Emulation and norming' pages 87 and 224), which is often ignored in social marketing exercises.

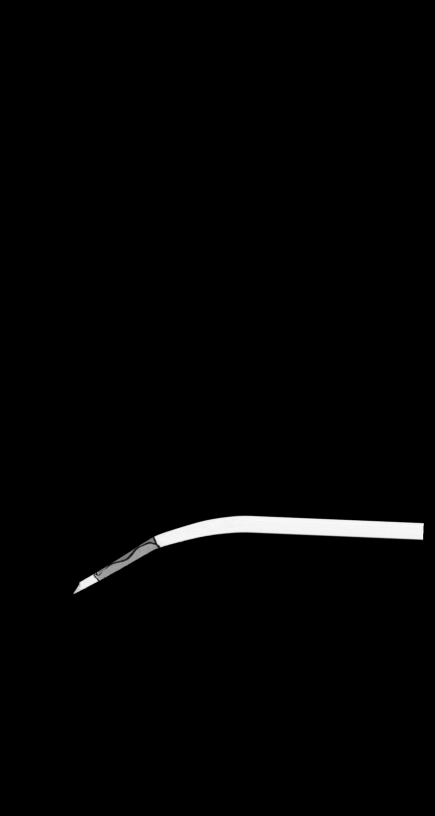

Case study: 'House'

While few social marketing exercises are models for campaigns, they are an increasingly rich source of examples of effective communications, at least in those cases where research has been used to create the design and execution. This is sometimes because the clients are public bodies with the budgets to hire in professional creative agencies who are increasingly applying similar techniques to campaigners, but many of the final 'deliveries' are things that campaign groups can do with far smaller paid-for resources.

In 2009, for example, a UK project for Kent County Council called 'House' won the APG Creative Strategy Gold Award for 'channel planning'. Like a host of other schemes, this set out to engage young people in order to reduce teenage pregnancies, sexual infections, and problematic drug and alcohol use. Unlike many others, the client and their agency (M&C Saatchi) took to heart the mass of research that shows that the context and the channel (see CAMPCAT page 25) are as important as the 'action' asked for in determining whether such communication is effective for these audiences. M&C Saatchi say:

> The idea was based on the premise (and extensive research) that if young people feel comfortable, relaxed and safe – they are more likely to open up and talk about 'stuff' with their mates and trusted youthworkers – on issues such as substance misuse and sexual health.

Consequently the agency involved young people themselves in helping transform disused high street venues (such as Kwiksave) in towns across Kent, turning them into 'an entertainment hub which looks like a mate's house' (it has a kitchen, bedroom, front room and so on). A diverse mix of activities went on in each house – careers chats, DJ mixing sessions, former drug users talking about their habit, alcohol education quizzes/games and so on. In other words, this moved youth/national health services out of institutional contexts such as doctors' surgeries, schools or dull youth clubs to co-created and fun places that young people actually wanted to be.

Marketing was virtually 100 per cent word of mouth (via ambassadors). Results after the first year included a reduction in youth crime and anti-social behaviour of 16 per cent (in Ashford), increases in young people accessing sexual health services, attendance by over 10,000 young people (including a high percentage of socially excluded groups), and more than one thousand attending interactive sessions on alcohol and drugs. Awards judge Craig Mawdsley noted: 'While digital would have been the obvious answer, the team went further, taking insights from the world of online but then applying them in the real world.'

APPENDICES

Climate Change Campaigning:
The Effect of Starting Conditions

The way you approach an issue, and then the sort of campaign proposition (see Chapter 7) you start to consider, depends of course on how it is framed (see page 28) – both by those communicating to you and yourself, based on your perceptions and experiences. In the case of 'climate change', the 'issue' was framed in science–government terms in the late 1980s. This in turn determined how the media framed it, leading to many problems in public communication, campaigns and achieving change. Responses, both in behaviours and in politics, have been held back by a media framing that is now out of date. Consequently, as of 2010, the by now vast community of climate campaigners faced a collective rethink as to their best way forward. This section looks at the effect of starting conditions and offers some ways forward in climate campaigning. A more detailed look at climate change campaigning can be found at www.earthscan.co.uk/onlineresources.

BEGINNINGS

I first came across climate change as a potential campaign issue in 1988. Like many other environmental campaigners, I had spent much of the previous decade working on acid rain and ozone depletion (caused by CFC, HCFCs and similar gases).[1] This meant that we automatically thought about the 'climate' or 'global warming problem' in terms of emissions of gases, international treaties (for instance, acid rain had the Convention on Long Range Transboundary Air Pollution, ozone had the Vienna Convention on Protection of the Ozone Layer and the Montreal Protocol, and both had EU Directives), and 'clubs' of countries setting themselves emission-reduction targets and subsequent action plans to implement them. In all three cases the UN played a pivotal role. It was an environmental-science regulator's model of society, with simple components of environmental media (air, water, soil and so on), sources, inputs and sinks. So, for good or ill, this architecture affected our thinking, and acted like a campaign template, and that, in turn, affected how we communicated campaigns. Initially, 'climate' was not much about everyday lives, homes or industries, products, services or choices.

Since then everything has changed and nothing has changed. Emissions have leapt up, and just the NGO delegations attending climate talks probably run into thousands. Some nations have adopted targets way beyond 20 per cent looking out to 2050, but most struggle to get anywhere close to it for 2020. What was only understood by a handful of scientists back in the 1980s, and then fairly dimly, had become widely known to NGOs, scientists and policymakers: namely that to keep the Earth within 'safe' ecological limits means cutting emissions effectively to zero, and that they must start to turn down by 2015.

CHALLENGES: NOT AN ISSUE DEFINED BY CAMPAIGNERS

Unlike most other 'environmental issues', it was clear even at Toronto that campaigners were not driving this process or defining the 'issue' – instead it was science and governments who made the running, with NGOs trailing along in their wake. A network of climate scientists effectively bounced their governments into recognizing the problem before potential opponents of action, such as the coal and oil industries, had time to get organized.[2] They used the Toronto meeting to break the issue into the media and made it impossible to suppress by bringing campaigning NGOs into the picture. When in September 1988 British Prime Minister Margaret Thatcher used a speech to the Royal Society in London to warn we had begun 'a massive experiment with the system of this planet itself', the issue was irretrievably launched onto the international political agenda, but as the property of political leaders, not NGOs.

This high level support was to have lasting consequences for how climate change campaigns were framed and communicated, many of which helped generate headlines but which have proved unhelpful in mobilizing broad public support.

The scientists involved were mainly atmospheric scientists, and a key role in setting up an institutional response had been given, almost accidentally, to the World Meteorological Organization.[3] Naturally they talked in terms of the science of gases and 'climate models' and on the scale of the planet and millennia. This started the process of first-explain-the-science, then make-the-case-for-action, then mobilize-to-support-the-action. This was about right for scientists talking to governments, but was not so effective with 'the public'. As I and others pointed out in 2005,[4] this repeated framing of climate change as 'an issue for political leaders', simply did not fit what the public was being asked to do (such as switch off electrical appliances), and that is without considering the equally ineffective instinct of physical scientists to try and motivate people to act by explaining the science, and revealing complexity (see page 23).

Even in 1988, reasons that the science did not seem likely to be sufficiently motivating included:

- The scenarios/projections looked 'on paper' like long slow gradual changes, with no disjunctions that might say 'decision time';

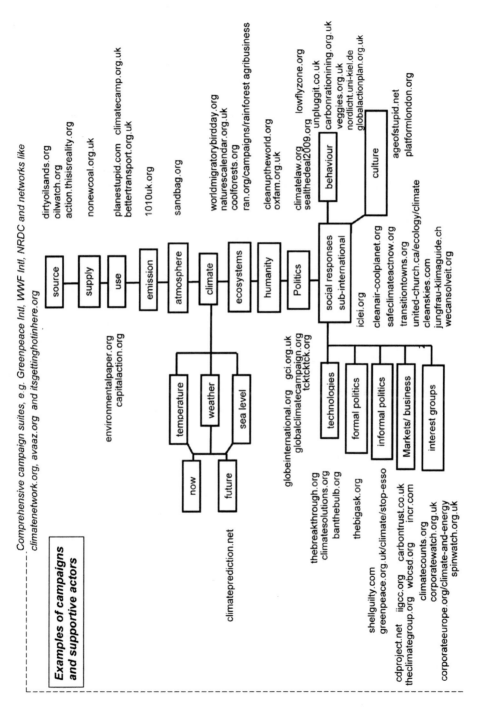

Figure A1.1 *Simplified map of 'the climate issue' by campaign*

- The global temperature changes were expressed as averages, and 1.5°C or even 4.0°C doesn't sound much when we are used to much bigger differences, month to month, day to day in the weather and in daily life, such as the temperature of 'hot water' (typically well over 40°C): hence the 'boiling frog' problem immediately came to mind – the slow gradual increase gets ignored;
- 'Climate' and 'atmosphere' were scientific abstractions and not media-friendly: they lacked human victims we could empathize with.

Very broadly speaking, the influences mentioned above created institutions that determined the way we acted on climate change. Science started it, and framed the problem, and hence (see pages 175 and 253) what the 'solution' looked like, in terms of gases, numbers and so on. Government and media and NGOs then all joined in, and science and government set up institutions that further framed the issue as one of international science–government processes.

These in turn led to talks on 'the scientific basis', 'adaptation' and 'mitigation', and that in its turn led to national and regional (for example EU) action planning and debates. This took place at very different speeds in different countries, and in fits and starts as different interest groups struggled to control agendas. From the early 1990s NGOs and some governments sought to engage businesses – Greenpeace, United Nations Environment Programme (UNEP) and the Alliance of Small Island States, for instance – quickly brought the insurance industry onto the side of those pushing for action. A simplified map of 'the climate issue' is shown in Figure A1.1, structured around the historical spine of science and government response, with some examples of current campaigns shown next to the relevant issues.

THE DIVERSITY OF CLIMATE CAMPAIGNS

The accumulated body of 'climate campaigns' now range in scope from those addressing the gaseous balance of the global atmosphere[5] to specific emission sectors[6] or personal behaviours,[7] and 'climate campaigners' span the social spectrum from straight-laced business people[8] or investors[9] to anti-globalization 'protestors' who even reject mainstream climate negotiations,[10] and cover topics from sea-ice to tropical forests,[11] from medicine and health[12] to 'social justice',[13] new technologies,[14] product design and ethics. There are climate campaigns to change particular towns, villages or cities,[15] climate campaigns to reach particular demographics[16] or psycho-demographics,[17] climate campaigns that promote favoured policy prescriptions,[18] campaigns against climate campaigns,[19] and climate campaigns[20] confined to the insides of institutions.[21] There are climate campaigns run by organizations that profess not to run campaigns,[22] and even campaigns that organizations encourage to be directed against themselves.[23]

Although nobody knows how many 'climate campaigns' there now are in the world, it must be many thousands. Political attention, media interest and scientific effort have followed a similar trajectory, and, with a lag of some years, so has the economic and industrial response.

Most campaigns have focused on achieving political regulation and that is having an effect. For example, in September 2009 the *Financial Times* reported[24] that the International Energy Agency (IEA) found global greenhouse gas emissions had dropped by 2.6 per cent since 2008, the steepest fall in 40 years. *ENDS Report* noted that 'for the first time, the impact of regulations checking greenhouse gases was clearly discernible, accounting for some 25 per cent of the reduction'.[25]

Before a nation state fully accepts the case for action, many campaigns focus on the 'regulatory battlefronts'. Nowhere is this still more true than in the US, where under G. W. Bush political action fell well behind that in Europe (although state-level action leapt ahead in the late 2000s). In 2008 the US Centre for Public Integrity reported[26] that there were four climate lobbyists (the great majority opposing climate action) for every Member of Congress.

The most obvious battlefronts are not, of course, always the best places to try and make a breakthrough. This is the point of using issue mapping (see page 95) and tools like force field analysis (see page 137). From the mid-1990s Greenpeace started to focus on market strategies and technologies, for example in its relatively successful 'Greenfreeze' campaign against HFCs in refrigeration, and pitching solar and wind against oil,[27] coal and tar sands. In the mid-1990s I argued inside Greenpeace that we needed a different approach to international climate politics from emission reductions at the UNFCCC. Starting in 1996 we used the 'carbon logic'[28] to frame campaigns against digging up more fossil fuels,[29] aiming to show a different political strategy – a carbon 'end game' bounded by bringing the atmosphere back into balance, rather than 'finger in the air' targets for incremental reduction driven by notions of feasibility and how much pain countries could bear to share (an example of taming the 'wickedness' of climate change, see page 99). For some years (1996–2000) Greenpeace tried to take this to the point of corporate responsibility – to the place where politicians authorized companies to add carbon to the stockpile (licensing for more fossil fuel extraction) – but my colleagues in the international political unit remained unconvinced, and after 2000 the campaign reverted to type.

The same basic knowledge was used in 2004 by Robert Socolow[30] to propose 'stabilization wedges', and in 2007 by the European Community in adopting its 2.0°C limit to climate change,[31] as well as in Peter Barnes's 'Sky Trust'[32] and by www.350.org.[33]

Ten years after our carbon logic excursion, US campaigners Michael Schellenberger and Ted Noordhaus made a point of criticizing American campaign groups for pursuing regulation[34] and instead advocated a different breakthrough[35] led by making renewable technologies cheap enough to exert a market-changing dynamic, which could then pull along regulation or create the space for it.[36] The question for campaign design is not which is 'right'

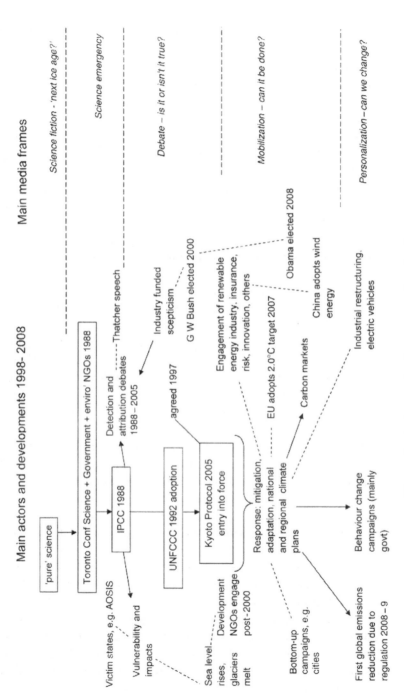

Figure A1.2 *Actors, developments and media frames*

Note: AOSIS = Alliance of Small Island and Low-Lying States

or 'wrong', or could work (Level 2, see page 9), but which can be *made* to work (a Level 3 campaign).

ISSUE DEVELOPMENT: MOVING FROM RAISING AWARENESS TO ACTION

It is impossible to adequately describe the development of the 'climate issue' in a page or two, but Figure A1.2 presents the main developments, actors and the changing media frames since 1988. It should be noted that throughout the history of the issue there have been bottom-up pressures from NGOs and others as significant as the top-down processes highlighted here. The 'worst case' science of the late 1980s has been gradually proved more right than wrong, so the generally accepted task has enlarged towards elimination of all climate pollution.

Over this time the main media frames and focus of campaigns have also changed. Throughout the 1990s, and up to the adoption of the Kyoto Protocol in 2005 (agreed in 1997 and ratified in the EU and Japan in 2002) and that of the 2.0°C target of the EU in 2007, many resources of environmental campaigns were devoted to a war of attrition against sceptics and reluctant governments. The gradual elimination of scientific uncertainties went on in the working groups of the IPCC and in the wider scientific community. The 2000s saw a widening of climate campaign alliances to include more active engagement by development and social groups: Al Gore's movie *The Inconvenient Truth* became a worldwide climate media phenomenon in 2007, the year that the IPCC unequivocally attributed global warming to human climate pollution.[37]

By 2009 many campaigns in developed nations had shifted from raising awareness of climate change and trying to counter sceptics[38] to holding governments to account so that their short-term actions tallied with their climate commitments.

BEHAVIOUR – THE HOME FRONT

Alongside 'traditionally' designed campaigns, the 2000s saw a slew of new 'climate campaigns' with a much more personal focus, on 'behaviour'. Some of the best have involved use of relatively simple 'heuristics' (see page 62). In line with similar initiatives in Holland and Japan, the UK Global Action Plan[39] (GAP) sets up 'eco-teams' in which neighbours discuss how much energy they could save using different domestic technologies, and agree to meet again to compare results. Often people then achieve better results than they committed to, driven by concern at what others might think of them. The effect is even bigger if the commitment is publicized. Although evidence of the efficacy of such approaches dates back at least to the German 'Negawatt for Megawatt' campaign of 1991,[40] many campaigns still do not employ them, and those that do are treated as news.[41]

Enter Web2 and personalization

By the mid-2000s a huge increase in use of mobile and personal internet access and 'social networks' led to a whole new raft of 'network' campaigns with little 'back office' infrastructure. For example the UK Climate Camp adopted an activist-gathering model from the 1990s UK roads protests, and 'flash mobbing' developed for advertising and PR, to create 'swoops' as a form of mass direct action.

Many more campaigns provided new engagement tools, with specific behavioural actions, for example online carbon footprint calculators.

Institutions on the move

An even larger set of climate initiatives do not sell themselves as 'campaigns' but have many of the same effects. Partly as a result of campaigns, the increasing amount of regulation and institutionalization around climate change creates new campaigning theatres, and changes the nature of the audience.

In one of its most effective projects ever, Friends of the Earth (England and Wales) ran a campaign called 'The Big Ask' in 2006–2007.[42] The Big Ask demanded a Climate Bill, and it succeeded, leading to the 2008 Climate Change Act, a world first. Thus the British government now sets[43] binding sectoral targets for reducing 'carbon emissions' to time-limited budgets (reducing emissions overall 80 per cent on 1990 levels by 2050). An independent Climate Change Committee advises on what more needs to be done.

Less than a year after the Act was passed, the UK government announced a 'Low Carbon Transition Plan'. *ENDS Report*[44] said it was 'an ambitious roadmap for meeting tough, legally binding carbon budgets requiring a 34 per cent cut in greenhouse gases by 2020 relative to 1990' and noted that 'the policy landscape' was 'transformed'. The Big Ask turned out to be a truly strategic campaign, with wide-ranging results in the UK. A 34 per cent cut on 1990 levels is of course greater than that 20 per cent cut by 2020 that seemed so optimistic in Toronto back in 1988.

Climate action is slowly becoming normal. Stimulated by the Act, the UK government has also set up the Carbon Reduction Commitment (CRC) to impose carbon cap-and-trade principles to 20,000 non-intensive energy users such as councils, hotels, banks and schools.

This begins to close the gap between individual consumers, and big business and national government. Slowly, bit by bit this will inevitably marginalize 'climate sceptics', as taking action to reduce climate pollution becomes 'business as usual'. In countries where similar legislation is introduced, future climate campaigns may then deal less with debates about climate science, principles and concepts, and more with the rights and wrongs of distribution, incentives, and ways of delivering 'carbon cuts'. In this way 'climate' will become a 'mature issue' like health or education, in which the 'if' question disappears in favour of 'how'.

FROM AWARENESS TO ALIGNMENT AND ENGAGEMENT

One way to think about the development of climate campaigns is to look at the overall development of the 'issue' in terms of the motivational sequence (see page 17) awareness → alignment → engagement → action.

At the end of the 1980s and in the early 1990s, the task for climate campaigners was mainly awareness-raising. The structured way in which the IPCC presented its findings framed an agenda of 'debate' and indirectly spawned a minor industry of professional sceptics, often funded directly or indirectly by the fossil fuel industry,[45] who devoted themselves to questioning the evidence. These belief-scepticism debates provided an easily available loop for those who didn't want to progress from awareness through to action.

A 2007 essay *Sustaining Disbelief*[46] identified the following types of such 'disbelief' debates:

- Existence – Could the models be right? Could large-scale human-induced climate change exist?
- Consequence – If it did exist, would that really matter?
- Detection – Can we find signs that the forecast climate change is really happening – a 'signal'?
- Attribution – If it's happening, can we find a 'fingerprint' of human influence?
- Response – Should we respond politically, for example by international government action, and socially and individually by changing the technologies we use and the lives we lead?
- Feasibility – Are the proposed solutions actually doable, technologically, economically, organizationally, politically?
- Efficacy – If we are trying them, are they really working?

The fact that all of these questions have been answered in the positive does not stop the debates being rekindled when the news media corrals and aggregates sceptic-sounding sentiments, and then simplifies and exaggerates them. As a result, even in the UK, the 'general public' seriously overestimates the amount of scientific doubt about climate change.[47] Some of the consequences of these debates are shown in Figure A1.3.

'Scepticism' can be found at any of these stages, although they mean very different things. So the different stages, or issues for debate, create a palette of beliefs and disbeliefs, which can be sampled by polling depending on the questions asked.

This is one reason why campaigning 'about climate change', as such, is a poor way to generate action. Campaign groups are in something of a quandary, because it is governments and scientific bodies who hold the ring on climate change. Because politicians and scientists have continued to use the global-climate-change frame and because the negotiations are

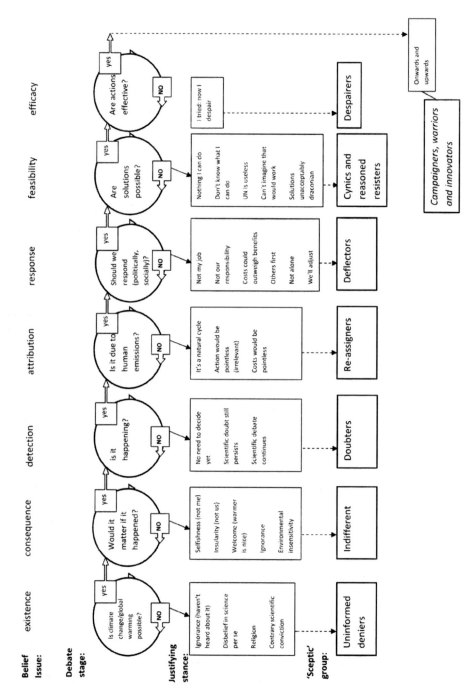

Figure A1.3 *Stages of scepticism*

structurally linked to science through the interaction of the IPCC and the UNFCCC, this difficulty persists.

In the late 1990s and early 2000s the focus of climate change campaigns was increasingly on alignment of audiences to particular impacts. In the North Eastern US, Clean-Air, Cool-Planet set out to reach fishers and hunters to raise awareness not of climate change at a global level, but in terms of its impact on their interest in forests and rivers of 'their region'. In Britain, the Woodland Trust developed[48] a project to make climate change a reality for the garden-loving British, enabling people to log the appearance of birds, plants and fungi as seasons changed.

CLIMATE CAMPAIGNS POST-COPENHAGEN: ESCAPING THE SCIENCE–GOVERNMENT FRAMING

At the Copenhagen Conference of the Parties of the UNFCCC in December 2009 (COP15), China and the US, which for different reasons had remained largely disengaged from the international 'climate process', became dramatically engaged but not by signing up to the laboriously prepared drafts for a global agreement. Instead, to the almost universal dismay of other countries and thousands of NGOs, they signed an independent 'Accord', a parallel agreement to do something, if not very much.

Around the same time, to the delight of the fossil fuel lobby and much of the media, a series of leaked emails and embarrassing admissions of errors in climate reports from the IPCC began to appear in the press. Sceptics were having a field day, although it seemed almost all governments recognized that the reality of human-made climate change was not in doubt. Faced with *force majeure* by the two most powerful nations in the world, supported by India, most other countries agreed it was best to embrace the Accord, and by the end of January 2010, 55 countries, together responsible for the majority of world climate pollution, had filed their pledges to cut or curb emissions with the UN.

Meanwhile, campaign plans and climate diplomacy had been thrown into disarray as the chess board of climate politics had been vigorously rearranged if not overturned. Should NGOs continue to focus their efforts on generating signs of public support for action through the international UN climate process, or should they adopt a different approach, and if so which?

There are innumerable blogs and opinions on the topic.[49] I believe that climate campaigning and parallel government efforts need to change (see *Climate Change Campaigns: Keep Calm But Don't Carry On*[50] for more detail). Strategies that primarily focused on the formal international UN climate talks are now out of date because, like the talks themselves, they are being overtaken by events. In short, the pro-climate action camp is has failed to realize potential support, and is using a communications and motivation model that has been repeatedly shown not to work.

The format of the 2009 talks and the 2009 campaigns had remained largely unchanged since the early 1990s but now, unlike then, millions of people, businesses and organizations are taking action consistent with cutting climate change pollution, and the major scientific uncertainties were resolved long ago. This spread of greener actions creates potential political space because of the VBCOP[51] principles (see page 143), which hinge on the consistency heuristic whereby people adjust their opinions (such as about whether climate change is a reality) to match their actions.

The consistency heuristic is itself part of a body of communications knowledge that has significantly developed since the UNFCCC started. This knowledge includes motivational values analysis, framing and heuristics. Such factors underlie the results of many studies that show, for example, that attempting to generate support for 'tackling climate change', either as a 'big picture' or through specific behaviours, is hardly ever best done by trying to explain climate change as an atmospheric and environmental process: yet this is exactly the assumption still made by many scientists, public bodies and even in some NGO campaigns.

Because opinions adjust to be consistent with behaviours, the development of greener industries and behaviours creates a large constituency for whom 'climate change' is a reality. Yet as of 2009/10 this reality has played little or no role in the UNFCCC process, which remains umbilically linked to the IPCC as if we were still at the stage where politics depended on resolving major scientific uncertainties. This in its turn perpetuates a media framing in which 'climate change' appears (falsely) to be a matter of great uncertainty, conjecture and scientific debate.

This sustains a playground for 'sceptics' and allows the media to continue to frame 'climate' as a social political question of 'belief', with stories fed by poll results about what we 'believe'.[52] As few people really understand the basis of the scientific consensus, they can only interpret 'debate' about 'climate science' by reflexive, emotional thinking using heuristics and driven by values (symbols, signs, rules of thumb, unconscious drivers). In addition, because of the IPCC–UNFCCC focus, climate scientists have been given a prominent place in the media and political dialogue but they, like many politicians, tend to be ignorant of how communications actually works, and end up unwitting facilitators of the communications strategies of those most opposed to taking action.

TEN PRACTICAL STEPS FOR DRIVING CHANGE

For examples and more details see the report *Climate Change Campaigns: Keep Calm But Don't Carry On*[53].

1 Create political space for necessary practical changes (for example renewables, efficiency, waste, different transport or food) by matching asks and offers to values, and then capturing and utilizing the consequent supportive opinions (VBCOP).

2 Create 'discourses' and dialogues around those changes – distributive, efficacy and risk issues, for example – to make news.

3 Do not try to sell 'big picture' Pioneer conceptions to Prospector and Settlers (values groups, see Chapter 3), for example 'a low carbon society': nobody was ever 'sold' a high carbon consumer society, it just happened and we embraced the benefits.

4 Focus much less attention on the international climate talks, and much more on making changes 'at home' (for example domestic renewables, electric cars, green fashions), and demonstrating that these are happening.

5 Educate the media about science and uncertainty and the basis of the construction of the consensus on climate change – best done as a peer-to-peer exercise.

6 Educate relevant scientists (and politicians and campaigners) about the basics of reflexive communications – framing, heuristics and values, for example – so, for example, they stop interpreting their progress or lack of through what the media says about opinion polling.

7 Government bodies and science institutions should give more scientific-policy attention to responses to impacts that are already happening (for example sea level rise, season change, acidification of the seas and melting glaciers) and explain these in terms that resonate with values, rather than publicizing the results of scenarios and models that are trying to push the outer limits of 'climate prediction' (where uncertainties are greatest).

8 Within the UN science–politics system, disengage the outer limits of science from the politics and stop politicians from using the elimination of uncertainty as a metric for taking political action.

9 Campaigners and politicians, and in particular their communications planners and social marketers, need to understand the dynamics of change in terms of values groups.

10 When talking about the 'big picture' of climate change to mixed audiences is unavoidable, use frames that are universal in terms of values. For example 'being a parent'.[54]

Where climate change campaigning goes now, and whether humanity manages to resolve the problem, nobody can know. The framing effect of how an issue starts and how to overcome this are just a few of many lessons that can be learnt from the climate issue. In this case the initial framing was something NGOs could do little about, but by offering alternative framings and shifting away from the government–science controlled issue of 'climate change' to specific actions – driving solutions – they may yet influence how it ends.

Appendix 2

Converting an Issue into a Campaign: The Case of WWF's Chemicals and Health Campaign

This is an example of a campaign set within a long-running issue. In this section we see how WWF converted the issue of chemicals into a discrete campaign on chemicals and health, and how their successful use of strategy and framing stories influenced EU legislation. An extended version of this section is at www.earthscan.co.uk/onlineresources.

In 2001, the stimulus to WWF's proposed campaign was the European Union's proposed new chemical regulation system 'REACH': Registration, Evaluation, Authorisation and Restriction of Chemicals.[1] The fundamental problem facing WWF was how to create a campaign that could work, rather than simply falling into the default mode of trying to publicize its ideas on how policies should be changed. For 18 months we (Campaign Strategy Ltd) held a series of brainstorms and workshops with WWF and conducted some formative and qualitative research to develop what became the 'Chemicals and Health Campaign (CHC)'.[2]

DEVELOPING THE CHC CAMPAIGN

Amongst WWF UK's[3] starting points was a management decision to run some sort of campaign on toxics, with these goals:

- By 2005, secure actions from at least two of the UK's top companies to reduce exposure of wildlife and humans to two endocrine disrupting chemicals (BFRs, BPA, Vinclozolin, phthalates and nonylphenols);
- By 2005, the EU Chemicals Regulation clearly incorporates WWF-UK's 'Four Tests' of environmental safety (substitution, precaution, the right-to-know and comparative assessment).

WWF started by discussing the instrumental objective but it also wanted to be *seen* to campaign (an organizational communications objective) and to increase its campaigning *capacity* (it also had a resource objective) – three of the five possible starting points on the 'campaign planning star' (see page 124). Each or any of these was a legitimate starting point for campaign development.

OPTIONS

We discussed several possible routes to change including:

- Trying to influence regulation at a UK and EU level; influencing markets through the interaction of business and consumers, either to deliver a specific result (for example a company drops chemical X), or to have a secondary impact on politics (business having a powerful influence over what politicians see as possible), or both;
- Influencing what was acceptable to the public: to create expectations and norms, which in turn would influence both business and politics.

This latter option, which is very hard to roll back, was the chosen option.

CHEMICAL INDUSTRY STRATEGY

It was soon agreed to avoid a campaign that played to the strengths of the chemicals industry, whose favoured defence had long been obfuscation and prevarication. This meant avoiding a straightforward head-to-head confrontation with the chemical makers.

When NGOs launched science-based campaigns, the usual result was at best a series of head-to-head debates between 'their experts' and 'our experts', often conducted in terms of chemical-speak that meant nothing to the public. Or else the debate was reduced to a dispute over what types of risk were faced, only to get lost in different meanings of 'risk'.

Campaigns based around wish lists of dangerous chemicals tended to lead into such a cul-de-sac. In addition, 'toxics' was already a 'mature issue': people had heard about pesticides and other chemicals for decades, so just providing more facts and figures was unlikely to have much new or additional effect.

WWF also considered other possible frames for the campaign, such as the Rights of the Unborn Child (on which there is a UN charter) and the 'right to know' but neither of these looked likely to produce an interesting and effective project.

A DISCOVERY STORY

To be easily communicable, a campaign needs to be visual and to present a story. The story of a campaign could be a physical journey, or a struggle to uncover something, and of course there are other forms of story. We decided to adopt the format search–discover–act, which can act as a 'frame' (see page 28) in which it follows that if you have searched or surveyed and discovered things, the next question is 'What is the consequence?' In the WWF campaign, we aimed to search for chemicals in human bodies. Finding something unpleasant or worrying in your body also invokes the 'grossness' factor. Whereas a list of chemicals in the environment is inherently dull and scientistic, finding that you or your nearest and dearest are polluted, is altogether more visceral.

We set up a blood testing programme. A leading WWF UK toxics lobbyist had already had her own fat tested and found high levels of persistent chemicals such as DDT, but WWF had not used it as a campaign mobilization tool.

A testing programme meant that the victims could become the messengers. People, unlike polar bears, can speak for themselves about how they feel about being forced to carry a burden of industrial chemicals. Rather than abstract notions of rights or concepts of ecosystem integrity, we would have a flesh and blood campaign with human interest and walking wounded.

COMPETING FRAMES

As the lobbying over REACH built up, the chemicals industry had tried to play on the idea of 'workability'. If they succeeded in triggering this frame, then because nobody would argue that the regulation *should* be unworkable, it sowed its own seed of success – after all, who other than the people actually making the stuff could say what was, or was not, workable?

The question raised by the blood sampling was very different. If these chemicals are getting into our bodies, then we need to know they are safe, beyond any doubt. It shifted the debate from a matter of degree, to one of presence or absence. In general, a 'black and white', either/or proposition is going to be better for campaigning than a 'how much' question (see page 181).

BLOOD TO BRUSSELS

WWF started its campaign by blood testing its own staff, on the principle don't ask others to do what you won't do yourselves. To give greater reach and weight to the campaign, we involved two partners – the National Federation of Women's Institutes (NFWI) and the 'ethically guided' Co-operative Bank.

WWF extended the survey from environmental activists to include ordinary families as well as politicians and other well-known figures. Each wave of blood testing repeated the same story of contamination but with a new twist. This generated repeated local, regional and national profile, and provided a diverse range of people who could talk about their experiences.

Figure A2.1 *Scenes from WWF UK Chemicals and Health Campaign*

Source: Justin Woolford

The WI members[4] then took their results and their opinions to Brussels, to lobby Members of the European Parliament (MEPs). Chartering a London bus and taking the Eurostar train, the 'blood tested grannies' created a visual story of a journey (Figure A2.1).

Blood (blood bags) and test results (people holding up papers) and family pictures of grandchildren also came with their own visual language: you could look at a picture and see what was going on, without so much need for words.

The Co-operative Bank ran an 18-month public campaign. In July 2003 the bank funded biomonitoring tests of over 150 volunteers including bank staff, Member of Parliament (MPs) and MEPs and mounted an awareness-raising Safer Chemicals advertising campaign that it calculated had reached one in three of the population.

By conducting a regional sweep of sampling, WWF was able to involve its network of local groups.[5] The chemicals found in the blood were reported at the WWF website. They tested for 78 chemicals including persistent and accumulative substances such as polychlorinated biphenyls PCBs and organochlorine pesticides but also newer chemicals such as polybrominated diphenyl ethers PBDEs, used as flame retardants in thousands of household products (from which they leak into our homes). Ninety-five per cent of those tested had ten chemicals and one person had two-thirds of them in their body.

WWF then extended its testing across Europe, and worked with Greenpeace to survey chemicals in the umbilical cords of babies. The tactic of testing brought cries of 'foul' from the chemical industry but engaged Members of the European Parliament as well as a much wider public audience than had participated in the issue before.

RESULTS

So far as REACH went, WWF's objectives were twofold: first to ensure that a class of very persistent and very bioaccumulative substances were included and listed as of high concern: some 30 professors and leading scientists signed a statement in line with this objective, which was achieved in the EC draft produced in 2003; and second to require their substitution (not yet fully achieved).

REACH was approved by the EU in 2006. As well as the WWF blood-testing exercise, Greenpeace had run tests on consumer products under the umbrella 'The Chemical Home'.[6] The European Consumers Association produced a Chemical Cocktail Website[7] and the NFWI had published a 'Simple Solutions' booklet[8] on avoiding chemicals. Friends of the Earth's 'Safer Chemicals' campaign had been aimed at companies that bought and sold products containing chemicals. FoE's European arm continues this work.[9] Retailers who had signed the pledge as of December 2002[10] were Marks & Spencer, the Co-op, Boots, B&Q, the Early Learning Centre, Mothercare, the Body Shop, Ikea, Homebase, Debenhams, Sainsbury's and Argos.

In 2008 *Ends Report*[11] re-surveyed these companies and found 'Many retailers are still using PVC, bisphenol A, phthalates and parabens despite making a commitment to Friends of the Earth (FoE) six years ago to phase them and other chemicals out.' On the other hand, many of these companies have stopped using some targeted chemicals, and it is now an active agenda with a degree of its own momentum.

REACH itself can be something of a regulatory angle-grinder, slowly but probably inexorably bearing down on the accumulated problem of an industry using tens of thousands of chemicals, about which little is often known.

Campaigners are now engaged in a war of attrition with some EU Member States and the Commission over issues such as criteria for reviewing and outlawing dangerous chemicals,[12] and have identified 267 substances they want withdrawn.[13] From time to time they will probably need to run more public campaigns again, but REACH at least ensures there is always an available 'theatre' to use as a battleground. The campaigns conducted in the run up to REACH also changed the players: when in 2008 an alliance of NGOs coordinated by Chemtrust produced their 'REACH Substitute It Now' (SIN) list, they were not alone but had the backing of companies including Boots, computer firm Dell, clothes-sellers H&M and construction company Skanska.[14]

Appendix 3

Formative Campaign Research: The 'Undersea'

T*his is an example of how qualitative research was used to inform design of campaign communications. An extended version of this section is at www.earthscan.co.uk/onlineresources.*

In 2009 a new conservation law was passed in the UK, The Marine and Coastal Access Act, giving new government powers to create offshore marine protected areas. Despite its maritime heritage and national love of the sea, at this the time England had only one fully protected undersea nature reserve of 3.3km² at Lundy. Working for government agency Natural England, Campaign Strategy Ltd commissioned perception research to test the

"I don't know why I don't care about the bottom of the ocean, but I don't."

Figure A3.1 *Public apathy as caricatured in* The New Yorker

Source: Charles Saxon, *The New Yorker* Collection, www.cartoonbank.com

Three Concepts connect primarily to 'topography'

GREAT highway of the north east

The **Great Highway** is special in that it is where the colder waters of the Northern seas meet the warmer waters of the South. It is defined by a glorious rolling sub-sea landscape of rocky planes, cliffs and caves.

The sub-sealandscape starts with chalk cliffs spilling into the sea, with inter-tidal reefs occasionally rising out of the water to form islands as the tide ebbs and flows, none more glorious than the historic island of Lindisfarne itself.

Dotted around this unique landscape are important habitats including open areas where scampis burrow and glades of kelp plants acting as a natural playground for families of seals feeding from the abundance of fish that live here.

LUNE DEEP GORGE OF THE NORTH WEST

The **Lune Deep** is a huge cavernous channel in the seabed at the entrance to Morecambe Bay and was formed over the course of the last ice age. It slides slope steeply from the seabed to a maximum depth of over 80 metres. In the bottom of the channel, boulders give way to tide-swept fine mud. On the upper slopes of the channel, there is hornwrack (which resembles seaweed) and a hydroid called an animal called 'sea beard', along with several interesting species of anemones. Further down the slope lives the distinctive peacock worm with the cobbles, pebbles and sediment forming the channel covered in a dense, furry 'turf' made up of tiny living marine creatures called hydroids and bryozoa. In the surrounding area, harbour porpoises can be found whilst a seabed consisting of sand and mud provides an ideal habitat for razor shells, with their shells washed up on the shores of the surrounding coastline in their thousands.

The Great Sand Dunes of the Dogger Bank

This part of the southern North Sea contains the biggest and best under water sand dunes in the sea around Europe. These magnificent dunes and covers an area bigger larger than Greater London- the peaks of the dunes are big enough to dwarf Big Ben and enough sand moves around every day to fill Wembley stadium three times over!

These mountains of sand are home to literally billions of Sand Eels -. fish that are a essential part of the food chain in the sea.

The Sand Eels help to provide the fantastic seafood that we all enjoy because they are eaten by cod, whiting and mackerel in huge quantities as well as feeding one of Britain's best most treasured seabirds- the Puffin.

Figure A3.2 *Example of stimulus material used by KSBR (www.ksbr.co.uk) in qualitative research on undersea landscapes*

theory that one reason for this was a lack of public engagement with the undersea as a 'place'. This might explain why attempts to mobilize public support for specific protected areas had melted away in the face of opposition from user interests such as fishing.

With qualitative researchers KSBR,[1] we conducted 18 focus groups around England of eight adults each. The groups were values segmented according to underlying motivations – Settlers, Prospectors and Pioneers (see Chapter 3) – with the objective of finding a common denominator way to convince all groups that there was something worthwhile protecting 'under the sea'. We also ran a subsequent quantitative baseline awareness study of over 3000 people, against a values-segmented quota (to the 12 Values Modes level).[2]

In the focus groups people were shown 'stimulus material' that described real undersea features and their life, for example kelp forests, seabed communities of reefs worms and anemones, the currents and rocky reefs of the north-east, and herring spawning 'creches' in the Thames Estuary. These were based on the ideas of Dramatic Topography (by analogy like dramatic scenery on land), Individuals and Communities (like villages, towns or cities) and Beauty Spots (another terrestrial equivalent).

RESULTS

We found a common ignorance about what actually lay beneath the sea across all segments (under one per cent could recall a real undersea place-based feature in the quantitative work) and pronounced differences between the values groups that were stronger and more consistent than demographic or regional differences. The English really had no idea of what lay under the sea. Around half were inspired to guess at the obvious – 'fish' and 'weed', for example – but there was clearly no understanding of the undersea of the type enjoyed by terrestrial landscapes. We also found that:

- All the groups, but especially the outer-directed Prospectors, felt ashamed that 'our seas' had got into a (largely assumed) state of disrepair and damage. Many spontaneously cited damaging activities such as pollution or industrial fishing in support of this and were inclined to believe there was 'not much there'. In addition both Settlers and Prospectors tended to think that seas in other countries were the only 'nice' ones (with the possible exception of south-west England), and there was a strong sense of fear and disgust about 'under the sea' – because it was dark, cold, slimy and dangerous. It was not something they had thought about or wanted to think about. These factors did not apply to 'the sea' when experienced as 'the coast' – hence the apparently contradictory poll findings that showed high public appreciation of things 'marine'. Unless something could bypass these factors, it would be hard to generate robust support for protecting particular undersea places.

- Pioneers reacted more positively to ideas or features of mystery and beauty and enthusiastically elaborated more possibilities. For Prospectors and Settlers, the unknowable triggered feelings of insecurity rather than interest: you might get entangled in a kelp forest, for example.
- Settlers, and to a lesser extent Pioneers, reacted positively to ideas of community: it was a 'result' to think that communities of little creatures were successfully living together in places around England. For Settlers this naturally translated into the thought that they ought to be left alone: they were of value simply for having survived.
- The only concept that engaged positive interest from Prospectors *and* worked for the other groups was dramatic topography. Prospectors could get enthusiastic about the scale of the Dogger Bank or the Lune Deep. Prospectors in particular wanted this proved – by seeing it, or better still, experiencing it: 'You should have a submarine to enable us to fly through it – zoom up and down it…'.

Mention of 'issues' or 'problems' quickly triggered a cut-out for Prospectors in particular: they did not want to know about anything 'political' and it triggered feelings of shame, guilt, fear and distaste. Communications starting from here are likely only to engage a small subset, mainly the Concerned Ethical Values Mode (a Pioneer group making up about 10 per cent of the population).

The very word 'environment' was associated by many Prospectors as a sign that criticism was on its way – they were about to be told not to do something. This provided another reason not to engage. Consequently the Natural England campaign was framed as a *Landscape* Awareness Campaign.

Less obviously, mention of what conservationists saw as solutions also had the same effect. The idea of more 'Protected Areas', while broadly understood, was taken to signify

Concept group	Sustenance	Outer	Inner
Topography	An exciting idea		
Individuals and communities	A compelling idea	A neutral idea	An interesting idea
Beauty Spots	A potentially worrying idea		A fascinating idea

Figure A3.3 *Simplified summary of results by Maslow Group*

that there were problems. There was also surprise that if there was anything worth protecting, it had not already been protected, potentially leading to a judgement against those in authority. This is why you first need to build awareness (in this case awareness that there is something there – an undersea landscape), before moving on to problems or solutions, let alone engagement for action based on perceiving problems and solutions (see Motivational campaign sequence, page 19).

The conventional advocacy mix talking about problems and solutions, issues, policies, laws, politics and the weird-and-wonderful mysterious creatures of the sea, had a chilling effect on the majority (60 per cent) of the population. England's great love of the sea reported in many surveys was not as much about the sea, and even less about the under-sea, as about *the coast* – a known and explored place where the perceived negatives of the undersea are kept at a safe distance. The high levels of concern about problems such as pollution, themselves probably generated or reinforced by decades of pollution campaigns, were consistent with the idea that the undersea around our coasts was 'empty and degraded'.

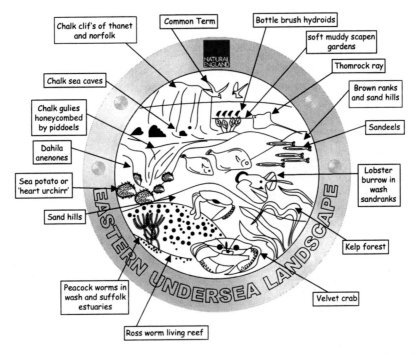

Figure A3.4 *Design for children's 'colouring in' window decal from Natural England Undersea Landscapes Campaign – Relates creatures to features of the landscape*

Source: Sam Symonds, www.anewleafdesign.co.uk, for Campaign Strategy Ltd; copyright Natural England

Communications activities designed using the research base

Using this research as a template for defining the communications most likely to be effective, the public strand of Natural England's Marine Campaign was designed to raise awareness of the undersea as a real place, a living landscape equivalent to the regional landscapes on shore, and to do this by 'taking people there', by:

- Showing them that such places exist visually (for example with maps and features and online films);
- Taking them on a journey as in a motion-ride experience;
- Enabling families and children to make and take home an undersea landscape in workshops (as we made it, it must exist);
- Enabling families and children to create and take away sea creatures with a particular geographic place-based relevance to their local undersea landscapes;
- To give these 'makes' relevance and enjoyable salience in their lives because they have a purpose (for example as kites to play with, as door guards, hair grips, pencil tops or finger puppets);
- To then show this to others via local media, and to expand the awareness of this through engaging councils, community groups, NGOs and others in creating and displaying signs of awareness of and engagement with such undersea landscapes, for example by 'adopting a landscape'.

Figure A3.5 *Making an undersea landscape in a box*

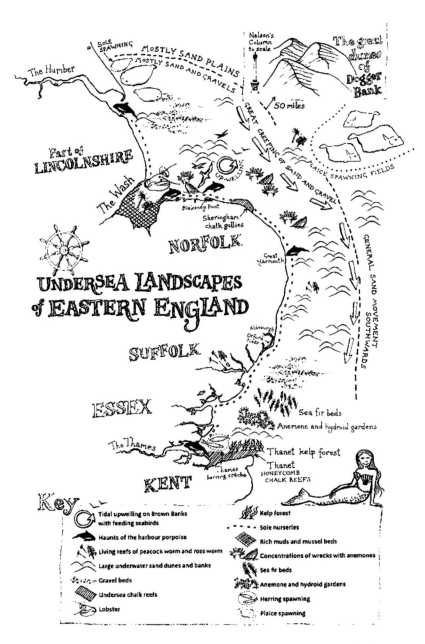

Figure A3.6 *Sketch for map of undersea landscapes – Regional identity*

Source: Download available at www.naturalengland.org.uk/ourwork/campaigns/default.aspx

At the time of writing, some of these steps had been implemented, such as the family workshops and the creation of maps and panoramas. The applicability of these particular findings outside England is unknown, but the principle of research to produce a communications campaign that resonates with motivational needs certainly applies more widely. In countries with clearer water and more divers and snorkelling, there will probably be far greater awareness that there is a landscape-under-the-sea. Transferable campaign design principles include:

- Do not rely on existing polling about an 'issue' to tell you what might work in a 'campaign';
- Use qualitative research to uncover perceptions (unlikely to be evidenced in polls);
- Divide up your audiences by motivational segments such as values, if you intend to try and get them to take an action, and use these segments to recruit research groups;
- Use research findings as a template for developing offers and asks;
- Do the qualitative research first in order to know the real meaning of questions in quantitative polling, and only do such polls after quantitative research.

Appendix 4

Obama Election Campaign:
A New Media Case Study

T*he story of how a young senator from Illinois came from left-field, without the traditional Washington powerbase and political infrastructure, gained the Democratic nomination and subsequently took the Whitehouse, has rapidly become a legend of 'how to campaign' and how to use new media in particular. Despite the singular nature of the US Presidential election, there are useful lessons for all sorts of campaigns in the analyses of the Obama campaign.*

Many studies of the Obama success reinforce the basics in this book. Whatever the technology involved, the essentials for effective communication to achieve an outcome remain the same: giving agency by getting the right message to the right people at the right moment. Other studies emphasize opportunities that arose through developments in communications technology: online tools that campaign groups can use to organize, provide engagement mechanisms and enable supporter communication involving large numbers of people.

Unlike the old 'mass media', online gave accessibility, but as the other candidates discovered, accessibility in itself is not enough. To exploit modern communication tools effectively requires a clear strategy, expertise, adequate resourcing, discipline and commitment.

Of course Obama was made for the moment. At the tail end of the Bush administration in the midst of a serious economic downturn, there was a widespread feeling in America that change was needed. Obama embodied an attractive alternative. Even so, the election result was not inevitable and there is no better model for demonstrating how strategic use of communication technology can engage by providing agency, provoking a self-sustaining chain reaction of participation to bring about tangible results.

This section does not attempt a full analysis of the Obama campaign – there are many books on the subject – but there follow a few salient points.

50 States

One of the key qualities of the internet (and, for example, multichannel satellite TV) is its capacity to enable 'narrowcasting' – that is to reach a specific segment of the population across a wide geographic area. In organizing terms – developing a campaign asset composed of followers or an aligned network – this means that the resources available to a campaign for organizing can do things that, without 'new media', would have been hard if not impossible. In the case of Obama's campaign, it meant that the Democratic Party could reach out and organize supporters in all 50 States, and attempt to fight an election across a broad front.

This '50 State Strategy' has its own webpage.[1] In past US elections, each party would focus its efforts in getting out the vote in its respective solid 'Democrat' or solid 'Republican' States and pour hundred of millions of dollars fighting it out over a handful of 'battleground states'. Thanks to use of online tools, the Obama campaign could redraw battle lines, and adopt a strategy built around online organizing and communication that enabled it to out-fight its opponent.

Strategy of tactical positioning

Although the techniques of targeted voter mobilization went back to the early days of US politics and to Republican Karl Rove, and the '50 States' to Democrat Howard Dean, the Obama campaign's big breakthrough was in the use of online media to facilitate it. This was their best tactic, and they planned a campaign around it (see page 33). In 2007 Obama adviser Robert Gibbs was reported as saying,[2] 'There are plenty of other people that can do "politics as usual" far better than we can. But I hope we have a campaign whose support continues to expand even faster than you can put a fence around it.'

Defining the problem

The problem (see P in RASPB propositions, page 175) the Obama campaign overcame is what has been called[3] 'the perpetual problem of Presidential politics: having one message to win over a party's most ardent supporters and another when trying to capture independents and UFGs ['up for grabs'] – the voters who decide a general election'. The problem was defined as past politics in which G. W. Bush and Bill Clinton were implicitly lumped together. The 'action' was plainly vote for Obama. The 'solution' was 'change', which in the Primaries worked against Hilary Clinton, and in the Presidential election campaign against McCain, without having to change a note. The 'benefits' could of course be safely tuned to specific audiences or left for voters to imagine. Campaigners should note that this was devised on the basis of extensive research on voter perceptions.

Resources – Money

During the primary contest that preceded the election competition with Republican John McCain, the Obama team realized that he had developed a very broad donor base, which could be directly tapped for funds. As a result, Obama rejected federal funding for his campaign and the financial limits that came with it. (During the Primary run off against

Hilary Clinton she loaned her campaign $5 million. As one commentator noted,[4] Obama's team 'responded by sending out an email to its supporters the next day that read, "We need to match this quickly, can you help?" Within 24 hours respondents donated $8 million.')

Resources and assets – People

The Obama campaign recruited a lot of technical expertise to define its 'online' strategy. Facebook founder Chris Hughes devised an innovative internet fund-raising system – the campaign eventually attracted more than three million donors. They donated about $650m (£403m) – more than both presidential contenders in 2004 combined. Other advisers on online included Google CEO Eric Schmidt.

The campaign was also masterful in getting out the vote. It ran a huge registration drive for likely Democrats – adding more than 300,000 people to the voter rolls in Florida alone. In the case of political campaigns, numbers are obviously key (not always the case in other campaigns).

In addition, realizing that so many new voters could overwhelm polling places on voting day, the campaign made early voting a priority in states where it was allowed. More people cast their votes before election day than ever before – over 29 million in 30 States.[5]

Resources – Communications technology

Obama met with Netscape founder Marc Andreessen to learn about social media in 2007 and then spent more than $2 million on hardware and software. The online team started at 11 people and rose to over 30.

Liking

The Obama campaign systematically exploited the 'liking' heuristic. People take more notice of people they perceive as like them, and who they like, such as friends (see page 26). David Plouffe, Obama's campaign manager, called it the 'persuasion army', getting grass-roots volunteers at a community level to talk to people who are 'like them, talk like them' to drive support in a way that advertising and direct mail cannot.[6]

Enthusiasm, credibility and feasibility

The Obama campaign succeeded in generating more enthusiasm and excitement than his opponent, John McCain. TV analysts, who tend to explain everything by what is easily seen on TV, focused on obvious personal differences such as age, ethnicity and personality, which undoubtedly played some role, but the campaign lesson is more about the proposition (see page 175) and its attractiveness in terms of feasibility (see the triangle, page 51) and the prospect of bridging the engagement gap (see page 60). As CNN commented,[7] 'It's hard to get your supporters ginned up for a national campaign if they see no infrastructure, especially local get-out-the-vote operations.'

The '50 State Strategy' ran against everything that conventional wisdom dictated as the objective was too large for the existing assets and resources of the Democrats, but the more the Obama campaign successfully involved potential voters in becoming party of Plouffe's 'army', the more credible it looked and the more reason there was to join in. This in turn generated enthusiasm and excitement. The impossible began to look possible.

In 2007 Obama strategist David Axelrod stated:[8]

> It's not just how he delivers the message but how we deliver the message, and what kind of relationship we develop with our supporters... If this campaign is what it should be, this is not going to be the hoisting of an icon. It's going to be the movement of millions of people.

This 'bootstrap' strategy relied on organizing and manifesting support and relentless use of a simple consistent message – change – which was not vulnerable to unpacking (see page 181) as it was relayed along the chain of organizers and volunteers because it remained fairly vague or elemental. It was also repeated across all media and channels.

As one observer noted:[9] 'You can't build a social network around something that people don't care about because no-one will have anything to say'. The 'Enthusiasm Gap' was said to be 61 per cent Democrat against 35 per cent Republican. Test this on your own campaign ideas – does it excite you? Is it the idea that is hard to stop talking about? Or is it just what we feel we ought to do?

Careful use of channels

The campaign knew that more than half of all adult Americans belonged to a social network but most only visit one. Obama created profiles on around 15 networks, including Facebook and MySpace, but was he also was the first presidential candidate with profiles on AsianAve. com, MiGente.com and BlackPlanet.com, influential ethnic networks. The campaign used these to direct supporters to MyBO, where it could present them with strategically useful activities.

Levels of engagement

Ultimately the Obama campaign required a lot of people to do one thing – vote – but it organized itself to get a lot to do much more, even achieving Stage 4 (see page 56), in which people change their lives for the cause. One report has it[10] that by the Primaries Super Tuesday, Obama's Field Director Jon Carson:

> *Called upon the volunteers – in particular, those he called the 'super-volunteers', people who had left their jobs or dropped out of school to help. He estimated that there were about 15,000 super-volunteers working full time for Obama.*

Letting people in

Plouffe rarely spoke to the media, but he communicated the strategy and progress with donors via amateur looking online videos – they could feel part of things, and it all helped sidestep the reframing and recoding effect that any campaign endures if it communicated via 'the media' (see pages 28 and 231).

User generation of content and activities

The password-protected campaign website 'MyBO' (my.barackobama.com) allowed supporters to create their own campaign content supporting the candidate. It held videos, speeches, photos, and how-to guides, leading over 400,000 to post pro-Obama videos at YouTube. By the end of the campaign, MyBO had 1.5 million registered web volunteers who had organized over 100,000 events, such as house parties.[11] This was complemented by centrally generated video at BarackTV. More than 1700 videos were posted here, about five times the number at McCain's site, and mostly featuring supporters activities rather than just Obama himself. The Obama campaign also used mobiles and Twitter, then in its infancy. By the end of the campaign, on Twitter, Barack Obama had 112,474 followers, while John McCain had 4603. On Facebook, Obama had 2,379,102 friends by November 2008 and McCain only 620,359. Texting was used to prompt action – such as voter turnout.

Recognizing people

The Obama campaign embraced support from specific groups and played it back to that group, those like them and wider audiences, saying again 'we like you'. User-generated videos on YouTube included Obama Girl's 'I got a crush… on Obama', which received more than 12 million views and the unofficial Facebook group Students for Barack Obama, started by a student in 2006, was incorporated into the campaign. Text messaging was used to relay personal messages straight from Obama back to supporters and to break news of important campaign developments through the supporter network rather than the news media. And he said thank you. Before his victory speech he sent this to Facebook fans:

> I want to thank all of you who gave your time, talent, and passion to this campaign. We have a lot of work to do to get our country back on track, and I'll be in touch soon about what comes next. But I want to be very clear about one thing – all of this happened because of you.

Using small steps

The campaign created a host of ways to take small actions that indicated support, knowing that (the consistency heuristic) this would be likely to potentiate more actions (especially if it involved sending or showing something to a friend). In building networks and manifesting support, this is important. As in fund-raising, those who focus increasingly only on 'high value' targets can end up losing their base and their future.

An event horizon

All electoral campaigns enjoy the benefit of having an event horizon – a defined moment that all efforts lead up to. This has enormous benefits in terms of engagement, not least because supporters know that their efforts will one day count (see page 167), even if a win is not certain. It has potential for drama (see page 1), with an outcome certain but unknown. It also meant that for a new candidate, pure hope could be fostered in the minds of the electorate, unsullied and untested by a track record or time in office. Campaigns based around a major event (such as the 2009 Copenhagen climate talks and www.1010uk. org, an organization that effectively used Copenhagen as an engagement template) can enjoy the same benefit. The downside is the potential emotional hangover and having to sustain momentum afterwards.

Table A4.1 *Effects of formats of 'donate' asks at a website*

Variations in text on button	Not signed up	Signed up	Donated
Donate now	0%	0%	0%
Please donate	+2.3%	+27.8%	+16.3%
Why donate	−27.8%	n/a	n/a
Donate and get a gift	+15.2%	-24.6%	+11.9%
Contribute	+8.51%	+2.9%	+18.4%

A campaign of calculation

Almost everything about the campaign was tested and retested. Some things could not be predicted but were tested and adapted as it went along. Table A4.1 shows, for example, the results of a test on different formats of 'donate' asks at a website.[12]

THE REAL LESSONS

The real lesson is that Obama's was not a 'new media' or 'online' campaign, but a campaign using new media. In communications terms, it sought specific outcomes, it engaged people, it kept its main message short and simple and valued small actions, it utilized heuristics, it was visual and created events, it told stories about real people and got them to tell their stories in ways that grew the scale of the campaign and sense of possibility, it was proactive not reactive, and it set the communications agenda in the outside world rather than being at the mercy of media framing.

The Obama campaign hit many of the principles of campaigning described in the first section of this book. It had moral legitimacy: a widespread feeling that change was needed; it engaged by providing agency, giving credible attractive ways to make a difference; it provoked a conversation in society in a self-sustaining chain reaction of participation (interesting methods); it had verve, élan, infectious energy that excited those it involved; it was strategic; it was communicable: remembered and reinvented visually; and it united people more than it divided them.

Appendix 5

Issues and Power Analysis:
Greening Apple Computers

This is an example of a successful campaign strategy informed by issues and power analysis, understanding industry dynamics and brands. An extended version is at www.earthscan. co.uk/onlineresources.

By 2006 Greenpeace and others had been pursuing the 'greening' of the computer industry for some years. Greenpeace had succeeded in starting something of a 'race' between manufacturers to comply with legal and voluntary standards and go further in removing toxic compounds such as heavy metals, PVC and brominated flame retardants. The emphasis and framing of the campaign had been on 'waste' and responsibility for waste, nearly all of which ended up in unregulated or little regulated smelting and scrap operations in India, China and other developing countries.

The campaign had created some environmental leaders on recycling and commitments to phase out some of the worst chemicals in the PC market: notably from Dell and Hewlett Packard, both fiercely competitive, and much larger than other producers, each with over 30 per cent of the market. All this had been achieved with little public engagement.

TARGETING INNOVATORS

Zeina Alhajj, the leader of the Greenpeace 'toxic tech' campaign, now wanted to push the sector further towards completely re-engineering electronics to design-out toxic components at source. Greenpeace had identified Apple and Sony as companies with disproportionate sector influence. Although their market shares were tiny (Apple at less than three per cent), they were the technical innovators, which the mass market 'box makers' imitated. If a step change was to come, then these were the obvious players to influence (see 'Issue mapping', page 95; 'Gathering intelligence', page 100; and 'The ambition box', page 134).

Sony had already made a commitment to phase out some chemicals and the campaign group therefore turned its attention to Apple. Its initial ideas for upping the ante were:

> *To expose the contamination which is hidden behind the sleek design of electronics and advertising. We want consumers to pressure industry leaders into creating durable products that are toxic free, last longer and are easy to recycle and dispose of.*

Greenpeace had already identified its primary target as consumers – suppliers, techies, young people (who get a new mobile on average every 18 months) and 30-somethings with disposable incomes – 'adaptors', and secondarily 'decision-makers' and regulators. It recognized that its campaign had to be as cool as the products: one campaigner wrote, 'We need to give Greenpeace "bling"!' An internal note added: 'The main strategy will focus on enraging the public about the "true" and dirty image of the industry.'

The traditional sorts of Greenpeace tools to do this include non-violent direct actions – such as 'return to sender' and investigations and exposés of contamination at plants and waste facilities. But would this be the best approach to change Apple?

INFLUENCING APPLE

The obvious route to attack Apple was a direct assault on its main brand attribute, the apple, or its high profile boss, founder and CEO Steve Jobs. Indeed various Apple-knocking images were already at large on the net: rotten Apples and so on. It was at this point that Campaign Strategy Ltd got involved to look at communications strategy. For a campaigns consultant it was a dream job as Greenpeace had already done three things right.

First, the underlying campaign strategy analysis was almost faultless. It had used consultants and its own resources to examine in detail the business strategies, models, interests, culture and policies of all the significant players in the computing and associated sectors. It had studied the interaction between companies and the ways in which innovation came about, as well as being on top of developments in UN and other forums where regulation was in development.

In other words, the PEST – political, economic, scientific and technical – factors were pretty well known, and the power analysis had been done, before Greenpeace turned its attention to communications strategy. The organization had done its homework looking at how the system worked that it was trying to influence.

Second, it recognized the need to fundamentally review its communications effort and was prepared to discard existing plans. All too often a campaign group tries to refresh or improve a campaign while continuing with existing projects on established tracks – a recipe for muddle.

And third, it was prepared to commit sufficient resources to the communications to give them a chance of really working.

We spent some time trying to understand the culture of Apple, its customer base and, in particular, its famous and idiosyncratic boss Steve Jobs. We asked around among people who worked in or consulted for the IT industry and who had done market research and product strategy for computing companies.

The first conclusion of this was that to engage consumers, as Greenpeace wanted, it needed to lift the focus of the campaign out of the 'waste' frame and relocate it in the retail and user environment. The campaign needed to live in the home, on the street (for example iPod) and in the office, rather than in 'a distant country' (where the 'waste stream' went). The battlefront needed to be in the consumer environment rather than, in this case, just where the problem actually had an impact.

For the consumer to engage with the 'issue' of toxic substances in their technology, it had to directly relate to their possessions as they experienced them – in this case mainly to their Mac – and not just to 'waste' or 'electronic waste', which was in the 'post-consumer' world. We noted that under the existing campaign model:

> It is a 'their world' not an 'our world' campaign for most potential campaign supporters and allows the industry to treat it as a policy issue (and the industry-wide working group proposed will tend to exacerbate this) ... it enables the retailers, and the retail setting, where both computer makers and retailers are most exposed to public values, to largely avoid the campaign (ie it happens elsewhere). It is not personalised to the user or owner of a computer, and it limits politics and media coverage in most countries to 'foreign pages'.

Consequently we suggested developing a market campaign track in the arena of retail alongside the waste track, and a solutions track (a geek-based design competition). The part that was operationalized was the market campaign that sought to:

- Make the product the problem (rather than just the waste);
- Make this real through consumer, retailer, market engagement;
- Personalize the campaign for the consumer-citizen;
- Make this real through their own products and their buying decisions.

In terms of style and feel, a campaign about Apple posed a fascinating communications problem. Apple was easy to identify and easy to reach but it was also media-savvy, cool and self-contained with legendary customer loyalty. It would be easy for Apple to 'stand above' most conventional campaign criticisms.

A SEDUCTION

The whole culture of geeks and net-heads, while not representative of mainstream consumers (even Apple customers), was also highly influential in the innovative part of the IT business and among the most fanatical and therefore most easily engaged but not necessarily easily influenced Apple customers. While they might be expected to see themselves as somehow 'green', their culture was individualistic, resistant to admonishment, even revelling in not being told how-to-be but liking to fix life themselves. Any external knocking or 'trashing' campaign would be an attack on their stuff and on themselves, because they 'lived the brand'.

So rather than a head-on attack on Apple, I advised that Greenpeace perpetrate a campaign of seduction, putting themselves in the shoes of the Apple consumer, and invoking the culture of the innovators, the geeks. Rather than going for outrage, we would be stimulating sorrow – these people loved (and often also hated) Apple, and the persona of Steve Jobs, but above all they were deeply wedded to it. Any 'boycott'-type campaign that asked consumers to sever their relationship with Apple would be likely to misfire like a well-meaning friend telling a moaning spouse simply to get a divorce.

On the other hand, a focus just on Apple's 'policies' would lead to an arid policy-wonk exchange – perhaps the optimal result for campaign resisters inside the company. Our advice noted:

> *Despite the distinctiveness of the Apple brand (which is arguably diminishing, in other words becoming sameier) and the prominence of Jobs (whose position and future is ultimately imponderable), the nature of the industry means that Apple is permeable to influences at large in the rest of the sector. This is especially true of the lateral geek- and engineer-worlds. These people – and Jobs identifies with them [one colleague of mine described the lure of the 'garage geek' for Jobs as 'the call of the wild'] – are drawn by technical brilliance and challenges, and lured by facilities and teams (though they are really lone operators who use teams to get ideas and approbation). They are not so much interested in an institutional home (in other words, as with other technically-led industries, it is permeable horizontally).*
>
> *Therefore we can assume that although Apple is like a closed citadel in terms of news media control, PR and product and policy info, it will rapidly absorb news of external events because this travels by the individual network. We should use this, and only reinforce it by direct overt approaches, which should be intended to echo, amplify or validate the conclusions that some inside Apple will be coming to.*

Direct attacks on the Apple brand will not easily work because Apple is equipped to deal with them. They will be like rain on the roof. Moreover, they may work against the project by alienating some potential participants. They may also make Greenpeace look naive and therefore lead insiders to discount other things Greenpeace does or says.

So:

- *'Try seduction first;*
- *Use the appeal of the future, emerging from the problems of the present;*
- *Use the geek doorways – lateral penetration;*
- *Juxtapose the complexity of toxic products with simplicity of good design;*
- *Use the intuition that good products are naturally green;*
- *Use personal, music, entertainment or other close to personal applications (emotional pitch).*

As a context:

- *Use the exposure to public and its supporters granted by Apple through running (and expanding) its retail shops (threat to coolness); and*
- *Avoid a head on GP assault on the Apple brand, subvertising or other outsider sneering or complaints. Instead stimulate a play on:*
  - *Internal engineer/designer doubts that they are doing the right thing;*
  - *Dilemmas for Mac/Apple users about the beauty of their products and the horror of the contents/its effects;*
  - *Dilemmas for Mac/Apple users (the loyalists who follow developments in the Apple world) about their expectations of the company cf its relative performance;*
  - *The self-myth of Apple that it can force through any innovation because of its people: 'I get to come to work every day and work with the most talented people on the planet. It's the best job in the world' [Jobs] and they hire 'the best of the best'.*

Greenpeace's response to this was to decide:

We won't 'attack' the Apple brand in the conventional sense. We'll use a bit of judo to 'jam the brand' and use the weight of their own brand values to get users to ask why they aren't being more environmentally responsible. We'll focus on positive messaging that doesn't defame the brand, but which exposes the gap between image and practice. Our messaging will ask more questions and make fewer demands or declarations.

By focusing on Apple's customers, we will engage them to help us change Apple for the better and push Apple to be an environmental leader and positive example for the whole consumer electronics industry to follow. By subverting, rather than challenging, Apple's own messaging, we applaud and encourage the values we share – achieving the seemingly impossible, challenging conventionality, doing things differently – and demonstrate how Apple's own values mandate a better policy toward the environment.

GREEN MY APPLE

What followed was Greenpeace's own creation, the 'Green My Apple' campaign (www. greenpeace.org/apple). For my part, I particularly liked the Steve Jobs presentation – in fact a spoof of his famously personal celebrity appearances at his own events. See 'Steve at Macworld 2007' written and voiced by Brian Fitzgerald of Greenpeace International at www.youtube.com/watch?v=2Uo_4kyrkDc.

The leading imagery deployed by Greenpeace focused on music (the iPod), close to the heart of Apple's corporate ambitions, rather than the keyboard. The campaign enlisted the creativity of Mac users in sending visual messages to Apple – a gallery of video letters from jilted Mac lovers. Here's some of what blogger Eva had to say at the website of the International Association of Business Communicators (http://evaapp.typepad.com/iabcuk/2006/11/reputation_in_a.html):

I have been paying a lot of attention to a recent Greenpeace campaign that urges Apple to create greener products and reduce its use of toxic chemicals, as an ongoing example of how digital media makes it easier to impact reputation.

Now, I am a big fan of Apple (the company – and fruit), which is probably why I really love the campaign. Its differentiator is that it uses the voice of an Apple fan to communicate its message, and targets that loyal and well defined community to pressure Apple to become greener (rather than the activist community or green lobby).

The campaign uses the tagline: 'I love my Mac/iPod/etc, I just wish it came in green'. So, while yes, it is critical of Apple, it is approaching the company from a positive position, and therefore enabling productive dialogue even among Apple enthusiasts.

The digital campaign centres around a website www.greenmyapple.com, which looks fantastically similar to www.apple.com.

The digital campaign (which also includes a video on YouTube) urges people to blog about the campaign (these blogs are then listed on the campaign website), to recommend the site by social bookmarks such as Digg or Del.icio.us, to send video e-cards to friends – especially Apple users – and to create games or digital animations promoting the campaign. This is virtuoso activism – with the best usage of online and digital media I have ever seen. From a digital communications perspective, I think that Greenpeace have really upped the ante with this one.

So far, online coverage is plentiful. A quick search found 2560 blogs linking to the campaign website (2561 when I post this one), and 116,000 Google results. Apple consumers seem to be generally supportive of the campaign, for example there is an editorial on MacUser (an online magazine for Mac computer users), which states: 'We should applaud Greenpeace for picking up on Apple's environmental record, as it means we could soon be enjoying its products with a clear conscience.'

As communicators, IABC members should be very interested in how Apple has chosen to respond to this campaign. Such a sophisticated campaign deserves a clever response. Well, so far, I can't find anything anywhere. There is nothing on the Apple website, and a Google search came up empty as well. The only thing I found was that Greenpeace was ejected from the MacWorld Expo in London last week (however, that may have had more to do with the event management, rather than Apple's official position).

So, again, as communicators, how do we think that Apple should respond? Well, personally, I think that the best response is to take the green suggestion seriously. Apple must know its demographic – chances are they're green. So, why shouldn't Apple try to make their products more environmentally sustainable. This could be what they are also thinking, which may explain why they have been keeping silent (the campaign launched in September). The company could be waiting until they can announce exactly what their green plans are.

Rather than responding to Greenpeace, Apple should respond directly to their users and fans. The message could be about how they realise this issue is important to their stakeholders, which is why they are reacting. Apple can then clarify their green strategy and future plans to improvement.

The worst response would be to attack the campaign. Some critics of the campaign have noted that Apple does not have the worst environmental record in the industry, or that other industries are most polluting. Maybe, but as Greenpeace says: Apple [could] be at the forefront of green technology, and show other companies how to do it the right way. So, rather than go on the defensive, Apple should engage in discussions about what 'green technology' means – with environmental groups, with users, with fans, with critics, with bloggers, with employees, even with competitors. A really innovative approach would be to incorporate the Greenpeace campaign (or something similar) into their own website, and open up an inclusive and boundless dialogue – both internally and externally – which investigates how the company could improve its products.

Figure A5.1 *Wallpaper created by JusHugo in support of the campaign*

Source: Flickr.com

It took nine months of online, in-store, at-exhibition and other offline campaigning for Steve Jobs to announce a change in policy. In May 2007[1] with the words 'A Greener Apple' on the front page of Apple's site, a message appeared from Steve Jobs[2] saying 'Today we're changing our policy'. In a classic U-turn (see 'How to tell when you are winning', page 210), Steve Jobs didn't acknowledge Apple had been wrong on its environmental policy but said Apple was changing its policy of not telling people about its plans to be greener – now it would. But Apple also committed to a series of substantive changes too. In victory, Greenpeace was positive: a campaigner wrote at their website:

> *It's not everything we asked for. Apple has declared a phase out of the worst chemicals in its product range, brominated fire retardants and PVC by 2008. That beats Dell and other computer manufactures' pledge to phase them out by 2009. Way to go Steve!*

Green My Apple was nominated for an award at South by Southwest Conferences and Festivals (SXSW) Annual Web Awards or 'Webbies'. Greenpeace used this to mobilize support for the campaign. A few weeks after Apple's announcement, a wider industry change was already starting as old rivals Michael Dell and Steve Jobs started trying to outbid each other

We love Apple. Apple knows more about "clean" design than anybody, right? So why do Macs, iPods, iBooks and the rest of their product range contain hazardous substances that other companies have abandoned? A cutting edge company shouldn't be cutting lives short by exposing children in China and India to dangerous chemicals. **That's why we Apple fans need to demand a new, cool product: a greener Apple.**

Figure A5.2 *Screenshot from Greenpeace campaign*

Figure A5.3 *Greenpeace online progress meter for Apple*

on green. Dell announced a free worldwide recycling policy and challenged the industry to follow. Steve Jobs declared a phase out of the worst chemicals in the Apple production line with a shorter deadline than Dell's, along with a new commitment to 'eco transparency'. Dell then declared it would become the greenest computer company in the world.

This continued to develop over the following years and in October 2009 Greenpeace celebrated victory on Apple toxics as the company cleared the last hurdle in eliminating toxic PVC plastic and is the first PC maker to completely eliminate hazardous brominated flame retardants in its new iMac and Macbook. Removing PVC from PC power cords was the last step. Greenpeace said, 'While removing the last use of PVC might not sound like a big deal, it means Apple's new products will be safer and easier to recycle and cause less pollution at the end of life.' The Green My Apple campaign is closed.

Postscript: Greenpeace has now moved on to a wider Information and communication technology (ICT) sector campaign – see www.greenpeace.org/international/campaigns/climate-change/cool-it-challenge.

Afterword

Although I favour campaigns planned as projects with critical paths, it has to be recognized that each path affects the landscape of an issue and gradually changes it. Your campaign is therefore benefiting (it is to be hoped) from previous efforts. Rick Le Coyte writes:

> *We shorten the odds by the day-to-day, year-on-year campaigning that not only exploits the consequences of [previous] actions but also helps create the context where ... actions lead to significant repercussions. Put more simply, opportunities arise partly because they are created.* (personal communication)

Notes

INTRODUCTION

1 Rose, C. (2004) 'Changing times, changing strategies', *Inside Track*, vol 7, available at www.campaignstrategy.org.
2 Sources removed – see original in Jim Coe and Tess Kingham, *Campaigning Effectiveness*, NCVO, London; see www.ncvo-vol.org.uk and http://tinyurl.com/yqdnh.
3 One of the best is Amnesty International (1997) *Campaigning Manual*, Amnesty International, London.
4 Lattimer, M. (2000) *The Campaigning Handbook*, Directory of Social Change, London; Dodds, F. and Strauss, M. (2004) *How to Lobby at Intergovernmental Meetings*, Earthscan, London.
5 In the UK, for instance, the excellent Friends of the Earth library of 'campaign guides', see www.foe.co.uk, and The CPRE Campaigners' Guide Getting Organised and Getting Results, See www.cpre.org.uk/library.
6 See www.frameworksinstitute.org.
7 Depending on the situation, many other forms of communication may be more important – for example, direct communication person to person, directly from an advertisement, from your campaign group via the internet, or by email directly to an individual.
8 'Dramatic polarities of the most unsubtle kind', journalist Simon Barnes describing the Brent Spar Campaign.
9 We used to use this with NGO clients at Media Natura, based on a system introduced to me by John Wyatt (johnwyatt@wyattandwyatt.com).
10 Tzu, S. (1981) *The Art of War*, Hodder and Stoughton, London; Wing, R. L. (1988) *The Art of Strategy*, new translation, Doubleday, London.
11 Saul Alinsky (1971) *Rules For Radicals*, Random House, New York.
12 The popular version of the story behind this saying is that the founder of the Salvation Army, William Booth, 'resolved to capture the hits of the day and turn them into choruses of salvation' after a visit to a revivalist meeting in a Worcester theatre in 1883. According to the Salvation Army:

> *There he enjoyed a song performed by converted sea captain George 'Sailor' Field – 'Bless His Name, He Sets Me Free'. He was surprised to be told afterwards that the tune was that of the popular music-hall song 'Champagne Charlie is My Name'. After reflecting on the impact it had had on the audience, the general turned to Bramwell Booth and said, famously, 'That settles it. Why should the devil have all the best tunes?' What is not so well-known, however, is that he was not the first to use that phrase. Rowland Hill, an*

*18th-century preacher, said the same a century earlier when turning 'Rule Britannia'
into a sacred song which began, 'When Jesus first at Heaven's command'.*

See www.salvationarmy.org.uk/music/VictHymn.html.

13 Public goods were first defined by economist Adam Smith in 1776, who noted that there were
products 'which though they may be in the highest advantageous to a great society are, however,
of such a nature that the profits could never repay the expenses to any individual or small
number of individuals, and which it therefore cannot be expected that any individual or small
number of individuals should erect' (from Musgrave, R. A. and Musgrave P. B. (2003) 'Prologue',
in Kaul, I. et al (eds) *Providing Public Goods: Managing Globalization*, UNDP, Oxford University
Press, Oxford).

14 Faye Scott and Green Alliance (2009) *Future Positive: Green Alliance's 2012 Strategy*, Green
Alliance; see www.green-alliance.org.uk.

15 Simon Bryceson – simon@bryceson.com.

16 Muir is celebrated in a small way but his legacy is largely overlooked, maybe because of two
weaknesses in the environmental and campaigning organizations. First, campaign organizations
set more store by 'elite' communication with institutions such as governments than by
communication with the public. Muir engaged with important people but he was first and
foremost a communicator to a 'mass' audience, and a maverick. Second, the dominant form of
campaign communication stresses the economic, the political, the scientific, the rationalistic
realms, rather than the psychological and the emotional ones. Consequently, campaigning lacks
heroes and, the environment movement at least, is much the weaker for it.

  You might argue that the closest it has come in the last 50 years have been interpreters of
nature and disaster and television advocates such as Jacques Cousteau or David Attenborough
on the BBC, and David Suzuki on CBC. In addition, there are organizations such as Greenpeace,
often seen as heroic, but for the most part studiously anonymous. An exception was the German
campaigner Monica Griefhan, who became a national TV figure (aka 'Mrs Greenpeace') in the
1980s and is now a minister in the German government. Among political 'greens', Petra Kelly
is perhaps the most heroic figure. David Brower, founder of Friends of the Earth (FoE) in the
US, and David McTaggart of Greenpeace are also heroes to some.

17 Obviously, numbers are important. Six is half a dozen, which always sounds a bit arbitrary and as
if it's a half-measure. Hollywood didn't go for the Magnificent Six. Nobody ever has useful lists of
eight. Three is the magic constructor of speeches, answers and arguments. Seven is a good upper
limit for something to actually remember. Ten is good for a 10-point plan and ticks the box
'comprehensive' but is not intended to be opened at the first sitting. Anything more than 10 in a
'plan' implies a failure to prioritize ('An 11-point plan' would only be OK if implementation wasn't
urgent – who remembers the Eleventh Commandment?). Nine might be seen as pedantic.

CHAPTER 1

1   Smith, P. R., Berry, C. and Pulford, A. (1997) *Strategic Marketing Communications*, Kogan Page,
London, p23.

2 Traci Madison of Unicorn Promotions, for example, claims we are exposed to 16,000 advertising messages every day. Others say hundreds of visual messages.

3 Wilson, D. and Andrews, L. (1993) *Campaigning: The A–Z of Public Advocacy*, Hawksmere, London.

4 You can start without the victim, but this only really works in policy or academic circles, where the ground rules for defining a problem already exist – for instance, when a pollutant or a social effect reaches a certain level. For public campaigning, though, you need to be able to show a victim, so start with the victim + problem.

5 I developed this sequence when working with Worldwide Fund for Nature (WWF) International in the 1980s, but many communicators use something like it and they didn't all get it from me.

6 See www.independent.co.uk.

7 Paul Slovic (2007) 'Genocide: When compassion fails', *New Scientist*, 7 April.

8 Leipold, Gerd (2000) 'Campaigning: A fashion or the best way to change the global agenda?', *Development in Practice*, vol 10, nos 3 and 4.

9 Ayerman, R. and Jamison, A. (1989) 'Environmental knowledge as an organizational weapon: The case of Greenpeace', *Social Science Information*, vol 28, pp99–119.

10 If you doubt this, try the group exercise used by Ed Gyde, a Director of Munro and Forster Public Relations. Ask people if they saw local TV news the night before. If they did, can they remember a story? If they can, do they recall the spokesperson/interviewee? And if they do, what was he or she saying?

11 Katie Aston, pers comm, katie.aston@ukgateway.net.

12 See *Campaign Strategy Newsletter*, no 18, 3 October 2005.

13 I told this story and a woman said to me that her mother came from a part of Tanzania that used chickens as currency, so perhaps it is true. I don't remember where I first heard it.

14 As a Friends of the Earth campaigner in a BBC radio show, Tony Burton of the CPRE and I assisted Chris Hall, then editor of *The Countryman* to make a case for planning controls to be extended to protect hedges, woods, ancient meadows and other features of the environment from agricultural intensification.

15 See http://news.bbc.co.uk/1/hi/england/oxfordshire/4558633.stm.

16 See more at Campaign of the Month (2006) 'What does your car say about you?', *Campaign Strategy Newsletter*, no 26, www.campaignstrategy.org.

17 Lippmann, W. (1921) *Public Opinion* (reissue available: Lippmann, W. (1997) *Public Opinion*, Free Press, New York).

18 See on Al Gore 'Don't say "people", think which people, and the message is, forget messages', *Campaign Strategy Newsletter*, no 24, 2006; UK Climate and Values Study Results in *Campaign Strategy Newsletter* no 12, 17 May 2005; and Chris Rose, Pat Dade, Nick Gallie and John Scott, *Climate Change Communications: Dipping a Toe into Public Motivation*, www.campaignstrategy.org.

19 'To be ten times richer in 2100 versus 2102 would hardly be noticed', and to meet the terms of the Kyoto Protocol would mean industrialized countries 'get 20 per cent richer by June 2010 rather than January 2010', when the costs of climate action are added to conventional 2 per cent growth forecasts. Pearce, F. (2002) 'Miserly attitude to climate rubbished', *New Scientist*, 15 June.

20 O'Connor, J. and Seymour, J. (1990) *Introducing Neuro-Linguistic Programming: Psychological Skills for Understanding and Influencing People*, Thorsons, London.
21 'Re-framing tax: Why it's a strategic target for campaigners', *Campaign Strategy Newsletter*, no 47, December 2008, www.campaignstrategy.org.
22 Mintzberg, Henry, Lampel, J. B., Quinn, J. B., Ghoshal, S. (1992) *The Strategy Process: Concepts and Contexts*, Prentice-Hall, NJ
23 Randerson, J. (2003) 'Nature's best buys', *New Scientist*, 1 March.
24 Dan Archer, a character in the long-running BBC Radio series *The Archers*, which for decades idealized farming as a benign and entirely wholesome activity. *The Archers* was originally started to promote farming after World War II, at the prompting of the UK Ministry of Agriculture.
25 Tzu, S. (1981) *The Art of War*, Hodder and Stoughton, London; Wing, R. L. (1988) *The Art of Strategy*, new translation, Doubleday, London.
26 One of the few examples of a campaign organization being wound up was Des Wilson's not quite one-man Campaign for Lead-free Air (CLEAR). This set out to eliminate leaded petrol in the UK, and once that had become inevitable, Des had it wound up. Few organizations have such a specific rationale or constitution, with such a domineering and incisive leader. Most will always find something else to do if an aim is fulfilled or an objective is achieved.

CHAPTER 2

1   Stewart, J. 'The basic theory of learning with stories', www.tms.com.au/tms10r.html.
2   Richard Dawkins, author of *The Selfish Gene*, coined the term 'meme' for a contagious information pattern that replicates by parasitically 'infecting' human minds and altering their behaviour, causing them to propagate the pattern (by analogy with 'gene'). Slogans, catchphrases, melodies, icons, inventions and fashions are all said to be memes. An idea or information pattern is not a meme until it causes someone to replicate it, to repeat it to someone else, like a gene.
3   Stewart quotes from Nelson Mandela's book *Long Walk To Freedom* to show the process, see www.tms.com.au/tms10r.html.
4   See www.tms.com.au/tms10r.html.
5   See www.knoxvilleopera.com/msgboard/read.php?action=print&TID=1.
6   McKee, R. (1999) *Story – Substance, Structure, Style and the Principles of Storytelling*, Methuen, London.
7   See www.storytellingcenter.net/resources/articles/simmons.htm with material from Annette Simmons.
8   See http://business.library.emory.edu/info/storytelling/index.html.
9   Rose, C. (1984) 'The first incidents report', Friends of the Earth, London, work now carried on by PAN-UK (Pesticides Action Network). PAN has an established system for helping people who become victims of pesticides. Anyone so affected should contact Alison Craig (alisoncraig@pan-uk.org), or visit the PAN website, www.pan-uk.org, to complete an online form and get the PEX briefings – Pesticide Exposure and Health.
10 Neuro-Linguistic Programming (NLP) identifies the main 'learning preferences' for receiving and taking in information as visual (by seeing), auditory (by hearing) or kinaesthetic (by touch).

In the US, 60–72 per cent of the population are said to generally prefer the visual route, 12–18 per cent the auditory and 18–30 per cent the kinaesthetic – see www.russellmartin.com/foodforbrain.asp.

A very useful NLP website is www.new-oceans.co.uk. NLP practitioners stress that these are not 'types' of people – you are not one or another. NLP also looks at how we evaluate information, whether our attention is generally attracted to problems or solutions, and a host of other factors very relevant to campaigns.

11 NLP practitioners say that people with an auditory preference tend to say things like: 'I can hear what you are saying', while those with a kinaesthetic preference – communicating best through touch, such as using 3D models – may say 'I get it'.

12 Starting with his 1983 book: Gardner, H., *Frames of the Mind*, Basic Books, New York.

13 See www.new-oceans.co.uk, NLP consultants New Oceans.

14 Gardner says most of us are comfortable in three or four (but not others) of the various forms of communication that are used to evaluate information.

15 Prescriptions from www.new-oceans.co.uk.

16 Known as Doctors without Borders in North America.

17 Dutch psychologist Frank van Marwijk notes that 'body language codes also differ between (sub) cultures'. He cites a story from Desmond Morris who, in *The Naked Ape*, describes a tragic incident in which people from another culture interpreted a simple hand gesture meaning 'come here' in the wrong way. According to van Marwijk:

> *Northern Europeans signal in a different manner than southern Europeans. In the North they signal with the palm of the hand upwards and in the South this is done with the palm downwards. Morris gives an example of two northern European men who were swimming in the sea and misinterpreted the hand gestures of several armed soldiers. The soldiers gestured that they had to come out of the water while they thought that they had to leave. The militaries shot them because they thought they were spies. This is a tragic example of miscommunication through a different frame of reference.*

See Bodycom Lichaamscommunicatie, The Netherlands – www.lichaamstaal.com/english/2main. html.

18 See www.kaaj.com/psych/index.html – 'Personality and emotion tests and software; psychological resources for researchers, clinicians and businesses', Albert Mehrabian, PhD.

19 In fact the studies on which this is based are very limited and it has been reshaped to have a wider firmer meaning (for example that it relates to receiving information, implying that most of that is non-verbal) than he originally intended, some say to become an NLP myth. See www. neurosemantics.com/Articles/Non-Verbal_Communication.htm 'Blasting away an old NLP myth about non-verbal dominance'. It's a good example of something that is too entertaining to be questioned. As Richard Ingrams, the editor of the satirical magazine *Private Eye* once said, 'This story is too good to check.'

20 See *Campaign Strategy Newsletter* nos 36 and 38.

21 See www.thebigask.com.

22 He said something like this. There is a lot of debate about exactly what he did say, but I am sure he would have agreed to be quoted.

23 'No impact from Energy Saving Day', http://news.bbc.co.uk/1/hi/sci/tech/7270218.stm.

24 'The danger of old ideas', *Campaign Strategy Newsletter*, no 38, 4 March 2008.

25 Activation of this model came about in a dramatic (and unexpected) way when a Greenpeace occupation of the redundant Shell North Sea oil installation the Brent Spar was supported by a massive Europe-wide boycott of Shell petrol stations.

26 It would be interesting to know if this hypothesis is borne out by more academic study, but it does seem to apply in many cases, and may be useful in designing campaigns.

27 UK examples include Bed Zed, one of Britain's largest 'carbon-neutral' housing project, with its own locally sourced wood-powered Combined Heat and Power (CHP) scheme, solar power, ecologically sensitive building materials and its own waste water system. Others include Tinkers Bubble near Yeovil, Somerset, described in Simon Fairlie's book *Low Impact Development Planning and People in a Sustainable Countryside* – see www.tlio.demon.co.uk/tinkers.htm – and the Hockerton project in London – www.hockerton.demon.co.uk. Eurotopia is a European directory of 336 intentional communities, many 'sustainable', in 23 countries throughout Europe – see www.eurotopia.de/englindex.html. Dozens of US communities, projects and networks are listed at www.ecobusinesslinks.com/sustainable_communities.

28 Some supermarkets originally saw GM foods as a profitable new line but quickly reacted to consumer hostility and became helpful to campaigners against it. This was not the case with all subjects.

29 See also *Campaign Strategy Newsletter* 25, August 2006 at www.campaignstrategy.org.

30 Lewis, J. (2001) *Constructing Public Opinion: How Political Elites Do What They Like and Why We Seem to Go Along With It*, Columbia Press, New York.

31 Jane Wildblood, pers comm.

32 See www.rprogress.org.

33 See also www.gpiatlantic.org for a Canadian version and the 17 October 1995 Senate speech of Senator Byron Dorgan –www.emagazine.com/may-june_1999/0599feat2.html.

34 See www.guardian.co.uk/science/2005/feb/24/4; http://blog-nca.chinese-medicine.co.uk/blog/_archives/2008/9/8/3874457.html; http://theliterarylink.com/metaphors.html (time is money metaphor); and www.via-web.de/time-concept/ – many based on original studies by Tom Cottle (the 'circles test' dating back to 1967).

35 *David Copperfield*, Chapter xii.

36 *Listen With Mother* – a 1950s BBC radio programme that began with the phrase that has now entered into popular culture, continued until 1980 on television as *Watch with Mother*.

37 Robert Cialdini, *Influence: The Psychology of Persuasion*, Collins, New York, 2007.

38 George Lakoff, *The Political Mind: A Cognitive Scientist's Guide to Your Brain and its Politics*, Penguin Books, New York, 2008.

39 Katya Andresen, Alia McKee Scott and Mark Rovner, *Homer Simpson For Nonprofits: The Truth About How People Really Think & What It Means for Promoting Your Cause*, Network for Good, at http://webofchange.com/blog/free-ebook-homer-simpson-for-nonprofits.

40 Much use is also made of heuristics in maths, software writing and design, for which a seminal work was George Pólya's book *How To Solve It*; see a useful table of techniques for problem

solving at http://en.wikipedia.org/wiki/How_to_Solve_It. Some of the most famous academic studies in heuristics were conducted by Daniel Kahneman and Amos Tversky, for example Amos Tversky and Daniel Kahneman, 'Judgment under uncertainty: Heuristics and biases', *Science*, New Series, vol 185, no 4157, 27 September 1974, pp1124–1131; http://psiexp.ss.uci.edu/research/teaching/Tversky_Kahneman_1974.pdf.

41 For example the gas saving campaign described by Cialdini, p101 in *Influence: The Psychology of Persuasion*, Collins, New York, 2007; the Eco-teams created by Global Action Plan, www.globalactionplan.org.uk; council-led projects such as in the London Borough of Barnet, http://news.bbc.co.uk/1/hi/uk_politics/8255153.stm; and the 1990 Negawatt Campaign in Kiel, Germany, A Consumer Initiative for Better Lighting and Energy Saving – Negawatt for Megawatt Friedemann Prose and Klaus Wortmann Paper given to 1st European Conference on Energy-Efficient Lighting, Stockholm, 28–30 May 1991, www.nordlicht.uni-kiel.de/nordlicht/prowo.htm.

42 Robert Cialdini (2007) *Influence: The Psychology of Persuasion*, Collins, New York, p171.

43 James Surowiecki (2004) *The Wisdom of Crowds*, Abacus, London.

44 See www.geert-hofstede.com.

45 See www.theyesmen.org.

46 See also *The Tipping Point*, Malcolm Gladwell, Little, Brown, 2000, Boston, New York and London.

47 Robert Cialdini and Kelton Rhoads (2001) 'Human behaviour and the market place', *Marketing Research*, Fall, www.imcdfw.com/docs/MarketingResearchJournal.pdf.

48 Robert Cialdini (2007) *Influence: The Psychology of Persuasion*, Collins, New York, p250.

49 Richard Layard, *Happiness: Lessons from a New Science*, Penguin, London, 2006.

50 David Straker, www.changingminds.org.

CHAPTER 3

1 See ACORN-type databases, for example, at www.upmystreet.com. These categories are based mostly on consumer purchases.

2 Others include 3SC Social Values 'tribes' by Environics in Canada and the US (http://erg.environics.net/), Y and R's 4Cs at www.4cs.yr.com, SRI's VALS at www.sric-bi.com/VALS and, in France, Sociovision's work at www.sociovision.com.

3 Abraham Maslow, *Motivation and Personality*, 3rd edition, Frager, Robert and Fadiman, James (eds), Longman, London, 1987 (first published 1954).

4 CDSM has tested it against Myers Briggs Type Indicator (MBT) I and other individual differences. Such preferences and 'traits' are probably genetic and largely fixed whereas Maslowian values exist more as a template through which people can move, so the particular Values Mode you are in reflects your life experience rather than your genes.

5 This better reflects the real relationships between the main Groups.

6 See Values and Voters Survey by CSL and CDSM: www.campaignstrategy.org/valuesvoters/index.html.

7 'Values and the politics of aid', *Campaign Strategy Newsletter*, no 51, May 2009.

8 Essentially an axis between SD and ID.

9   Ronald Inglehart and Christian Welzel, *Modernization, Cultural Change and Democracy: The Human Development Sequence*, Cambridge University Press, Cambridge, 2005, www.worldvaluessurvey.org.

10 See *Campaign Strategy Newsletter*, no 36, 2007, and Chris Rose, Pat Dade and John Scott, *Research Into Motivating Prospectors, Settlers and Pioneers to Change Behaviours That Affect Climate Emissions* at www.campaignstrategy.org/articles/behaviourchange_climate.pdf.

11 See *Campaign Strategy Newsletter*, no 37, 2007, and www.100ideashouse.com.

12 Chris Rose, Pat Dade and Les Higgins, *Who Gives a Stuff About Climate Change and Who's Taking Action?*, www.campaignstrategy.org/whogivesastuff.pdf.

13 *Consumer Power: How the Public Thinks Lower-Carbon Behaviour Could Be Made Mainstream*, Reg Platt and Simon Retallack, IPPR 2009, www.ippr.org.uk and www.cultdyn.co.uk/ART067736u/Now_People_0.pdf.

14 For a more detailed example of a change that may be at the cusp of tipping see *Resolving Koo's Paradox: A Non-Profit Opportunity?*, Chris Rose at www.campaignstrategy.org.

CHAPTER 4

1   See www.cleverworkarounds.com/2009/03/04/the-one-best-practice-to-rule-them-all-part-4/.

2   See www.cleverworkarounds.com/2009/03/04/the-one-best-practice-to-rule-them-all-part-4/ and www.sevensigma.com.au/.

3   In its analysis, WWF UK sent a survey to over 300 organizations, from house builders to local authorities and social NGOs, and held dozens of meetings with government and industry, to distil the information in the problem map. This was then tested and refined at a workshop with representatives of house builders, industry research bodies, social housing providers, investors and developers.

4   Rittel, H., 'On the planning crisis: Systems analysis of the "first and second generations"', 3 90-396 BEDRIFTSOKONOMEN NR. 8 – 1972.

5   Sandra S. Batie, 'Wicked problems and applied economics', *American Journal of Agricultural Economics*, Dec 2008, http://findarticles.com/p/articles/mi_hb6673/is_5_90/ai_n31043946/.

6   Of course pollution with such gases has already modified ecosystems – such as melting tundra releasing methane (more wickedness) – so it is not possible to return to exactly what we had before but it is still a rational objective. We'll know what sort of solution it is if we achieve it.

7   See http://unfccc.int/essential_background/feeling_the_heat/items/2914.php.

8   In the 1980s the Stockholm Environment Institute (SEI) convened the Advisory Group on Greenhouse Gases (AGGG) for the United Nations Environment Programme and the World Meteorological Organisation. It served as a precursor to the Intergovernmental Panel on Climate Change (IPCC). Leading roles were played by SEI's Executive Director Gordon Goodman and chairman of SEI's Board, Professor Bert Bolin, who would later become the first chairman of the IPCC, which was awarded a Nobel Peace Prize, http://tinyurl.com/y9vnu7b.

9   For example see www.goingcarbonneutral.co.uk.

10 When I worked for WWF International we were kept well supplied with intelligence on the European timber trade by a small NGO that seemed to specialize in such trawls.

11 A cardinal rule for interviewees is to beware the moment that the interview 'ends' and the journalist lays down their pad, closes it and puts away the pen, or switches off the TV camera.

At this point it is natural for your guard to drop and to lapse into friendly chat mode. This is often when the interviewee lets drop some key point which they had been careful not to state in the actual interview. If interviewed in your office, try to have someone else show the journalist out, for exactly this reason.

12 See www.ran.org.

13 At this time I was running the consultancy and charity Media Natura. Greenpeace asked us to look into what might change and explain the UK policy.

14 *Campaign Strategy Newsletter*, no 13, 2005, at www.campaignstrategy.org.

15 Contact him via www.bryceson.com.

16 British or Australian slang for someone who tries too hard to show that they are clever, in a way that annoys other people, www.urbandictionary.com.

17 For example, MOx – mixed oxide fuel – instead of uranium.

18 Or perhaps not, and that is the industry's greatest asset: it is so bizarre and ridiculous that it makes its critics sound implausible. 'It can't really be that bad…' but it is. And being impossible to believe, few politicians get the true measure of it. Not surprisingly, when the UK government authorized the MOx plant to start in October 2001, thereby putting more plutonium into circulation, few politicians seemed to notice. The Royal United Services Institute said it 'beggars belief' that UK ministers could take 'a reckless decision' to launch an export business expanding global trade in plutonium 'at such a time of global insecurity' (*Environment Watch*, 12 October 2001, p3).

19 Aerial emissions from, for example, the THORP plant have become a growing part of Sellafield's emissions.

20 Dry storage is the least polluting option for nuclear waste, holding it in stores where it is recoverable and can be monitored and, if necessary, moved and repackaged. The industry is gradually moving to this position, and reprocessing at Sellafield will eventually shut down. Subterranean 'out-of-sight-out-of-mind' options, such as pursued by the nuclear dump-makers Nirex, in which waste would be deposited in caverns and then glued in using a high-tech version of tile grout, are also gradually losing credibility.

21 See, for example, Lewis, J. (2001) *Constructing Public Opinion: How Political Elites Do What They Like and Why We Seem to Go Along With It*, Columbia Press, New York.

22 MORI (April 1986) *Public Attitudes Towards Charities and the Environment*, MORI, for WWF.

23 The newspaper's chosen topic was animals, and it gave extensive coverage to the seal distemper virus epidemic in the North Sea, which was linked by many to pollution. This, along with dramatic pictures of algal red tides encouraged by nutrient pollution, undoubtedly helped sensitize Conservative Party opinion on the environment. Combined with news of global warming and back bench disquiet over new road building, it helped convince Mrs Thatcher to go 'green'. A year later (14 November 1988) *The Daily Telegraph* reported that Gallup found damage to the environment ranked as 'the greatest threat facing mankind'.

24 See www.environics.ca and www.environicsinternational.com.

25 A useful website is at www.mapfornonprofits.org, where Carter McNamara has compiled a large resource of papers. See www.mapnp.org/library/grp_skll/focusgrp/focusgrp.htm#anchor365840. Another helpful site is the commercial Market Navigator of George Silverman and Eve Zukergood at www.mnav.com.

26 'Client Guide to the Focus Group' at www.mnav.com.

27 I was told this by a researcher – I think he was serious.

28 It produced and lobbied heavily for chlorofluorocarbons (CFCs) and hydrochlorofluorocarbons (HCFCs).

29 'Focus groups' have a bad name because of their abuse and misuse in politics. Many political focus group exercises are hopelessly superficial, but the real problem is where they are used to create propositions irrespective of the values of an organization.

30 See discussion in *Campaign Strategy Newsletter* no 48, January 2009.

31 John Scott, pers comm, john.scott@ksbr.co.uk.

32 A 2007 survey by AA Personal Loans found that a fifth of holidaymakers are planning to take holidays in Britain to reduce their carbon footprint. Eleven per cent said they wanted a driving holiday in Europe because of the environmental impact of flying. Three per cent of people have cancelled their holidays altogether because of climate change concerns. Fewer than half of the respondents said they were sticking to plans to take short-haul flights to Europe. See www.mailonsunday.co.uk/pages/live/articles/news/news.html?in_article_id=455481&in_page_id=1770.

33 *Campaign Strategy Newsletter* no 18, 3 October 2005.

34 Matthews, R. (1999) 'Get connected', *New Scientist*, vol 164, issue 2215, 4 December, p24.

35 Cohen, D. (2002) 'All the world's a net', *New Scientist*, vol 174, issue 2338, 13 April, p24; Matthews, R. (1999) 'Get connected', *New Scientist*, vol 164, issue 2215, 4 December, p24.

36 The Ozone Campaign – research by Diagnostics for Greenpeace UK, unpublished.

37 Source: Steve Park of the UK Crime and Disorder Reduction Partnership.

38 See http://creatingminds.org/tools/tools_ideation.htm for a long list of links.

CHAPTER 5

1 A good one is SOSTAC, standing for Situation, Objectives, Strategy, Tactics, Action, Control (source: Smith, P. R., Berry, C. and Pulford, A. (1997) *Strategic Marketing Communications: New Ways To Build and Integrate Communications*, Kogan Page, London). Their system is intended for commercial marketing. A difference between most commercial organizations and some campaign groups is that the values and methods of NGOs are closely entwined. What they are determines how they work. What they deliver is as much intangible – maybe a spiritual touchstone, an icon, sustaining a hope – as it is a tangible service or product. Their choice of strategy and tactics then becomes constrained by who and what they are. They may pick objectives with principles, plan them with strategy and then run them with tactics that express the values that supporters share with the organization. In this sense they may be more comparable to religions than businesses.

Another is the ten-point plan invented by Steve Shalhorn (steve.shallhorn@dialb.greenpeace.org) and Jo Dufay (my extracts only):

(i) Claim moral ground. Present a persuasive moral argument – choose your ground carefully so as to deny the opponent any moral ground.

(ii) Clarify goal and message. Your goal may not be the same as outright victory – you may just want to weaken your opponent. Getting your message out might be the most important thing. Your campaign may be just one element in a long-term struggle.

(iii) Know what a win looks like. Who has the power to make the changes you need – exactly how can they yield to your campaign demands?

(iv) Organizational context. Be aware of your weaknesses. It is usually easier for your opponent to attack your organization and its credibility than your moral ground.

(v) Assess the players. If you can, try to deny your opponent the support of its allies. Try to enlist neutral organizations to your cause.

(vi) Choose target. Your target is not necessarily the same player as your opponent but should be in a position to deliver the change you want, or a significant part of it.

(vii) Strategy. A plan that integrates goals, policies and actions into a cohesive campaign.

(viii) Tactics. A finite event or activity, used towards achieving your goal. Leave your opponent little room for counteraction.

(ix) Win. Assess a win realistically. In issue campaigns, unlike elections, an outright win is rare. Refuse false offers of compromise but be looking to take a win – people are attracted to victors. Celebrate.

(x) Evaluate. What worked well, what didn't meet expectations, what could be improved next time.

2   Unless, of course, they devote their time solely to this. The need is to avoid uninformed interference in what should be an evidence-based design process.

3   Critical path planning has its origins in the oil industry. Engineers wanted to know which steps were critical – those that absolutely had to take place, and in which order, to complete a project safely and on time. Campaign planning usually deals with softer, less-predictable material than an engineering project made of steel and concrete, but critical paths are an extremely useful tool in sorting out what has to happen and in which order.

4   Rose, C. (1998) *The Turning of the Spar*, Greenpeace, London, available from info@greenpeace.uk.org.

5   Currently enjoying archived status at http://archive.greenpeace.org/~odumping, see also Brent Spar pages at http://archive.greenpeace.org/~comms/brent/brent.html and photo library at http://archive.greenpeace.org/~comms/brent/phopho.html.

6   In *The Greenpeace Story*, Michael Brown and John May (1989), Dorling Kindersley, London, give an account of how Pete Wilkinson first came across ocean dumping of radioactive waste, off the south-west of the UK.

7   In this as in many other campaigns, the perceived awfulness or wrongness of the act is as much down to the irresponsibility of those causing it, as it is down to impact of the act. Campaigns are about responsibility not just impacts.

8   Controlling dumping in the North-East Atlantic area.

9   Although many others such as WWF and Friends of the Earth were also involved in this and in preventing POPs.

10 Now with consultants Varda – www.vardagroup.org.

11 The Spar was a floating storage unit in the Brent field, used before that field was served by pipelines, shaped like a vast vertical biscuit tin.

12 Rather than oil installations, the main agenda focused on pollution entering the sea from rivers and the air. Greenpeace argued that as direct dumping was prohibited, the next logical step was to stop the same pollutants entering by direct discharges via rivers, and so on. This became the next successful campaign objective in the OSPAR-level critical path. On 23 July 1998 in Lisbon, Portugal, the Oslo–Paris Commission environment ministers voted for a full ban on the dumping of steel oil installations at sea, to avoid the production of new chemicals, and to remove hazardous toxic chemicals from the marine environment within a generation. Substantial reductions in radioactive discharges had to be made by the year 2000 and by 2020, while radioactive concentrations added to the seabed must be close to zero.

13 See Note 4.

14 The Spar was a huge structure, twice the height of London's Nelson's Column, weighing over 14,000 tonnes empty, including 7700 tonnes of steel and 6800 tonnes of haematite (iron ore) mixed with concrete and used for ballast. It had six tanks that stored 43,000 tonnes of crude oil altogether, which it would receive from rigs on the Brent oil field, before passing it on to tankers for shipment. In 1991 it ceased operation. The top end of its 137 metres height emerged from the sea like a vast steel turret, while 109 metres remained iceberg-like below the waves. Huge chains and concrete blocks held it in place. A number of men had died in accidents on the Spar, and life on board couldn't have been much fun in winter – a wave height recorder on board suggested waves had sometimes reached almost a hundred feet in height, and in any sort of swell, the structure groaned and creaked and swayed.

15 This had been the plan when it was first anchored in the mid-North Sea, before changes to UK Petroleum Revenue Tax had tipped the balance in favour of dumping instead of a return to shore. That, coupled with a spat between oil companies and the heavy-lifting firms over pricing for removal, had set Shell on a collision course with Greenpeace, when it opted for the largest single act of littering ever seen in the Western world.

16 Gladwell, M. (2000) *The Tipping Point: How Little Things Can Make a Big Difference*, Little, Brown and Co, Boston, New York and London.

17 Colegreave, S. (2002) 'The Brent Spar story', *Critical Marketing: Cause Related Marketing*, winter issue. Colegreave writes:

> *From 1995 onwards there was a change in corporate and pressure-group marketing, advertising and PR. The following years were to see the introduction of cause-related marketing and 'green' summits and conferences that brought corporations and interest groups together for the first time. This development was a direct result of a confrontation between the environmental pressure group Greenpeace and the multinational oil company Shell.*

18 For an example of change in a commercial context see the useful website at www.mindtools. com/pages/article/newTED_06.htm.

19 Jim Coe and Tess Kingham, *Campaigning Effectiveness*, NCVO, London, 2005, www.ncvo-vol. org.uk.

20 Deborah Arnott and Ian Willmore (2006) 'Smoke and mirrors', *The Guardian*, 19 July, http:// society.guardian.co.uk/health/story/0,,1823348,00.htm and www.munroforster.com/case_ bigsmoke.cfm.

21 See www.forestonline.org.

22 *Campaign Strategy Newsletter* no 29, 2006, www.campaignstrategy.org.

23 See www.campaigncc.org.

24 Christopher Tchen, Partner at Carbon Limiting Technologies, christopher.tchen@carbonlimitingtechnologies.com.

25 First published at www.campaignstrategy.org.

26 Thomas E. Mann and Norman J. Ornstein (2000) *The Permanent Campaign and Its Future*, AEI Press, Washington, DC.

27 See www.incpen.org/resource/data/incpen1/docs/27%20June%2005%20Green%20intentions, %20but%20misplaced%20actions.pdf.

28 See for example the large review of transport-related behaviours by Jillian Anable et al: *An Evidence Base Review of Public Attitudes to Climate Change and Transport Behaviour*, The Robert Gordon University for UK Department of Transport, London, July 2006.

29 Louise Gray (2008) 'Credit crunch sparks a rise in wood burning stove sales', *Daily Telegraph*, 12 October.

30 See www.worcester-bosch.co.uk/homeowner/our-company/news/solar-sales-mock-the-recession.

31 For the 'West of England' project into motivating people to take domestic climate behaviours, see Chris Rose, Pat Dade and John Scott, *Research Into Motivating Prospectors, Settlers and Pioneers to Change Behaviours That Affect Climate Emissions* at http://documents.campaignstrategy.org/uploads/behaviourchange_climate.pdf.

CHAPTER 6

1 See www.commonground.org.uk – specializing in the celebration of place and localness.

2 Daniel Elkan (2009) 'Winners wear red: How colour twists your mind', *New Scientist*, 28 August, www.newscientist.com.

3 See http://news.bbc.co.uk/1/hi/in_depth/uk/2001/foot_and_mouth/1199183.stm.

4 Fred Pearce (2008) 'Bring on the solar revolution', *New Scientist*, 21 May.

5 1997–2000 – see http://archive.greenpeace.org/climate, the 1999–2000 campaign at www.greenpeace.org.uk and Note 4.

6 Hare, B. (1997) *Fossil Fuels and Climate Protection: The Carbon Logic*, Greenpeace, London.

7 At the June 1997 UN General Assembly Special Session on the environment – unfortunately, internal differences in Greenpeace meant this didn't happen, robbing the campaign of some political salience.

8 With other NGOs.

9 The campaign suffered several shortcomings. Public engagement mechanisms never developed very effectively, and it was ended before it became widely known in the UK outside Scotland. Among its successes the campaign put the term 'fossil fuels' into the political dictionary used in discussing climate change for the first time, and led to significantly increased political backing for renewables in Scotland.

10 The 2001/2002 London 'countryside marches' mobilized a pro-hunting lobby around the classic security-driven proposition of 'defend our (rural) way of life'. The first march made politicians panic at its size, but the second underlined that almost the whole lobby, well organized, had been bussed to London – a 'that's-all-there-is' moment – which was unimpressive.

11 Ward, B. (1966) *Spaceship Earth*, Columbia University Press, New York.

12 Was any of this deliberate? If so, it was impeccable use of visual language for PR.

13 George Lakoff is professor of linguistics at the University of California at Berkeley. See his work at www.frameworksinstitute.org and also Metaphors of Terror, www.press.uchicago.edu/News/911lakoff.html.

14 Ed Gyde now at Ed.Gyde@audiencecommunications.com.

15 While I was director from 1988 to 1992, we undertook hundreds of projects for NGOs large and small. I have also seen similar results from other studies of NGO support.

16 Take John Pilger's book, an update of the imperialist 'great game', *The New Rulers of the World*, 2003, Verso, London. Pilger is a journalist for whom I have great respect, but in *The New Rulers of the World*, I reached the bit about the continuing refusal of the Australian Prime Minister to apologize for a century of degrading treatment of Aboriginals by the white Australian establishment, the theft of their land, the denial of human rights, the withholding of reparations called for by the British, the children torn from families by police in a programme to 'breed out' colour from mixed-race families, the continuing underfunding of aboriginal health as opposed to whites – this came after the 1967 carve-up of Indonesia's economy by the US, UK and multinationals, doling out the tropical forests of Sumatra (mostly gone now) to US, French and Japanese companies, the copper, gold and bauxite to the Americans; and after the 35,000-strong CIA training programme Operation Cyclone, which helped form al-Qa'eda and the Taliban, the US White House activities of Paul Wolfowitz, Richard Perle and others in planning 'total war' to 'let our vision of the world go forward' and achieve 'full-spectrum dominance' of the planet; after the mass murders in Indonesia and East Timor for long disguised as good news by the media of Australia and the US; after the use of 300 tonnes of depleted uranium in the 1991 Gulf War and the cancer wave that has followed – and there was still more to come … and at this point I gave up.

17 It was this realization that led Greenpeace UK to initiate systematic 'solutions campaigning' in 1993. See Rose, C. (1994) 'Beyond the struggle for proof: Factors changing the environmental movement', *Environmental Values*, vol 2, pp285–298.

18 The campaign against chlorine bleaching converted much of the industry to 'ECF' paper – which is 'elemental chlorine-free' and significantly reduces the total load of pollutants. Fewer users, however, have opted for totally chlorine-free paper. This emphasizes that, while commercial and market mechanisms may create rapid and innovative change where industrial–political regulations were deadlocked, they are relatively unreliable at delivering a complete solution. For that, government regulation is still required.

19 UK Prime Minister's speech to CBI/Green Alliance, 24 October 2000.

20 For recent developments regarding HFCs, see www.mipiggs.org the website of the Multisectoral Initiative on Potent Industrial Greenhouse Gases. It is the dominant domestic refrigeration technology in Europe. Yet in the US, the chemicals industry had succeeded in using supposed safety concerns over hydrocarbon flammability to keep out the technology – this in a country

so enthusiastic about gasoline, and despite the fact that there had been a million accident-free fridge years of operation in Europe by 2000. The US Environment Protection Agency has actually given out prizes to HFC manufacturers on 'environmental' grounds.

21 The first Greenpeace boat.

22 Brown, M. and May, J. (1989) *The Greenpeace Story*, Dorling Kindersley, London.

23 During the Amchitka voyage, for example, Bob Hunter of the Vancouver Sun and Bob Metcalfe of the CBC were both on board, along with a photographer. Like marine versions of John Muir, they made regular reports to radio stations and newspapers. Later, Greenpeace broke new ground in the techniques and technology of 'running film' and, eventually, transmitting still and TV pictures by satellite with its 'squisher', technology now in commercial use worldwide.

24 This formulation was invented by Nick Gallie, a small Scotsman whose contributions included the famous David Bailey 'fur coat' advertisement: 'It takes up to 40 dumb animals to make a fur coat. But only one to wear it.'

24 This also implies that emotional and rational are exclusive, and that there is only one form of rationality; both of which are obviously untrue.

25 These are preferences not absolutes, but are reflected in the number of neural net connections in the brain – so individuals really are more one than the other. Visit www.mtsu.edu/~devstud/advisor/hemis.html for a description and an online right/left brain hemispheric dominance inventory to test yourself.

26 Speech by Heinz Rothermund, Managing Director of Shell UK exploration and Production at the 1997 Celebrity Lecture for the Institute of Petroleum at Strathclyde University, 20 May 1997.

27 In 1996, Professor John Shepherd, chairman of the UK Natural Environmental Research Council was asked by the UK government to report on the arguments over the 'science' of the Brent Spar. Unusually for an 'official scientist' Shepherd wrote: 'if people have an emotional response to pristine areas like Antarctica or the deep sea, and want them to remain unpolluted, it is not up to scientists to say this is irrational'. This stood in great contrast to the gales of political and media criticism that lashed Greenpeace on grounds that it was 'unscientific' or 'wrong'. Perhaps Shepherd could do this because he was the boss and didn't feel threatened by the idea that emotion (including aesthetics, morals, ethics) and rationality were not opposites, or maybe he'd just thought about it more?

28 See www.campaigncc.org/.

29 See www.beyondshelter.org/EmergencyCampaign/EmergencyCampaign.shtml.

30 See www.newportcathedral.com/.

31 See www3.unesco.org/iycp/uk/uk_visu_projet.asp?Proj=00280.

32 See www.visualexpert.com/Resources/psychwarnings.html.

33 Dennis S. Mileti and Lori Peek (2000) 'The social psychology of public response to warnings of a nuclear power plant accident', *Journal of Hazardous Materials*, vol 75, pp181–194.

CHAPTER 7

1 I am indebted to media trainer Sara Jones, smcjones@blueyonder.co.uk, for pointing this out.

2 New Oceans say: 'Perceptual Filters are patterns of behaviour, not types of people.' You can try its sample online 'personality profilers' for learning and sorting preferences (NLP), and the

psychometric MBTI (Myers Briggs Type Indicator) and right/left brain tools at the same website, www.new-oceans.co.uk.

3   See www.new-oceans.co.uk.

4   Jon Gertner (2009) 'Why isn't the brain green?', *New York Times*, 19 April, www.nytimes.com.

5   See www.wyattandwyatt.com.

6   They included alkylphenols, phthalates, brominated flame retardants, chlorinated paraffins and organotin compounds.

7   Britain's biggest-ever protest.

8   Palast, G. (2003) *The Best Democracy Money Can Buy: The Truth About Corporate Cons, Globalization and High-finance Fraudsters*, Plume Books, New York.

9   Which took over the Union [Carbide] plant.

10 Roszak, T. (1992) *The Voice of the Earth*, Touchstone, New York.

11 Ibid.

12 *The Changing Face of Environmental Campaigning: Greenpeace and Business*, audio of speech by Gerd Leipold of Greenpeace to Yale University Environment Center, 6 April 2009, at http://tinyurl.com/yj8qh5g; Ray A. Goldberg and Jessica Droste Yagan, *McDonald's Corporation: Managing a Sustainable Supply Chain*, Harvard Business School, at www.favaneves.org/arquivos/mcdonalds-hbs-2008.pdf.

13 See http://media-newswire.com/release_1055564.html - Instituto Socioambiental (www.socioambiental.org), Greenpeace Brazil (www.greenpeace.org.br), Instituto Centro de Vida (www.icv.org.br), Instituto de Pesquisa Ambiental da Amazônia (www.ipam.org.br), The Nature Conservancy (www.tnc.org.br), Conservation International-Brazil (www.conservation.org.br), Amigos da Terra-Amazônia Brasileira (www.amazonia.org.br), Imazon (www.imazon.org.br), and WWF Brasil (www.wwf.org.br).

14 See www.greenpeace.org.uk/blog/forests/slaughtering-amazon-20090529.

15 For more information visit www.greenpeace.org.uk/forests/amazon and campaigners blogs at that site.

CHAPTER 8

1   By which I mean the edited media, the press, newswire, TV, radio and internet channels where someone else owns and controls the communication channel, which you may influence but can't directly control unless you buy advertising. In contrast, direct communication involves no intermediaries between you and the audience, for example, direct mail, events, face to face, telephone calls.

2   As Dan Rather, US news anchor put it, 'as addictive as crack cocaine'.

3   From Basic Media Briefing, developed for local groups – you can contact FoE via www.foe.co.uk.

4   Cohen, N. (2003) 'The defeat of the left', *New Statesman*, 5 May, pp16–17.

5   Underwood, M., Communication Cultural and Media Studies Infobase at www.cultsock.ndirect.co.uk/MUHome/cshtml/index.html.

6   *The Observer*, 11 June 2000.

7   BBC *Today Programme*, 12 May 2003.

8   Fiske, J. (1987) 'Film, TV and the popular', Bell, P. and Hanet, K. (eds), *Continuum: The Australian Journal of Media & Culture*, vol 12, http://kali.murdoch.edu.au/continuum (see Note 5).

9   McShane, D. (1979) *Using the Media*, Pluto Press – now out of print.

10 Based on material from Ed Gyde, pers comm ed_gyde@munroforster.com.

11 I was once talking to Charles Clover, now environment editor of the *Daily Telegraph*, outside the dockland offices of that newspaper, when his then editor, Bill Deedes, came up. 'Good editorial, Clover,' he said. 'Thank you sir,' said Charles. 'Know what was wrong with it though?' asked Deedes. Clover intimated that he didn't. 'Two facts, Clover – that's one too many. The readers don't like more than one fact – confuses 'em – and with that he walked off. One number, not more. What's true of *Daily Telegraph* readers is true of most of us.

12 See *Campaign Strategy Newsletter* no 36, 21 November: 'Be interesting – Or be ignored', at www.campaignstrategy.org.

13 Public Affairs consultant Peter Sandman has a formula for 'outrage' that he supplies to corporations wanting to understand why the public gets upset with them (and how to avoid that).

14 Cohen, N. (2002) 'National parks, state schools and hospitals, laws against pollution: All could be under threat from the World Trade Organisation', *New Statesman*, 2 December, pp20–22.

15 Figures from www.drugscope.org.uk, 'Deaths from Drug Use' 2000 data for England and Wales, using IDC 10 and not double counting, is available from the National Programme on Substance Abuse Deaths (np-SAD). The data found the following: cocaine 57 deaths, amphetamine 19, ecstasy 27, opiates 486, alcohol 353, GHB 2.

16 Which became the London Wildlife Trust.

17 Example taken from my website: www.campaignstrategy.org.

CHAPTER 9

1   I was accused of this by the *Evening Standard* over a campaign by the London Wildlife Trust to stop an office block being built on the 'Chiswick Triangle', now a nature reserve.

2   See www.ncvo-vol.org.uk/count-me-in/banadvocates.

3   In 2003, WWF International's ingenious web and real-life lobbying campaign for fisheries, organized by Martin Hiller and Karl Wagner, took the sea to Brussels with a rather magnificent lighthouse constructed just outside the main conference, and set up a virtual protest that attracted 20,000 participants. What effect it had beyond good press pictures is harder to pin down.

4   BBC news website: Saturday, 21 December 2002, 'Fisheries cuts spell disaster',www.bbc.co.uk.

5   BBC news website: Saturday, 21 December, 2002, 'EU ministers agree fishing reform', www.bbc.co.uk.

6   'Fishing for trouble' (2003) *The Ecologist*, April, pp18–19.

7   Leipold, G. (August 2000) 'Campaigning: A fashion or the best way to change the global agenda?', in Eade, D. (ed) *Debating Development: NGOs and the Future*, Oxfam, Oxford, p234.

8   See www.grist.org/article/doe-intro.

9   *Campaign Strategy Newsletter* no 14, 5 July 2005.

10 A friend, Andy Stirling, says: 'Guessing off the top of the head and slightly conservatively that about a quarter of stations are interconnections (say 60) and that these typically link to an average of one tenth of the interconnections (say 6), my final total guess is therefore that the final number lies somewhere between a lower bound of 60×6! (i.e. 60×6 factorial $= 60 \times 6 \times 5 \times 4 \times 3 \times 2 \times 1 = 43,200$) and the boggling upper bound of 272 factorial (272!). This is larger than the number of elementary particles in the Universe ('Q' $= 10^{80}$) and would apparently be the number of possible journeys if you could move in any sequence between stations without using the lines.'

11 Although these studies did not look at motivation, it's a fair assumption that many of this 'sensitive' group are the Prospectors in Dade's model. By and large, NGOs have not been very successful with these people, partly because their engagement mechanisms have been designed to encourage a 'ladder of activism'. To involve these people requires alternative chains of engagement such as lifestyle change, rather than activism.

12 This picture is a composite impression based on many surveys and research projects I saw conducted for groups such as WWF, Greenpeace and a renewables company. For some published data in this area, see www.mori.com and, internationally, www.environics.com.

13 The 'supporter' numbers are not comparable as organizations differ in what they count. Some count each family member as a member, while others do not, and some count any sort of a donation as support.

14 'What does Katrina mean for campaigns?', *Campaign Strategy Newsletter* no 16, 9 September 2005.

15 Lisa Roner, 'Wal-Mart – An environmental epiphany?', 7 December 2005, www.climatechangecorp. com/content.asp?ContentID=4009.

16 'Air travel and NGOs', *Campaign Strategy Newsletter* no 28, 24 October 2006.

17 Climate and Air Travel Issue, *Campaign Strategy Newsletter* no 30, 27 December 2006.

18 Jeff Randall, 'Why it is better to lose your money than your reputation', www.telegraph.co.uk/finance/comment/jeffrandall/2804285/Why-it-is-better-to-lose-money-than-your-reputation.html.

19 Nathan Skinner, 'Be prepared', www.stratfor exampleicrisk.co.uk/story.asp?storycode=380873.

20 Ronald Inglehart and Christian Welzel (2005) *Modernization, Cultural Change and Democracy: The Human Development Sequence*, Cambridge University Press, Cambridge, UK.

21 'The 4x4 is here to stay – On and off-road', 29 June 2004, www.smmt.co.uk/news/DetailedArticle_pop.cfm?login=1&articleid=8281&printfriendly=undefined&CFID=408022&CFTOKEN=99447893.

22 See www.dailymail.co.uk/news/article-1024482/Chelsea-tractors-abandoned-green-car-sales-rise-120pc.html#ixzz0fdqJQSET.

23 Richard Headland, 'Time to ditch the 4x4?', *Which? Car*, 20 February 2009.

24 For instance, the proportion of household waste recycled or composted in England rose from 7 per cent to just 11 per cent in the four years to 2000/01, *ENDS Report* 330, July 2002, pp28–32, 'Household waste recycling: How high should we aim?' (FoE proposed a 60 per cent recycling rate was achievable.) See www.endsreport.com.

25 *ENDS Report* 352, May 2004, pp14–15, 'Morley uses health study to urge building of new waste facilities'.

26 *ENDS Report* 416, September 2009, pp17–18, 'Leading English councils hit 70 per cent recycling rate'; *ENDS Report* 420, January 2010, pp28–31, 'Should England up its recycling target?; *ENDS Report* 419, December 2009, pp20–21, 'Surrey ditches plans for two new incinerators as waste arisings decline'; *ENDS Report* 420, January 2010, pp17–18, 'Hampshire broadens its incinerator inputs'.

27 For more details see Chris Rose, *Climate Change Campaigns: Keep Calm But Don't Carry On,* February 2010, at www.campaignstrategy.org.

28 *ENDS Report* 409, February 2009, p16, 'DEFRA urges caution on 2020 landfill forecasts'.

CHAPTER 10

1 Friday, 1 November 2002, 'News audiences "declining" in UK', http://news.bbc.co.uk/1/hi/ entertainment/tv_and_radio/2385625.stm – 'New news, old news', report conducted for the Independent Television Commission (ITC) and Broadcasting Standards Council (BSC) by Ian Hargreaves and James Thomas.

2 British Market Research Bureau.

3 See www.thisisbournemouth.co.uk/dorset/bournemouth/media/07.pdf.

4 See www.naa.org/marketscope/databank/tdnpr1299.htm.

5 According to the Federation of International Editors of Journals, www.ulsterbusiness.com/ current/items/item-16.htm.

6 Office of National Statistics news release, 16 February 2009, www.statistics.gov.uk/pdfdir/ st0210.pdf.

7 See http://pewresearch.org/pubs/1066/internet-overtakes-newspapers-as-news-source.

8 See www.culture.gov.uk/images/publications/digital_britain_interimreportjan09_annex1.pdf.

9 See www.investigationsfund.org.

10 See www.flatearthnews.net/.

11 For example http://people-press.org/report/444/news-media.

12 See www.journalism.co.uk/5/articles/536178.php and www.nytimes.com/2009/10/19/ technology/internet/19link.html.

13 See http://weblog.greenpeace.org/makingwaves/archives/2009/10/trafigura_background.html.

14 See www.edelman.com/trust/2010/docs/2010_Trust_Barometer_Executive_Summary.pdf.

15 Burgess, J. (1987) 'Landscapes in the living room', *Landscape Research Group*, vol 12, no 3.

16 True at least with Greenpeace UK.

17 Klein, N. (2000) *No Logo*, Flamingo, London.

18 For instance: http://e-strategyblog.com/2008/12/barack-obamas-use-of-social-networking/, www.epolitics.com/learning-from-obama/, http://fairsay.com/blog/how-to-ecampaign-like-obama and www.rollingstone.com/news/story/19106326/the_machinery_of_hope/print.

19 For example www.facebook.com/pages/Veterans-for-Obama/40333288128; www.facebook. com/pages/Obama-Pride/55618600602#!/pages/Obama-Pride/55618600602?v=info.

20 For example www.blackplanet.com/barack_Obama/; www.migente.com/barack_Obama/; www. eons.com/members/profile/barackobama.

21 Sean Larkins (larkins.miah@btinternet.com).

22 Gladwell, M. (2000) *The Tipping Point: How Little Things Can Make a Big Difference*, Little, Brown and Company, London, New York.

23 Conservative Party Chairman Kenneth Baker, quoted p5 in *The Great Car Economy Versus The Quality of Life*, Greenpeace, 1990.

24 Douglas Hurd, 'Quality of life: The big issue of the next decade', *Sunday Correspondent*, 12 November 1989.

25 Nicholas Comfort and David Nicholson-Lord, 'Tories put green slant on next election', *Independent on Sunday*, 11 February 1990.

26 George Jones and Charles Clover, 'Veto on plan for carbon tax to cut pollution', *Daily Telegraph*, 27 July 1990.

27 See 'An example of a campaign', pp182–183 in Chris Rose, 'Achieving Change' chapter in *Conservation in Progress* (1993) Goldsmith, F. B. and Warren, A., Wiley, Chichester, UK.

28 *Why Britain Remains the Dirty Man of Europe*, Chris Rose, Greenpeace, 1990.

29 See www.fair.org/counterspin/index.html.

30 See www.gla.ac.uk/Acad/Sociology/media.html.

31 Summary of their book *Market Killing* at www.gla.ac.uk/Acad/ Sociology/Market.htm.

32 Nick Davies, *Flat Earth News*, Vintage 2009 (first published in 2008 by Chatto and Windus).

33 'New media' is often taken to include such technologies as websites, including interactive chat sites and newsgroups, the internet, weblogs, bots/robots, web crawlers and browsers, intelligent agents, email (including sound, messages, pictures), video-telephony, local networks such as Bluetooth, combining interfaces, digital TV, webTV, DVD, databases, extranets and intranets, all seen in the context of the network economy, and the growing application of artificial intelligence.

34 Cox, D. (2003) *New Statesman*, 20 January, p49.

35 Replacement of materials with design or information value.

36 See http://petewarden.typepad.com/searchbrowser/2010/02/how-to-split-up-the-us.html.

37 See www.wired.com/wired/archive/5.09/newrules_pr.html and Kelly, K. (1998) *New Rules for the New Economy: 10 Radical Strategies for a Connected World*, Viking Press, London.

38 These figures were for the period 1999–2001 and will change rapidly. Many commercial agencies publish data on who watches what and when.

39 See www.nfoeurope.com/ib/ThoughtLeadership.cfm?lan=en.

40 See www.wired.com/wired/archive/7.09/nokia.html.

41 See www.saga.co.uk/radio 'music and lifestyle-oriented speech catering for today's over-50s'.

42 Sean Larkins, pers comm, study COI/Mediavest March 2001, Sean Larkins (larkins.miah@btinternet.com).

CHAPTER 11

1 See the study 'Now Hear This' at www.fenton.com.

2 Marr, A. (1995) *Ruling Britannia: Failure and Future of British Democracy*, Michael Joseph, London.

3 patrick.branigan@homeoffice.gsi.gov.uk.

4 katie.aston@ukgateway.net.

5   Simmons, J. (2003) *The Invisible Grail*, Texere, London.

6   The late John Grey, chairman of Media Natura, director of Halpin Grey Vermier, who taught me about visual language and who was a great communicator.

7   Apply triage: is what you are assuming as a critical path or final objective simply too difficult to be practically achievable? Focus not on what will change anyway, or is impossibly hard to change, but on things that may change if you act on them.

8   The fuel duty escalator introduced by the UK John Major government as a 'carbon tax' measure. Retained by the 1997 Tony Blair government, it yielded large revenues for the Treasury, which were not spent specifically for either transport or climate-change measures, such as renewable energy – although it was 'counted in' by the environment department of the government as one of its climate policy measures designed to help meet international commitments for the UK to reduce CO_2 emissions. It was never clear that the tax was set at levels that actually deterred use of fuel. Petrol prices rose as a result of world oil price rises, and an aggressive campaign of direct action was organized by truckers and farmers.

9   Organizer Brynle Williams told the BBC in 2002 that protests had achieved 'the reduction of some fuel duty in this year's budget, as well as big reductions in licence costs for hauliers. The wagon-owners had a dramatic reduction, the cost of fuel has come down by approximately 10 per cent', http://news.bbc.co.uk/1/hi/uk/1533218.stm. Fuel duty was subsequently frozen in two budgets.

10 Between September 2000 and January 2001, the price of Brent crude oil dropped by 30 per cent and petrol prices followed, though dropping much less – Wednesday, 3 January 2001, 'Should petrol be cheaper?', http://news.bbc.co.uk/hi/english/business/newsid_1098000/1098985.stm.

11 A few weeks after protests dominated the headlines, polls showed that attitudes to environment and fuel on the one hand, and the price of fuel and the protests on the other, were not aligned on the same axis. MORI, for instance, found 58 per cent supporting protest action, while the RSPB found 51 per cent believing petrol should be taxed for environmental reasons, with 46 per cent wanting taxation to limit greenhouse gas emissions. 'The public's intimate relationship with their car as a second skin' is what drives their irrational fuel protests – Coward, R. (7 November, 2000) 'Special report: The petrol war', *The Guardian*.

12 A 'pro war' swing began after the war started, but the choice and consequences of 'no war' or stopping the war once begun, are very different and incomparable.

13 Terrorist threat to countries outside Iraq, weapons of mass destruction inside Iraq, the same but maybe exported from Iraq, the intention to use them or the potential to use them, threats to the region, contacts with al-Qa'eda, harbouring al-Qa'eda, and the 'failure' of the United Nations to resolve various Iraq-related problems, ending up with humanitarian abuses by the Iraqi regime.

14 President Bush had a much less critical and a more poorly informed public and media, along with a popular desire for revenge, almost any sort of revenge, post 9/11. The subtext rationale for Blair's position was to contain or moderate Bush, and that might have been a more effective explanation to use if it had not been for the fact that war without a convincing rationale seemed to many to be at least unwise (that is, he had failed to moderate Bush beyond the US waiting for the UK to join in the war).

15 One could argue that chlorine never had a visual identity in the campaign.
16 See www.wwf.org.uk/chemicals.
17 See case study in *Campaign Strategy Newsletter* no 52, June 2009; 'The Gurkhas campaign: Lessons from Lumley', www.campaignstrategy.org.

CHAPTER 12

1 There are a host of mostly very dull books about this. For me, one of the more interesting approaches, and one that can be applied to non-governmental organizations, is organizational psychology, such as William Bridges' book – Bridges, W. (1992) *The Character of Organizations: Using Jungian Type in Organizational Development*, Davies-Black Publishers, Palo Alto, CA.
2 'We' in this case was Chris Williams, then marketing director, Nick Gallie, then creative director, and myself, but the process of developing an organizational communications strategy also involved dozens of other people, such as Annie Moreton.
3 Pat Dade, thegurupat@aol.com pers comm – see also www.cultdyn.co.uk.
4 See www.utne.com/web_special/web_specials_archives/ articles/2246-1.html.
5 I don't mean to encourage the invention of brands for specific campaigns. That's usually a mistake. Brands are what define you as different, and trying to define one campaign as different from the rest of your organization only raises questions and doubts about both of them. Resist the temptation to establish vanity brands for individual campaigns – stand out by what you do, not by superficial things like new logos or graphic design. The real campaign value of a brand lies in its heritage of past accomplishments and journeys that you and its supporters have been on.
6 Psychological, political, corporate, and so on, often by acting as indicators of what may come if they are ignored.
7 In *Cod* (Jonathan Cape, London, 1998), his history of the cod, Mark Kurlansky writes:

> *The real revolutionaries were middle-class Massachusetts merchants with commercial interests, and their revolution was about the right to make money ... the ability to make decisions about their own economy... Massachusetts radicals sought an economic, not a social revolution. They were not thinking of the hungry masses and their salaries. They were thinking of the right of every man to be middle-class, to be an entrepreneur, to conduct commerce and make money. Men of no particular skill, with very little capital, had made fortunes in the cod fishery. That was the system they believed in.* (p93)

Some may say that the more recent American practice of demanding free access for its goods abroad while protecting its own markets at home, is evidence that this tradition is alive and well.
8 Conventional NGOs were present on the sidelines – for example, FoE – or behind the scenes, as with Greenpeace, which gave limited help but exerted no control.
9 One remarkable success for FoE was in 2002 at Hastings, where a bypass scheme was defeated. The A556(M) in Cheshire has also been scrapped.
10 Roger Higman, pers comm, rogerh@foe.co.uk.

11 Although any internet search will retrieve large amounts of material from *Schnews* and elsewhere.

12 Of course within 'their' world, the campaigns did have brands, such as – in Britain at least – Reclaim the Streets, the magazine *Schnews*, and the Union Jill, a rainbow version of the Union Jack. But these were not used to recruit or lever support from outside the activist circle, so are not campaign brands in the sense used here.

13 This term may date from a book by Philip Selznik published in 1952: *The Organizational Weapon: A Study of Bolshevik Strategy and Tactics* (Rand series), McGraw-Hill, Maidenhead, UK.

14 Kingsworth, P (2003) *One No, Many Yeses*, Free Press, London.

15 'Communicating global interdependence', a FrameWorks Message Memo, www.frameworksinstitute.org.

16 Rose, C. (1998) *The Turning of the Spar*, Greenpeace, London.

17 See http://news.bbc.co.uk/1/hi/uk/536533.stm Thursday, 25 November 1999 – 'BBC apologizes to Greenpeace'.

18 Despite conventional wisdom in environmental circles, that was considerable. The Ministry of Agriculture's laboratory at Burnham-on-Crouch, Essex, wrote about the contents of the Spar in a memo leaked to Greenpeace: 'The chemistry of this water is such that it has to be considered very toxic to marine biota (life). It should be treated as hazardous waste and any discharge prohibited.' Clearly, this could not be done if it was dumped at sea. One of the scientists added a comment: 'The bottom line is that the waste cannot be dumped at sea. The only option is to take ashore and treat.'

19 Beck, U., *Risk Society* (1986), *Counterpoison* (1991), *Ecological Enlightenment* (1992) and *Ecological Politics in an Age of Risk* (1994).

20 Tudge, C., 'Mad, bad and dangerous', *New Statesman*, 4 March 2002.

21 Stirling, A. (1999) *On Science and Precaution in the Management of Technological Risk*, University of Sussex, Brighton, a synthesis report of studies conducted by Professor Ortwin Renn and Dr Andreas Klinke of AFTA Stuttgart, Professor Arie Rip of CSS Twente, Professor Ahti Salo of HUT, Helsinki and Dr Andrew Stirling of SPRU Sussex. EC Forward Studies Unit Final Report of a project for the EC Forward Studies Unit under the auspices of the ESTO Network, commissioned by Dr Michael Rogers, CdP, Brussels; oversight by Silvio Funtowicz, JRC, Ispra. Final Report, May 1999.

22 Milliband, E. (10 March 2003) 'The house Jack couldn't build', *New Statesman*, pp16–17.

23 Marr, A. (1996) *Ruling Britannia*, Penguin, London.

24 Reinicke, W. H. (1998) *Global Public Policy: Governing Without Government?*, Brookings Institute, Washington, DC.

25 See, for example, Burke, J. and Ornstein, R. (1997) *The Axemaker's Gift*, Tarcher Putnam, New York.

26 But not in the US. The proportion of security-driven people has increased rapidly in recent decades. It seems because deteriorating real prospects have caused many formerly esteem-driven people to 'retreat' to a security-driven state. See more at www.campaignstrategy.org.

27 For example, the loss of old social allegiances based on security-driven politics has reordered the power base of both left and right in Britain, resulting in a shift towards the centre, which fails to satisfy the inner-directeds, and an overemphasis on esteem-driven voter propositions, which annoys the others.

28 See http://archive.greenpeace.org/~comms/vrml/rw/text/z02.html.

29 See 'The world will never be the same again... because of Jubilee 2000', a justifiably self-congratulatory report at www.jubilee2000uk.org.

30 For example, John Elkington at Sustainability, www.sustainability.com.

31 See http://travelindia.com/TI_Guides/garhwal/garhwal_html/chipko_movement.html.

32 McSpotlight – www.mcspotlight.org – gets well over a million hits a month. The McLibel trial was an infamous British court case between McDonald's and Helen Steel and Dave Morris, a postman and a gardener from London. It took two-and-a-half years; the longest-ever English trial. The judge declared in June 1997 that McDonald's 'exploits children' with its advertising, produces 'misleading' advertising, is 'culpably responsible' for cruelty to animals, is 'antipathetic' to unionization and pays its workers low wages. But he also ruled that the campaigners libelled McDonald's and they should pay £60,000 damages. They refused to pay, and McDonald's did not pursue it.

33 Compare the centralized UK or US with highly federal Switzerland, for example.

APPENDIX 1

1 See Chris Rose, *The Dirty Man of Europe: The Great British Pollution Scandal*, Simon and Schuster, 1990.

2 Whether this was by accident or design is debatable but it certainly had that effect. Many books have been written about it but see www.iiasa.ac.at/Admin/PUB/Documents/IR-97-034.pdf; Wendy E. Franz, 'The development of an international agenda for climate change: Connecting science to policy', ENRP Discussion Paper E-97-07, Kennedy School of Government, Harvard University, August 1997.

3 Following a request by the UN General Assembly to the Executive Heads of WMO and UNEP, the IPCC was established by the 40th Session of the WMO Executive Council in 1988, where it was given its initial mandate and terms of reference – Review of the terms of reference of the IPCC, IPCC-XXVI/Doc. 4 (29 March 2007), www.ipcc.ch/meetings//session26/doc4.pdf. Negotiations on what became the UNFCCC were launched in December 1990 by the UN General Assembly. An Intergovernmental Negotiating Committee (INC) was convened to conduct these negotiations, which were concluded in 15 months. The Convention was adopted on 9 May 1992, and opened for signature a month later at the UN Conference on Environment and Development in Rio de Janeiro, Brazil. It entered into force on 21 March 1994, after receiving the requisite 50 ratifications. See www.unfccc.int.

4 'Climate change communications – Dipping a toe into public motivation', Chris Rose with Pat Dade, Nick Gallie and John Scott, May 2005, www.campaignstrategy.org/valuesvoters/climatechangecommunications.pdf.

5 For example www.350.org.

6 For example www.planestupid.com.

7 For example Rob Bell's www.unpluggit.co.uk aimed at mobile phone stand-by.

8 For example the AISE 'Washright Campaign' reported at www.wbcsd.org.

9 For example www.iigcc.org, www.incr.com, www.igcc.org.au.

10 For example www.climate-justice-action.org/.

11 For example www.tropicalforestgroup.org/, www.tropicalforesttrust.com, http://ran.org/ campaigns/rainforest_agribusiness/ and www.greenpeace.org/international/news/forests-for-climate-indonesia-06102008.

12 For example, in a letter to the *British Medical Journal* and then *Lancet* in 2009, the heads of 18 colleges of medicine in the developed and developing world warned of catastrophic health effects if tough greenhouse gas emissions cuts were not agreed. 'Copenhagen failure would be a "health catastrophe"', *ENDS Report* 416, September 2009, p6, www.endsreport.com.

13 For example www.cafod.org.uk/climatejustice.

14 For example www.thebreakthrough.org/.

15 For example Cities for Climate Protection, www.iclei.org.

16 For example www.oxfam.org/en/campaigns/climatechange/sisters-planet; www.wen.org.uk/ climatechange/resources/manifesto.pdf.

17 For example www.globalcool.org.

18 For example 'contraction and convergence', www.gci.org.uk/contconv/cc.html.

19 See for example Exxon's activities: www.guardian.co.uk/environment/2009/jul/01/exxon-mobil-climate-change-sceptics-funding.

20 For example www.peopleandplanet.org/gogreen/unis.

21 For example The Carbon Trust's 'One Million A Day' campaign aimed at Small and medium enterprises (SMEs): www.carbontrust.co.uk/News/presscentre/one-million-a-day.htm.

22 For example see www.bbc.co.uk/bloom, which seems to advocate action, and contrast with Peter Barron, editor of the BBC flagship news programme *Newsnight*: 'It is absolutely not the BBC's job to save the planet. I think there are a lot of people who think that, but it must be stopped' – 'BBC drops climate change special', John Plunkett, *The Guardian*, 5 September 2007.

23 In a series of emails in the months before the 2009 COP15 climate summit in Copenhagen, Ed Miliband, at the time Minister for Energy and Climate in the UK Parliament, encouraged contacts to 'vote' by email on various 'options' facing Prime Minister Gordon Brown as to how he should spend his time. One of these involved being proactive about the climate talks – effectively a minister encouraging a campaign aimed at his own government.

24 'Recession results in steep fall in emissions', Fiona Harvey, *Financial Times*, 20 September 2009.

25 In an interview for the *Financial Times*, IEA's chief economist Fatih Birol said effective measures included the EU's climate package, which calls for a 20 per cent cut in emissions by 2020 relative to 1990, tighter US car emission standards and energy efficiency policies in China.

26 See www.publicintfor examplerity.org/investigations/climate_change/.

27 See for example *The Turning of the Spar*, Chris Rose, Greenpeace UK, 1988.

28 Bill Hare, 'Fossil fuels and climate protection: The carbon logic', http://archive.greenpeace. org/~climate/science/reports/fossil.pdf.

29 See http://archive.greenpeace.org/climate/science/reports/fossil.pdf.

30 Robert Socolow, 'Stabilization wedges: Mitigation tools for the next half-century', Keynote Speech on Technological Options at the Scientific Symposium on Stabilisation of Greenhouse Gases 'Avoiding Dangerous Climate Change', 1–3 February 2005, Met Office, Exeter, UK, at www.stabilisation2005.com/Robert_Socolow.pdf, and references therein.

31 See http://europa.eu/rapid/pressReleasesAction.do?reference=MEMO/07/16.

32 See www.skybook.org/; www.grist.org/article/sky-trust-explained/.

33 350 says (2009): 'What does the number 350 mean? 350 is the most important number in the world – it's what scientists say is the safe upper limit for carbon dioxide in the atmosphere. Two years ago, after leading climatologists observed rapid ice melt in the Arctic and other frightening signs of climate change, they issued a series of studies showing that the planet faced both human and natural disaster if atmospheric concentrations of CO_2 remained above 350 parts per million' (currently at 390).

34 See www.thebreakthrough.org/PDF/Death_of_Environmentalism.pdf and for other views search Grist Magazine, for example www.grist.org/article/markey-spokesman-questions-breakthrough-institute1; Chris Rose, 'Commentary on death of environmentalism', at www.campaignstrategy.org/resources.html; *Campaign Strategy Newsletters* nos 1 and 4, 2005, at www.campaigsntrategy.org.

35 Their organization is 'The Breakthrough Institute' where 'The Era Of Small Thinking Is Over'.

36 For example Josh Freed, Avi Zevin and Jesse Jenkins, 'Jumpstarting a clean energy revolution with a national institutes of energy', *American Energy Innovation*, September 2009.

37 See www.newscientist.com/article/dn11088-blame-for-global-warming-placed-firmly-on-humankind.html.

38 For an analysis of 'climate scepticism' see *Sustaining Disbelief* at www.campaignstrategy.org.

39 See www.globalactionplan.org.uk/.

40 The campaign 'Negawatt for Megawatt' took place from November 1990 until Easter 1991 in Schleswig-Holstein (Northern Germany) and succeeded in promoting purchase of compact flourescent lightbulbs, including by using the 'commitment heuristic', in over 200 towns, and cutting nearly 1mkwh a year in electricity use, www.nordlicht.uni-kiel.de/nordlicht/prowo.htm.

41 Martin Rosenbaum, 'Can politicians shape our behaviour?', http://news.bbc.co.uk/1/hi/uk_politics/8255153.stm.

42 Discussed in *Campaign Strategy Newsletter*. See issues 36 and 38 at www.campaignstrategy.org.

43 See www.foe.co.uk/resource/briefings/briefing_deliver_cc_act.pdf.

44 Low-Carbon Transition Plan published for UK, *ENDS Report* 414, July 2009, pp40–41, www.endsreport.com.

45 See for example www.edf.org/article.cfm?ContentID=4870 and www.sourcewatch.org/index.php?title=Global_warming_skeptic.

46 See www.campaignstrategy.org/articles/sustaining_disbelief.pdf.

47 In a 2008 IPSOS MORI study for DEFRA, 60 per cent agreed that 'many scientific experts still question if humans are contributing to climate change' – www.ipsos-mori.com/Assets/Docs/Publications/sri-environment-public-attitudes-to-climate-change-2008-concerned-but-still-unconvinced.pdf.

48 See www.naturescalendar.org.uk.

49 For example, *The Copenhagen Accord: A Stepping Stone?*, WWF, http://assets.panda.org/downloads/the_stepping_stone_final_280110.pdf; 'After Copenhagen', Tom Athanasiou at www.ecoequity.org/2010/01/after-copenhagen; Climate Interactive at http://climateinteractive.org/scoreboard/scoreboard-science-and-data; '*Copenhagen 2009*, failure or final wake-up call for our leaders?', Benito Muller at www.oxfordenergy.org/pdfs/EV49.pdf; 'The Copenhagen

Conference: A post-mortem', Social Science Research Network at http://papers.ssrn.com/sol3/
papers.cfm?abstract_id=1553167; Jeremy Leggett at www.jeremyleggett.net/triple-crunch-log/;
John Sauven of Greenpeace at www.guardian.co.uk/commentisfree/2010/feb/16/climate-
change-global-solution-greenpeace; Oliver Tickell at www.guardian.co.uk/commentisfree/cif-
green/2010/jan/25/carbon-market-copenhagen-climate; 'Climate groups grapple for a path
forward from Copenhagen', Jonathan Hiskes (US) at www.grist.org/article/2010-01-28-climate-
groups-grapple-for-a-path-forward-from-copenhagen/.
50 See www.campaignstrategy.org/climate_campaigns_keep_calm.pdf.
51 See http://campaignstrategy.org/newsletters/campaignstrategy_newsletter_49.pdf.
52 See www.campaignstrategy.org/articles/sustaining_disbelief.pdf.
53 Chris Rose, 2010, www.campaignstrategy.org/climate_campaigns_keep_calm.pdf.
54 *Campaign Strategy Newsletter* no 50 – 'It's the children stupid'.

Appendix 2

1   REACH started life in 1998 – see for example an EU account at http://tinyurl.com/ygm52br
    and http://assets.panda.org/downloads/reachin5minutes.pdf.
2   See www.wwf.org.uk/chemicals; Justin's video, http://tinyurl.com/yjpose5; see also www.
    forumforthefuture.org/greenfutures/articles/602336; www.thewi.org.uk/standard.aspx?id=10982.
3   Like Greenpeace and, to a lesser extent, Friends of the Earth, WWF UK's effort was part of a
    wider campaign, in this case involving a number of its European offices.
4   See www.thewi.org.uk/standard.aspx?id=10982.
5   See, for example, Scotland, http://news.bbc.co.uk/1/hi/scotland/3235102.stm, and Wales
    http://tinyurl.com/yht3wjf.
6   See www.greenpeace.org.uk/Products/Toxics/campaign.cfm.
7   Formerly at www.chemical-cocktail.org/index_en.asp.
8   Still available at www.thewi.org.uk/standard.aspx?id=10982.
9   See www.foeeurope.org/safer_chemicals/Index.htm.
10 See www.foe.co.uk/resource/press_releases/1212xmas.html.
11 'Retailers struggle to phase out risky chemicals', *ENDS Report* 402, July 2008, pp22–23.
12 See, for instance, 'PBT criteria under REACH spark internal battle', *ENDS Report* 408, January
    2009, pp52–53.
13 'Green groups publish chemical blacklist', *ENDS Report* 405, October 2008, pp24–25.
14 'ECHA starts work on REACH candidate list', *ENDS Report* 402, July 2008, p21.

Appendix 3

1   See www.ksbr.co.uk.
2   Natural England Research Reports, NERR019, http://naturalengland.communisis.com/
    naturalenglandshop/docs/NERR019.pdf.

APPENDIX 4

1   See www.democrats.org/a/party/a_50_state_strategy/.
2   See www.washingtonpost.com/wp-dyn/content/article/2007/02/04/AR2007020401343_2.
    html.
3   See www.newyorker.com/reporting/2008/11/17/081117fa_fact_lizza#ixzz0hcYMZxRC.
4   See http://adage.com/campaigntrail/post?article_id=127508.
5   See http://obama.3cdn.net/277bb8792237d562f2_9gm6bnupn.pdf.
6   See www.realclearpolitics.com/articles/2008/06/obamas_50_state_strategy.html.
7   See www.bozkurtihsan.co.uk/2008/POLITICS/10/28/martin.election/index.html.
8   See www.washingtonpost.com/wp-dyn/content/article/2007/02/04/AR2007020401343_2.
    html.
9   See http://publicrelationssydney.com.au/?p=514.
10 See www.newyorker.com/reporting/2008/11/17/081117fa_fact_lizza#ixzz0hcYMZxRC.
11 Lorien C. Abroms, and R. Craid Lefebvre, 'Obama's wired campaign: Lessons for public health
    communication', *Journal of Health Communication*, vol 14, pp415–423, 2009.
12 See www.slideshare.net/dsiroker/how-we-used-data-to-win-the-presidential-election-by-dan-
    siroker.

APPENDIX 5

1   See www.greenpeace.org/international/news/tasty-apple-news-020507.
2   See www.apple.com/hotnews/agreenerapple/.

Basic Campaign Checklist

The guidelines below were summarized from my website www.campaignstrategy.com by the organizers of the 'Communicate' Conference in 2006 (see resources at www.festivalofnature. org). A checklist can't replace a book – and all these ideas are explored in more detail in the main text – and a book can't replace what you will discover from experiencing campaigns, but some users have found these guidelines useful, especially if an organization has not campaigned before.

1. Do you really need to campaign?

Campaigning can be fun, but it's often hard, dull, frustrating and unsuccessful. Campaigning is usually only done when all else has failed. It involves a conversation with society, persuading people to take an unusual interest in supporting a move that would not normally happen. It means setting up and sustaining processes that are not normal or 'business as usual'.

If politics is the 'art of the possible', campaigning is the science and art of changing what is possible. Do it right and a campaign succeeds in inspiring its followers to go on to the next target. But unstructured or poorly focused campaigns are hot air balloons kept aloft by burning idealism and goodwill, until they suffer 'burn out'.

So before you go any further stop and ask yourself: 'Do I really need to campaign? Or can I get what I want by other means – "business as usual" – can I buy it, can it be delivered by simply asking politely, or through quiet lobbying, or by trading or through politics?'

2. Motivation not education

Campaigning lowers the barriers against action and increases the incentives to take action. Education, in contrast, is a broadening exercise. It uses examples to reveal layers of complexity, leading to lower certainty but higher understanding.

Campaigning maximizes the motivation of the audience, not their knowledge. Try using education to campaign, and you will end up circling and exploring your issue but not changing it.

Campaigns do have some 'educational' effect, but it is education by doing, through experience, rather than through being given information. Information is not power until it leads to mobilization.

3. Analyse the forces

You know what needs to change. Ask this: 'Why hasn't it happened already?' Try mapping out the forces for and against what you want to happen. Draw a map of the problem – the people involved, the organizations, the institutions – and work out exactly what the mechanisms are for the decisions you want to change.

Then identify potential allies and opponents and work out who your target audience is for each step (see Guidelines 4, 5 and 6). Look at it from their point of view.

Check – how will you now change the balance of forces for and against action in order to overcome the obstacle? If you don't know the answer to this, how can you specify an objective to be achieved?

4. KISS (Keep It Simple, Stupid)

Campaigns are needed because there is an urgent problem that has to be made public in order to be resolved. Effective motivation needs simplicity in message and purpose.

Communicate only one thing at a time. Use a simple unambiguous 'call to action' that requires no explanation.

5. Right Components – Right Order

You need to follow the sequence: awareness → alignment → engagement → action.

The campaign involves a deliberate series of revelations or communication exercises to take the 'audience' from a state of ignorance, through interest and then concern (components of awareness), into anger and engagement (motivation), and finally into a state of satisfaction or reward. If that happens, the campaign participants or supporters will be ready for more.

Communicate them all at once and there's no involvement in the 'story' of the campaign. A good campaign has to be like a book or a drama – the outcome must be important but unknown.

Showing a problem may lead to concern, but in itself that won't lead to action. Show them now is the opportunity to force a change, to implement the solution, and give them a way to act – and you have the conditions for engagement.

6. Start from where your audience is

A marketer finds out what you want, what you already do and think, and creates or finds a product that fits you.

When it comes to communication, do your market research. Say you need to persuade a group of councillors to take a particular decision about a forest. You may think it's important for frogs or as a watershed. But what do they see? What if they use it for jogging or 50 per cent of their constituents are woodcutters? You may see a forest but they may see timber, or an exercise area. Put the issue in their terms.

7. Construct a critical path

All issues are complex, but your campaign must not be. Complexity demotivates; it makes people feel confused – and if they feel confused, they will think you are confused, and not worth listening to.

Your campaign cannot be the 'whole picture'. Instead it has to be a way, a trail, stepping stones, a critical path. Do not try to communicate 'the issue', however tempting it may be. Communicate your campaign – what you think, the problem as you see it, the solution as you see it, the opportunity as you see it – and only that.

Stick with each stage until it is achieved. Each stage is a target or objective in itself. Resist the temptation to talk ahead by giving 'the whole picture'. Plan a campaign as a series of steps where one leads to the next – like dominoes.

Try mapping out the forces for and against what you want to happen. Draw a map of the problem – the people involved, the organizations, the institutions – and work out exactly what the mechanisms are for the decisions you want to change.

8. Campaign against the unacceptable

Your campaign may be 'about an issue', but to engage people it will need to have a much more specific 'battlefront'. Choosing that battlefront is a crucial task.

A campaign strongly supported by a tiny part of the population may sustain a vigorous organization. It may survive for decades – for as long as its supporters have the energy. But to succeed, most campaigns need to attract much broader support – and to do that, you often need to narrow the focus.

Normally the task is to find the pieces of an issue or concern that are unacceptable to a big enough group of people to get the effect you need. In general it is better to campaign against a small part of a big problem, where that part is 99 per cent unacceptable to the public, than to campaign against say half of the overall problem, where that is only unacceptable to one per cent of the population.

9. Make real things happen

Don't argue, do. Events are the stuff of politics – whether formal politics, business politics, personal politics or the politics of the dung heap.

News is not about ideas or concepts; it is about things that happen. Ask yourself every day, what is this campaign doing? What's the verb? Is it starting something, publishing, blocking, rescuing, occupying, marching, lobbying, painting... What are you doing?

Too often campaigns become absorbed in collecting information or circulating it to people who already agree with the cause.

Some of the most powerful events are direct actions, especially where these are non-violent and can be justified on moral and 'scientific' or 'economic' grounds. That way they gain widest support. But there are many other powerful ways to campaign.

10. Say what you mean

Directly or indirectly, a campaign consists of persuading others not just that you are right but that you are so right that they must take some form of action.

Everyday we are exposed to many thousands of messages. Almost all are ignored or immediately discarded. Very few things 'stick' and anything that makes a message hard work to understand makes it less likely to stick.

The simplest thing you can do to help your message is to be direct and straightforward. Forget about being 'clever'. When all else fails (as it probably will), say what you mean. (Try telling a relative – when they 'get it', use their way of saying it.)

11. Find the conflicts in events – Make the news

This is often misunderstood. Conflict is inherent to campaigns. Without a conflict of interest, a campaign would not be needed.

Campaigns make news when they create change, make a difference, or threaten to do so. A conflict formed just of ideas is of interest only to academic or political theoreticians. What counts for the rest of us is who comes out on top, what gets changed, how does it affect me, my family, my life and how it can be lived? In other words 'outcomes'.

News connects with politics through events. Events are also the things that change our views. A campaign is about forcing a change to the status quo. Conflict is therefore built into it, indeed almost defines campaigning.

12. Communicate in pictures

At every level, think out your campaign in steps, leading back from the objective you want to achieve.

Create a chronological storyboard – your critical path – and work out how you will make that happen. If you can't, then change your objective. But don't try to do the job of the press. Don't try to create 'cartoons'.

Things that aren't real, for example, are 'addressing the issue', 'working on ... the subject', 'developing awareness' and 'reaching the public'. Things that are real could include occupying a tree, releasing a dove, conducting a survey in a shopping mall, visiting your MP, writing a letter, sending an email, speaking to a crowd, or invading the Sellafield nuclear reprocessing plant.

Create events that actually generate those pictures – or lead them to occur. Then make sure you communicate in pictures, not just words.

If you find this difficult at first, try involving a local photographer. Take them through your campaign plan and get them to say whether they could tell the story in pictures. As a rule, if there's nothing to photograph, there's no actual activity, no objective to achieve, and no campaign to join in with, report or support.

Pictures are far more powerful than words. Good ones tell the story and the best need no caption. And pictures cannot be interrogated or argued with. Make your campaign speak in characters and symbols that are larger than life. The only things stronger than images are face-to-face contact and direct engagement in doing the campaign.

ADVANCED TIPS – IF YOU HAVE BEEN CAMPAIGNING

Campaigning is a creative and a technical process – an art and a science. It's all too easy to get 'too close' to the subject and to lose perspective. Sometimes it's good to step back and reconsider, to try a different tack, to go round an obstacle instead of through it – and even, when you're winning, to remember that running the current campaign is not an end in itself.

There are three things you might try in self-diagnosis of your campaign if it 'isn't working'.

1. Testing a strategy

Ideally no campaign should be started until you have tested your strategy. In reality campaigns often 'just grow', and the opportunity to properly test them never arises.

I recommend testing a strategy with two types of research – qualitative research to investigate language and 'political' research to investigate obstacles, decision-making, attitudes of key individuals, potential allies and opponents.

Qualitative research should not be confused with quantitative opinion research conducted by groups such as Gallup, NOP or IPSOS MORI. Quantitative or 'polling' research tells you how many people think something. Qualitative research tells you why they think something.

The best known type of qualitative research is 'focus groups' – in other words mediated discussion groups run by a skilled mediator. This research is essential for getting beneath the skin of 'issues' and past the initial responses people will give based on trying to 'be helpful' to the questioner, what they've been 'told' to think about it in the press, or the influence of the group. In my experience good qualitative research throws up major challenges to any campaigner's assumptions about what messages are 'effective'.

A company with extensive experience of qualitative research on environmental issues is KSBR at www.ksbr.co.uk.

Most campaign groups ought to be able to conduct their own 'political' research. It is mostly a question of gaining access (often this just involves a phone call and a visit) to the people who know, and following up every lead. A huge 'public affairs' industry exists to help businesses do such research, but public interest organizations ought, with common sense, to be able to use goodwill among politicians, business people, journalists and officials to find out what they need to know.

2. The scandal equation

Does your campaign rely on a sense of scandal or outrage? Often this is the case – or the campaigners think it ought to be.

If your campaign 'isn't working', consider changing your focus. Note that scandal is not just composed of awfulness. This is the thing journalists and the press usually focus on. 'Just how bad is it?' they ask as they try to turn a disaster into a more newsworthy claim of 'catastrophe'.

On its own, though, an awful problem can be a tragedy but not a scandal. To be a scandal it has to be avoidable. This is the component that campaigners more often overlook. It has two parts – what can be done about it and what is being done about it. The more that could be done, and the less that actually is being done, the greater the scandal. If nothing can be done, or if everything possible is being done, it's not a scandal at all.

3. If you've been campaigning: Are you being co-opted?

Do you understand your opponent well enough?

Officialdom (and some companies) will try to marginalize those who can cause real 'damage' to their interests, use those who have uniquely useful information or expertise, and simply patronize the rest.

The latter two are both forms of co-option, which for most groups is the main danger. Ask yourself these questions:

- Is your campaign regarded as 'constructive' and 'responsible' by your opponents?
- Do those with power to make the decisions you want to change give you grants or other help?

- Do you rely on them for information?
- Has your campaign resulted in greater access to officials or politicians or executives but still no real result?
- Have you been invited to join a task force or working group or commission (or other) in which no decision will actually be taken?

If the answer to any of these is 'yes', then you may well be on the way to co-option.

A campaign should get its resources – its capital of funds and information and support – from the public, not from other institutions. It needs to remain free to act and with the legitimacy that comes from expressing a public sentiment rather than an institutional interest.

Learn the ways of your opponent. Learn their language – get to know ex-politicians or ex-officials or people from inside a company who understand the culture and way of thinking. All too often, the government is acting not in the public interest but to keep the public from affecting some entrenched commercial interest or to defend the power of officials or politicians.

Acronyms and Abbreviations

AGGG	Advisory Group on Greenhouse Gases
AGM	annual general meeting
AOSIS	Alliance of Small Island and Low-Lying States
BC	British Columbia
BSC	Broadcasting Standards Council
BSE	bovine spongiform encephalitis ('mad-cow disease')
CAMPCAT	channel, action, messenger, programme, context, audience, trigger
CAR	Concern, Action, Reassurance
CDSM	Cultural Dynamics Strategy and Marketing
CEO	chief executive officer
CFCs	chlorofluorocarbons
CHC	Chemicals and Health Campaign
CHP	Combined Heat and Power
CLEAR	Campaign for Lead-Free Air
CO_2	carbon dioxide
CRC	Carbon Reduction Committee
CSR	corporate social responsibility
DEFRA	Department of Environment, Food and Rural Affairs
EC	European Commission
ECF	elemental chlorine-free paper
FAB	Families Against Bush (Climate)
FAIR	Fairness and Accuracy in Reporting
FoE	Friends of the Earth
FSC	Forest Stewardship Council
FTSE	Financial Times Stock Exchange
GAP	Global Action Plan
GM	genetically modified (food)
HCFCs	hydrochlorofluorocarbons
HFCs	hydrofluorocarbons
HR	human resources
ICT	information and communications technology
ID	inner-directed

IEA	International Energy Agency
INC	Intergovernmental Negotiating Committee
IPCC	Intergovernmental Panel on Climate Change
IPPR	Institute of Public Policy Research
IQ	intelligence quotient
ITC	Independent Television Commission
M+F	Munro and Forster
MBTI	Myers Briggs Type Indicator
MEP	Member of the European Parliament
MIPIGG	Multisectoral Initiative on Potent Industrial Greenhouse Gases
MMR	measles, mumps and rubella vaccine
MOx	mixed oxide fuel
MP	Member of Parliament
MSC	Marine Stewardship Council
MSF	Médecins Sans Frontières
NASA	National Aeronautics and Space Administration
NFWI	National Federation of Women's Institute
NGO	non-governmental organization
NLP	Neuro-Linguistic Programming
np-SAD	National Programme on Substance Abuse Deaths
NVDA	non-violent direct action
OD	outer-directed
OECD	Organisation for Economic Co-operation and Development
OSPAR	Oslo and Paris Commission regulating the disposal of wastes in the North East Atlantic
PAN	Pesticides Action Network
PCB	polychlorinated biphenyls
PEP	point, evidence, point
PEST	political, economic, scientific and technical
PEX	Pesticide Exposure and Health
PM	Prime Minister
POPs	persistent organic pollutants
PR	public relations
PSB	Problem, Solution, Benefit
RASPB	Responsible party, Action, Solution, Problem, Benefit
REACH	Registration, Evaluation, Authorisation and Restriction of Chemicals
SD	security-driven (or sustenance-driven)
SEI	Stockholm Environment Institute
SIN	Substitute It Now

SME	small and medium enterprises
SMS	Short Message Service
SOSTAC	Situation, Objectives, Strategy, Tactics, Action, Control
SUV	sports utility vehicle
SXSW	South by Southwest Conferences and Festivals
TCF	totally chlorine-free paper
THORP	Thermal Oxide Reprocessing Plant (Sellafield)
UNEP	United Nations Environment Programme
UNFCCC	United Nations Framework Convention on Climate Change
UNICEF	United Nations Children's Fund
VBCOP	Values, Consistency, Behaviour, Opinion, Politics
WRI	World Resources Institute
WTO	World Trade Organization
WWF	Worldwide Fund for Nature

Index

35

20-21   144   Fairline
151   200
    188   58   193   13